THE
COMPETENT ORGANIZATION

MANAGING WORK AND ORGANIZATIONS SERIES

Edited by Dr Graeme Salaman, Professor of Organisation Studies in the Faculty of Social Sciences and the Open Business School, The Open University

Current titles:

THE
COMPETENT ORGANIZATION
A PSYCHOLOGICAL ANALYSIS OF THE
STRATEGIC MANAGEMENT PROCESS

Gerard P. Hodgkinson
Paul R. Sparrow

Open University Press
Buckingham · Philadelphia

Open University Press
Celtic Court
22 Ballmoor
Buckingham MK18 1XW

email: enquiries@openup.co.uk
world wide web: www.openup.co.uk

and 325 Chestnut Street, Philadelphia, PA 19106, USA

First Published 2002

A catalogue record of this book is available from the British Library

ISBN   0 335 19903 8 (pbk)   0 335 19904 6 (hbk)

Library of Congress Cataloging-in-Publication Data
Hodgkinson, Gerard P., 1961–
    The competent organization: a psychological analysis of the
    strategic management process/Gerard P. Hodgkinson, Paul R. Sparrow.
        p. cm – (Managing work and organizations series)
    Includes bibliographical references and index.
    ISBN 0-335-19904-6 (hardcover) – ISBN 0-335-19903-8 (pbk.)
    1. Strategic planning.   2. Organizational effectiveness.
    I. Sparrow, Paul.   II. Title.   III. Series.
HD30.28   H62 2002
658.4′012–dc21   2001054512

Typeset by Type Study, Scarborough
Printed in Great Britain by The Cromwell Press, Trowbridge, Wiltshire

For Dorothy, whose love, wisdom and support are my inspiration and without which none of this would have been possible, and Ben, David and Rebekah, my lovely children.

For Sue, the one I love, who continues to give me the freedom to write.

CONTENTS

Contents

Contents

xi

FOREWORD

Gerard Hodgkinson and Paul Sparrow have made a significant step towards a trans-disciplinary understanding of strategic management in this accessible, well-written book which provides an attractive new vocabulary for understanding how organizational competencies are generated by cognitive processes. It is a much needed next step in making the tools and insights of cognitive psychology as available to strategic management as the contributions of economics and behavioural science.

I admire how the book is organized. From the first chapter, managerial competence is tied to the need for 'knowledge that is actionable' (Argyris 1999) in the disordered, turbulent, demanding context of our times. For example, an artful blend of academic and practical concerns can be found in the Chapter 2 discussion of organizational learning and tacit knowledge, which leads to Chapter 3s coverage of organizational memory. Typically, the discussion is subtle, as in their discussion of the advantages as well as disadvantages of forgetting. Attention moves from micro processes to team, organizational and macro concerns throughout the book, and work from a wide range of ontological and epistemic perspectives is covered.

But this book also points out shortcomings in work to date, and resists the impulse to claim that cognition provides easy answers to problems unsolved by economics, socio-political or other approaches. The authors note that cognitive theorists have too often reiterated established findings, or overly simplified complex sources. There are many useful suggestions for new studies here, as well as a useful summary of a great deal of past work.

In short, Gerard Hodgkinson and Paul Sparrow provide a much needed, multi-level analysis that is more comprehensive and detailed than any survey of cognitive contributions to management yet available. It is a pleasure to commend their efforts to a wide range of readers, from both the academic and practitioner communities.

Anne Sigismund Huff
Director
AIM – The Advanced Institute for Management

Professor of Strategic Management
Cranfield School of Management and the University of Colorado

PREFACE

According to Johnson and Scholes (1999: 10): 'Strategy is the direction and scope of an organisation over the long term, which achieves advantage for the organisation through its configuration of resources within a changing environment, to meet the needs of markets and to fulfil stakeholder expectations'. Building on this definition, they argue that strategic management is concerned with three broad sets of issues: analysis, choice and implementation. Strategic analysis involves understanding the strategic position of the organization, its environment, resources, values and objectives. Strategic choice involves the formulation of possible courses of action/options, evaluation of their suitability or fit and selection of the strategy to be followed. Finally, strategic implementation is concerned with the translation of strategy into action, resource planning, designing the organizational structure to carry through the strategy and adapting the people and the systems used to manage the organization.

In this book we set out to demonstrate how the development and application of scientifically sound psychological theory and research can contribute to an understanding of the strategic management process, thereby enhancing organizational effectiveness through the design of interventions that foster strategic competence. We define such competence as the ability of organizations (or more precisely their members) to acquire, store, recall, interpret and act upon information of relevance to the longer-term survival and well-being of the organization. Our analysis of the strategic management process is thus primarily cognitive in nature. We draw upon an extensive body of work from the burgeoning field of managerial and organizational cognition, in order to develop a multi-level perspective on the strategic management process. We consider the rapidly changing context in which modern work organizations are now operating and the demands that this is placing on key individuals and groups as they seek to skilfully steer the organization over the longer term. Backed by theory and research from the fields of industrial, work and organizational psychology, social cognition, cognitive psychology and differential psychology, we identify a number of ways in which organizations might attempt to meet the psychological challenges posed by this unprecedented period of organizational and social change. Our purpose in writing this book is thus twofold:

- to provide a reasonably comprehensive overview of the psychology of strategic management, as viewed from our own perspective as active researchers and consultants working in this new sub-field;
- to consider the limitations of the work that has been conducted thus far, in order to identify what we consider to be the principal directions for future research and scholarship.

The central message of our book is that while considerable inroads have been made in legitimizing the psychology of strategic management as a field of study in its own right, and in the mapping of its principal boundaries, there is still a considerable way to go before research on this topic reaches a level of sophistication and maturity which is comparable to the better-established areas of industrial, work and organizational psychology. In particular, there are several non-trivial methodological hurdles that have yet to be confronted if many of the theoretical notions and tools of intervention discussed in this book are to be adequately scrutinized through the rigours of empirical research. As we shall see, many of the procedures currently in use for mapping strategic knowledge have yet to be screened in terms of their basic psychometric efficacy, both as basic research methods and for the purposes of organizational intervention. The vast majority of these procedures have been designed to elicit conceptual knowledge that is immediately accessible through verbal report and/or other forms of conscious awareness. However, even the most cursory glance at the voluminous work that has emerged from experimental psychology and the wider field of cognitive science in general over recent years reveals that we can delineate many forms of knowledge, some of which are amenable to investigation through such direct methods of elicitation, the majority of which are not. Although the relevance of some of these forms of non-conscious knowledge for the theory and practice of strategic management has yet to be tested, it is clear that current methods of assessment are only scratching the surface and not getting at 'deep cognition' within organizations. While the analysis of various explicit forms of procedural and declarative knowledge is an obvious starting point for getting this new field of study under way, in order to assist in the management of knowledge, facilitate organizational learning and to challenge the deeply held assumptions and beliefs of key organizational actors, we need to expand our repertoire of investigative techniques. Precisely how intuitions and the other non-conscious forms of tacit cognition that drive the strategic motives and behaviour of modern organizations should be assessed using reliable and valid procedures is, in our view, the most pressing problem facing the field at this point in time.

This book is the product of an intellectual journey and friendship that began approximately 14 years ago, in 1988, when we met for the first time at an annual occupational psychology conference of the British Psychological Society, held at the University of Hull, UK. To the best of our knowledge, at that time, we were the only industrial, work and organizational psychology academics in the UK who were engaged in the study of strategic management from a psychological perspective. Gerard was employed as a full-time researcher at Manchester Business School, University of Manchester, investigating the nature and significance of managerial mental models of competition, while Paul was engaged in full-time research into strategic change and human resource management at the newly launched Centre for Corporate Strategy and Change, Warwick Business School, University of Warwick. As we embarked on our journey there were very few fellow travellers indeed. Hambrick and Mason's (1984) seminal article on top management teams

Publisher acknowledgements

had not long been published as we worked on our respective projects, both of which had been fully completed before Anne Huff published her now classic edited volume: *Mapping Strategic Thought* (Huff 1990). Looking back, it now seems inconceivable that attempts to apply psychological theory and research to the field of strategic management were so underdeveloped in those early days that an extensive trawl of the extant literature on competitive strategy revealed just two published sources (Dess and Davis 1984; Gripsrud and Gronhaug 1985) of direct relevance to Gerard's emerging work on the cognitive analysis of competitive industry structures, with two others in the pipeline (Fombrun and Zajac 1987; Porac *et al.* 1987). The extensive list of references incorporated in this volume bears strong testimony to how far the field has advanced over the years that have followed.

Although our respective early work was concerned with the analysis of two very different problems, what united us from the outset was a conviction that the mainstream approaches to the study of strategic management – a field historically dominated by the discipline of economics and, latterly, sociology – were essentially limited as a basis for furthering understanding of the strategic management process. The way in which the strategy field has developed over the intervening years has more than confirmed our initial judgement; it has been most gratifying not only to witness the birth of a new sub-field, the psychology of strategic management, but also to have been actively involved in its development, virtually from its inception. We hope that readers of this book will share the sense of intellectual excitement and curiosity that has driven us to combine our efforts in the writing of this book.

Needless to say we are indebted to a great many colleagues whom, directly and indirectly, have assisted one or both of us at varying points during the course of our journey. It is invidious to single out particular individuals in these circumstances. Nevertheless, a number of people have played a highly influential role in helping us to refine our thinking about the issues addressed in this book. Neil Anderson, Kevin Daniels, Peter Herriot, Anne Huff, Gerry Johnson, John Maule, John McGee, Nigel Nicholson, Roy Payne, Andrew Pettigrew, Jo Porac, Howard Thomas, and George Wright have had particularly formative influences on Gerard's work, through sustained dialogue and constructive feedback over many years. Paul is similarly indebted to Cary Cooper, Susan Jackson, Randall Schuler, Roy Payne, Andrew Pettigrew, Chris Hendry, Richard Whipp and his brother, John Sparrow for the insights that they have brought to his work and the signposts through their own work in this area. Others have assisted in our journey through their collaboration in the design and execution of various specific projects, culminating in the co-authorship of a number of our previous publications, upon which this book inevitably draws. In this connection, we are particularly grateful to Nicola Bown, Keith Glaister, Jo Padmore, Alan Pearman, Anne Tomes, and, once again, Kevin Daniels, Gerry Johnson, John Maule and George Wright, whose direct involvement at varying stages in our work has enabled us to achieve far more than would have been possible working in isolation. We are extremely grateful to all of you for the part that you have each played, knowingly or unknowingly, in helping us to shape our thinking in the preparation of this volume.

We also grateful to Mandy Robertson for her assistance with the figures and tables in the preparation of our final manuscript; your patience and attention to fine detail in ensuring that the many illustrations were all converted into camera-ready copy is much appreciated, and to Lorraine Friendship for tracking and formatting the extensive referencing for this book. John Skelton at Open University Press is also deserving of particular mention for his unstinting support of our project from its inception, despite the fact that we continually failed to meet numerous deadlines along the way.

Finally we are grateful to Dorothy and Sue, our respective spouses, and Ben, David and Rebekah (Gerard's children), whose patience and forbearance has been stretched well beyond reasonable limits (however liberally defined!), over the two-year period that it has taken us to finally complete the writing of this work. Yours has been the greatest sacrifice of all, and it is to you that we dedicate this book.

Gerard P. Hodgkinson   Paul R. Sparrow
Business School   Business School
The University of Leeds   The University of Manchester

March 2002

ACKNOWLEDGEMENTS

In general, permission to reproduce specific figures and tables from published works is acknowledged at the appropriate places in the text. In addition, however, we are grateful to our own respective publishers for permission to incorporate material directly or in adapted form from the following sources:

Hodgkinson, G.P. (1997a) The cognitive analysis of competitive structures: a review and critique, *Human Relations*, 50: 625–54. © The Tavistock Institute.

Hodgkinson, G.P. (1997b) Cognitive inertia in a turbulent market: the case of UK residential estate agents, *Journal of Management Studies*, 34(6): 921–45. © Blackwell Publishers Limited.

Hodgkinson, G.P. (2001a) The psychology of strategic management: diversity and cognition revisited, in C.L. Cooper and I.T. Robertson (eds) *International Review of Industrial and Organizational Psychology*, Volume 16, pp. 65–119. Chichester: Wiley. © John Wiley & Sons Limited.

Hodgkinson, G.P. (2001b) Cognitive processes in strategic management: some emerging trends and future directions, in N. Anderson, D.S. Ones, H.K. Sinangil and C. Viswesvaran (eds) *Handbook of Industrial, Work and Organizational Psychology*, Volume 2: *Organizational Psychology*, pp. 416–40. London: Sage. © Gerard P. Hodgkinson.

Hodgkinson, G.P. and Johnson, G. (1994) Exploring the mental models of competitive strategists: the case for a processual approach, *Journal of Management Studies*, 31: 525–51. © Blackwell Publishers Limited.

Sparrow, P.R. (1994) The psychology of strategic management: emerging themes of diversity and cognition, in L. Cooper and T. Robertson (eds) *International Review of Industrial and Organizational Psychology*, Volume 9, pp. 147–81. Chichester: Wiley. © John Wiley & Sons Limited.

Sparrow, P.R. (1998) Information overload, in K. Legge, C. Clegg, and S. Walsh (eds) *The Experience of Managing: A Skills Workbook.* London: Macmillan. © Macmillan Press Limited.

Sparrow, P.R. (1999) Strategy and cognition: understanding the role of management knowledge structures, organizational memory and information overload, *Creativity and Innovation Management,* 8(2): 140–8. © Blackwell Publishers Limited.

Sparrow, P. (2000) Strategic management in a world turned upside down: the role of cognition, intuition and emotional intelligence, in P.C. Flood, T. Dromgoole S.J. Carroll and L. Gorman (eds) *Managing Strategy Implementation.* Oxford: Blackwell. © Blackwell Publishers Limited.

THE COGNITIVE PERSPECTIVE
COMES OF AGE

In June 1985 The Prudential Assurance Company, one of the largest and most successful life assurance companies in the UK, entered the residential estate agency sector by acquiring Ekins, Dilley and Hanley, a small, 12-branch chain located in the East Anglia region of England. The chain was relaunched in January 1986 as Prudential Property Services. Eighteen months later, at the peak of the UK housing market boom, Prudential had amassed some 800 branches, through an extensive nationwide programme of mergers and acquisitions. Unfortunately, the performance of residential estate agency businesses is inextricably linked to the state of the housing market. House prices began to fall rapidly in response to dramatic increases in the interest rate during 1990, followed by rising unemployment in 1991. As sales fell to barely half their normal annual total, estate agents began to drastically cut the scale of their operations, to the extent that more than 20 per cent of the 20 leading estate agents' offices were closed. The Prudential Assurance Company withdrew from the sector altogether, with trading and purchases losses estimated to be in excess of £300 million. How could an organization with such a high profile and historically successful track record have fallen prey to such a catastrophic chain of events?

This book is concerned with describing the growth of interest among organizational psychologists, strategic management scholars, management consultants and organizational researchers in the application of psychological concepts, theories and techniques to the field of strategic management. It attempts to refine theoretical and practical understanding and outline the models that are being used to explain the managerial mind and the knowledge content that it processes.

Unfortunately, high profile cases like Prudential, replicated across a number of different types of organization, spanning both the private and public sectors, have been all too common over recent years. Partly in reaction to this, and partly from evidence gathered through systematic research and theorizing, academics and practitioners have increasingly called into question a number of key assumptions which have hitherto underpinned the field of strategic management from its inception. For example, the assumptions that:

- strategic decision makers are inherently rational actors who seek to maximize outcomes, first seeking all available information, then weighing up the various alternatives in order to select the best course of action;
- business environments are objective entities waiting to be discovered through the application of formal analytic procedures;
- successful strategies are invariably the product of deliberate planning;
- the locus of strategy making invariably resides in the upper echelons of the organization, while implementation is everyone's business.

Drawing on some of the latest developments in the fields of cognitive and industrial, work and organizational psychology, the primary aim of this book is to provide an in-depth, psychological analysis of the strategic management process, in order to distil what we consider to be the key lessons for researchers and practitioners in this newly emerging field of study, which we have termed 'the psychology of strategic management' (Sparrow 1994; Hodgkinson 2001a, 2001b), and highlight some of the significant challenges that lie ahead. It is important to note at the outset that although this book is predominantly psychological in emphasis, such is the complexity of the issues with which we are dealing that we must draw upon theory and research from a range of base disciplines, primarily from within the psychological sciences, but also incorporating elements of anthropology, industrial economics and the sociology of organizations. The central defining concepts of this book are *strategic competence* and *managerial and organizational cognition*. Our key message is that cognitive competence is crucial to strategic responsiveness and the organization's capacity to learn and renew itself in these turbulent times. In our view, a strategically competent organization equates ultimately to being a learning organization. In practice, this means being agile, open to the environment and capable of picking up those weak signals that are indicative of the need for change. These signals must not only be detected, but also filtered, stored, recalled and interpreted in a fashion that enables the organization to respond appropriately. In all but the very smallest of organizations, knowledge management is thus central to this process. In cases where strategic competence is highly developed, the organization is able to proactively develop additional competencies and stake out new strategic territories. Conversely, where the organization fails to develop such strategic competence, it responds reactively in an ever-vicious circle, which at best enables it to defend its existing markets, products and services.

The interrelated notions of knowledge management, organizational learning and the learning organization have received widespread coverage in the popular management literature over recent years. In this book we demonstrate how these notions can be harnessed in order to develop strategic competency, through an exploration of scholarly theory and research spanning individual, group, organizational and inter-organizational levels of analysis. In our view much of the literature on knowledge management, organizational learning and the learning organization has been tantamount to little more than a repackaging of established concepts, theories, frameworks and tools and techniques from other, better established areas of the management disciplines. Nevertheless, through a careful analysis of the strategic management process from a psychological perspective, we seek to demonstrate how the 'hype' and 'rhetoric' often associated with these terms can be translated into 'actionable knowledge' (Argyris

3

1999) – i.e. knowledge which is at one and the same time scientifically rigorous and useful to practitioners.

Managing in times of disorder

The Prudential case illustrates the fact that many organizations are now managing in times of severe disorder. D'Avini (1994) has coined the term 'hypercompetition' to characterize the increasingly typical organizational response to this state of affairs. This concept suggests that the disorder, stress and unpredictability confronting modern organizations are profoundly affecting the nature of rivalry between firms. Managerial perceptions are being driven by this kind of competition. Drawing on the fields of cognitive and organizational psychology, Sparrow (2000) has argued that the many changes currently taking place within the world of work are placing unprecedented informational burdens upon those responsible for strategy formulation and implementation. Hence, there is a high level of strategic risk associated with managing under these conditions.

Hypercompetition is not the force driving the changes currently experienced by many contemporary organizations, but the response expected to these changes. Organizations are experimenting with a range of new organizational forms and strategies to adapt to or manage this unprecedented change (Ghoshal and Bartlett 1990; Bartlett and Ghoshal 1993; Brown and Eisenhardt 1997, 1998; Nohria and Ghoshal 1997; Floyd and Woolridge 2000). The economic cycles that have created this period of hyperturbulence are long-wave in nature with disorder created at the interface between the end of the cycle of economic growth based on the post-war economy and the beginning of a cycle based on new technological drivers of information, communication and biotechnology. The economic opportunities are immense and the social disruptions challenging to say the least. Academics of course disagree over the scale of this disorder. Business economists and strategic management researchers such as Porter (1996) argue that these changes are constrained only to particular sectors, while organizational behaviour specialists and organizational analysts such as Zohar and Morgan (1998) suggest that corporate anarchy will be the result of the economic and competitive forces that have been unleashed. A three-year collaborative project involving several hundred strategic management, marketing, international management and business policy specialists, organizational scientists and social psychologists organized by the US Academy of Management and the journal: *Organization Science* produced a series of outputs, including conferences and workshops. In introducing the resultant book, Ilinitch *et al.* (1998: xxi) point out that:

> The language and metaphors of today's managers make one point abundantly clear: they are experiencing the strongest and most disruptive competitive forces of their careers. Rather than a game, business has become war. Rather than an honourable fight with the best firm winning, the goal has become extermination of the enemy. CEOs from industries ranging from telecommunications to auto parts describe the competition they face as 'brutal', 'intense', 'bitter' and 'savage'. In the words of Andrew Grove, the CEO of Intel, 'only the paranoid survive' in a world of hypercompetition. Increasingly, managers are turning to academics and consultants to understand why the nature of competition is changing and for insights about how to compete in chaotic and disorderly times.

Few managers would disagree with this sentiment. For academics and practitioners, however, it raises some important challenges. The very act of organizing is an attempt to create stability and reduce uncertainty through structures and processes. Strategic management has been driven by the need to reduce rivalry, through effective competitive positioning and the restriction of entry into profitable market niches. Yet from the perspective of those researching the new organizational forms (e.g. Ghoshal and Bartlett 1990; Bartlett and Ghoshal 1993; Nohria and Ghoshal 1997; Ilinitch *et al.* 1998), a number of critical questions need to be addressed, such as the following:

- How can organizations manage their actions to exploit flexibility and knowledge creation?
- How can firms reinvent themselves as they become more flexible?

- What do disposable organizations really look like?
- What factors are driving the new cycles of competitive escalation and de-escalation?
- How do some firms succeed in rewriting the industry rules?
- What models of strategy will become obsolete in the future and what form(s) might the replacement models take?

It is the inability of conventional theories, frameworks and techniques to address such questions adequately that has led scholars and practitioners to search elsewhere in the quest for new and greater insights.

Strategy as 'content' versus strategy as 'process'

Recognizing that all organizational strategies, whether deliberately planned or emergent (Mintzberg and Waters 1985), are ultimately the product of a negotiated order (Walsh and Fahay 1986) developed in the context of a socio-political arena (Pettigrew 1973, 1985; Mintzberg 1983; Johnson 1987), within the past two decades or so there has been an explosion of scholarly interest in the application of psychological concepts, theories and techniques in an attempt to better understand the strategic management process (see, e.g., Porac and Thomas 1989; Huff 1990; Walsh 1995; Finkelstein and Hambrick 1996; Hodgkinson and Thomas 1997; Eden and Ackermann 1998; Eden and Spender 1998; Flood *et al.* 2000; Huff and Jenkins 2002). This rapidly developing body of work forms the focus of the present book. In particular, we centre on the analysis of socio-cognitive processes in strategic management, processes through which those responsible for all aspects of strategizing acquire, store, share and act upon information, knowledge and beliefs concerning those issues that have an ultimate bearing on the longer-term direction of the organization as a whole.

As noted above, a major unifying theme throughout our analysis is the question of 'competence'. In particular, we consider what precisely it means for an organization to be deemed 'strategically competent' in these turbulent times, the various factors that determine strategic competence and ways in which such competence might be fostered. As we shall see, a key lesson to be derived from our analysis is that there are undoubtedly some fundamental limits to the levels of competency attainable, but also there are various steps that can be taken to foster strategic competence among individuals and groups. Hopefully, the application of this knowledge will help to minimize the sorts of strategic blunder highlighted at the outset of this chapter.

The emergent body of theory and research on the psychology of strategic management has shifted the focus of attention away from a preoccupation with traditional 'content' issues in strategy – for example, questions about the merits of various strategies such as organic growth versus mergers and acquisitions, related versus unrelated diversification and so on – towards a focus on 'process' issues – i.e. questions concerning *how* particular strategies come to be formulated and implemented within organizations. For example:

- By what processes and mechanisms do industry and market boundaries and competitive practices evolve and change?
- How do the information processing limitations of decision makers impact upon their understanding of strategic issues and problems?
- How do the mental representations of strategic issues and problems held by senior managers and other stakeholders impact upon decision processes and individual and organizational performance?
- How can we harness accumulated knowledge concerning the cognitive capabilities and limitations of decision makers in order to enhance the strategic management process in organizations?

It is an analysis of these sorts of questions that forms the focus of this book.

The nature and purpose of theory and research

Earlier we noted that, like Argyris (1999), we see the ultimate purpose of social scientific theory and research as being the creation of knowledge that is 'actionable'. However, such are the levels of complexity and turbulence confronting modern organizations that the recent explosion of interest in the development and application of psychological knowledge within the strategy field has been accompanied by an intense debate among academics about the ultimate relevance of management research as a whole to broader issues of policy and practice (see, e.g., Tranfield and Starkey 1998; Huff 2000; Whitley 2000; Anderson *et al.* 2001; Hodgkinson 2001c; Hodgkinson and Herriot 2002). Against a backdrop of increasing financial stringency on the part of government funding bodies, together with a growing awareness of the many challenges posed by rapidly changing business environments, in recent years organizational psychology and management academics have been concerned to articulate and defend the distinctiveness of their fields of study. Although the questions that they have addressed may sometimes have seemed irrelevant to practitioners, or appeared to create artificial divisions or barriers to understanding between the different academic sub-fields involved, this questioning process has also served to raise awareness of a series of hidden problems or assumptions, and has highlighted the dangers of making managerial prescriptions based on a limited knowledge base. Indeed, an awareness of the theoretical and methodological shortcomings of some of the empirical work underpinning the development of the psychology of strategic management as an emergent field in its own right is essential if we are to avoid the very pitfalls that led strategy researchers to turn to organizational psychology and the cognitive sciences in the hope of gaining fresh insights and new tools capable of meeting the pressing problems confronting contemporary organizations.

The managerial and organizational cognition perspective

As noted at the outset, the recent upsurge of interest in the psychology of strategic management has arisen primarily from a fundamental conviction that the strategy field has hitherto placed too much emphasis on the largely unquestioned assumption that the strategy process is an inherently rational phenomenon (although for notable exceptions see Chaffee 1985; Johnson 1987; Mintzberg 1994; Mintzberg *et al.* 1998). Drawing on theory and research from a variety of interrelated fields, especially cognitive and organizational psychology, social cognition and organizational sociology, a new approach to organizational analysis has developed over the past 15–20 years or so: the managerial and organizational cognition perspective (see, e.g., Porac and Thomas 1989; Meindl *et al.* 1994, 1996; Hodgkinson and Thomas 1997; Spender and Eden 1998; Lant and Shapira 2001a). Faced with a complex, ambiguous and continuously changing environment, organizational actors have to absorb, process, make sense of and then disseminate a bewildering flow of information in order to make decisions and solve problems. Managerial and organizational cognition research is concerned with the analysis of these processes. Over recent years, a rapidly growing army of social scientists, gathered under the managerial and organizational cognition umbrella, have concerned themselves with the way in which managers and other organizational actors construct aspects of their life at work, develop theories of knowledge and represent such knowledge. This is a very broad arena. A number of disciplines have developed language systems and constructs that are heavily laced with cognitive connotations. For example, industrial economists have examined how the behaviour of industries and firms is dependent on the way in which managers combine information on costs, demands, competitors and profits, while sociologists have given importance to the norms and taken-for-granted beliefs that shape organizational practice.

This interdisciplinary body of work has laid important foundations for conducting a psychological analysis of the strategic management process. Research conducted from a managerial and organizational cognition perspective has directly challenged the fundamental assumption of rationality, on which many of the dominant theoretical perspectives within the strategy field – such as the design school (Christensen *et al.* 1982), the planning school (Ansoff 1965; Steiner 1969; Ackoff 1983) and the positioning school (Porter 1980, 1985) – are to varying extents implicitly or explicitly based. Indeed, Spender and Eden (1998) have argued that *the* defining question for the field of managerial and organizational cognition is based upon a negative assertion – that the existing body of knowledge about managerial decision making is inadequate, as are the theories of rational expectations and managerial choice that dominate business school syllabi. As observed by March (1999), rational theories are characterized by four common assumptions:

- that the decision maker has knowledge of the alternatives for action;
- that the decision maker has knowledge of the consequences of the alternative actions, at least up to the point of being able to derive a probability distribution;
- that there is a consistent preference ordering, or set of values, by which alternative courses of action can be compared;
- that there is a decision rule by which single, alternative actions can be selected.

In sum, rational theories of decision making are predicated on the assumption that managers perform complex strategic analyses, free from inherent bias, giving each piece of information equal attention (P. Johnson et al. 1998). The idea that managers work on complete data, well-defined objectives and logical information processes does not, however, accord with the everyday realities of organizational life. Managers have neither full information or knowledge, nor the competence and capacities to process the myriad of information that is readily available (March and Simon 1958). Nor do they all have the same perfect knowledge of strategic issues. The managerial and organizational cognition approach to strategic management, therefore, differs from previous traditions in that it focuses on the models that drive actual managerial action, rather than on abstract, rational models.

Given the cross-disciplinary nature of managerial and organizational cognition research one problem is the need for scholars to simplify and agree upon a common language. As observed by Meindl et al. (1994), over a remarkably short time period, managerial and organizational cognition scholars have employed a rich diversity of complex terms, each highly similar on the surface, but which actually have very different connotations within the respective fields from which they have ultimately originated.

The basic principles of the managerial and organizational cognition perspective can be summarized as follows:

- Individuals are limited in their ability to process the rich variety of stimuli contained in the external world – stimuli which are exceedingly complex in nature.

- Consequently, they employ a variety of strategies in order to reduce the burden of information processing that would otherwise ensue.

- This culminates in the development of a simplified understanding of reality which is encoded within the mind of the individual.

- Once formulated, these 'mental representations' act as filters through which incoming information is subsequently processed, which in turn can lead to biased and inappropriate decisions.

Origins of the managerial and organizational cognition perspective

The foundations of the managerial and organizational cognition perspective were originally laid with the development of cognitive psychology as a major sub-field of study within academic psychology. In an attempt to render psychology a truly scientific endeavour, behaviourists (e.g. Skinner 1938; Mowrer 1947) argued that concepts relating to 'under the skin phenomena', such as 'perception,' 'attention' and 'memory,' should be eschewed in favour of the analysis of stimulus → response (S → R) connections, on the grounds that the latter could be readily subjected to direct observation and measurement. In practice, however, it became increasingly difficult to account for all but the most simple of behaviours without recourse to cognitive terms. Rejecting the central theoretical tenets of behaviourism, cognitive psychologists (and cognitive scientists in general) have focused on the analysis of the various intervening mental processes that mediate responses to the environment.

Although the application of cognitive theory and research to managers and organizations is a relatively recent phenomenon, the need for a cognitive approach to managerial and organizational analysis was implicitly acknowledged in a number of 'classic', earlier works on strategy and organization theory. Hence, Stubbart (1989) contends that research on managerial and organizational

11

cognition provides a vital missing link between environmental conditions and strategic action, a link that was implied strongly in the work of early strategy scholars such as Hofer and Schendel (1978) and Andrews (1971), while Weick (1995) notes that Chester Barnard's seminal text on the functions of the executive (Barnard 1938) introduced the notion that organizations can be viewed as systems of action, consciously coordinated by controlled information processing and communication. However, Simon's (1947) classic work, *Administrative Behaviour*, is generally acknowledged as having laid the main foundations of modern cognitive theory and research in organizational settings. In this work, Simon introduced the notion of 'bounded rationality' which suggests that actors are unable to take decisions in a completely rational manner, due to the fact that they are constrained by fundamental information processing limitations. Nevertheless, they strive for rationality within the limits of their cognitive capacities.

March and Simon's (1958) *Organizations* is another classic book which has profoundly influenced the development of the managerial and organizational cognition perspective by highlighting the ways in which organizational routines free up attention that can then be used to concentrate on non-routine events (see also Cyert and March 1963). While the origins of the cognitive perspective in strategic management and organization studies can be traced back to these earlier works, it is over the past 15–20 years that the study of managerial and organizational cognition has come of age.

Having outlined the relevant background that has led to the explosion of scholarly interest in managerial and organizational cognition research within the strategy field, in the remaining sections of this chapter we briefly introduce some of the key concepts, theories and frameworks underpinning this approach. This material provides a useful foundation for understanding many of the issues to be addressed in subsequent chapters.

The human information processing model of skilled performance

In order to aid understanding of the complex mental processes performed by the brain in response to environmental stimuli, cognitive scientists have found it useful to conceptualize these operations as a sequence of activities (see, e.g., Broadbent 1958; Welford 1976). Figure 1.1 presents a human information processing model taken from Wickens (1984). Although highly simplified, this general model, or framework, captures the essential processes associated with virtually any task involving human cognition. The model suggests that the way in which individuals act is driven ultimately by the way in which they interpret their worlds (perception), this in turn being shaped in part by their past experiences and learning.

Often, in an effort to reduce the amount of cognitive activity required, past experience, stored in long-term memory, is influential in determining an individual's responses to current situations or stimuli; actions that worked in the past are routinely applied to the present so as to free up mental capacity. Cognitive psychologists employ the term 'top-down processing' to denote this type of activity. Researchers have also identified another type of activity, known as 'bottom-up processing'. This occurs when incoming stimuli influence actors' cognitions and actions directly, without reference to past memories. In practice, at a given point in time, information processing may be affected by what an individual brings to the task at hand (e.g. prior expectations, influenced by previous experience and contexts) and/or key features of the stimuli present in the current task environment. Clearly, the balance between bottom-up (stimulus driven) and top-down (conceptually driven) information processing strategies is likely to vary across tasks and situations; however, in the contexts in which senior managers operate it is the latter approach that is likely to predominate – see Walsh (1995) for detailed explanations as to why this is the case.

Heuristics and biases in strategic decision making

Another major body of psychological theory and research that has led to the development of key insights into the strategic management process is drawn from the field of behavioural decision research (e.g. Tversky and Kahneman 1974; Fischhoff 1975; Fischhoff *et al.* 1977; Kahneman *et al.* 1982). This work builds on

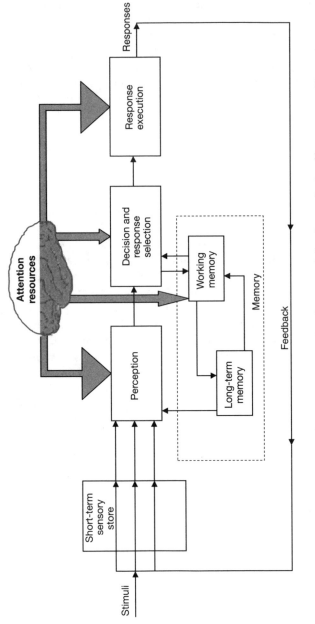

Figure 1.1 A basic information processing framework for the analysis of human cognition

Source: reproduced by permission of the publisher from Christopher D. Wickens (1984: 12), *Engineering Psychology and Human Performance*. Columbus, OH: Charles E. Merrill Publishing Company. © Bell & Howell Company.

the insights of computational models, such as that outlined in Figure 1.1, which depict decision makers as limited capacity processors of information. Behavioural decision researchers have amassed an impressive volume of evidence demonstrating the fact that in order to render the world manageable, decision makers employ a variety of 'rules of thumb', known as 'heuristics'. Heuristic processing strategies enable the decision maker to cut through the welter of information bombarding them by imposing a number of simplifying assumptions on the data.

Simon (1957) identified one such heuristic, known as 'satisficing'. Faced with a number of choice alternatives, decision makers select the first alternative that meets their minimum requirements, rather than choosing the best from all the alternatives on offer. Satisficing is much simpler in terms of its cognitive operations, thus placing fewer demands on scarce mental resources. Subsequent research has identified other heuristics that, in common with satisficing, involve less mental effort (see, e.g., Svenson 1979; Payne *et al.* 1993) and there is strong evidence suggesting that heuristic modes of reasoning underpin human judgement processes, particularly in the context of judgements involving the assessment of risk and uncertainty (Kahneman *et al.* 1982).

Although the use of heuristics reduces the information processing requirements on the decision maker, there are also risks involved in that their deployment may lead to sub-optimal outcomes. In the case of satisficing, for example, once an 'acceptable' option is found, the search for and evaluation of additional potentially viable alternatives ceases. Consequently, 'better' options that have not been considered will be ignored.

Behavioural decision researchers have also identified a number of cognitive biases in human judgement and decision making that might have a bearing on the strategic management process. One such bias, known as the 'framing bias' (Kahneman and Tversky 1984) is illustrated in Box 1.1.

The inconsistencies highlighted in Box 1.1 map onto a large body of literature showing that people tend to be risk averse when outcomes are considered in terms of gains, and risk seeking in the domain of losses (see Kuhberger 1998). This phenomenon demonstrates that choice behaviour may be crucially affected by the form in which decision alternatives are presented, or 'framed'

Box 1.1: Illustration of the framing bias

Consider the following problem:

A large car manufacturer has recently been hit with a number of economic difficulties, and it appears as if three plants need to be closed and 6000 employees laid off. The vice-president of production has been exploring ways to avoid this crisis. She has developed two plans:

Plan A: This plan will save one of the three plants and 2000 jobs.

Plan B: This plan has a ⅓ probability of saving all three plants and all 6000 jobs, but has a ⅔ probability of saving no plants and no jobs.

Which plan would you select?

Now reconsider this problem, replacing plans A and B with the following:

Plan C: This plan will result in the loss of two of the three plants and 4000 jobs.

Plan D: This plan has a ⅔ probability of resulting in the loss of all three plants and all 6000 jobs, but has a ⅓ probability of loosing no plants and no jobs.

Which plan would you select?

An analysis of each pair of decision choices (Plans A and B versus Plans C and D) reveals that they are objectively identical (A is same as C, and B is the same as D). Nevertheless, when presented with the first pair of choices, an overwhelming majority of individuals express a preference for Plan A, whereas Plan D becomes the favourite when presented with the second set of choices. Thus, the way in which problems are framed, or presented, can dramatically alter the way in which outcomes are evaluated.

Source: Bazerman (1984: 333–4)

---

rather than a systematic analysis of the expected outcomes of these alternatives. An explanation of this bias lies outside the scope of this book (interested readers should consult Kahneman and Tversky 1984; Bazerman 1998; Hodgkinson and Maule 2002). However, we shall return to the framing bias in Chapter 7, when we consider some of the ways in which research into managerial and organizational cognition might be utilized for practical purposes as a basis for intervening in the strategy process, with a view to enhancing the quality of strategic decision making. In the meantime, it is interesting to note that a number of studies have rigorously demonstrated that the framing bias is likely to occur in the context of strategic decision making (Bateman and Zeithaml 1989a, 1989b; Hodgkinson *et al.* 1999; Hodgkinson and Maule, in press). Accordingly, attempts to develop techniques for overcoming

Table 1.1   An evaluation of selected heuristics and biases in terms of their effects on strategic decision making

Heuristic/bias	Effects
1 Availability	Judgements of the probability of easily recalled events are distorted
2 Selective perception	Expectations may bias observations of variables relevant to strategy
3 Illusory correlation	Encourages the belief that unrelated variables are correlated
4 Conservatism	Failure to revise sufficiently forecasts based on new information
5 Law of *small* numbers	Overestimation of the degree to which small samples are representative of populations
6 Regression bias	Failure to allow for regression to the mean
7 Wishful thinking	Probability of desired outcomes judged to be inappropriately high
8 Illusion of control	Overestimation of personal control over outcomes
9 Logical reconstruction	'Logical' reconstruction of events which cannot be accurately recalled
10 Hindsight bias	Overestimation of predictability of past events

Source: adapted from C.R. Schwenk (1988: 4) The cognitive perspective on strategic decision making, *Journal of Management Studies*, 25: 41–55. © Blackwell Publishers Limited. Reproduced by kind permission of the publisher.

this bias are well justified. Meanwhile, more generally, Schwenk (1988) has usefully summarized the ways in which a variety of heuristics and biases might have a bearing on strategic decision processes (see Table 1.1).

As observed by Schwenk (1984), different biases tend to come to the fore during different stages of the decision process. Early on, when identifying the problem, individuals seek information that confirms their initial beliefs. When generating alternatives they use these beliefs to anchor or restrain their judgements. Feelings of personal responsibility can also lead to group convergence, in an attempt to diffuse such responsibility. The effectiveness of the initial judgement is affected by the representativeness of the analogies that they draw with other, similar situations. Consequently, some alternatives tend to be preferred from the outset, while others are discussed in negative terms. It is easy to then justify preferred alternatives on the basis that they do not involve trade-offs. In the final evaluation stage of a group decision, managers use analogies to justify their point of view, but this can lead to an overestimation of the extent to which past experiences are applicable, partial descriptions of strategic alternatives and the devaluation and dismissal of vitally important information by the group. The deployment of heuristics can also result in decision makers being over-confident in their decisions, and can create a misdirected search for certainty and a consequent *illusion of control* (Fischhoff 1975; Langer 1975; Fischhoff *et al.* 1977; Willman *et al.* 2001).

The non-rational escalation of commitment to a failing course of action

Another important contribution of behavioural decision research to the debate on rationality in strategic decision making has been made by Staw and his colleagues (e.g. Staw 1981, 1997): the notion of 'the non-rational escalation of commitment to a failing course of action'. This is the tendency for organizations to 'throw good money after bad' in the event that the benefits anticipated from a decision that has already been taken fail to materialize. Often in these circumstances, rather than abandoning the chosen course of action, organizations commit ever-greater sums of money and other resources in a series of successive steps, in the hope that matters will eventually improve, to the point where the benefits anticipated at the outset eventually materialize. Such escalation behaviour becomes non-rational at the point where the levels of resource committed exceed those that a rational model of decision making would prescribe. Arguably the case of Prudential Property Services exemplifies this phenomenon. Despite evidence that major losses were accruing (to the tune of £1 million per week), the board of directors continued to sanction the current strategy, until the £300 million threshold had been passed. The recently blighted Millennium Dome project in the UK is perhaps another example of this problem.

A considerable literature has amassed on the escalation of commitment (both at the individual and group levels of analysis), with explanations ranging from the accumulation of cognitive biases (of the sort illustrated in Table 1.1) (Schwenk 1986) and framing effects, to impression management and related conceptions. While a detailed consideration of these competing explanations lies beyond the scope of this book, as Wright and Goodwin (1999: 315) have observed: 'Clearly the social processes causing escalation of commitment will tend to magnify any inherent inertia toward a currently-followed strategy'. (For recent reviews of the voluminous literature on this phenomenon see Staw 1997; Bazerman 1998.)

The conflict theory of decision making

Janis and Mann (1977) devised a theory of decision making known as the *conflict theory*, which is especially relevant to the analysis why organizations are so often characterized by the tendency to adhere rigidly to extant strategies in the face of major environmental threats (see also Staw *et al.* 1981). This theory asserts that there are various coping mechanisms that can come into play, depending on the differing levels of conflict (decisional stress) experienced. Only one coping pattern, *vigilance*, is actually functional. Under high levels of stress (characterized by hesitation, vacillation, feelings of uncertainty and signs of acute emotional distress each time the decision comes to the fore), dysfunctional information processing strategies are likely to be adopted in an effort to reduce the stress to acceptable levels.

Three such defensive coping patterns have been highlighted which are likely to lead to a dysfunctional adherence to the strategic status quo (strategic inertia). These are *procrastination* (involving the postponement of a decision), *buck passing* (shifting responsibility for the decision to a third party), and *bolstering*. The latter involves overemphasizing the benefits to be gained from the current strategy at the expense of an appropriate consideration of the down-sides. Two other coping patterns have also been highlighted by Janis and Mann: *unconflicted adherence* and *unconflicted change*. These patterns both occur under conditions of low decisional stress and are non-problematic in terms of the present context. (For an application of this theory in relation to a failed intervention in an organization seeking to bring about major strategic change see Hodgkinson and Wright, in press.)

Before concluding this discussion of the contribution of behavioural decision research to a psychological understanding of the strategic management process, it is worth returning briefly to our earlier discussion concerning the nature and role of research in the management field more generally. In this connection, it is important to note that much of the foundational work in the field of behavioural decision making has been conducted in the context of highly controlled experiments, under laboratory conditions. This has led some scholars (e.g. Eden and Spender 1998) to question its utility as a basis for furthering understanding of the strategic management process. However, following Schwenk's (1982) plea for strategic management research that meets the twin imperatives of rigour and relevance, others have sought to explore directly the applicability of concepts and theories from behavioural decision research using a variety of techniques, including laboratory experiments, field studies and the analysis of documentary sources (see, e.g., Barnes 1984; Schwenk 1984, 1985, 1986; Bukszar and Connolly 1988; Huff and Schwenk 1990; Golden 1992; Lant *et al.* 1992). While there is undoubtedly considerable scope for further work, the overwhelming conclusion to be drawn at this point in time is that many of the insights generated initially by behavioural decision researchers in the laboratory are highly applicable as a basis for furthering understanding of the strategic management process (for recent reviews see Schwenk 1995; Das and Teng 1999; Hodgkinson 2001b; Maule and Hodgkinson, 2002).

Mental representations: schemata, cognitive maps and mental models

Precisely how knowledge is represented in the mind and what types of computations can be carried out on these representations in order to bring about such activities as remembering, perceiving, reasoning, problem solving and decision making are the fundamental questions to which basic and applied research within the field of cognitive science is ultimately addressed (see, e.g., Anderson 1990; Johnson-Laird 1993). Not surprisingly, therefore, much work has been devoted to operationalizing the notion of mental representations to shed light on issues of primary concern to strategy scholars and organization theorists more generally.

It is useful at this point to introduce three further preliminary concepts: the related notions of *schemata* (Bartlett 1932), *cognitive maps* (Tolman 1932) and *mental models* (Johnson-Laird 1983). Schemata may be broadly defined as follows:

> Schemata contain collections of knowledge derived from past experience which serve the function of directing perceptual exploration towards relevant environmental stimuli. Such exploration often leads the perceiver to sample some of the available stimulus information. If the information obtained from the environment fails to match information in the relevant schema, then the information in the schema is modified appropriately.
>
> (Eysenck and Keane 1995: 81)

The notion of cognitive maps, which originated from work on the ways in which animals and humans navigate the physical world, is similarly intended to capture the idea that knowledge is internally represented in a form which both simplifies reality and provides a basis for subsequent action. Likewise, Johnson-Laird's theory of mental models, and the pioneering work of Kenneth Craik upon which it is based (e.g. Craik 1943), asserts that:

21

The psychological core of understanding . . . consists in your having a 'working model' of the phenomenon in your mind. If you understand inflation, a mathematical proof, the way a computer works, DNA or divorce, then you have a mental representation that serves as a model of an entity in much the same way as, say, a clock functions as a model of the earth's rotation . . . Many of the models in people's minds are little more than high-grade simulations, but they are none the less useful provided that the picture is accurate . . .

(Johnson-Laird 1983: 2–4)

Managerial and organizational cognition scholars have tended to use these notions interchangeably to convey the general idea that actors develop internal representations of their worlds, which in turn are linked to organizational action (see, Huff 1990; Walsh 1995; Reger and Palmer 1996). Arguably, they are sufficiently similar in meaning to justify this general usage. In the remainder of this book, therefore, we use the terms 'schemata', 'cognitive maps' and 'mental models' synonymously, to capture the over-arching idea that individuals internalize their knowledge and understanding of organizational life in the form of a simplified representation of reality. In so doing, however, we must be mind-ful of the fact that these terms were originally developed for differing purposes by researchers pursuing a variety of problems in cognitive psychology, albeit sharing a common, general focus: the question of mental representation.

A similar range of concepts has evolved in order to convey the idea that over time groups of organizational actors come to develop shared representations of reality. As observed by Walsh (1995), the number of terms employed by managerial and organiz-ational cognition researchers in an effort to capture the nature and significance of individual and collective mental representations of reality has proliferated massively over recent years. Table 1.2 lists some of the many concepts now in common usage within this field in an attempt to capture the general notion of individual and collective knowledge structures.

In sum, individual and collective knowledge structures act as mental templates which can be imposed upon an information-rich environment in order to give it meaning (Walsh 1995). Like

Table 1.2 Constructs illustrating the diversity of concepts employed in an attempt to capture individual and collective knowledge structures in cognitively-oriented management theory

Construct	Construct
Attentional fields	Managerial perceptions
Belief structures	Managerial thought structures
Cause maps	Mindscapes
Cause-effect beliefs	Negotiated belief structures
Cognitive frameworks	Organizational ideologies
Cognitive maps	Organizational knowledge
Cognitive perceptions	structures
Collective cognitions	Organizational schemata
Collectively shared interpretations	Organizational cause maps
Construed reality	Organizational prototypes
Core causal beliefs	Overriding concern
Distilled ideologies	Provinces of meaning
Dominant logic	Quasi-theories
Folk theories	Shared appreciative systems
Frames of reference	Shared perspectives
Givens	Strategic frames
Implicit theories	Symbolic domains
Implicit thought structures	Tacit understanding
Industry recipes	Team mental models
Interpretation	Templates
Interpretative schemes	Theories of action
Issue categories	Thought worlds
	World views

Source: after Walsh, J. (1995) Managerial and organizational cognition: notes from a trip down memory lane, *Organization Science*, 6(3): 280–321.

heuristics, they also act as simplification devices, helping managers to overcome the limitations of short-term memory when they search long-term memory for relevant information (Daniels *et al.* 1995). When these knowledge structures are organized appropriately (i.e. contain high quality information, rich and sophisticated linkages built around deep predictive constructs), and when they are utilized by highly competent managers, then a series of benefits accrue. The manager is able to attend to the most meaningful events in their environment, can encode and retrieve information more effectively, can make more appropriate and accurate interpretations and can solve problems more readily. However, as illustrated in Table 1.3, an over-reliance on such top-down knowledge structures can also produce many negative consequences and actually limit the manager's understanding of the environment. The potential liabilities include stereotypic thinking, miscontrolled information processing, inaccurate filling of data gaps, the rejection of apparently discrepant but important information, a refusal to disconfirm cherished hypotheses and

Table 1.3 Constructs illustrating the diverse range of concepts employed in an attempt to capture the dysfunctional consequences of top-down, schematic information processing in the development of cognitively-oriented management theory

Construct
Bias screen/search
Blind spots
Blinkered perceptions
Cognitive biases
Cognitive inertia
Cognitive trails
Collective blindness
Collective strategic myopia
Competitive blind spots
Functional fixedness
Grooved thinking
Impoverished views of the world
Managerial lenses
Personal bias
Perceptual filters
Selective perception
Self-serving biases
Strategic myopia
Strategically-sensitive blind spots
Tunnel vision
Quasi-satisfying

Source: after Walsh, J. (1995) Managerial and organizational cognition: notes from a trip down memory lane, *Organization Science*, 6(3): 280–321.

the inhibition of creative problem solving. The paradox is that 'schematic information processing can be at once enabling and crippling' (Walsh 1995: 282).

Enactment, sense-making and the enacted environment

Another key foundation underpinning recent managerial and organizational cognition research has been laid by Weick, through his development of the interrelated notions of *enactment*, *sensemaking* and the *enacted environment* (see, e.g., Weick 1969, 1979a, 1979b, 1995, 2001). Many of the sequential information processing models advanced by cognitive psychologists (such as that presented in Figure 1.1) imply that the environment is an objective entity, and that the reason subjective differences in perception occur is because the objective environment can only be partially comprehended, due to limited processing capacity ('bounded rationality'). Weick's work challenges this limited view of the environment (which he terms 'the perceived environment'), arguing that theories stressing the notion that reality is selectively perceived overemphasize the object → subject relationship, at the expense of the idea that often the subject exerts considerable influence on the object:

> Managers construct, rearrange, single out, and demolish many 'objective' features of their surroundings. When people act they un-randomise variables, insert vestiges of orderliness, and literally create their own constraints . . .
> There is a reciprocal influence between subjects and objects, not a one-sided influence such as implied by the idea that a stimulus triggers a response. This reciprocal influence is captured in the organizing model by the two-way influence between enactment and ecological change.
> (Weick 1979a: 164–6)

By drawing attention to the fact that the environmental constraints and opportunities faced by organizations are actively constructed by the actions of particular individuals and groups, the notions of enactment and the enacted environment have laid an important conceptual foundation for understanding the strategic management process (see Smircich and Stubbart 1985). According to Weick, reality within organizations is relative. In contrast to the computational model of information processing outlined in Figure 1.1, choices within a Weickian framework are not seen as being correct or incorrect, as judged against an abstract mathematical equation. Probabilities represent just one of the many benchmarks that may be used to determine a quality decision. The 'correctness' of a decision is dependent upon the point of view that is being used to evaluate it.

Sense-making is partially dependent on the perceptions of what Weick calls 'communities of believers' who have their own 'local rationalities' or 'interpretative stances' (Weick 1995). These local rationalities are in turn embedded in larger 'systems of meaning' – some of which are individual and some of which are shared by the group. The important point is that they predominate at the time a decision is made. Consequently, if we are to explain organizational choice we have to unpack these rationalities.

Combining the computational and interpretive perspectives

Two major perspectives can be discerned within the body of work on managerial and organizational cognition: the first, 'the computational perspective', exemplified by the work of March and Simon and behavioural decision researchers, originates primarily from the field of experimental cognitive psychology; the second, the 'interpretive perspective', is exemplified by the work of Weick. The principal contribution of the former approach has been to draw attention to the fundamental information processing limitations of organizational actors and the strategies they employ in an effort to overcome these limitations, while the latter has contributed to an understanding of the ways in which organizational realities are socially constructed. Whereas from the former perspective organizations are viewed as systems of *information*, from the latter they are viewed as systems of *meaning* (Lant and Shapira 2001b, 2001c). This is a very important distinction. In the words of Lant and Shapira (2001c: 369–70.)

One needs meaning and interpretation to set goals; determining what types of outcomes are important is an interpretive process. One also needs meaning and interpretation to make sense of the outcomes and events that occur (e.g., is this a normal event or a cause for concern?). To take volitional action, however, actors must, at least for certain periods of time, fix their goals and decide on a certain interpretation of outcomes. Without momentary certainty of this kind, it seems that purposeful action would cease. Given a set of goals, one can gather information to one's advantage, leverage it, create knowledge, and disseminate knowledge so organizations are more effective. Organizations and their actors move in and out of these different processes continually by asking questions such as: How did we do? How should we do? How best to do it?

Hence, while this basic distinction between the *downstream* choice or calculation process associated with decision making and the *upstream* process of sense-making is important, nevertheless in practice *both* perspectives are ultimately required if we are to develop adequate theoretical accounts of the ways in which strategic competence is developed and utilized in organizations.

As an illustration of how the computational and interpretive perspectives can be usefully combined, consider the work of Lant *et al.* (1992), which investigated the ways in which managers explain poor performance records. This work has demonstrated that within turbulent environments, organizational actors are more likely to attribute past poor performance records to external factors, whereas in stable environments no such tendency is observed. On the basis of these findings, Lant concluded that such biased sense-making leads ultimately to poor adaptation, not least because managers fail to learn from their experience (see also Bettman and Weitz 1983; Staw *et al.* 1983; Huff and Schwenk 1990; Clapham and Schwenck 1991; Gronhaug and Falkenberg 1998).

Structure of the book

Before concluding this chapter it is useful to outline some of the principal issues and themes to be addressed in the remainder of the book. As we shall seek to demonstrate throughout, the adoption of a managerial and organizational cognition perspective is beginning to shed light on a number of long-standing problems within the wider strategy field.

A truly comprehensive psychological analysis of the strategic management process is impossible within the confines of a single volume. As Hodgkinson (2001b) has observed, the range of issues that legitimately fall within the thematic purview of this rapidly developing specialty is potentially as broad as the wider field of strategic management as a whole, covering all aspects of strategy formulation, choice and implementation. In recent years, researchers have investigated topics as varied as the psychological impact of mergers and acquisitions (Cartwright and Cooper 1990, 1993; Hogan and Overmyer-Day 1994), cognitive processes in the boardroom (Forbes and Milliken 1999), strategic issue processing, image and organizational identity (Dutton and Jackson 1987; Jackson and Dutton 1988; Dutton and Dukerich 1991; Jackson 1992; Gioia and Thomas 1996), psychological aspects of entrepreneurship (Frese et al. 2000; Rauch and Frese 2000) and psychological processes underpinning organizational learning and strategic renewal (Barr and Huff 1997; Barr 1998; Brown and Starkey 2000; Floyd and Lane 2000). Indeed, such has been the scale of the many advances that have occurred over recent years, that the literature on virtually all of the topics to be addressed in this book is now sufficiently well developed that they could each form the sole focus of attention of the entire volume. Consequently, our coverage must be selective, both in terms of the range of topics addressed and which particular issues we highlight.

In the next two chapters, we continue our analysis at the organizational level, commencing with a chapter on organizational learning (Chapter 2). Sense-making and learning are two inseparable concepts. Organizational learning is also seen to lie at the heart of competitive strategy. In this chapter we explore two types of competency. While the work surveyed in this chapter touches upon some of the *individual* behavioural competencies that are needed in order to manage organizational learning processes, our main focus is at the *organizational* level. What do organizations need to do in order to manage learning across the organization as a whole? We make some important distinctions between the learning organization and the process of organizational learning. A series of perspectives on organizational learning are introduced. The role of implicit or tacit knowledge is also introduced. We focus on how organizations can elicit this hidden knowledge by examining a variety of communication and knowledge management processes within the learning organization, and linking these processes to the knowledge structures that exist within the organization. We examine the way in which knowledge can be transferred effectively across networks of people and consider how communities of effective practice can be developed. We also introduce the opposite of organizational learning: organizational forgetting. Indeed, throughout this book it will be seen that in order to better understand the competencies needed for the effective strategic management of organizations, often we must also comprehend the dysfunctional processes that can occur within these settings.

It is important to note that strategic management is not solely the preserve of the top management team. In Chapter 3 we consider the contextual factors that shape strategic cognitions in a wide variety of team settings, homing in on the interrelated concepts of organizational memory, knowledge management and distributed cognition. We consider ways in which strategic knowledge is distributed throughout the organization as a whole. In particular, we consider the utility of the notion of 'team mental models' and examine the processes by which teams within the lower reaches of the organization develop and share their strategic knowledge. Many teams (or individual managers) now work across distributed networks. We introduce the ways in which cognition can be managed, first across networks of people and then in the context of human-machine interaction in team settings. Having developed the argument that cognition can reside outside the individual manager (i.e. within the wider social and physical workplace environment), we examine organizational culture as a form of collective cognition. Drawing upon the organizational culture literature, we illustrate some of the ways in which taken for granted routines and procedures can serve as repositories of organizational memory. We also highlight the fact that increasingly individual managers are acting as knowledge brokers within the informational market-place.

We continue our journey in Chapter 4 with a consideration of environmental analysis, which is often viewed as the logical starting point of strategic analysis. We demonstrate how psychological research concerned with actors' mental models of competition sheds light on the socio-cognitive processes through which organizations, both individually and collectively, create their own industry and market structures, and competitive niches. This chapter also highlights the ways in which the processes by which competitive territory comes to be defined and protected (through the social construction of isolating mechanisms, i.e. entry and mobility barriers) can also become a major barrier to subsequent learning. Cognitive inertia is a very real danger that can arise in the context of well-established competitive fields, which serves to inhibit organizational learning and strategic renewal. We conclude with a review of other research on competition and cognition that has drawn attention to the need to better understand the micro-processes that shape strategic cognition at the level of the individual strategic decision maker and within the wider top management team.

In Chapter 5 we take a closer look at the processes through which executives (both as individuals and in the context team functioning) develop mental representations of strategic issues and problems in general. As we shall see, a great volume of research has accumulated over recent years concerned with the ways in which the cognitive processes of the 'dominant coalition' serve to determine the strategic choices and outcomes of the organization. However, it is only very recently that researchers have begun to study executive cognition directly, much of the previous work having studied the functioning of executive teams 'from a distance', using demographic variables as a proxy for cognition.

Continuing our analysis at the level of the individual, in Chapter 6 we explore a number of individual differences that ultimately have a bearing on the ways in which actors process strategic information. We consider directly the question of what it means to be strategically competent as an individual and how such competence might be fostered, through training and development interventions, or selected for, through the use of psychometrically sound assessment procedures.

Having thoroughly explored the nature of organizational learning and strategic competence, the factors that shape such competence (at the individual, group, organizational and interorganizational levels of analysis), in Chapter 7 we provide an overview of the various techniques that have been developed over recent years, both in an effort to further understand the nature of strategic cognition and to facilitate organizational learning and strategic renewal.

In Chapter 8 we draw together the main lessons from our analysis for researchers and practitioners/consultants, and highlight what we consider to be some of the most pressing priorities for future research.

2

ORGANIZATIONAL LEARNING

We argued in the opening chapter that organizational learning is seen to lie at the heart of strategic competence. Gottlieb Daimler and the Karl Benz Foundation sponsor interdisciplinary research groups to form a *Kolleg* (series of lectures) on critical management issues. From 1994 to 2000 the Ladenburger *Kolleg* brought together more than 30 academics, managers and consultants to consider the issue of organizational learning. It was found to be a central strategic topic in the context of the worldwide processes of business transformation that we are currently witnessing (Dierkes *et al.* 2001). Indeed, competitive advantage for organizations is considered to flow from the creation, ownership and management of knowledge assets-based enterprises (McKeen 2001). This view is predicated on the assumption that knowledge-based enterprises are more efficient than markets at gathering information and disseminating understanding because they have reduced communication costs and heightened capabilities to support individual learning and the management of knowledge. In short, knowledge-based enterprises have to convert social capital into intellectual capital, and organizational learning is central to this transformation process.

We begin this chapter by giving consideration to the different ways that academics from the main strategic management schools of thought each consider the process of organizational learning. Van der Heijden and Eden (1998) have provided a useful analysis in this respect, drawing on three contrasting schools of thought that Mintzberg (1990) and Whittington (1993) argue have become dominant in the field of strategic management: the *rational*, *evolutionary* and *processual* schools of thought (see Box 2.1).

Box 2.1: Organizational learning as viewed from the perspective of three contrasting schools of thought on strategic management

The *rational school* of thought on strategy considers that the strategist thinks on behalf of the whole organization in order to determine the best way forward (analysis and choice). Thought and action (implementation) are seen as being distinct from each other, with action being seen as a problem of implementation. The strategist is therefore faced with a task of predictability and setting clear objectives and intentions. Implementation follows from formulation. It is assumed that reasonable people will do reasonable things, and that implementation according to plan is achievable as long as full understanding is communicated throughout the organization.

The *evolutionary school* of thought, by contrast, considers that organizational behaviour is complex and that many aspects of it are beyond the bounds of rational thinking. Strategy is a perspective or label that can be put on emergent behaviour, and successful strategies can best be articulated after the fact. Organizations can develop a memory that captures previously successful strategies and this can be transmitted to managers. Strategy is, however, a process of random experimentation, filtering priorities and learning by doing. Strategic change is driven by the emergence of new forms of organizational power, and strategic thinking is consequently valued by managers as a source of influence and personal power.

The *processual school* takes the middle ground. Strategies cannot be worked out in a rational way, but a series of processes can be created and managed by strategic leaders in order to make the organization more flexible, adaptable and receptive to change. Organizations, therefore, are able to learn from their mistakes.

Source: Van der Heijden and Eden (1998)

Pettigrew and Whipp (1991), who consider strategic management from a processual perspective, argue that organizational learning lies at the heart of competitive strategy, and that the ability to learn equates to the ability of an organization to reconstruct and adapt its knowledge base (comprising skills, structures and values). In order to accomplish such learning, organizations have to be capable of creatively destroying outmoded practices and attitudes: 'The ability to learn faster than competitors may be an organization's only sustainable advantage' (Pettigrew and Whipp 1991: 290).

By necessity, this chapter has to cover a very wide territory. It also has to convey a number of competing perspectives. This is because during the 1990s academics from the fields of management science, production management, cultural anthropology, strategic management, sociology, psychology and organization theory *all* incorporated concepts of the learning organization or organizational learning within their disciplines (Easterby-Smith 1997). There has been an increasing convergence of interests between researchers from very different disciplines. Philosophers, cognitive scientists, computer scientists, social psychologists and anthropologists have all made important contributions to our understanding of the topic (Spender 1998).

It is important to note at the outset that the basic distinction between 'organizational learning' and the 'learning organization' is much more than a subtle play on semantics. As Argyris (1999: 1) has observed:

We divide the literature that pays serious attention to organizational learning into two main categories: the practice-oriented, prescriptive literature of 'the learning organization', promulgated mainly by consultants and practitioners, and the predominantly skeptical scholarly literature of 'organizational learning', produced by academics. The two literatures have different thrusts, appeal to different audiences, and employ different forms of language. Nevertheless, they intersect at key points: their conceptions of what makes organizational learning 'desirable', or 'productive'; their views of the nature of the threats to productive organizational learning; and their attitudes toward whether – and if so, how – such threats may be overcome.

The learning organization is seen as an institution that identifies, promotes and evaluates the quality of its learning processes inside the organization (Tsang 1997). Organizational learning, on the other hand, is a process that is evidenced by the degree to which individuals acquire chunks of knowledge, develop and spread

---

Box 2.2: Key definitions and characteristics of organizational learning and the learning organization

In this box we illustrate the rich diversity of definitions and features that the many writers working on this topic have variously highlighted.

- A process of detecting and correcting error (Argyris 1977).
- A process of improving actions through better knowledge and understanding (Fiol and Lyles 1985).
- Encoding of inferences from history into routines that guide current behaviour (Levitt and March 1988).
- Shared insights, knowledge and mental models that build on past knowledge and memory (Strata 1989).
- An organization which learns and encourages learning in its people (Handy 1989).
- The synthesis of a diverse set of assumptions or beliefs into a commonly shared understanding (Ginsberg 1990).
- The expansion of an organization's capacity to create its own future and the results it really desires. A process whereby people continually learn how to learn together (Senge 1990a).
- The processing of information in order to change the range of potential behaviours. The acquisition of knowledge that is recognized as potentially useful to the organization (Huber 1991).
- The creation of new knowledge (making tacit knowledge become explicit), dissemination of it throughout the whole organization and embodiment of it into new technologies, products and services (Nonaka 1991).
- The creation, acquisition and transfer of knowledge, and the skilful modification of the organization's behaviour to reflect new knowledge and insights. Seeing the world in a new light. Learning from the organization's own experiences and history, and the experiences and best practices of others (Garvin 1993).

---

this knowledge within the organization, gain acceptance of it, and recognize this knowledge as being potentially useful (Huber 1991). Not surprisingly, there has been a proliferation of increasingly varied definitions of both of these terms, as illustrated in Box 2.2.

The learning organization

Two major perspectives on the learning organization have emerged, although they are by no means mutually exclusive:

- providing a values proposition and a logic for managing and organizing;
- requisite managerial competencies for a learning organization.

In this section we consider each in turn.

Providing a values proposition and a logic for managing and organizing

Arvedson (1993) argued that most concepts of the learning organization draw upon and stress the importance of the search for a 'new logic for managing and organizing', as well as a set of desirable values that enabled this new logic for managing and organizing to happen. Building on the argument that the learning organization is an idealistic, values-laden goal, he pointed out that it is not so much that we *have to* create learning organizations (i.e. for strategic or competitive reasons) but that we *want to* (i.e. the concept suits the organizational zeitgeist or values of our time). The more that managers become aware that there are many different (but equally successful) ways of organizing and managing, the harder they find it to adopt an analytical, scientific view of management. They replace this scientific perspective with a view that considers management as an *art*. This perspective stresses the importance of assumptions, guesses and underlying values in any learning process. The task of building a learning organization reinforces the values that people want in work. What are these values? Two core principles seem to be valued within the learning organization literature:

- Organizations should become platforms for individuals, rather than individuals becoming resources for organizations;
- People are more effective when they are intrinsically motivated to take action and to learn (unless the organization systematically deprives them of the opportunity to do so), rather than extrinsically motivated through such things as reward.

Hence, the learning organization, when viewed from the 'a logic for managing and organizing' perspective, is seen as a context for people – an ideal type of organization where effective learning (in the eyes of its practitioners) takes place. Consequently, much of the literature is geared towards measuring and calibrating institutions against this ideal, concentrating on the diagnostic and evaluative tools that can promote the quality of learning processes inside organizations (Tsang 1997). The purpose of this work has been to develop normative models that facilitate change in, and then improve, learning processes within the organization. These models have been developed from either a technical or a social perspective (Easterby-Smith and Araujo 1999). Those who take a technical perspective emphasize the measurement of learning outcomes – typically through the use of production cost learning curves, product quality indicators and employee attitudinal or behavioural data (Argote et al. 1990; Garvin 1993).

Requisite managerial competencies for a learning organization

Much early work also focused on the characteristics of a learning organization (from either a technical or social perspective). These characteristics tended to suggest a series of necessary managerial competencies. From a technical perspective, as observed by Adler and Cole (1993), writers stressed the development of organizational competences that facilitate the:

- introduction of information systems to collect relevant metrics;
- standardization of information; and
- rapid sharing of problem solutions across relevant work units.

In this book we give most attention to the social perspective on the learning organization, exemplified the work of Senge (1990a), Isaacs (1993), Peters and Waterman (1982), and Swieringa and

Weirdsma (1992). These writers take the ability of individuals to learn from their experiences or from others in the work setting as their starting point. They have developed models of the learning process, or have outlined a series of phases through which organizations have to pass in order to learn. They tend to delineate a series of linear, progressively desirable, hierarchical stages through which organizations progress, or a number of cyclical phases that enable organizational practices or processes to be classified as being increasingly effective (Easterby-Smith and Araujo 1999).

Some important distinctions were drawn in this early work. For example, many academics would acknowledge that while they work in *learned* organizations (institutions that are full of clever and educated people), they might not consider that they work in *learning* organizations. Universities, for example, are often very traditional, institutionalized and rigid places. Adaptation makes the difference between learning and just being learned. De Geus (1988) argued that in a changing environment the only organisms that survive are those which adapt. Salaman (2001) too notes the use of metaphors that imply evolutionary dynamics within organizations. Peters and Waterman (1982) used this sort of biological analogy to capture the essence of the learning organization when they argued that their 'excellent companies' had managed to maintain adaptability over a longer time period than their competitors because they 'intentionally seeded evolution'. This seeding of evolutionary processes within the organization was achieved by creating internal market-places that encouraged competition. According to Peters and Waterman (1982), these market-places led to:

- higher levels of experimentation;
- provision of the permission to fail;
- duplication and overlap;
- the facilitation of small-scale organization and team learning;
- the encouragement of interaction with the most sophisticated internal and external customers; and
- the creation of an information-laden environment that diffused ideas that work.

The social perspective is therefore strongly values-laden. This is perhaps nowhere more evident than in the work of Senge, who in defining the learning organization argues that 'first, you must realize that the very idea of a "learning organization" is a vision' (1990b: 58). He weaves together general ideas about the motivation to learn, team learning, leadership and managerial mental models into what constitutes a basic value proposition and competency specification for the learning organization (see Box 2.3). These values in turn suggest a series of important behavioural competencies that are needed to enable this vision. A number of other writers have emphasized the importance of systemic knowledge in this context (Checkland and Scholes 1990; Kim 1993; Richmond 1993; Balle 1994).

Salaman (2001) sees parallels between Senge's notion of the learning organization and features of Nonaka and Takeuchi's (1995) 'knowledge creating company' (discussed later in this chapter) and the work of Quinn (1992) on the 'intelligent enterprise'. These writers stress the role of an 'alert senior management cadre capable of anticipating and understanding environmental developments and then being able to redesign the organization quickly and efficiently to ensure its compatibility with strategy' (Salaman 2001: 346).

To summarize, Senge (1990a) argues that organizations are the way they are because of the way that their people think. A necessary building block for the learning organization is a set of individuals who take responsibility for their own learning (Arvedson 1993). Although individual learning is not enough to ensure learning at the organizational level, the learning organization can only become a reality when individuals allow themselves to be stretched, willingly challenge their own assumptions, reflect on events, relate their learning to insights, take risks, become emotionally involved with the organization and act through changed behaviour. From Senge's perspective, then, the learning organization is very dependent on the individual competencies of the managers within it. Different authors have highlighted different competencies. For Senge (1992) (and Isaacs, another member of the MIT Organizational Learning Center) these competencies are driven by the skills associated with generative learning, leadership in a knowledge-based organization and the creation of dialogue. For Peters and Waterman (1982) the

---

Box 2.3: Senge's perspective on the learning organization

Senge (1990a) draws attention to the transformation away from the 'resource-based organization' towards the 'knowledge-based organization'. Arvedson (1993) outlines a series of key elements in Senge's thinking that differentiated resource- and knowledge-based organizations across five basic tasks that are central to all organizations:

Tasks and key characteristics	Resource-based organization	Knowledge-based organization
Setting direction	Achieved by creating a vision at the top.	Achieved through creating shared visions. Can emerge from many places. The role of the top is to ensure that a vision exists, not necessarily to create it.
Thinking and executing	The top thinks, the local managers act.	Thinking and acting are merged at all levels.
Nature of thinking	Atomistic thinking.	Systemic thinking.
Conflict resolution	Conflict is mediated politically.	Dialogue is set up to integrate diverse views and build shared mental models.
Role of leadership	Leaders motivate people toward attainment of the vision through rewards and recognition, make the key decisions and create the structures to control local actions.	Leaders build a shared vision, empower people, inspire commitment and enable good decisions to be made throughout the organization by designing learning processes. The leader acts as designer of the organization, teacher, coach, facilitator and steward.

Senge argues that in the resource-based organization people have to know their jobs, but do not need to know how these jobs interrelate with one another. Knowledge- or information-based organizations, on the other hand, require more systemic thinking in order to avoid any devolution of power simply leading to chaos. Senge draws attention to two types of competencies: learning and leadership competencies.

Maintaining the survival and biological metaphor, he distinguishes between different types of learning: what he calls 'survival' or 'adaptive learning', and 'generative learning'. Adaptive learning is about coping. It is seen as a necessary and important form of learning, but one that is insufficient for the learning organization. Generative learning, by contrast, enhances our ability to create. It requires the capability to see the systems that control events: 'the key to seeing reality systemically is seeing circles of influence rather than straight lines . . . every circle tells a story' (Senge 1990a: 75). It is this insight into systems that control events that enables managers to develop new ways of looking at the world (Senge 1992). Few managers are skilled in generative learning.

For Senge, another reason why the learning organization is so hard to create is because the majority of managers do not have the appropriate leadership competencies. Leadership competencies have historically been couched in terms of individualistic and non-systemic worldviews, stressing the importance of charismatic decision making. Senge argues that leadership instead needs to be more distributed throughout the organization in order to ensure learning. Moreover, given that most knowledge in organizations is based on subjective insights, intuitions and hunches, mutual understanding is needed before any significant conceptualization, experimentation and reflection can take place. In order to create knowledge, managers need to tap the tacit knowledge of their subordinates. To do this they have to learn the discipline of managing mental models (their own models and other peoples') – surfacing, testing and improving the internal pictures that people have of how the world works. Four skills are important for managers in articulating these mental models:

- recognizing leaps of abstraction – i.e. jumps from observation to global generalization;
- exposing and articulating what is normally not said – i.e. implicit assumptions;

- balancing inquiry and advocacy when learning from failure;
- noting the difference between what is said (espoused theory) and what is done (theory in use).

attitudes, skills and competencies associated with the acquisition and capture of knowledge from customers, outsiders and each other are central to the learning organization. For Garvin (1993), it is competencies in systematic problem solving, experimentation with new approaches, learning from one's own experience and past history and the experiences of others, and the ability to transfer knowledge quickly and efficiently throughout the organization, that form the essential components.

Organizational learning

To some observers the linear/sequential view associated with work on the learning organization (from either a technical or social perspective) is overly simplistic. By the early 1990s, concerns were growing that the concept of the learning organization had become over-exploited and in many ways was being trivialized (Arvedson 1993). The work of theorists such as Senge (1990a, 1990b, 1992), Pedler *et al.* (1989) and Field and Ford (1995) had become commercially significant for organizations and had spawned several consulting approaches aimed at developing the learning organization (Easterby-Smith and Araujo 1999). The attractiveness of the approach lay in the fact that most organizations agreed on the need to adapt to a changing environment, to learn from the past, and finally anticipate and then respond to threats and opportunities through continuous innovation (Ayas 1999). However, conclusive empirical evidence to support interventions seeking to develop the learning organization is hard to find. Easterby-Smith and Araujo (1999) note that of 150 papers on the learning organization published by 1997, only 10 per cent were based on empirical data, and most of these were founded on action research and personal interventions by the authors.

As noted earlier, however, a distinction is frequently drawn between the concept of the learning organization and organizational learning. The latter is an academic field of study that has examined the process of individual and collective learning (and unlearning) within or across organizations (Easterby-Smith and Araujo 1999). In searching for the theoretical underpinnings of the topic, Prange (1999) outlined the main concepts that have been used to capture the construct of organizational learning (see Table 2.1).

Within the organizational learning literature, as with the learning organization literature, a distinction can be drawn between those who take a technical view and those who take a social view (Easterby-Smith and Araujo 1999). The work of people from each of these perspectives emphasizes the importance of very different sets of organizational and individual competencies, and very different routes to gaining these competencies.

The distinction made in Chapter 1 between the computational and interpretative perspectives on managerial and organizational cognition is also echoed within the organizational learning literature. Hence, the *social perspective* on organizational learning, seen in the work of Brown and Duguid (1991) and Orr (1990), examines the way that people make sense of their experiences at work. Easterby-Smith and Araujo (1999) note that the experience base and source of learning may be explicit (e.g. based on hard information) or may be more tacit (e.g. the 'feel' experienced by a craftsperson, or the intuition of a skilled strategist). Learning is, however, seen as a political process embedded in the culture of the organization. Data have no significance until people determine what they mean. Formal instructions about how to do a job are inadequate (Brown and Duguid 1991). New entrants learn the unwritten rules about how to perform competently through informal exchanges between experienced and less experienced people, the use of anecdotes, metaphors and war stories (Orr 1990). From this perspective, eliminating organizational politics is seen as both naïve and idealistic. The presentation of internal and external information to stakeholders in a way that suits the purpose of a business unit is not viewed, in a negative way, as 'spin'. Rather, it is seen as a necessary competence. Organizational learning is not something that takes

Table 2.1 Building blocks in organizational learning (OL) theory development

Author(s)/year	Definition of OL	Who? (Content of OL)	What? (Content of OL)	When? (Incentives for OL)	With what results? (Efficiency of OL)	How? (Processes of OL)
Cyert and March (1963)	Organizational learning is adaptive behaviour of organizations over time	Aggregate level of organization	Standard operating procedures and organizational rules	Slack resources	Adaptation to changing environmental states; improved adaptation as prerequisite for survival	Adaptation of goal, attention and search rules; learning from experience
Cangelosi and Dill (1965)	Organizational learning consists of a series of inter-actions between adaptation at the individual, or sub-group level and adaptation at the organizational level	Individuals and sub-groups in organizations	Complex management decisions	Stress stimulates learning, both sub-system and total system learning, separately and together	Reduction of stress, and improved decision making	Adaptation to conflicting patterns of behaviour caused by stress
Argyris and Schön (1978)	Organizational learning is the process by which organizational members detect errors or anomalies and correct them by restructuring organizational theory in use	Individual learning in organizations	Organizational theories in use or theories of action	Match or mismatch of expected outcomes or discredit of organizational theories in use	Link between learning and improved action	Assumption sharing; individual and collective inquiry constructs and modifies theories in use; exact process remains unclear

Duncan and Weiss (1979)	Organizational learning is defined as the process within the organization by which knowledge about action out-come relationships and the effect of the environment on these relationships is developed	The individual is the only entity who can learn. However, they must be seen as a part of a system of learning with exchanges of what is learned among individuals	Organizational knowledge base	Slack resources	Depends on available organizational knowledge for decision making; adaptation to changing environmental states	Development of action-outcome-relations via: (a) sharing (b) evaluation (c) integration
Fiol and Lyles (1985)	Organizational learning means the process of improving actions through better knowledge and understanding	Organizational learning is not simply the sum of individual learning	Patterns of cognitive associations and/or new responses or actions (cognitive vs. behavioural change)	Tension between constancy and change; crisis (especially for higher-level learning)	Environmental alignment; future performance improvement	Low-level learning as repetition of past behaviour, high-level learning as development of complex associations

Table 2.1 Continued

Author(s)/year	Definition of OL	Who? (Content of OL)	What? (Content of OL)	When? (Incentives for OL)	With what results? (Efficiency of OL)	How? (Processes of OL)
Levitt and March (1988)	Organizations are seen as learning by encoding inferences from history into routine behaviour	Organizational learning is more than individual learning; there is an 'emergent' component	Routines which include rules, procedures, frameworks, cultures, belief structures, paradigms etc.	Outcomes in response to aspiration level	Adaptation to changing environmental states; balance between exploration and exploitation	Learning from direct experience; learning from the experience of others; learning of paradigms for interpretation
Huber (1991)	An entity learns if, through the processing of information, the range of its potential behaviours is changed ... Let us assume that an organization learns if any of its units acquires knowledge that it recognizes as potentially useful to the organization	Concept of entity, which include individuals, groups organizations, industries, society	Information/ knowledge	Probably not intended as author aims to describe a whole range of learning sub-categories	Range of potential behaviour change, not necessarily resulting in *observable* changes	Information processing: acquisition, distribution, interpretation and storage of information; the related *processes* of organizational learning remain unspecified

		Connections	Behaviour/actions	Necessity for nearly error free operations, e.g. aircraft carriers	Decrease of organizational errors	Heedful interrelating via:
Weick and Roberts (1993)	Organizational learning[1] consists of interrelating actions of individuals; that is their 'heedful inter-relation' which results in a 'collective mind'	between behaviour, rather than people				(a) contribution (b) representation (c) subordination

1 In fact, Weick has never used the label 'organizational learning' in his work. He has used concepts which may substitute for learning, such as: improvisation, interpretation, assimilation, variation, selection, heedful interrelation etc. Weick (1979a, 1991) and Weick and Roberts (1993) take it for granted that some kind of memory for something is available, and then try to understand what people do with it. Thereby, they work farther downstream than do many scholars of learning.

Source: reproduced by permission of the publisher from C. Prange (1999) Organizational learning – desperately seeking theory? in M. Easterby-Smith, J. Burgoyne and L. Araujo (eds), *Organizational Learning and the Learning Organization.* London: Sage. © Christiane Prange.

place in the heads of individuals, but is accomplished through interaction (Easterby-Smith and Araujo 1999).

The *technical perspective* on organizational learning can be seen in the work of Huber (1991), Argyris and Schön (1978) and Zuboff (1988). From this perspective, organizational learning centres on the effective processing of information (acquisition, storage, interpretation and retrieval). This view is more or less commensurate with our opening definition of strategic competence. Information is assumed to be both explicit and generally available within the public domain, and learning is created through a process of 'informating' (i.e. making information more available to all).

The technical view of organizational learning recognizes the problem of politicking within organizations as being persistent, but this is considered to be a problem that can be nullified. However, it is hard to discuss the issue of learning in isolation of organizational politics. Organizational competency sets that de-emphasize politicking and generate 'healthy risk perceptions' are important in the creation of competent organizations. Levinthal and March (1993) argue that in many situations organizations have to find a balance between the exploration of new technological products or processes (which can lead to new strategies and knowledge in the long term) and their exploitation (which can lead to high profitability in the short term, but provide no foundation of wealth). This is to be expected. However, problems occur for organizations when people do not behave according to rational calculations, but follow their own political (and often risk-laden) agendas. Political processes can affect access to and ownership of information as well as the ways in which meaning is generated from that information. All too often, managers do not act in the best interests of the wider organization; they distort or suppress information to support preferred agendas, and use information selectively to validate decisions that serve their personal interests (Coopey 1995).

Psychologists have used the analysis of disasters to gain insight into both risk-taking behaviour and learning in organizations. Disasters such as the Piper Alpha accident (Paté-Cornell 1993) and the *Challenger* space shuttle accident (Heimann 1993; Vaughan 1996; Starbuck and Hedberg 2001) have revealed important sources of cognitive bias and constraints on learning. Vaughan (1996) analysed the *Challenger* disaster and identified the way in which the culture within NASA and its suppliers brought about a process of 'deviance normalization' whereby managers and engineers could interpret potential technical problems as if they were not problems. They were able to make regular formal redefinitions of acceptable and unacceptable risks in which the whole engineering community were willing to participate. Similarly, DiBella *et al.* (1996) showed that the Chernobyl disaster was caused by a radical departure from existing operational parameters as engineers were experimenting with a new form of online refuelling. Had these engineers been successful in their work they would have achieved a major scientific breakthrough and would have been praised for having the courage to engage in 'double-loop learning' (Easterby-Smith and Araujo 1999).

Cognitive change and commonly shared understandings

It is generally held by those who take a technical view of organizational learning that organizations do not learn as entities, but their members do. Cognition and learning are seen as two sides of the same coin. Individuals act on a stage – which is the organization – and learn from this acting (Hedberg 1981). Many writers, therefore, project models of individual learning directly onto the organization. In so doing, some believe that cognitions can be mapped as if organizations themselves were unitary actors (Porac *et al.* 1987; Spender 1989) while others argue that cognition can only belong to individual managers (Bougon 1992; Eden 1992). We shall return to this complex issue of individual versus collective cognition in later chapters. For the moment is it enough to note that despite such differing assumptions, many writers (e.g. Inkpen and Crossan 1995; Leroy and Ramanantsoa 1997) use the idea of cognitive (and behavioural) change as the elementary basis for understanding organizational learning (cf. Starbuck and Hedberg 2001).

For Argyris and Schön (1978) learning entails the construction, testing and restructuring of 'theories of action'. Organizations learn as their individual members learn, in their capacity as agents of organizational action. Knowledge is acquired and developed by individuals and is embedded in an organizational memory (see Chapter 3). Several other writers also view learning as the development of causal action-to-outcome relationships (e.g. Duncan and Weiss 1979; Hedberg 1981; Fiol and Lyles 1985).

Organizational learning is also seen as the degree to which members acquire chunks of knowledge and recognize them as being potentially useful (Huber 1991). The existence of organizational learning for Huber is evidenced by the development of knowledge among individual members. The spread of this knowledge represents the breadth of organizational learning. Organizational learning is seen as a two-way process (as is made clear in the discussion of 'dialogue' later in this chapter). Huber views organizational learning in terms of its:

- *Elaborateness* – i.e. the variety of organizational knowledge. Learning accelerates as knowledge becomes more varied and elaborate and the possibilities for action are expanded.
- *Thoroughness* – i.e. the degree to which the comprehension and interpretation by various individuals is uniform.

Elaborateness is very similar to early psychological concepts of cognitive complexity at the individual level, and to Ginsberg's (1990) ideas about socio-cognitive complexity within management teams (see also Chapter 5). Thoroughness can be related to Ginsberg's ideas about socio-cognitive consensus within top teams. For Ginsberg (1990), the socio-cognitive consensus of top teams is an important element of organizational learning, which revolves around the synthesis of commonly shared understandings (see his definition in Box 2.2). In order to learn, top teams need diverse perspectives (socio-cognitive complexity) and, paradoxically, shared interpretations of reality. Fiol (1994) sees this socio-cognitive consensus in terms of the level of agreement in respect of the frames of reference used to interpret situations. The meaning attributed to objects and events is related to the context of actors' schemata, and the context within which these are employed (we shall return to the issue of cognitive consensus and the factors that shape it in Chapters 4 and 5).

Tacit knowledge and the competent mindlessness of the individual

So how do organizations develop this socio-cognitive consensus? The organizational learning literature has traditionally emphasized the need to inquire into *implicit intelligence* – forms of knowledge, processing and learning that lie outside the conscious, rational model of cognition (Spender 1998). Sociological theory and research has played an important role in building early understandings about this implicit form of knowledge, known as *tacit knowledge* (Polanyi 1967). The interest of sociologists has been in the sheer quantity of what people have to learn in order to partake in what are complex social tasks within organizations. They have considered the possibility that although there is a qualitative difference between the explicit knowledge of which we are aware and the implicit knowledge that often guides our action, both forms of knowledge are necessary for skilled performance (see also Chapter 6). Polanyi studied the nature of scientific discovery and distinguished between objective knowledge and tacit knowledge, with his often quoted conclusion that 'people know more than they can tell' (Polanyi 1967: 4). For him the issue was one of the communicability of this hidden, implicit knowledge. He defined 'tacitness' as a quality of the communicability of knowledge. Tacit knowledge is of a different degree of articulation rather than knowledge of a different type (Spender 1998).

In order to build on the idea of implicit knowledge we have to move for a while into the world of cognitive psychology, and work by learning and developmental psychologists who have looked at the development of individual-level knowledge. Cognitive psychologists now believe that the evidence for there being an alternative mode of human cognizing is overwhelming, and in Chapter 6 we consider this view in the context of intuition and intuitive decision making. Cognitive psychologists argue that there is also knowledge and intelligence of a different type and not just of a nature that is hard to articulate (Schultz 1953, 1972; Reber 1993). Reber (1993: 5) defines implicit learning as 'the acquisition of knowledge that takes place largely independently of conscious attempts to learn and in the absence of explicit knowledge about what [is] learned'. It has been argued that while managerial decisions are not considered to be irrational, they are made using processes that do not take rational elements into account. People make choices correctly, but do so by drawing upon knowledge that they are unaware of (Scribner 1985, 1986). This is known as competent mindlessness. It is defined as a 'state of flow', driven by automatic processing (Csikszentmihalyi and Csikszentmihalyi 1988), from whence we get the concept of skilled performance based on insight about when it is important to 'go with the flow'. If there are parallel forms of information processing (be they conscious or unconscious) then it seems equally possible that there are also explicit and tacit aspects of memory and learning. For Reber (1993), implicit memory is evidenced when an individual displays a memory of an earlier experience without being conscious that the experience took place. While the notion of implicit memory remains somewhat controversial, there is evidence to suggest that areas of the brain are locally specialized to different forms of memory and researchers have concluded that there are alternative systems of knowledge, complete with their own means of knowledge representation, learning, storage, recognition, retrieval and computation (Lewicki 1986; Lewicki *et al.* 1987, 1988; Spender 1998).

Eliciting tacit knowledge: organizational knowledge creation processes

To what extent does the existence of a tacit and unconscious form of individual memory, learning and knowledge apply to the collective and organizational context, and what are the implications for developing competence in organizational learning? Lubit (2001) notes that competitors in industries as varied as watches, cars, cameras, industrial robots, financial services, computer chips and consulting services each faced a sector that was initially dominated by a company with specialized knowledge. However, in every case, the dominant organization rapidly lost its lead as other companies acquired the knowledge needed to compete. Knowledge has an increasingly transient value, such that: 'core competencies can turn into core rigidities impeding performance, if changes in an industry, or advances by one's competitors, are not countered by the ability to rapidly develop and spread new knowledge' (Lubit 2001: 165).

Nonaka (1991) argued that any organization that wants to compete on the basis of knowledge must learn how to create new knowledge. He used Japanese techniques of knowledge creation to highlight the competencies that are needed (see Box 2.4). Knowledge creation has to be the centre of an organization's human resource strategy because 'new knowledge always begins with the individual' (Nonaka 1991: 97). Nonaka criticized the

---

Box 2.4: Four patterns of knowledge creation

The distinction between tacit and explicit knowledge suggests four basic approaches to the creation of new knowledge in any organization:

- *From tacit to tacit*: one individual shares tacit knowledge directly with another, learned through observation, imitation and practice. This process requires organizational competence in *socialization* (learning tacit knowledge).
- *From explicit to explicit*: discrete pieces of explicit knowledge are combined into a new whole – i.e. synthesized information. This process requires organizational competence in *combination* (standardization of knowledge).
- *From tacit to explicit*: the most powerful form of knowledge creation. This process requires organizational competence in *articulation* (translating tacit knowledge into a communicable form).
- *From explicit to tacit*: new knowledge that once shared becomes internalized in the minds of employees and is used to broaden, extend and reframe their own tacit knowledge. This process requires organizational competence in *internalization* (intuitive understanding and expansion of one's own tacit knowledge base).

According to Nonaka, all four processes and their associated competencies must exist in the knowledge-creating organization. They serve as modes of knowledge conversion and 'crystallize' and 'amplify' knowledge beyond the individual to other parts of the organization.

Source: Nonaka (1991), Nonaka *et al.* (1996)

---

view propounded by Simon (see Chapter 1), that organizations act as information processing machines, in which the only useful knowledge is hard, quantifiable data, coded procedures and universal principles. Tacit knowledge consists partly of hard to pin down technical skills called 'know-how'. It also has an important cognitive dimension, and consists of the mental models, beliefs and perspectives that are ingrained in the minds of employees. Drawing on insights into the innovation process within firms such as Honda, Canon, Matsushita, NEC, Sharp and Kao, Nonaka argued that there was a unique approach to the management and creation of new knowledge, which he believed involved 'Tapping the tacit and often highly subjective insights, intuitions and hunches of individual employees and making those insights available for testing and use by the company as a whole' (1991: 97).

Gaining tacit knowledge requires 'a way of behaving' and the use of processes of 'self-renewal' within the organization, because knowledge has to be mobilized and even embodied within the actual technologies and products. It is these that ultimately provide the firm with competitive advantage, not just the intellectual property of the managers who devise the products. Figurative language and symbolism is one of the most powerful ways of making tacit knowledge explicit. Cryptic slogans, analogies and metaphors can create images and symbols in the minds of employees that can lead to a more holistic approach to knowledge creation. The use of metaphor is key in this process:

> Metaphor is a distinctive method of perception. It is a way for individuals grounded in different contexts and with different experiences to understand something intuitively through the use of imagination and symbols without the need for analysis or generalization. Through metaphors people put together what they know in new ways and begin to express what they know but cannot yet say. As such, metaphor is highly effective in fostering direct commitment to the creative process in early stages of knowledge creation.
>
> (Nonaka 1991: 100)

Nonaka identifies three individual-level functions critical to organizational learning. By establishing a connection between two areas of experience through *metaphor* to form an inclusive image or symbol, a discrepancy or tension is set up. The multiple meanings and contradictory logics can jump-start the creative process. The next step is *analogy*. Whereas metaphor is driven by intuition, analogy is a more structured process of reconciling contradictions and making distinctions – an intermediate step between pure imagination and logical thinking. The last step is the development of an actual *model*, which is far more immediately conceivable than a metaphor. Contradictions are resolved and developed into concepts, and these become transferable through the use of consistent and systematic logic. Organizations can manage these individual-level functions first by understanding their importance to the knowledge creation process. More importantly, they need to create:

- Organizational designs based on principles of redundancy and overlapping business processes. This requires the conscious overlapping of company information, business activities and managerial responsibilities. The duplication and waste encourages frequent dialogue, communication, the transfer of tacit knowledge and therefore a 'common cognitive ground'.
- Internal competition generating team structures. Competing groups must be allowed to develop different approaches to the same project and argue over the advantages and disadvantages.
- Strategic rotation through different functional areas and business processes to make organizational knowledge more 'fluid'.
- Free access to organizational information, reducing internal 'information differentials' in terms of access to and insight into information.
- Knowledge management systems based on single, integrated databases.

Organizations need to manage carefully the exposure of employees in different roles to the information needed for knowledge creation. This can be done through the design of appropriate human resource management systems. Although prescriptive, and in reality highly aspirational given the current competencies possessed by the average employee, the recipe is as follows. Frontline employees are immersed in day-to-day details, expert in the realities of a business but deluged with highly specific information. Signals from the market-place are vague and ambiguous and the broader context is hard to see. Employees in these roles need to be constantly challenged to re-examine what they take for granted, and allowed time for reflection during periods of crisis or breakdown. New knowledge is born out of chaos. Managers have the role of orientating this chaos towards purposeful knowledge creation. Their role is to provide conceptual models and give voice to an organization's future by asking questions and articulating metaphors, symbols and concepts. Senior managers must also set the standards that are used to justify the value of knowledge. These have to be qualitative, rather than based on hard economic and strategic metrics. Team leaders and/or middle managers need to act as the intersection between these vertical and horizontal flows of information, mediating between the 'what is' and 'what should be'. They are the true 'knowledge engineers'. Their ability to synthesize the tacit knowledge of frontline employees and senior managers and to embody it within new technologies and products is the ultimate test of organizational learning.

However, not all knowledge acquired by individuals is added automatically to the organizational knowledge base (Bood 1998). It first has to be exchanged and accepted by others within the organization (both cognitively and socially) before it is considered to be relevant (Duncan and Weiss 1979) or is 'pasted' into the organizational knowledge base (see Chapter 3 for an outline of knowledge-based systems). We therefore now move onto a very important notion that is beginning to shape much of our thinking about organizational learning and the competent organization: the notion of 'communities of practice'.

Communities of practice and collective learning

Recently attention has turned to the unsystematic and unintentional ways in which organizations learn (Brown and Duguid 1991; Huber 1991; Lave and Wenger 1991). This has come to be known as the *social constructionist perspective* (Huysman 1996) alluded to earlier in the present chapter and discussed in general terms in Chapter 1. Central to this perspective is the idea of communities of practice, through which members create new ideas and insights about work at hand. Often, there may be several communities within a single organization. The learning processes take place during day-to-day activities and are considered to be all the more successful by virtue of being unplanned (Huysman 1999). Organizational learning is seen to be an evolutionary rather than systematic and planned process. Learning is seen as an inevitable part of participating in social life and practice through membership of communities and the attempts that these communities make to improve the skills of their members (Elkjaer 1999). It is more than just effective information processing and the transmission of the 'right' attitudes and culture. Work practices develop through processes of social construction – i.e. they are given meaning through storytelling and narration (Orr 1990). Learning therefore requires an effective process of conversation which enables actors to compare, challenge and negotiate strategic cognitions. A variety of cognitive mapping techniques may be used to model these cognitions, and these are detailed in Chapter 7.

However, at this stage we build on our earlier discussion of Nonaka's views about the power of metaphor and focus on the need for successive rounds of dialogue, which has become a central element of much of the recent thinking about organizational learning (see Box 2.5). The word 'dialogue' has two Greek roots, *dia* and *logos*, suggesting 'meaning flowing through'.

It is important to note that different writers have employed the term 'communities of practice' in a variety of different ways. Some have used the term to mean communities of practitioners – i.e. different groups of actual learners and employees often associated with an existing profession, function or knowledge base. Others have defined such communities in terms of informal, rapidly changing constituencies of people brought together by a series of interactions that might take place around a particular work practice, business process or problem solution (Elkjaer 1999). Lave and Wenger (1991) have defined the boundaries that surround such communities of practice in terms of *legitimate peripheral participation* (LPP). In a similar vein to an apprenticeship system, it is participation in the practice and engagement in the performance (even though there may be no visible signs of teaching activities)

Box 2.5: The role of community or collective dialogue

Dialogue is variably referred to as 'organizational inquiry' (Duncan and Weiss 1979), 'rumour and conflict' (Schön 1983) and 'strategic conversation' (Van der Heijden and Eden 1998). Collective or community dialogue is an idea that has been associated with researchers from the MIT Center for Organizational Learning. It is based on the premise that the existence of knowledge is often achieved through the use of metaphors (Nonaka 1994) – i.e. the understanding and experiencing of one concept in terms of another (Lakeoff and Johnson 1980). Successive rounds of dialogue lead to the exchange and testing of individual knowledge and the creation of new knowledge (Bood 1998). Central to the idea of collective learning is that of community dialogue in which members 'speak the truth of [their] experiences, listen with [their] hearts, slow things down so more can happen, and notice [their] inner voices' (Dixon 1999: 49). The exchange of metaphors is particularly useful in conveying tacit knowledge and personal perspectives. Collective dialogue, however, is different from collective discussion (Senge *et al.* 1994). Discussion or debate (the linguistic root of which is 'to beat down') has the purpose of telling, selling or persuading as two or more parties attempt to find agreement. Both parties maintain their certainties and both suppress deeper inquiry (Isaacs 1993). It implies the defence of assumptions and attempts to convince of the merit of ideas. Dialogue, on the other hand, is about improving the quality of communication. People operate within shared fields of assumptions, which tend to be unstable, fragmented and incoherent. In order for dialogue to be effective, actors must first learn to perceive, seek, inquire into and allow the transformation of these fields. New insights are forged through the creation of shared meanings, and understanding of the whole. In turn, this requires that actors' assumptions are uncovered (Senge 1990a; Isaacs 1993). In contrast to discussion, which preserves the status quo for individuals, dialogue is a communal activity through which collectives learn and change (Preskill and Torres 1999). Effective dialogue does not necessarily need groups to reach agreement or consensus, but the way in which disagreements and tensions are managed is crucial.

that create learning. Another body of theory which is highly relevant to this discussion is known as *activity theory* (see Box 2.6). From this perspective, the most effective communities of practice are those that engage more people in the process of knowing, and those that engage people from different communities of knowing.

Since the focus is not on individual learning and cognition, not surprisingly, much of this work has been carried out by sociologists and educational theorists, although there have been parallel concerns within the psychological literature, seen in particular through work on distributed cognition (Salomon 1993) (see Chapter 3). At this point it is important to note that there is a clear link between the individual psychology of managers and the sociological context in which organizational learning takes place: 'The vitality of how a community knows depends on the vigour of interactions that take place between the cognitive processes of

---

Box 2.6: Activity theory and collective knowing

Engestrom (1987, 1991, 1993) developed activity theory as a means of analysing the way that collectives or communities develop and learn. This theory suggests that knowledge should not be viewed as a commodity that individuals or organizations have or acquire. The term 'knowing', rather than 'knowledge', is used because knowledge often implies the existence of a timeless, uncontroversial body of fact, whereas knowing implies the passive absorption of such knowledge (Blackler *et al.* 1999a). Activity theory explores 'how people do their knowing,' rather than exploring their personal knowledge and skill. The culture of an organization provides an 'infrastructure of knowing' – the concepts, tools and technologies shared by members of a community of activity. Hence, competence or expertise includes not only cognitive and technological aspects, but also social aspects. Activity theory argues that the important questions for the study of organizational learning are:

- Who do people do their knowing with?
- Under what circumstances can people learn to collaborate with others who have been schooled in different communities of knowing?

---

individual members and the infrastructure of knowing that they use' (Blackler *et al.* 1999a: 208).

Spender (1998) argues that activity theory itself can be traced back to the work of the developmental psychologist Vygotsky (1962), who studied the evolution of thought and language in the newborn child as it progressed to adulthood in a social context. No amount of instruction can create the higher-level functions unless the child itself becomes actively engaged in the development process. Activity creates a form of conscious learning, and therefore 'performance precedes competence' (Moll 1990: 3). Adults have to manage developmental activity within a controlled space – called the *zone of proximal development* (ZPD) – to socialize the child and allow the higher-level functions to emerge. Not surprisingly, organization theorists see analogies between this view of learned competence and the need for collective learning in organizations.

Does activity theory add anything more than an interesting observation about the phenomenon of collective learning? What does it imply for creating the learning organization? Proponents of this perspective argue that we need to shift the organization's attention away from the development of competent individual managers. Instead, organizations need to recognize that the focus of their learning efforts should be moved towards generating and managing the frameworks that govern the LPP within a business process or work practice. Organizations need to introduce practices that allow communities within themselves to learn through the development of their own identities, professions and skills. Many of these identities and professions are of course supra-organizational in nature. Intriguingly, there are some parallels here to work on the psychological contract and organizational commitment, which argues that managers are more committed to, and trust, their colleagues and their profession rather than their organization (Sparrow 1999b). In order to create the 'engaged participation' and partnership in organizational projects that communities need in order to learn, as Elkjaer (1999) has observed, organizations have to:

- include employees and middle managers in decisions about where the organization wants to go;

- allow communities to understand their own trajectories (where did we come from, where are we now, where do we want to go next and how are we going to get there?).

Social constructionists argue that organizational learning occurs slowly, and through the experience of trying, doing and thinking about the consequences of actions. Elkjaer (1999) quips that awaydays and courses at fancy resorts that neatly package the organization's strategy are far removed from this type of process. Ideas about communities of practice are closely associated with and influenced by ideas about collective learning. Dixon (1994, 1999) identifies six principles of collective learning that represent a pragmatic project intervention perspective on how best to create community dialogue:

- *Teams and organizations as the unit of learning.* Learning is not simply the sum of individual competencies or cognitions. Competence and knowledge are also the product of collective, system-level interactions and as such can only be acquired through collective units. Whole team participation learning methods can be used to build such competence and knowledge.
- *Organizational assumptions.* These are limiting, and limit effectiveness. However, groups are often unaware of their assumptions (Argyris and Schön 1978). Paired team reflections and appreciative inquiry can be used to test such assumptions.
- *Co-inquiry.* All parties across organizations have to be in a learning role, rather than in pre-defined expert-student relationships (Freire 1994).
- *Collective intelligence.* Individual knowing can be organized collectively and meaningfully. When groups think together they can create powerful solutions which individuals could not construct on their own (Weisbord 1992). Joint planning forums can help to create collective intelligence.
- *Learning occurs over time.* Systems change over periods of months and years, and so does learning. Planning, implementing, reflecting and re-planning are all necessary acts of learning (Revans 1982). Consequently, projects with timespans greater than one year are important.
- *Collaborations and alliances.* Organizations need to recognize that they can learn from each other, through joint ventures,

benchmarking, study visits and joint supplier-customer train-ing. Community dialogues can also be used to build support.

Box 2.7 illustrates how these principles have been put into effect at the Ford Motor Company.

The problem of collective forgetting

The pragmatic project-intervention perspective on organizational learning seen in the work of Dixon (1999) has been complemented by research into learning within strategic teams. We are not talk-ing here about research on top-level management teams, which will be covered in Chapter 5, but more functional teams that are engaged in strategically important implementation tasks. A number of researchers have analysed collective learning within project teams. Returning to the promise of developing more sophisticated corporate memories and the outline of communities of learning in Box 2.7, it should be noted that knowledge sharing processes are not foolproof. We address the complexities of collec-tive cognition and knowledge management in the next chapter. To build a link to that discussion, we would note that Ford and Fire-stone recently experienced a catastrophic failure in the sharing of knowledge, resulting in a mismatch of tyres in the Ford Explorer vehicle. Vital information was scattered in different places within each company. If Ford is so good at knowledge sharing then why did no one know about the underlying problem? There are two possible explanations:

- Knowledge is best shared within communities because people with something in common talk more than strangers. The social network at Ford and Firestone was not rich enough to support the level of cross-company communication that might have uncovered the problem.
- The greater the dispersion of knowledge the more powerful are the forces required for it to be pooled effectively. A strong magnet is needed to pull key facts together, such as a business model. If there is no such magnet the required dialogue will not take place.

Box 2.7: Knowledge worth $1.25 billion: communities of learning at Ford

In 1995 the vice-president of manufacturing at Ford travelled to his European plants and realized that there were ideas that could be used in his US plants, and vice versa. He introduced a process designed to share best practice. At the same time, a re-engineering group known as process leadership (PL) was adapting General Electric's WorkOut programme, incorporating key elements within their own process called RAPID (rapid actions for process improvement deployment), used in a series of workshops in an attempt to eliminate minor inefficiencies. In 1996 the leaders of the two processes met and shared the best elements of each process. An exchange visit between plant managers identified 31 'I didn't know you could do it that way' improvements. Ford's best practice replication process was created. In four and a half years this resulted in the sharing of 2800 proven ideas across manufacturing operations valued at $850 million, with another $400 million to be won from work in progress. Portions of the process were patented and it has been licensed to Royal Dutch Shell and Nabisco. The process snowballed from an early low-tech reliance on narratives, based on 4- by 6-inch photographs, and quick descriptions of each improvement in terms of what it cost, how to do it and who to call, into a more sophisticated form. When the physical volume of knowledge became too large, it was placed on the web and intranet, and rules were introduced to manage the system. Distinct roles and responsibilities were introduced to manage the system, no practice was allowed onto the system unless proven and every improvement was described in the language of the work group involved. Ford recognized the work groups as communities of practice. They exist within several manufacturing communities: central engineering, body assembly, final-area assembly, paint, materials and logistics. Each group has a company-wide community administrator who spends half a day a week serving the community and acting as a focal point. They look for a new practice, or act as contact point for inventors. Inventors make up picture sheets using a webpage template and email them to the community administrator, who then compares them with those of the other plants, and, if they pass the tests, immediately posts them on the web and emails them to every focal point in the community. One way or another, each focal point must report a decision in respect of each innovation: adopt, adapt or

---

reject, by when, with what investigation and for what reason. Score-cards are displayed for each plant summarizing how much they are adding to or adopting from the shared pool of knowledge.

Source: Stewart (2000)

Attention has therefore been focused on the tensions and dilemmas that such teams face. This type of research has attempted to reveal the cultural and organizational infrastructures used by project teams (or more accurately the communities of practice, extending beyond the team) and the extent to which such teams can avoid the pitfall of *collective forgetting*. Blackler *et al.* (1999a, 1999b) studied engineering design teams in high-technology defence companies. They applied the activity theory perspective (see Box 2.6) to the study of organizations. Collective forgetting is the converse of collective learning. It occurs when a community infrastructure for learning disintegrates or falls into disuse (Engestrom 1991). In the words of Blackler *et al.* (1999a: 210): '[Collective] forgetting occurs when relationships cease or fragment through silence or solitude or through disassociation and disorientation'.

Systems of activity change through time as new technologies, procedures and social groupings develop in response to new circumstances. In times of rapid change, communities lose touch with their intellectual and practical heritage, become disconnected with their view of the future and allow disputes to arise about how they should respond, which create the conditions that culminate in organizational forgetting. Box 2.8 outlines a classic example of this highly dysfunctional process.

A new project leader summed up the reality behind the events outlined in Box 2.8:

The memories of others is the only possible navigation system for this data and it's all a bit random. At the moment people perceive it to be easier and cheaper to reinvent the wheel than go and try and find out what others have done. Word of mouth and coffee breaks are the only form of dissemination [and now] time pressure is so great . . . even coffee break learning is threatened.

(Blackler *et al.* 1999a: 203)

Box 2.8: Right First Time: a story of forgetting and organizational dementia

Blackler *et al.* (1999a) studied a series of design and production teams in a high technology firm in the defence sector. A drive for cost reduction and improved delivery times was linked to a four-phase move towards computer integrated manufacturing, which entailed improved coordination, process control, widespread automation and systems integration based around continual improvement and learning. The manufacturing function achieved big improvements in efficiency. However, the company seemed to have got stuck after the process improvement stage. The receipt of a new order for a Mark II product meant that the company was keen to learn lessons from the problems experienced with the Mark I product. A delta team was set up to act as a vehicle for learning and innovation, intended to import new approaches to other teams, review new practices and support innovations. The team comprised a small number of experienced and respected design engineers. They identified a series of significant costs of failure associated with high levels of rework, categorizing the causes of design changes and identifying human errors under the banner 'Right First Time'. Team learning was to be translated into organizational learning through procedural and technical changes, measured by the average cost per design change. Looking back on the early work, engineers and managers evaluated its success in different ways, but despite diligent work the teams had not produced the results expected, nor had they championed the cause of Right First Time design practice. The investigation into the events that actually transpired revealed that there was little formal documentation – just a few copies of various presentations and conflicting memories of the various outputs achieved by the team. A 'clear desk' policy had reinforced the destruction of hard copy documents, with a reduction in the amount of material archived to computer and/or coded inboxes. Moreover, only 'box owners' or their predecessors had accessed the boxes or knew what was in them. Within a couple of years of a major strategic development the learning that had taken place within the company in terms of design rework avoidance, along with some vital technical lessons, had been lost.

Source: Blackler *et al.* (1999a)

In explaining the process of organizational forgetting, Blackler *et al.* (1999a) noted that in practice engineers had questioned the Right First Time philosophy. Design engineers saw their work as a series of trial and error episodes, whereby designs were built, tested and modified in an iterative fashion. To design out setbacks, rethinking, new ideas and mistakes was to design out experimentation, risk and technological innovation – the very competitive strengths of the company.

So how might the organizational competence of collective learning (as opposed to forgetting) be developed? We address this in detail in the next chapter. The research discussed in this chapter has suggested some of the following more immediate and practical activities. Communities of practice transcend conventional organizational boundaries and bring practitioners and functional experts together in an informal way. From the above examination of theory and practice, it is clear that a collective infrastructure for knowing, with an emphasis on community dialogue, re-engagement and reorientation needs to be engendered. This can be accomplished by taking the following steps:

- Treating the tensions and paradoxes experienced by communities as a major opportunity to learn, and initiating a dialogue between the community and strategic managers to explore alternatives at the project definition stage.
- Rather than just accelerating learning, teams need to expand learning. Multidisciplinary teams with good social skills need to be created within organizations and tasked with developing a dialogue that addresses an underlying problem in the business model or philosophy.
- Capturing and recording knowledge through the use of debriefing exit interviews for leavers, retirees and even managers making significant cross-project moves.

Competency traps and progressing organizational simplicity

We end this chapter with a discussion of organizational learning, adaptation and the use of knowledge resources as portrayed in the strategic management literature. This stream of research suggests that in the absence of positive attempts to trigger organizational learning, organizations will naturally revert to rigid, narrow and simple knowledge bases. We introduce two concepts from this literature: the notions of *competency traps* (Levitt and March 1988) and *progressing organizational simplicity* (Miller 1993). Organizations have a natural tendency to repeatedly use their knowledge bases, but over time their ability to adapt becomes hampered when environmental conditions change and alternative responses are demanded. It is this state of affairs that has been characterized as the competency trap. Organizations also have a tendency to become preoccupied with a single goal, strategic activity or worldview – this is the phenomenon known as progressing organizational simplicity.

In order to avoid the competency trap, organizations need to strike a balance between two strategies (March 1991; Levinthal and March 1993):

- Exploration, which is the search for new knowledge. This is a costly process.
- Exploitation, which is the ongoing use of the organization's existing knowledge base. This helps the organization to refine its routines and recoup the initial investments in exploration.

However, the tendency is for organizations to focus on exploitation – of the knowledge and routines that contribute most to organizational success – and filter out those routines that are less successful in the current setting (Cyert and March 1963). Opinions about what works and why become more firmly settled in the minds of managers each time the organization's knowledge base is applied (Nelson and Winter 1982; Levitt and March 1988). Knowledge that is deemed to be less successful in a particular setting gradually disappears from the organization's memory. Information search strategies and information processing routines (what Miller 1993 refers to as 'infosystems') become more limited, and the creation of new knowledge and routines less likely (Huber 1991). Two immediate problems follow from this: the domination of a strong but more homogeneous culture (Harris 1994; Miller 1994); and the loss of secondary skills, because their practitioners of these skills fail to gain power and respect (Milliken and Lant

1991). As the organization's infosystems and routines begin to reflect a narrower range of skills and concerns, resources become more focused on one central tactic or activity. Step by step, the pursuit of an exploitation strategy reduces variety in the organization's knowledge base and promotes ossification through the process of progressing simplicity: 'Before long, there is no noise left in the system: no court jesters, no devil's advocates, no iconoclasts with any say, no counterveiling models of the world. This progressing conformity decreases flexibility, engenders myopia and blocks learning and adaptation' (Miller 1993: 134).

It is also important to note that theorists adopt a number of different perspectives on how the competency trap may be broken at the organizational level. *Radical change theorists* (e.g. Tushman and Romanelli 1985) believe that long periods of inertia are punctuated by short periods of immense and generally painful change. These short periods serve to synchronize the organization's knowledge base and routines with the external environment (Vermeulen and Barkema 2001). *Organizational renewal theorists* (e.g. Brown and Eisenhardt 1997) believe that organizations can administer limited shocks to their system that serve to renew and refresh their technological knowledge base at regular intervals, in particular through controlled strategies of new product or geographical market entry (Miller and Chen 1996; Barkema and Vermeulen 1998), or through forging alliances (Ingram and Baum 1997).

Returning to the challenges that this creates for strategic leaders, Pettigrew and Fenton (2000) warn that bipolar concepts such as exploitation and exploration are often seen as dichotomies, paradoxes, contradictions and dualities. When March (1999) discusses the duality or bipolar concept of exploration and exploitation, for example, he argues that it is difficult, if not impossible, for firms to define an optimum mix between the two. It is perhaps better to view them as opposing forces that must be balanced (Evans and Doz 1992). The creation of such balance is viewed as an art form, but one that can be furthered by seeking the complementarities between apparent opposites: 'Innovative forms of organizing are creating new levels of uncertainty and complexity for management' (Pettigrew and Fenton 2000: 297). The strategic choices made about the scale, pace and sequencing of change, and the judgements about how to balance these complementarities, fell within the remit of leaders and top teams. They require more holistic forms of thinking and executive action, and this explains why we give so much attention to the skills necessary for managers to take action in Chapter 6.

However, we must first turn our attention to the management of knowledge and the development of a more balanced approach to exploration and exploitation. We shall return to the issue of competency traps and progressive simplicity in Chapter 4, and again in Chapter 5.

Concluding remarks

The interrelated notions of the learning organization and organizational learning tend to attract passionate supporters and protagonists. They have been used to inspire many organizational change projects, and to help managers surface, confront and assess the (in)adequacies of their current organizational practices (Salaman 2001). But the more our understanding of the learning organization develops, the more distant the dream it promises may seem. Consequently, in recent years, a more critical perspective has also emerged, principally because of awareness of the gap between the current design of organizations and the expressed aspirations to generate more effective learning. For example, Spender (2000: 444) asserts that much of the discussion on organizational learning and the learning organization amounts to little more than 'ungrounded musings', while Weick and Westley (1996) argue that the very notion of organizational learning is an oxymoron. There is a conflict between learning, which is to disorganize and increase variety, and organizing, which is to forget and reduce variety. The structure of an organization defines boundaries and levels, which in turn imply differentiated specialization and focus, power and rewards. These political and structural divisions become informational divisions. They influence and distort the nature of, and flow of, information. The political influences on informational boundaries cut across at least three aspects of the learning organization, namely: free exchange within, across and between different communities of practice;

networked knowledge and experience; and open dialogue (Salaman 2001). Learning is, therefore, the antithesis of organizing. Snell (2001) too has criticized the notion of the learning organization from an ethical perspective, arguing that the moral foundations required for the characteristics of a learning organization to emerge and be sustained tend to be absent from most organizations. Moreover, learning organizations have to entertain multiple, socially constructed realities and discourses. There are no single, all-embracing versions of the truth. Such ambiguity does not sit well with a managerial mindset focused on best practice and benchmarking.

Given the above criticisms we must return to our definition of strategic competence, as outlined in Chapter 1. These criticisms notwithstanding, we maintain that the strategically competent organization *is* one that engages in processes of organizational learning. While we acknowledge that a range of constraints, both practical and ethical, often prevent the attainment of such competence, it is still a useful notion for academics to pursue. The dialogue that has taken place has opened the minds of researchers and practitioners alike to the need to manage at least four types of knowledge – and the creation of this knowledge – within organizations. In this chapter we have made distinctions between explicit and tacit knowledge and learning, and knowledge and learning that resides within the individual or within collectives. We build on the latter distinction in the next chapter in particular, and show that such a distinction oversimplifies the nature of cognition within organizations. There is also a practical need to continue the exploration of organizational learning. We also point to the growing importance of the so-called knowledge-driven economy and highlight ways in which organizations are seeking to create organizational designs intended to broker information across internal and external markets. Such developments make the need to understand the complexities of organizational learning all the more evident, for with or without theory, such changes to the design of organizations will occur and the consequences will have to be managed. The more that we can learn about the processes of organizational learning, the more that we shall be able to effectively furnish advice on the competencies that should be developed within organizations. Clearly, research on organizational learning needs to be strengthened. It also needs to be fed into work on the learning organization. These two areas of research can enrich each other, and should, in our view, become more integrated, rather than being treated as separate fields of study.

3

DISTRIBUTED COGNITION, ORGANIZATIONAL MEMORY AND KNOWLEDGE MANAGEMENT

In Chapter 2 we outlined the nature of organizational learning and discussed the role of knowledge as a source of competitive advantage. The knowledge-components of a firm's distinctive competence are considered by a number of writers to offer above normal returns and considerable competitive advantage (e.g. Spender 1996; Teece 1998). The more tacit the organizational knowledge base is, however, the higher the causal ambiguity in terms of what is really providing the firm with its competitive advantage. It is this ambiguity that is considered to increase the amount of time that it takes competitors to replicate organizational knowledge (Reed and DeFillippi 1990). Although the knowledge assets of organizations might be hard to replicate, nevertheless, they may still be supplanted by the development of new knowledge (McEvily *et al.* 2000).

While the concept of a knowledge-driven economy is not new (Alfred Marshall first outlined it in the 1890s, in his book *Principles of Economics*), knowledge has assumed heightened importance over recent decades. Turuch (2001) presents four reasons for this, all of which demonstrate the risks associated with poor knowledge management:

- The bulk of fixed costs associated with knowledge-based products and services accrue in respect of their creation, as opposed to their dissemination or distribution.
- As knowledge grows, it tends to branch and fragment. Rapid and effective recreation of knowledge can represent a source of competitive advantage.
- The value of investments in knowledge can be difficult to estimate, with outcomes ranging from disappointment of expectations through to extraordinary knowledge development.
- Even when knowledge assets create considerable economic value, it is hard to predict who will capture the lion's share of these investments.

It is on the basis of these sorts of observation that knowledge-based assets are assumed to form the foundation for success in the twenty-first century (Offsey 1997; Turuch 2001). A series of attempts have been made to conceptualize the firm in knowledge-based terms, including Spender's (1996) dynamic theory, Nonaka and Takeuchi's (1995) notion of the 'knowledge creating company' and Nonaka's (1991, 1994) related conception of the organizational knowledge-creating process, Tsoukas's (1996) notion of the firm as a distributed knowledge system, and various other theoretical models in which the firm is portrayed as an institution designed to protect knowledge from expropriation by competitors (Liebeskind 1996). However, it must be made clear that despite the best efforts of leading scholars from a number of disciplines, there is as yet no commonly accepted knowledge-based theory of the firm, nor indeed are there any commonly accepted theories of how knowledge-based assets should be managed. That it is important to distinguish between these two types of theoretical endeavour becomes apparent when we consider the potential contribution that psychologists might make to this rapidly evolving area of research: they are unlikely to make much of a contribution to the development of a knowledge-based theory of the firm. They are, however, in a strong position to contribute meaningfully to the latter endeavour.

Another useful distinction that can be drawn is between knowledge creation as a process that primarily resides within individuals, and knowledge creation as a process that occurs within institutions. Grant (1996) notes that writers such as Levitt, March, Huber, Spender and Nonaka all see organizational knowledge creation essentially as an individual-level activity which is then directed towards the production of goods and services. Fenton and Pettigrew (2000) note that organization theorists who adopt this perspective tend to focus on the ways in which individual creativity and learning can be facilitated, and the ways in which the resultant knowledge can be transferred into value-added outputs, such as products and services. This body of work gives attention to the various 'integration mechanisms that can bring the varied knowledge of small numbers of individuals together to deliver organizational solutions' (Fenton and Pettigrew 2000: 29). There are two main paths that organizations tend to follow in an attempt to create sustained advantage through knowledge:

- acting to spread internally tacit knowledge that other organizations find almost impossible to copy (Nonaka and Takeuchi 1995); or
- creating superior knowledge management capabilities that foster innovation (Lubit 2001).

Other theorists have adopted a more institutional perspective. For example, Liebeskind (1996) views the firm as a knowledge-integrating institution that must be designed and administered in ways that create, capture, protect and integrate knowledge. This approach takes a much broader view of the nature of knowledge (see, e.g., the discussion of the work of Collins and Sackmann later in this chapter). The institutional perspective directs attention to the ways in which the firm's administrative structure (which includes the design of the organization and the processes that this engenders) can itself institutionalize knowledge. Researchers have posited several organizational designs that might facilitate this dynamic process of knowledge creation, capture, protection and integration. Some of the better-known examples are to be found in Daft and Lewin's (1993) discussion of modular forms of organization that are intended to interconnect and coordinate self-organizing business processes – see also Sanchez and Mahoney (1996) and Tsoukas's (1996) discussion of the firm as a distributed knowledge system.

Again, psychologists can contribute to the development of both perspectives. We have already outlined work that positions the individual within organizational knowledge creation processes in Chapter 2. The main contribution psychologists can make to the institutional perspective is to:

- Provide a reality check on the work of organizational design theorists. There are many grand and sophisticated designs which look good on paper, but which prove unworkable and unsustainable, given the capabilities and competencies of individuals. The discussion of information overload later in this chapter demonstrates the practical limitations that we face in this respect.
- Help to articulate the processes through which knowledge flows to and from individuals to deeper institutional structures, by uncovering what takes place in distributed networks and collective work settings, and how individuals interact with the knowledge-embedded artefacts that surround them.

These are the themes that we will explore in this chapter, building upon the material already presented on organizational learning. We begin by looking at the nature of shared cognition. Work on team mental models can be used to highlight the way in which shared cognition can be used effectively in the competent organization. We then move on to the more complex and contentious issue of distributed cognition. Arguably, cognition might not only be distributed between a series of human agents across computer networks, but may also be distributed across technologies and human agents. The work of cognitive ergonomists and cognitive anthropologists is used to introduce the idea that facets of cognition can surround the manager and other organizational actors, built into the physical environments in which they work. In the short term the issue is one of ensuring an appropriate distribution of cognitive load between human agents and the surrounding technologies. In the longer term the boundaries between human cognition and artificial intelligence will be called into question, although this is not an issue that we go into here. What we do address is the obvious next step from considering cognition built into the technologies that surround managers and employees – to consider cognition built into the organization itself. We inquire whether the organization itself can display knowledge and have a memory, above and beyond the cognition of its individual managers. We also consider the ways in which knowledge might be stored within the organization. We introduce the interrelated notions of organizational knowledge structures and organizational memory and discuss work on the link between culture and different types of organizational knowledge. As we shall see, organizational culture can serve to provide a form of organizational memory. We outline the ways in which culture may codify such memory, and draw upon work on high reliability organizations in order to demonstrate the ways in which culture can be exploited in the development of a form of mindful performance. We examine communication and knowledge management processes in the learning organization, and link these to the knowledge structures that exist within such organizations. We also outline the impact that new forms of work organization and information and communication technologies are having on organizations and the role of organizational memory information systems is introduced. Attention is given to a number of knowledge management initiatives in organizations. We examine some of the recent speculation that organizations are becoming more dependent on the efficient operation of internal information markets, and consider the role of managers within such organizations.

Having developed the argument that organizational-level knowledge structures, cultures and information systems can serve both as a form of collective memory and organizational learning, it becomes necessary to detail some of the dysfunctional aspects of organizational cognition. One of the most pressing issues is the problem of information overload. We outline the nature of overload and some of its causes and focus on the way key information interactions are designed, and the associated level of risk that can be built into an organization when managers make decisions in the context of information overload. Finally, we discuss modern organizational forms and the need to consider the factors that enable the effective distribution of knowledge across the internal networks of modern organizations.

Team mental models

We begin this chapter with a discussion of work on team mental models with three aims in mind. First, we wish to look at shared cognition in diverse team settings. In Chapter 5 we shall concentrate solely on work that has specifically examined top management teams, but we begin, here, by considering teams in general. Second, we need to build on the basic distinctions that we made between explicit and tacit knowledge and individual and collective knowledge in the previous chapter, by considering the complexity of shared cognition in terms of the questions that arise about its content, structure and the processes of transfer. Third, ideas about team cognition can help move us towards the concept of distributed cognition, which is covered in the next section. This material serves a vital link to our later discussion of new organizational forms and the role of managers in knowledge-driven organizations.

From a strategic management perspective, three reasons have been advanced as to why we need to better understand the nature and significance of collective cognition (Gibson 2001):

- effective collaboration in the use of information is a principal source of competitive advantage;
- more and more employees are now employed in the domain of knowledge work;
- organizations utilize increasingly collective processes, including team-based organizational designs, for accomplishing work and business strategies.

In Chapter 2 we noted that it has been argued that teams are the fundamental unit of learning in modern organizations (Nonaka and Takeuchi 1995). As Gibson has observed, 'understanding collective cognition processes has important implications for organizational knowledge management and learning' (Gibson 2001: 122). The notion that shared cognition benefits team and organizational performance has been around for over 20 years (Cannon-Bowers *et al.* 1993; Klimoski and Mohammed 1994; Cannon-Bowers and Salas 1998) and much of our insight into team mental models comes from human factors experts and specialists in military training environments, for whom the study of team cognition is a necessity. However, in a recent special issue of the *Journal of Organizational Behavior*, Cannon-Bowers and Salas (2001) noted that some important questions remain to be answered conclusively:

- *What* is shared?
- What does *sharing* mean?
- How should sharing be *measured*?
- What *outcomes* should result from shared cognition?

Shared cognition within teams is an important indicator of a team's readiness or preparedness to take on a strategic task. Its value in coordinating behaviour is fivefold (Cooke *et al.* 2000):

- It furthers understanding of the process of performance by articulating how team members should interact with each other.
- Once cognition and knowledge are shared, cues can be interpreted in a similar manner, and individual decisions and actions can be more compatible.
- It results in better task-specific performance, in terms of greater accuracy, efficiency, quality of output and volume or timeliness.
- It leads to better team processes and task-related performance through more efficient communication, more accurate expectations and predictions, greater consensus levels, more highly similar interpretations and better coordination.
- It generates more positive outcomes, including motivational outcomes such as greater cohesion and trust, higher morale and greater satisfaction with the team. It also enhances collective efficiency.

However, it would be misleading to assume that simply by sharing cognition these benefits result automatically. There is considerable confusion about what the concept of team cognition actually means. Collective cognition is defined in terms of the group processes involved in the acquisition, storage, transmission, manipulation and use of information (Gibson 2001). The key to understanding this form of cognition is to examine the patterns of connections between individuals and the weights that are put on them: 'collective cognition does not reside in the individuals taken separately, though each individual contributes to it. Nor does it reside outside them. It is present in the interrelations between the activities of group members' (Gibson 2001: 123). As noted in Chapter 1, numerous terms have evolved in an effort to capture the nature and significance of individual and collective cognition in general. Specifically in the team context, no fewer than 20 labels have been used to outline various concepts of shared cognition, such as collective cognition, team knowledge, team mental models, shared knowledge, transactive memory and shared mental models (see Box 3.1 for an outline of the richness of the team mental models concept). Indeed, the reality is that 'in any given team, some knowledge will have to be shared, other knowledge similar, and yet other knowledge distributed and complementary' (Cannon-Bowers and Salas 2001: 199).

The organized understanding of relevant knowledge that is shared by teams is a phenomenon that has been studied by work, social and cognitive psychologists, and experts in decision making and organizational behaviour. These researchers have in common an interest in understanding the fluid and implicit coordination that can be observed in effective teams (Mohammed and Dumville 2001). However, this is a field in which empirical study is considerably less advanced than is conceptual development. In part this is because the various concepts captured by the notion of team mental models are difficult to measure at the team level (see Chapter 7 for an overview of some research methods that might prove helpful in this connection.)

We now consider a number of important processes that seem to facilitate the development of these mental models. In an attempt to enrich and expand theoretical understanding in this area, Mohammed and Dumville (2001) highlighted work on three important concepts: *information sharing*, *transactive memory* and *cognitive consensus*. These processes have their counterparts at the organizational level of analysis and parallels should be drawn to earlier work on organizational learning (see Chapter 2).

Group information sharing (sampling behaviours)

The first key concept introduced by Mohammed and Dumville (2001) is that of information sharing. Stasser and Titus (1985) studied information pooling behaviours in groups. In particular, they examined the ways in which these behaviours could either

Box 3.1: Reflections on team mental models: what is shared and how?

The concept of team mental models can be broken down into a series of important questions and answers. The first key question is *what* is it that teams need to share? The answer seems to be four main things:

- *Task-specific knowledge*: team members can act on the knowledge that they each hold without the need to discuss it. They can develop compatible expectations of performance based on highly task-specific knowledge of procedures, sequences, actions and strategies (Cannon-Bowers *et al.* 1993).
- *Task-related knowledge*: common knowledge about task-related processes such as teamwork. This knowledge contributes to the team's ability to accomplish the specific task, but also holds true across other similar tasks (Rentsch and Hall 1994).
- *Knowledge of team-mates*: this includes transactive memory – i.e. knowledge of the distribution of expertise within the team, enabling individuals to adjust their own behaviour in accordance with the expectations of others and compensate for their individual strengths and weaknesses (Moreland 2000).
- *Attitudes and beliefs*: shared beliefs, leading to compatible perceptions about the task and environment, and the cognitive consensus necessary in order to reach decisions (Mohammed *et al.* 2000).

These four facets of knowledge and belief have to be shared. However, even the word 'shared' has at least four different connotations:

- *Shared or overlapping*: where two or more members need common portions of knowledge (but not redundant knowledge). This applies to task-specific knowledge, e.g. a surgeon and a nurse in an operating theatre.
- *Similar or identical*: where team members must have similar if not identical knowledge. This applies more to attitudes and beliefs, e.g. where certain attitudes and beliefs are essential to drive performance.
- *Complementary or compatible*: beyond requiring portions of common knowledge, specialized roles require compatible yet different knowledge around the team. This can lead to accurate expectations about behaviour, e.g. multidisciplinary teams such as aid workers.

- *Distributed:* adequate coverage of knowledge and effective appor-
  tionment of knowledge. Where systems and tasks are so complex
  that it is impossible for any one team member to hold all the
  knowledge necessary to succeed, e.g. in the case of forced coordination and interdependence among military combat teams.

Source: Cannon-Bowers and Salas (2001)

produce better decisions or lead to detrimental collective *information sampling behaviours*. Group discussion is known to lead to
biased sampling and the introduction of favoured shared information (i.e. information held by all group members before discussion began) at the expense of unshared information (i.e.
information held by one or more members prior to discussion)
(Gigone and Hastie 1993; Stasser *et al.* 1995). Our earlier discussions of the necessary skills for the creation of true dialogue and
on communities of practice (see Chapter 2) should be seen in the
context of attempting to overcome the limitations of collective
information sampling behaviours. Shared information not only
has a sampling advantage, it has a repetition and recall advantage
over unshared information (Larson *et al.* 1996; Stewart and Stasser
1998). Shared information tends to be considered during the
earlier stages of group discussions, and information discussed
later on tends to have less impact on the final decision (Larson
et al. 1994). Leadership, expertise and status can negatively impact
on information sampling behaviours, as can information load –
i.e. the amount of information processed (Stasser and Titus 1987).
The issue of information overload is covered later in this chapter.

Research on information sampling behaviours has tended to
focus on the frequency of information sharing, free recall of
information and the use of information in the context of group
and individual decisions. However, we also need to know what
impact such behaviours can have on actual knowledge and on
knowledge convergence. Rather than just focusing on the communication of distinct pieces of information, what impact does
sampling have on the way knowledge is organized and interconnected by managers? Some work is beginning to emerge on
this issue and in Chapter 6 we examine the role of unshared

knowledge in managers' cognitive maps as a source of intuitive insight. Some empirical work has also been conducted showing the value of information exchange. For example, aircrew communications research has found that effective and less effective crews differ in terms of the communication sequences they follow (Bowers *et al.* 1998). At this point, however, work on information sharing behaviours serves to highlight the dangers of focusing exclusively on shared information and the importance of effective information pooling behaviours and dialogic skills.

Transactive memory (and transactive knowledge)

In organizational research, this concept was used initially to understand team members' knowledge of one another, having been introduced previously by Wegner (1987) to explain aspects of the behaviour of intimate couples. It has since found its way into the study of skilful team performance (Moreland 2000) and the analysis of organizational knowledge.

In complex organizations the management of knowledge is seen as a key source of competitive advantage (Rulke and Zaheer 2001). This is because distributed local knowledge only becomes organizational when the different parts of the organization possess or know where to acquire the knowledge (Lessard and Zaheer 1996).

Insight into the nature of transactive memory started from the observation that individuals in continuing relationships are often able to 'utilise each other as external memory aids to supplement their own limited and unreliable memories' (Mohammed and Dumville 2001: 93). Rather than focus on shared overlapping knowledge and processes of convergence, similarity, agreement, compatibility or overlap among team members' knowledge, this approach focuses on complementary overlapping knowledge. Memory is viewed as a social phenomenon. Transactive memory is often observed in the context of *skilled team performance* (Moreland 2000). Over time, team members come to understand the distribution of expertise within the wider team. This improves performance because team members compensate for one another, can predict each other's actions, provide information before being asked, and allocate resources according to member expertise. An obvious example of this phenomenon occurs in the world of football. The 'blind pass' is a move made by highly skilled players. It depends on the player's ability to accurately predict where their team-mates are likely to be. This understanding is a form of task-related knowledge which can be used in a variety of situations.

Mohammed and Dumville (2001) note that there are no simple correlations between the degree of team mental model convergence and the various dimensions of team performance. This may be because researchers have underemphasized the distributed nature of collective knowledge. Overlapping knowledge in teams with large pockets of distinct knowledge may be inefficient. Mohammed and Dumville argue that future research should specify 'the domains and conditions under which distributed and common knowledge will aid or hinder team performance' (2001: 96). They provide the examples of legal defence teams (where effective performance requires some overlapping knowledge and some unique insights among legal experts challenged by the action of the courtroom), and dyadic and triadic teams, such as nurse, surgeon and anaesthetist (where some knowledge must be highly accurate and identical, and some can be unique and complementary).

Transactive knowledge, a very closely related concept, is defined more as a set of individual memory systems which combine the knowledge possessed by particular members with a shared awareness of who knows what (Wegner 1987). It is the knowledge required for the effective functioning of a group or collective (Liang *et al.* 1995). According to Gibson, the interdependencies fostered by effectively functioning groups demand a 'knowledge holding system' that is larger and more complex than any one individual's own memory system: 'To utilise knowledge, groups must be able to recall information shared in previous interactions. A transactive memory system – the set of individual memory systems in combination with the communication that takes place between them – facilitates this process' (Gibson 2001: 124). Two dimensions of such transactive knowledge are frequently identified:

- *self-knowledge* (knowledge situated within the individual about the strengths and limitations of available expertise at the unit level); and

- *resource knowledge* (knowledge about where the expertise lies) (Rulke and Zaheer 2001).

There are three additional notions closely related to the concepts of transactive knowledge and memory which are worthy of brief mention (see Cooke *et al.* 2000; Cannon-Bowers and Salas 2001):

- *interpositional accuracy* – i.e. the accuracy of one's knowledge concerning the roles of others;
- *knowledge distribution metrics* – reflecting gaps in an individual's knowledge that can be compensated for by knowledge of other team members;
- *schema accuracy* – i.e. the accuracy of one's knowledge about others' knowledge.

In the same way that team members need to be able to retrieve, use and rely on the knowledge of others within the team, managers need to understand what knowledge their units require and where this knowledge is to be found. This understanding about where knowledge resides within a group is referred to as *meta-knowledge* and is seen as a precondition for effective knowledge transfer (Larson and Christensen 1993). Diffusing or sharing resource knowledge across geographically dispersed organizations, where there may be little face-to-face interaction, is a major challenge. Psychological research has shown that the effective sharing of meta-knowledge can result in the creation of group memory systems that are richer than the sum of individual members' memories (Wegner 1987). Extrapolating from work at the individual level, this accumulation of prior knowledge facilitates the subsequent assimilation new material. As observed by Sutcliffe (2001: 148), 'The more objects, patterns, and concepts that are stored in memory, the more readily people acquire new information and the better they are at using the information in new settings'.

Paralleling work at the team level, strategic management researchers have also examined the role of transactive processes in facilitating the effective retrieval of knowledge (both unique and shared) across organizational units. For example, Rulke and Zaheer (2001) recently conducted a study to investigate this phenomenon in food retail stores. Unfortunately, however, a number of hypothesized relationships between elements of managers' cognitive maps and efficiency and performance (innovation) failed to materialize in this study.

Clearly, the learning channels or communication media used to convey transactive knowledge play a crucial role in facilitating knowledge transfer, and an effective transactive system is needed in order to foster organizational learning. However, not only is knowledge distributed across multiple organizational units and media, so too are important aspects of the actual cognitive task. With the advent of new communication media, such as computer-networked environments, we need to better understand the nature of distributed cognition (Hollingshead 1998), an issue we consider later in this chapter. First, however, we consider the nature and significance of cognitive consensus.

Cognitive consensus

Gibson (2001) notes that research from the fields of information processing, group development and communication indicates that there are four process phases involved in the development, or cycle, of collective cognition, which in turn comprise several key elements and sub-processes:

- *accumulation* (perceiving, filtering and storing);
- *interaction* (retrieving, exchanging and structuring);
- *examination* (negotiating, interpreting and evaluating); and
- *accommodation* (integrating, deciding and acting).

Cognitive consensus involves the exchange of a multiplicity of views and the development of mutual perspective-taking. It becomes important in particular during the fourth stage of accommodation, when the perceptions, judgements and opinions of group members become integrated to a greater or lesser degree through processes of consensus building. Once integrated, decisions and actions become easier. Groups that have reached consensus share common expectations of the task and group, and can predict the behaviour and resources needed more accurately. This is known variously as 'realised consensus' (Walsh *et al.* 1988), 'consensus frame' (Corner *et al.* 1994) and 'sharedness' (Klimoski and Mohammed 1994).

Groups have to maintain a state of equilibrium between conflict and consensus (Gibson 2001), for there can be negative consequences in the form of biased information sampling or poor decisions caused by 'groupthink' (Janis 1982). Group members can overlap to the point where their shared cognitions become a liability (Cannon-Bowers *et al.* 1993) and the potential for individual contributions is lost. In a laboratory investigation of the schemata employed by strategic decision-making groups, Walsh *et al.* (1988) found that groups marked by low consensus outperformed those marked by high consensus.

In the business world, one area to which ideas about cognitive consensus have been applied is new product development (Brown and Eisenhardt 1998; Mohammed *et al.* 2000). In this domain, successful groups have to work through a delicate balance between deliberation and decision. While agreement and integration are important factors in collective cognition, conflict and debate also serve a necessary role in prompting the group to act outside routines and to go beyond the controlled processing of information. Gibson (2001) proposes that the greater the amount of conflict in groups, the more time that is spent on examination activities (negotiating, interpreting and evaluating knowledge) and on interaction activities (retrieving, exchanging and structuring knowledge). The establishment of consensus leads to more time being spent on accommodation activities (integrating, deciding and acting). We shall return to this issue in Chapter 5, when we consider some of the research that has begun to investigate a number of factors that might predict cognitive consensus in top management teams and the effects of such consensus on organizational performance.

Distributed cognition: networks of people and technology

In the last section we considered the issue of shared cognition across individuals and teams. We concluded that cognition in modern organizations is distributed across different work groups and their respective decision domains. In the next section we shall discuss the concept of cognition residing *within* organizations. Cognition might reside within an organization without the need for complex higher-level information processing. For example, scientists have recently applied the tools of complexity theory (the science of complex systems) to the design of business models using the analogy of social insects and the ways in which they work without supervision. Teamwork in this context is largely self-organized and coordinated through a variety of interactions among individuals within the colony. These interactions might be primitive (one ant merely following the trail left by another) but taken together they can result in efficient (and apparently intelligent) solutions to difficult problems. Using simple rules, ants forage and find the most effective routes to food sources across a myriad of possible paths. This collective behaviour, which can be used to optimize operations, has been called 'swarm intelligence' (Bonabeau and Meyer 2001). It draws on three principles:

- *flexibility* (adaptation to a changing environment);
- *robustness* (when one or more individuals fail, the group can still perform their task); and
- *self-organization* (activities are neither centrally controlled nor locally supervised).

Senior managers tend to relate to the first two of these principles, but often have to be convinced that they result from the third. However, potentially significant business gains can be achieved through the application of these principles. SouthWest Airlines, for example, was able to cut freight transfer rates by 80 per cent and workloads by 20 per cent at its busiest cargo stations through the insights of swarm intelligence. Unilever, McGraw-Hill and Capital One have also applied these principles to tasks as varied as the scheduling of factory equipment, role allocation, organization and even the plotting of strategy for firms wishing to enter new markets (Bonabeau and Meyer 2001).

In order to build a bridge between ideas about cognition shared across teams, and cognition shared across organizational artefacts and technology, in this section we need to consider the proposition that the competent organization also has to deal with cognition that is distributed across and shared between systems, artefacts and human actors. In recent years human-computer interaction specialists, responsible for designing and modelling interactive and collaborative information technology (IT) systems, have begun to reconsider and build upon concepts from the distributed cognition literature (Wright *et al.* 2000). Designers of human-computer interaction systems used to focus on 'tasks' (goals, methods, knowledge structures or semantics) as their basic unit of analysis in modelling the interaction between people and technologies. However, with the growth of computer-supported cooperative work (CSCW) their focus has begun to shift away from individual users of single computers towards groups of individuals communicating through a variety of technologies (Rogers and Ellis 1994). The most appropriate unit of analysis to understand this is 'the network of people and technological artefacts involved in the work' (Wright *et al.* 2000: 3). The label 'distributed cognition' has been employed by researchers investigating the way in which these shared entities (information transformations) are represented, and then used to coordinate collaborative work. It has been used to understand activities as varied as navigating warships, landing aircraft or solving children's puzzles (Nardi 1996). Distributed cognition is explained as follows. As information is propagated around networks, it is transformed. Different interaction strategies (between the human and technological facets of distributed systems) exploit different information structures, and these in turn act as the 'principal resources for action'. As the load shifts between the human and technological resources, so too does the level of cognition on the part of human agents and the resultant necessary competencies.

There are two distinct intellectual traditions that have informed the analysis of distributed cognition (Wright *et al.* 2000). The first comes from the field of cognitive anthropology. Researchers have emphasized the need to study the role that artefacts play in the practice of work in real-life settings. Hutchins (1995) argued that cognition should not be studied as an individualistic mental phenomenon – i.e. information processing occurring inside the head of a solitary thinker. It must be considered as a joint activity involving a network of human and technological agents. Information can be represented across this network and is transformed as it flows between agents, generating new information and changing tasks. Work on aircraft landing and warship navigation has shown how computations are distributed across individuals in teams and technological artefacts. Different cognitive tasks (sensing, recording, computing) are distributed between the agents. Effective cognition is viewed as a process of distributing internal and external representations in order to design a robust information processing system, and the whole network has to be designed in order to maximize error recovery or minimize the impact of error.

The second tradition comes from the field of cognitive psychology. Cognitive psychologists have studied the role of the individual in technological environments and have drawn a number of important distinctions between knowledge that resides in the head and knowledge that resides in the external world (see Box 3.2). This approach, known as cognitive engineering, has been applied to a wide range of problems, including the design and analysis of aircraft failure management interfaces (Hicks *et al.* 1999) and the modelling of virtual work environments (Smith *et al.* 1999).

What relevance does this work have for managers? The main message lies in terms of what it now takes to be intelligent in modern organizations, when working in an environment in which cognition is distributed across networks of managers (as individuals or as teams) and technologies. Managers employ a variety of interaction strategies (i.e. they use the informational resources at their disposal, inherent within the distributed system of which they are a part, in different ways) in order to arrive at a decision. In other words, they adapt their problem-solving strategies to exploit the constraints and opportunities built into their particular environments. Sternberg and Wagner (1994) have been associated with this *interactionist view* of intelligence. We consider in further detail the question of what it now means to be intelligent in modern organizations in Chapter 6.

Organizational-level knowledge structures and organizational memory

We noted in Chapter 2 that it is not organizations that learn as entities, but individuals. However, research attention is increasingly being devoted to the topic of organizational-level knowledge

---

Box 3.2: Cognitive engineering and the networked manager

The cognitive engineering approach is founded on the basic premise that information embedded in technological artefacts is as important to achieving a task as information residing within the mind of the user (Norman 1988). Well-designed artefacts and objects can reduce the need to remember large amounts of information and reduce cognitive effort. This has been termed 'cognitive offloading' (Scaife and Rogers 1996). The rules needed to operate effectively in a distributed system may be represented externally (physical symbols, objects, dimensions, rules, constraints, physical relationships) or internally in the problem solvers' memory (Zhang and Norman 1994). External representations can be designed so that they can be picked up, analysed and processed by a manager's perceptual systems alone, which creates less cognitive demand than when internal representations (schemata and plans that have to be retrieved from memory) are called upon. Deductive processes can also be assisted by the distribution of cognitive elements. Traditionally, deduction has been seen as operators having to create an internal model of the environment, and simply using the information from some external representation to cue the appropriate internal condition or rule of action. Recent work, however, suggests displays of information in the environment can be designed to:

- reduce the difficulty of the task by supporting recognition-based memory and perceptual judgements (Hutchins 1995);
- Trigger appropriate problem-solving strategies and inferences (Zhang 1996, 1997).

---

structures and organizational memory. Work on distributed cognition has led to a recognition that in an effective organization, physical systems can themselves carry a degree of cognitive load and be designed to maximize error correction (Wright *et al.* 2000). It is an obvious next step to ask whether the representation of information in the external environment can also serve as useful knowledge, and whether in fact organizations themselves can be designed to have effective memories.

In the early 1990s a series of questions were being asked about organizational memory. To what extent is there an organizational wisdom or mind? How is this linked to individual managers' schemata? To what extent does this 'mind' benefit from having a diversity of backgrounds within the top management team? Unfortunately, there have been very few empirical attempts to answer such questions (Sparrow 1994). The interrelated notions of organizational memory and organizational-level knowledge structures have been addressed mainly from a theoretical standpoint.

Lyles and Schwenk (1992) theorized various links between top management, strategy and organizational knowledge structures. The concept of schema (and its plural derivative: schemata) introduced earlier in this book refers to individual-level knowledge structures. Lyles and Schwenk argued that the schemata of top managers become encoded, stored and retrieved, and thereby influence the organization's knowledge structures. At the organizational level, the term 'knowledge structure' refers to the shared beliefs that define the expected relationships, behaviours and actions of organizational members. Organizational-level knowledge structures differ from individual-level schemata because they are socially constructed, a manifestation of consensus (see our discussion of the processes through which communities learn in Chapter 2). Lyles and Schwenk argue that organizations, like their top teams, develop shared frames of reference, recollect past events, stories and myths, learn and unlearn, and have memories. Figure 3.1 illustrates the process by which these organizational-level knowledge structures are hypothesized to develop over time.

Lyles and Schwenk (1992) argue that earlier sociological conceptions of *organizational mind* tended to focus on the ways in which behaviours and social processes affect the cognitions of the individual manager. They contend that a more psychologically orientated approach to organizational knowledge structures is needed if we are to further our understanding of their detailed features. To this end, they distinguish between core and peripheral elements within organizational structures. Core elements comprise knowledge about the organization's mission, the justification for its existence and its basic business aims. They act as underlying 'mental scripts' that serve to shape expectations and delimit the events and behaviours that are appropriate to the

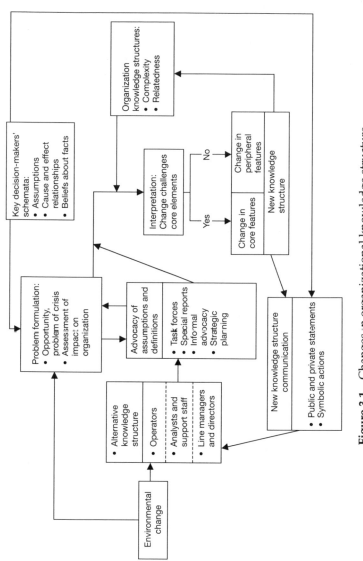

Figure 3.1 Changes in organizational knowledge structure

Source: reproduced by kind permission of the publisher from M.A. Lyles and C.R. Schwenk (1992), Top management, strategy and organizational knowledge structures, *Journal of Management Studies,* 29(2): 155–74. © Blackwell Publishers Limited.

organization and the people within it. Peripheral elements differ from core elements in terms of their content and the extent to which they are underpinned by consensus. The peripheral elements are open much more to debate within the organization. They include knowledge about how to achieve the expectations encapsulated within the core elements, and how to interpret the actions of competitors and other signals from the external environment. They are the cause-and-effect beliefs that interrelate core knowledge to the organization's sub-goals and behavioural strategies (or means) that are necessary to implement them.

Strategic analysis and organizational memory

The previous sections have raised a series of questions about organizational memory. Indeed, the theoretical proposals about organizational knowledge structures advanced by Lyles and Schwenk (1992) presuppose that there *is* some representation of complex events stored within the collective memory or knowledge base of the organization. A series of important questions have been raised by such theoretical discussion. To what extent do individuals and organizations actually recognize and store strategic information in a holistic pattern, and what mechanisms are involved? In addressing such questions, organizational scientists have borrowed much of their language and concepts from the field of cognitive psychology. As we have seen, attempts to clarify the role of the individual in processes of organizational learning, and developments associated with the concept of the learning organization, have led some writers to assume that it is legitimate to extend the use of concepts from human information processing theory to the organizational level of analysis. *Organizational memory* may provide yet another basis for understanding the nature and significance of organizational knowledge (Stubbart and Ramaprasad 1990). Mintzberg (1973) asserted that individual managers spend little time in reflection. Weick's (1979b) analysis of cognitive processes in organizations was intended to counter this assertion. He argued that 'an organization can be a body of thought through the higher-order reference signals in terms of which people organize their behavior' (p. 61). Organizations are, however, more than just bodies of knowledge. They contain 'sets of thinking practices' embodied in such things as 'standard operating procedures that can be smarter than their operators' (Weick 1979b: 70). It can be inferred from Weick's analysis that if an organization is to learn anything, then the distribution of its memory, the accuracy of that memory and the conditions under which that memory is treated as a constraint become crucial characteristics of organizing.

Early theorists, then, viewed organizational memory simply as the embodiment of standard operating procedures. However, later definitions also included structural artefacts such as the roles allocated to employees. By the mid-1980s a number of writers had attempted to list the contents of organizations' memories (e.g. Daft and Weick 1984; Hall 1984; El Sawy *et al.* 1986). It was generally recognized that a number of cognitive and structural artefacts within the organization could serve to store elements of its history and, therefore, have consequential effects on organizational performance through their bearing on current decisions.

However, the extension of the concept of memory to the organizational level of analysis has been fraught with ambiguity and problems of anthropomorphism (Walsh and Ungson 1991). Opinions have ranged from the notion that organizational memory is only a metaphor, acting as an aid to the interpretation of events (Argyris and Schön 1978), to the view that organizations are mental entities capable of thought – i.e. they literally do remember (Sandelands and Stablein 1987). Lyles and Schwenk (1992) point out that one does not have to believe that organizations actually have minds in order to appreciate that they nevertheless do have knowledge structures that may be stored and retrieved over time. However, as seen in the previous chapter, there are some compelling theoretical arguments, and, to a certain extent, empirical support, for the contention that organizational-level knowledge structures can and do influence organizational and individual behaviour, not only in terms of strategic analysis and choice, but also in terms of the preferred modes of implementation.

Walsh and Ungson (1991) argued that information that 'reflects the organization' is stored and processed by the individuals who comprise the organization, the organization itself (through its systems, operating procedures and routines), or the dominant coalition (typically the top team, or board). They examined the historical treatment of the concept of organizational memory in order to refine the notion, and developed an accompanying conceptual framework in which the functions of organizational information processing systems are portrayed in terms which are *similar* in function to the functioning memory of individuals. In so doing, however, they were careful not to ascribe the psychological properties and behaviours of individuals to organizations. They see a threefold utility to the notion of organizational memory:

- providing information and facilitating effective decision making in the pre-choice stage of strategic analysis;
- reducing implementation costs by pointing to the 'whats' and 'hows' that have efficiently shaped individual behaviours; and
- creating a source of independence, the means by which groups in power can influence others by enhancing, sustaining or challenging their power bases as required.

The process by which information is acquired forms the core of an organization's memory over time. Information that is encoded and returned by individuals is an interpretation of organizational decisions (in the form of who, what, when, where, why and how) in relation to various decisional stimuli (problems) and subsequent consequences (responses). Acquired information is filtered to form the individual and organization-level schemata, interpretive schemes and frames of reference (Shrivastava and Schneider, 1984) described elsewhere in this book.

Using storage metaphors drawn from individual-level memory processes, Walsh and Ungson (1991) have identified six storage bins or *retention facilities* that comprise the structure of organizational memory (see Figure 3.2). These are distributed across different parts of the organization:

- *Individuals* retain information (based on their own direct experiences and observations) in the form of memory, belief structures, causal maps, assumptions, values and articulated beliefs. Of all five retention facilities, it is only individuals who have the cognitive capability to fully understand the 'why' of a decision in the context of an organization's history.

95

- *Culture* acts as a learned and transmitted way of perceiving, thinking and feeling about problems. Schein (1993) clearly establishes culture within the realm of organizational memory. Cultural information is stored in language, shared frameworks, symbols, stories, sagas and the grapevine. Some information is therefore retained in a 'supra-individual' collectivity (Douglas 1986).

- *Transformation logics* are used to convert inputs (e.g. raw materials or new people) into outputs (e.g. finished products or company veterans). They also contain embedded information. The retrieval of information from past transformations guides current transformations. Standard operating procedures are one representation of such transformation logics. Others include work design practices, selection standards, socialization activities, and budgeting and strategic planning processes. Such transformation systems act as mechanisms for capturing and preserving knowledge.

- *Organizational structures* also represent a repository for retaining information. Roles not only serve to label positions and define expectations, they also frequently carry formal and informal codifications of 'correct behaviour' and reflect an appropriate interaction sequence (Walsh and Dewar 1987). Although they are less powerful than culture in acting as a 'bin' for organizational memory, facets of structure may nevertheless contain information about an organization's response to problems in terms of who does what.

- *Workplace ecology* (i.e. the physical structure of the organization's environment) encodes and therefore reveals a good deal of information, reflecting the status hierarchies that help to shape and reinforce particular behaviour patterns, especially in terms of 'where' to behave and 'how'.

- As shown in Figure 3.2, *external archives* also act as repositories of information concerning the organization's past; former employees, competitors, business historians and archival sources all hold encoded data of a form which may be retrievable.

The theoretical argument that organizations contain storage bins of information beyond individual memory is well supported in the literature. However, the practical application and benefits

The management of knowledge

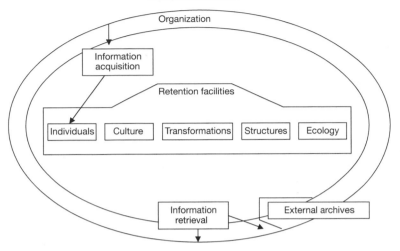

Figure 3.2   The structure of organizational memory
Source: reproduced by kind permission of the publisher from J.P. Walsh and G.
Ungson (1991) Organizational memory, *Academy of Management Review*, 16(1):
57–91. © Academy of Management Review.

from tapping into this organizational memory depends on the
ease with which the information can be retrieved and usefully
interpreted. Schemata formed from past experience can facilitate
information processing in information-rich decision environments, but retrieving the information in an uncontaminated way
is not easy, as we shall see in Chapter 7. Work on autobiographical
memory and the ability to recall historical events (Brown *et al.*
1986; Schuman and Scott 1989) has shown that recollections of
experiences and decisions are usually constrained, biased towards
greater coverage of the distant past and are often a source of
multiple and conflicting individual memories. However, some
researchers argue that more comprehensive retrieval processes
can be generated by growing what Ackermann and Malone (1990)
describe as 'answer gardens' in organizations, or by developing
computer-based organizational memories (Huber 1991).

In reviewing the utility of work on organizational memory,
Walsh and Ungson (1991) noted that there are both positive and

negative implications arising from the decoding of such memory and bringing it to bear on strategic decisions. Business history provides abundant examples of organizations chastised for not letting go of their pasts. On the other hand, organizations often fail to learn from their history. Organizational memory may thus blind strategists if examined, or mock them if incorrectly retrieved or not retrieved at all. Walsh and Ungson (1991) conclude that the role of organizational memory in relation to the strategic management of organizations is as yet unclear. A clear view of the past at the organizational level might well obscure the development of an accurate view of problems in the present by importing from the past established biases of individual decision makers who had a number of blind spots, limited worldviews and belief structures.

Protagonists of course argue that organizational memory can increase efficiency and effectiveness by: avoiding a repetition of past mistakes (Walsh and Dewar 1987); adding legitimacy to new decisions that otherwise would be rejected (Kantrow 1987); drawing on history to frame sharper questions (Neustadt and May 1986); and helping to control and coordinate implementation (Walsh and Ungson 1991). Until case studies of decoded organizational memory are carried out, however, we shall not really know whether this notion has any utility.

Linking organizational learning to knowledge structures

It is clear from the preceding sections that, while organizations do not think, knowledge certainly resides at the organizational level (Löwstedt 1985; Clark and Staunton 1989, Weick 1990). Swan and Newell (1998) see organizational knowledge as that which is socially recognized and codified. It is embedded in either organizational systems (such as rules, procedures for communication and strategies) or technical systems (hardware, software and technical operating procedures). It is considered to operate in much the same way that knowledge operates at the individual level – i.e. it serves as an interpretive scheme, the purpose of which is to inform managerial action (Bartunek 1984; Daft and Weick 1984). However, such organizational knowledge can only develop when organizations (or rather their members, via systems, structures and cultures engineered through the actions of managers) perceive, interpret, reconstruct and communicate new information (Rogers and Ellis 1994).

At the beginning of this chapter we drew attention the institutional perspective on the knowledge-based firm. At this point it is useful to revisit this perspective, in particular the work of Collins and Sackmann, each of whom have attempted to derive taxonomies of knowledge. Collins (1993) distinguishes between encultured knowledge (shared understandings); embedded knowledge (systematic routines); encoded knowledge (conveyed by signs and symbols); embrained knowledge (dependent upon the conceptual skills and cognitive abilities of the organization's members); and embodied knowledge (action-orientated). One of the earliest attempts to specify the content of encultured knowledge was that made by Sackmann (see Box 3.3). She approached the problem by trying to codify the nature of *cultural knowledge*.

As multiple individuals acquire the sort of knowledge outlined in Box 3.3, it becomes embedded in the 'organizational memory'

Box 3.3: Organizational learning and cultural knowledge

Sackmann (1991, 1992) studied the nature of cultural knowledge in organizations. She identified four kinds of cultural knowledge:

- *Dictionary knowledge*: definitions and classifications of objects and events (i.e. procedural in nature).
- *Directory knowledge*: information on how things are done (i.e. descriptive in nature).
- *Recipe knowledge*: information on how things should preferably be done (i.e. prescriptive in nature).
- *Axiomatic knowledge*: fundamental beliefs or final causes that cannot be reduced any further.

Organizational learning involves changes to the way in which events or objects are described. This means changes to the content of the schemata of managers as a whole – in their descriptive theories of action, prescriptive theories of action, and/or fundamental beliefs.

(Argyris and Schön 1978) or 'pasted' into an 'organizational knowledge base' (Duncan and Weiss 1979). If this knowledge is particularly deeply rooted it is referred to an 'organizational paradigm' (Pfeffer 1981a; Johnson 1987). However, the depth of organizational learning embedded in such knowledge has to be questioned, because much of this learning represents only 'directory' or 'recipe knowledge' in Sackmann's (1991) terms. Weick (1995), however, warns that we should consider two questions before we get caught up in the imagery that is created by discussions of organizational knowledge:

- What is the *substance* of this *process* of sense-making?
- *What is the content* that is being processed?

Organizational learning as mindful performance

Can an organization's culture make up for weaknesses in the competencies of its individual managers? Can tacit knowledge be synthesized in ways that belie the constraints of the organization's design? One of the ways in which researchers have tried to understand knowledge creation processes has been through the study of culture. In particular, the study of high reliability organizational cultures has led to the development of ideas about the creation of organizational competence through *collective mindful performance*.

It has been generally assumed that many modern organizations such as nuclear power stations or genetic research laboratories are liable to fail by design (Perrow 1984). They combine 'tight coupling' (whereby minor failures can propagate rapidly through the system) with 'interactive complexity' (in which information and communication – who talks to whom – flows in multiple directions and through multiple media). However, the work of Weick and Roberts has shown that organizational cultures can be created through which it is possible to contain the uncertainties inherent in such organizational designs (Weick 1987; Roberts 1989, 1990; Weick and Roberts 1993). High-risk organizations such as the US Navy, for example, have managed to have the least number of nuclear accidents, despite the fact that they operate the greatest number of nuclear reactors in high-pressure systems (Bierly and Spender 1995). According to Weick and Roberts, this has been accomplished through the development of a 'collective mind'. A central observation is that some organizations through their cultures have to be concerned with reliability. Consider, for example, the almost impossible challenge of ensuring safe operations on an aircraft carrier, as described in the work of Rochlin *et al.* (1987: 78), quoted by Weick and Roberts (1993) at the beginning of their analysis:

> Imagine that it's a busy day, and you shrink San Francisco Airport to only one short runway and one ramp and one gate. Make the planes take off and land at the same time, at half the present time interval, rock the runway from side to side, and require that everyone who leaves in the morning returns that same day. Make sure the equipment is so close to the edge of the envelope that it's fragile. Then turn off the radar to avoid detection, impose strict controls on radios, fuel the aircraft in place with their engines running, put an enemy in the air, and scatter live bombs and rockets around. Now wet the whole thing down with seawater and oil, and man it with 20-year olds, half of whom have never seen an airplane close-up. Oh and by the way, try not to kill anyone.

Such organizations have to enact collective mental processes that are more fully developed than those that are only concerned with efficiency. As their work developed, Weick and Roberts began to use culture not just as a loose metaphor for organizational cognition, but also as a specific model of collective mind (Spender 1998). They argued that team-level cognition was more than just the result of there being a shared understanding. Rather, collective mind can only be understood by paying close attention to the communication processes that have to take place between a group's members. Weick and Roberts (1993: 260) observe that 'reliable systems are smart systems'. They draw attention to a number of ways in which fully developed mental processes enable organizations preoccupied with reliability to spend more time and effort organizing for (and understanding) the complexity that they face, while making few errors, including controlled information processing (Schneider and Shiffrin 1977) (see Chapter 6), mindful attention (Langer 1989), and heedful action (Ryle 1949). In developing their ideas about collective mind, Weick and Roberts have argued that organizations do not have the ability to think or cognize for themselves, but they can develop cultures that display the qualities of 'mindfulness' or 'heedful practice'.

In a similar vein, Roberts and Bea (2001) have studied the consequences of rapidly developing crises or systems failures. Like the earlier work of Weick and Roberts, this latest research has highlighted the importance of heedful interactions. It is argued that when individual managers take heed, they act carefully, critically, consistently, purposefully, attentively, studiously, vigilantly and conscientiously. These adjectives can easily be converted into action verbs that form the collective basis of the competent organization. Three aspects of the social interrelationships between managers create the overall competence of 'collective mindfulness'. These are the way that managers:

- contribute (the way as a group they construct the activity);
- represent and envisage the activity;
- subordinate (interrelate actively with the system that they envisage).

As managers hear about the organization's stories and myths, they begin to comprehend and enter into this heedful organizational mind, and the storytellers themselves rediscover that in telling the stories 'they [have] more thoughts than they thought they did' (Weick and Roberts 1993: 367). For Weick and Roberts the notion 'heedful interrelating' suggests that each performance is novel and that organizational actors are forever learning. Their ideas here are akin to those outlined earlier about Senge's generative knowledge (see Chapter 2). Problems only arise when, as groups mature, they allow the interrelationships between managers to become institutionalized – i.e. routine and habitual:

> Performance becomes less mindful when individuals represent others in less detail, when contributions are shaped by less understanding of others' needs, and when the boundaries of the activity system are narrowed. Dysfunctions arise as attention is focused on local issues rather than on the system as a whole. Inter-relating becomes careless and the collective mind dissipates.
>
> (Spender 1998: 20)

Communication and knowledge management in learning organizations

Learning organizations also have to rely on complex thought processes and the creation of *ongoing dialogues* between people (Schein 1993). These dialogues are not easily captured in organizational memory. Moreover, as we have seen, information processing has become both complex and widely distributed in the typically decentralized and dispersed organizations that people work in today (Bartlett and Ghoshal 1993). Organizations are composed of many diverse, interdependent work groups, such as new product development teams and manufacturing planning teams, all of which have unique decision domains, and all of which develop unique perspectives in response to the different tasks, goals and environments they face. Although managers can act autonomously within each of these decision domains, they are affected by each other's actions. Mechanisms of integration are needed above and beyond the simple summation of the different perspectives that exist within the organization. Knowledge has to be *managed*. But what does this actually mean?

There has been an explosion of interest in the topic of knowledge management in recent years. Here, we can only provide a selective overview of some of the main issues and themes. Fortunately a number of highly accessible literature reviews have recently been published on this topic (e.g. Cross 1998; Scarbrough *et al.* 1999; Staples *et al.* 2001), to which interested readers should refer. Scarbrough and Swan (2001) cite a KPMG survey that suggested 43 per cent of 100 leading British firms were undertaking some kind of knowledge management initiative. Organizations have attempted to exploit the benefits of Internet technology to overcome problems of intra-organizational communication and to promote information sharing across disparate sites and businesses. Newell *et al.* (2001) point out that intranet technology is, therefore, often seen as a solution to the problems of managing knowledge. They examined the development and impact of this type of technology within a European financial services company. Far from serving as an important integrating mechanism that encouraged communication and knowledge-sharing, however, the technology was employed symbolically and as an instrument 'of sub-unit power and autonomy, thereby reinforcing divisions across groups' (Newell *et al.* 2001: 107). Tensions exist between the integrity of the social communities within which knowledge is embedded, and the desire to support a diversity of knowledge through different perspective-taking; and between a desire for a centralized and standardized IT approach and the homogeniz-ation and de-skilling of different knowledge groups. A series of 'internal electronic fences' were thus created by the technology, as the users sought to defend the integrity of the social community in which their knowledge was embedded.

It is highly noteworthy that there is considerable overlap of interest among those wishing to explicate the learning organiz-ation notion and those concerned with knowledge management. However, there has been little overlap of interest between infor-mation systems and human resource management professionals and scholars. With regard to the latter communities, very separate dialogues and academic discourses are currently taking place. Indeed, there is currently little discussion between the psychol-ogy, economics and knowledge engineering research communities active in this area. Spender (2000) notes that the proliferation of published material on knowledge management indicates that there is a widely felt need to understand the phenomenon, but also maligns the fact that fragmentation is beginning to occur. This is hardly surprising in view of the wide range of methods and ideas now being imported into this area:

> We can wonder whether there has ever been a previous occasion where so varied a community – currently including hard science computer specialists, new wave management gurus, biologists, chaos theorists, forward-looking accoun-tants, cultural anthropologists and epistemologists – all think themselves engaged in so similar an enterprise.
>
> (Spender 2000: 443)

Gallupe (2001), on the other hand, argues that the diverse work now taking place on knowledge management systems is begin-ning to force some clarity of definition. What is knowledge? It is considered to be an extension of information, because it is infor-mation embedded within a context. Davenport and Prusak (1998) define knowledge as information combined with experience, context, interpretation and reflection. Knowledge is exceedingly complex, however, as evidenced by the sheer number of taxonomies that have been proposed over the years. Several of these have been highlighted already, while others will be considered in Chapter 7. In the meantime, another useful distinction worthy of brief mention at this point is that highlighted by Zack (1999), who divides knowledge into:

- declarative or descriptive knowledge (describing what something is);
- procedural or process knowledge (describing how something is done);
- causal knowledge (describing why something happens).

Clearly, this threefold classification scheme bears a striking resemblance to the fourfold taxonomy developed by Sackmann (1991, 1992) in respect of the varieties of cultural knowledge.

Several writers have focused on the knowledge capabilities that are deemed necessary to support a knowledge-based enterprise (see, e.g., Nevis *et al.* 1997; Ruggles 1998; Beckman 1999). Staples *et al.* (2001) have grouped these capabilities into three clusters:

- *Knowledge acquisition and creation:* the acquisition or creation of new knowledge fundamental to the long-term viability of the enterprise.
- *Knowledge capture and storage:* the creation of an inventory of knowledge so that the organization knows what knowledge it possesses and where it resides. The maintenance of current knowledge in usable form so that it remains valuable.
- *Knowledge diffusion and transfer:* the subsequent mobilization and flow of knowledge within the organization that creates knowledge-based value.

In Chapter 2 we explored a number issues associated with the first and third of these capability clusters. We are concerned here with knowledge capture and storage capabilities, which are often highly reliant on IT. Increasing attention is being given to how *knowledge management systems* (KMS) can handle and support tacit knowledge capture and transfer, which lie at the heart of organizational memory. The latter requires the capability to identify, package, retrieve and update knowledge (Davenport and Prusak 1998).

As we saw in Chapter 1, psychological and decision theory research shows that there are a number of weaknesses in human intelligence, not least the inability of humans to integrate different pieces of data, the tendency to overvalue information which is readily available and the tendency to view new information through pre-existing mental models. Knowledge-based information systems therefore attempt to augment human intelligence in two ways:

- Information is organized, analysed and presented in ways that provide the user with an alternative view (through executive support systems and data visualization techniques).
- Humans tend to retrieve information from memory through association, whereas automatic retrieval systems do so through matching. Studies show that while an automatic retrieval system may bring to light irrelevant material, providing this information is appropriately presented, humans are able to quickly and effectively screen out excesses, resulting in a superior information base, especially in the case of competitive intelligence systems (Drott 2001).

Given the obvious importance of the interrelationships between knowledge and the flow of information and understanding throughout the organization, it is clearly useful for us to briefly explore how human-computer interaction specialists, think about the problems created by the need for an organizational memory and the management of knowledge. For human-computer interaction specialists, organizational memory consists of information systems that combine a semi-formal organizational knowledge base with formal meta-knowledge (understanding) that can be applied to the knowledge base. It is only when these two elements are combined that organizational memory can be said to be operating.

The challenge is to design information systems that capture problem-solving expertise, experiences gleaned from people and business processes and the lessons learned from technical problems encountered. Typically, these are articulated initially in the form of documents, models and 'war stories', as well as other artefacts. They are then converted into a form that can be retrieved easily without losing the true value of the knowledge (Staples *et al.* 2001).

Economists, psychologists and knowledge engineering professionals are all currently examining how KMS or organization memory information systems (OMIS) can contribute to knowledge-intensive work processes such as strategic planning and product design (Decker and Maurer 1999). The growth of organization-wide email has led to the creation of increasingly weak ties among people working on common business processes, often doing so with little or no knowledge of one another. Rich communication media are needed not only because of the higher levels of complexity in communicated messages, but also because of the need to understand their content. Organizations such as Chase Manhatten Bank have explored the role that email communication can have in knowledge management and have funded research on OMIS (Schwartz 1999). It is argued that distributed artificial intelligence programming techniques can provide ways of preserving, distributing and reusing knowledge accrued by the organization (Schwartz 1999). However, people are central to the task of knowledge management within organizations because knowledge cannot be disembodied from the people and the situation in which it is applied.

OMIS are regarded as a prerequisite for any knowledge management within organizations, but they are not sufficient in themselves. They tend to be used to capture learning from business processes that rely on continuous process improvement, such as design engineering. They are more advanced than the early knowledge-based systems (KBS), which simply served the function of storing the knowledge of experts in the form of rules or cases and then provided that knowledge to novices or other experts. Organizational memory has to support a collection of different business processes rather than simply contain solutions to single tasks. OMIS have to support people (and their reasoning processes) by providing them with access to relevant knowledge, which typically includes best practices, design rationales, process knowledge and formal knowledge bases. Finally, the knowledge inside the system also has to be communicated and disseminated to employees. Some of the many knowledge management initiatives that are currently being undertaken by organizations are highlighted in Box 3.4.

Box 3.4: Lest we forget: knowledge management initiatives in organizations

Much attention has been given recently to the firm's intellectual capital as evidenced by its collective knowledge, under the banner of corporate or organizational memory. 3M call this 'the shadow organization'. Most organizations have done little to capture and record this knowledge, either to pass it on to newcomers or allow existing managers to draw on it for instruction. However, the dangers of corporate memory loss are now most acute. In an era of downsizing, outsourcing and re-engineering, the average tenure of employees has been shortened considerably, to around six years – a period that is less than the average trade cycle of most organizations (i.e. approximately eight years). Consequently many organizations are now being run by managers who have no memory of previous major upturns or downturns within the market-place, a highly dangerous state of affairs. Business history is under-emphasized in the West. There are three professors of business history in British business schools, compared to 400 in Japan.

Since 1984, Kraft Foods in the USA has had an archives manager who has responsibility to conduct half-day exit interviews for managers with more than 15 years of experience and all managers upon retirement. Each manager's career is researched and questions prepared on relevant subjects. At retirement, the history is still recent enough to be recalled. Interviews are preserved in the form of written transcripts, edited only for lapses in grammar. These are indexed, stored and archived for reference purposes, and are used to speed up the induction process for newcomers. The Kraft organization has material dating back to 1780 when the company's first product was introduced. The call for more professional archives management was led by the company's PR and legal departments, advertising staff needing to create campaigns that drew upon the product and company's heritage, and staff engaged in strategic reviews of project planning or making decisions about the merits of growth through acquisition or through product development.

There are business history consultancies that offer to build up oral histories by interviewing key individuals at regular intervals during their employment, or track important projects as they unfold. Decision makers are debriefed through the use of oral diaries to reveal sequential evidence of how and why decisions were made at the time. Independent functional experts then produce a learning audit that specifies lessons that can be applied in the future. Boeing made good use of such learning audits in its three-year Project Homework, carried out by senior employees before the development of its 757 and 767 aircraft. They studied management failures and successes associated with past development processes. Several members of the project were transferred to the 757 and 767 start-up projects, with the result that Boeing had the most problem-free product launch in its history.

Fuji-Xerox incorporates archives into a 'registered know-how' system. Management consultants Booz-Allen and Hamilton developed a knowledge programme in 1995 headed by a chief knowledge officer and some 12 to 15 knowledge managers, or 'super-librarians'. The programme is based around a core knowledge team. Over 3000 documents are constantly augmented on an intranet to capture knowledge created by global innovation teams (teams of senior staff seconded for two years at a time and charged with developing the firm's intellectual capital), and by client engagement teams. Such programmes imply a cultural shift within organizations towards greater openness, which is a considerable challenge in itself.

Source: Van de Vliert (1997)

Intra-organizational information markets

Until recently our ability to manipulate and process information and data outstripped our ability to communicate and interact, but managing the quantity and quality of *interactions* made possible by KMS and OMIS is a key strategic management skill. All interactions not only have the same economic purpose – the exchange of goods, services or information – but they also place different cognitive demands on actors in terms of their requirements for data gathering and information search, coordination, communication, collaborative problem solving and the monitoring of transactions. Interactions occur in many forms and each medium is associated with a different load and richness of information. Managers have to seek the right party with whom to exchange information, arrange the presentation of the information, manage its brokerage, integrate it with information from other databases and monitor the performance of the interaction. In short, managers act as information brokers, managing a web of natural interactions that take place within the organization. This web has come to be known as the 'intra-organizational information market'. The current explosion in 'electronic connectivity' and the number of interactions that now surround many organizations is expected to increase the information load associated with many jobs. Research by McKinsey consultants shows that the overall 'interactive capability' in developed countries is set to increase markedly over the next decade (Butler *et al.* 1997). Workers will be able to process existing interactions in less than half the time that it currently takes. As we have seen, these interactions are shaped increasingly by computing and communications technologies, but they are also being shaped by a number of evolutionary developments in strategic organizational form that are currently taking place.

Recent work at Harvard University supports the emergence of this new form of market and highlights the innovative ways in which managers are now having to transact and compete (Hansen 1999; Hansen *et al.* 1999; Hansen and Haas 2001). Clearly, electronic documents represent just one form of information currently being traded, but the rapidity with which they can be disseminated serves to illustrate the dynamic nature of these new internal markets. Four theoretical assumptions are made about these markets:

- Employees search internal databases and information media to help them complete their tasks.
- There is a distinct set of suppliers of information, such as practice groups and business functions. These individuals or subunits are responsible for gathering, selecting, editing, codifying and publishing codified knowledge.
- Both information suppliers and information users receive rewards for their participation in the internal knowledge market (and the creation of documents that are attended to) through performance evaluations and social rewards such as enhanced status.
- There is a significant problem in matching dispersed sets of users and suppliers of information documents.

But what do these intra-organizational information markets look like? To what extent and in what ways do they draw upon principles of knowledge management? We need to return to the popular business literature in order to understand the context within which these markets operate. Towards the end of the 1990s organizations began to consolidate all of their internal trans-actional systems into one or two enterprise-level resource planning systems (ERP). Coupled with initiatives in business process re-engineering, the net effect was to streamline the organization's back-end processes (Kocharekar 2001). As a consequence, many organizations came to appreciate the fact that their intellectual capital was beginning to surpass their physical capital in substantial terms. Paradoxically, the new forms of process being adopted rendered these organizations *more* dependent on the remaining human agents in the value chain (Sparrow 1999a). Moreover, the increased availability of computing and communication technologies enabled more geographically dispersed knowledge transfer, at least in theory. Organizations, therefore, have begun to seek better ways to invest, manage, and harvest their intellectual capital. They have responded broadly on two fronts:

- *E-commerce initiatives*, in an attempt to foster greater efficiency in their transaction processes. Such initiatives include attempts to better link the internal transactional systems and processes to the outside world, using different models (e.g. business to business and business to consumer) that link the internal and external stakeholders of the organization.
- *Knowledge management initiatives*, in an attempt to leverage their intellectual capital by turning attention away from the pursuit of streamlined internal transactions, towards a focus on internal collaborative endeavours that facilitate the sharing of information and knowledge.

A plethora of technical developments have taken place under the knowledge management umbrella. It is necessary to speculate a little about their consequences in order to understand the re-positioned role of managers within the strategic management process of modern organizations. Business intelligence systems or intelligent data mining systems are being used as analytical tools for senior managers, while notes-based applications are being used to foster self-managing teams. Intranet portals serve the role of bringing this information together. It is argued that, ultimately, the two (currently unconnected) strategic drives towards transaction efficiency and intellectual capital effectiveness will need to converge, as more and more commerce becomes knowledge-based. Kocharekar (2001) defines this desired convergence as a *k-commerce business model*. Organizational processes are being created that, hopefully, will enhance the value of information, since it is being conveyed through appropriate communication channels – i.e. channels that match the information richness to the communication medium selected (Daft and Lengel 1984).

Not only must the internal processes be linked to each other, they also need to be linked to a series of parallel processes at work among external partners (be they suppliers of material, financial services or support services). The organizational processes that are being integrated not only cross inter-organizational boundaries, but also operate across a number of internal boundaries. Increasingly, these processes are being interlinked through internal hierarchies. At the basic level, transactional processes are carried out that may be concerned with activities such as procurement. These are generally not totally passive, and frequently have built-in intelligence in order that they may adapt, for example by having the automatic capability to negotiate transactions. This is the current level of capability inherent in many e-commerce systems. As the transaction level becomes more 'adaptive', greater importance will be given to the support processes that operate at the next level up. These support processes serve to extract information from transactions, glean trends and provide guidance to managers. The support level comprises functional experts and information systems that monitor and analyse information. Systems are available to broker this support information upwards into senior management processes, which are focused on enabling strategic direction, providing business partner information, business intelligence and decision support systems, and building industry or sector communities. In practice, each of these sets of processes may be linked through market intermediaries or brokers, whose role is to add value to the communication or information flows by augmenting them. If the market intermediaries or brokers cannot add such value, then it is argued that they will be bypassed. Many of these developments are reflected in current business architectures. The difference in the near future, however, is that the processes outlined are expected to become more integrated as information systems advance.

There are two immediate issues created by this new organizational context. First, managers will need to have a 'good' mental model of how knowledge and information is shared across the people with whom they need to interact (in order to deliver an important business process, product or service) (Sparrow 1999a, 2000). This need becomes paramount as we move towards virtual forms of organization (Sparrow and Daniels 1999). Second, as observed in Chapter 1, in information-rich environments the most scarce resource is not information but the amount of *attention* individuals can allocate to information search, filtration and interpretation (see Ocasio 1997). Simon (1997: 40) notes that when competing for attention in knowledge markets, the real problem is that '[a] wealth of information creates a poverty of attention'. Suppliers of electronic documents within and between organizations are thus competing with one another to gain the attention of users in an internal market for knowledge. Another key challenge, therefore, will be to ensure that managers have the information and knowledge handling skills needed to carry out these processes.

Managers will have to learn how to work with and manage organizational processes over which they will not have full control. It is the ability of the human mind to categorize, associate, extrapolate, interpolate, interpret and transform that turns information into knowledge (Drott 2001). While the interactions associated with intra-organizational information markets are not the only source of information overload (time spent in individual analysis and data processing also plays a role), they represent the largest and most rapidly expanding element of most managerial work. In one sense, then, it is the strategists, organizational designers and systems analysts who have first created – and are now trying to deal with – problems of information overload. It is to this issue that we turn next.

The problem of information overload

In our discussion of heuristics and biases in Chapter 1, we highlighted the fact that in practice managers not only have to make decisions under conditions of *information inadequacy* (a source of uncertainty) (Spender and Eden 1998), but also under conditions of *information overload*. Brooks *et al.* (2001: 335) note that information overload is 'frequently conceived of as a supply of information that exceeds needs or perhaps more subtly as information presented at a rate too high to process'. Similarly, Hansen and Haas (2001) define information overload as a very high ratio of readily available information to the information needed to complete a task. Five key developments have led to the communication of more complex information within organizations (Fulk and DeSanctis 1995):

- increased speed of communication;
- dramatic reduction in communication costs;
- increased communication bandwidth;
- vastly expanded connectivity;
- integration of communication through computing technologies.

Ultimately, organizations must analyse some of the structural reasons why information overload has come about in the first place (Sparrow 1999a). Networking technologies make it more 'economic' to share a piece of information with a colleague or group, or to work with different people inside the organization, or with customers or suppliers outside the organization. Often these different parties are geographically dispersed around the world. Each additional node in a network required to implement strategy effectively increases the scope for interactions exponentially, not arithmetically (Butler *et al.* 1997). In many modern organizations, however, emails flow freely, bypassing traditional hierarchies and functional and vertical communication routes. It is estimated that 60 per cent of information communicated through email would never reach the recipient if not for computer-based mail systems (Fisher 1993). An employee at Sun Microsystems typically receives 120 messages a day, a 50 per cent increase from the early 1990s. Hansen and Haas (2001) cite a 1997 Pitney Bowes study, showing that the average Fortune 1000 worker receives more than 50 email messages a day, and a *Wall Street Journal* analysis indicating that the amount of corporate data stored on computers is doubling every 12 to 14 months. A Reuters study found that 61 per cent of 1000 employees surveyed reported that they were presented with too much information relative to the needs of their job (Reuters 1998). The problem is that email systems tempt managers to act faster, thereby doubling the impact on information load. Managers used to be able to rely on secretaries as an information filter, but today there are 14 per cent fewer secretaries in the USA than a decade ago, while there are many more managers connected to electronic systems.

Electronic documents may contain numerical data (e.g. market numbers), textual information (e.g. market analyses) or more complex forms of knowledge (e.g. know-how about how to enter markets) (Hansen and Haas 2001). In distinguishing between data, information and knowledge, Daft (1995: 299) defines information as 'that which alters or reinforces understanding'. But when there is too much information around it can have the opposite effect. Information load is defined as 'a complex mixture of the quantity, ambiguity and variety of information that people are forced to process. As information load increases, people take increasingly strong steps to manage it' (Weick 1995: 87). As observed by Weick, the *supply* perspective suggests that information overload should be typically measured in terms of:

- the number and difficulty of decisions and judgements the information requires;
- the time available to act;
- the quality of information processing required;
- the predictability of the information inputs.

Much of the information that managers are faced with is problematic in this regard. Four properties of information are associated with overload: low quality, low value, high ambiguity and an ever-decreasing 'half-life' in terms of the currency that the information carries (Sparrow 1998a). These properties increase information load in a number of ways:

- low quality information requires the manager to add the mental effort to make it of any worth to the issue at hand;
- low value information requires an assessment of its explanatory power in relation to other sources of information;
- ambiguous information requires an assessment of what must remain ambiguous and what can be deduced to be certain;

- information that only has a short period of relevance requires rapid processing and dissemination.

Not only do many of these actions waste time, they pose a number of potentially serious problems. For many managers, *the* problem is one of general information overload. Earlier, we argued that there are significant risks associated with relying on the knowledge structures of managers, and risks associated with outsourcing, which can lead to problems of organizational memory loss. We discussed the use of rich communication in combination with organizational memory as a way of ensuring that organizations can still learn in this highly volatile environment. However, in many organizations, individual managers consider that they rarely have the time to apply even what knowledge they have. We need to consider the problem of information overload at both the level of the individual and the organization.

At the individual level, problems of overload are now inherent in many managerial roles. This adds a significant element of strategic risk because of the potential it creates for dysfunctional analysis, decision making and problem solving. Sparrow (1998a) outlines problems of information overload which can lead to managers feeling that they are 'drowning' in a sea of information (this syndrome is also called 'communication pollution' or 'information anxiety'). At the personal level, information overload is associated with feelings of an inability to cope and inadequacy of knowledge and has been identified as a source of stress. The problems associated with this syndrome have not yet received much attention in the strategic management literature. Overload implies an excessive burden and encumbrance that is sustained with difficulty. The potential for dysfunctional decision making is clear when the effect that overload has on cognition is outlined. Managers cease to operate effectively as the load increases and begin to demonstrate dysfunctional behaviour. In coping with the volume of information (let alone its complexity and ambiguity) they begin to neglect large portions of it and try to 'punctuate' its flow in predictable ways. This 'punctuation' begins with omission, then greater tolerance of error, miscueing or mis-attributing the source of information, filtering its message, abstracting its meaning, attempting to use multiple channels to decode and transmit its content, and, finally, seeking escape! These punctuation strategies serve to highlight the residual information, and therefore heighten the impact of misperceptions on subsequent 'sense-making'.

Closely related to 'volume induced' information overload is 'complexity induced' overload (Huber and Daft 1987). Uncertainty is increased because of three elements: *numerosity* (the number of separate elements to be dealt with); *diversity* (the range of information sources and media); and *interdependence* (the complexity of causal relationships between the information elements). Employees may be exposed to information that conveys a great number of diverse elements that interact in a variety of ways. The greater the complexity, the more the untrained person searches for and relies on habitual and routine cues. This creates the potential for disaster, as in the nuclear industry, where the combination of a reliance on complex technologies, numerous transformation processes and inexperienced operatives makes the unexpected commonplace.

In terms of organizational consequences, managers become blinded to more important matters and divert attention to irrelevant issues. The ill-conceived actions of overburdened managers can also generate the potential for unjustified risk-taking and error. The increased volume and load of information forces managers to devote far more time to the process of information search (a skill that has become critically important in many roles) and far too little time to processing or learning from the information. A key management challenge is to find ways to utilize the available brain power of the organization's employees, while not getting them bogged down under a welter of data.

So how can organizations deal with this problem of information overload? A series of popular psychology techniques aimed at lessening the impact of work on memory and decision strain have been outlined by Lewis (1999). Managers may also use heuristics as a possible strategy in certain situations. However, for organizations the challenge is to reduce the dysfunctional levels of overload currently being placed upon their managers. Early work on information load has suggested that organizations might modify the information processing demands of work by providing buffers against uncertainty and complexity. Sparrow (1998a), for example, has suggested that secretaries can be trained to recognize optimal information loads and shield their managers by acting as filters. Computer-based communication can also be designed to allow operators to select from a variety of systems, each matched to a particular cognitive style (Robertson 1985). Ultimately though, it comes down to organizational form and design.

Although we have focused in this section on information overload from a 'supply-side' perspective, it is important to note that this can be misleading. Brooks *et al.* (2001: 335) point out that:

> Information is not a single object that is added sequentially to some internalised information pile. Information is received, filtered, rejected, interpreted, modified, simplified and often, forgotten. It may alter or reinforce existing views, it may come from different sources and carry different weight and authority, different degrees of accuracy, and may be more or less timely.

What might be useful information to one person may be regarded as unnecessary by another. From this perspective, a message must first have been processed, its underlying meaning having been evaluated, or at the very least one must have contemplated processing the message prior to the experience of overload (Stohl and Redding 1987). We should only consider information overload in the context of informational expectations, which in turn means that we have to understand informational needs (Brooks *et al.* 2001).

Summary and conclusions

In this chapter we have argued that the level of and the need for both non-routine and non-structured communications has increased within organizations. However, it is clear that each of the perspectives introduced views the problem of information overload slightly differently:

- From the cognitive engineering perspective (Norman 1988), the level of load is linked to the design decisions built into distributed cognitive systems and the particular demands made by the interactions required of the manager.

- From an organizational memory perspective, the problem becomes a simple one (Dworman *et al.* 1997). As information pertinent to the task in hand passes through the organization, how is it best captured, and if it is captured, how can it best be retrieved effectively and brought to bear on the present task?
- For human-computer specialists studying knowledge management systems, the problem of overload cannot be separated from the equally difficult challenge of providing the 'rich communication media' that facilitate organizational learning across highly distributed and decentralized operations. In an environment of high uncertainty and high novelty, it is argued that routine information processing has to be made more thoughtful, and communication has to be enriched through the use of appropriate media (Daft and Lengel 1984).
- From an organizational learning perspective, information overload is linked to the problem of organizational forgetting. In Chapter 2 we outlined the pressure on design teams and the problem of organizational forgetting when even 'coffee break learning' was under threat from time pressure.

From a general industrial, work and organizational psychology perspective, the ability to manage information overload and cope with information anxiety is seen as a key management competency (Wurman 1989; Stewart 1994). However, to expect all managers to improve their cognitive capabilities to cope with information overload is considered to be a route to chaos. Not all managers are capable of such development, the organization might not have enough depth of talent capable of being developed, and even the most competent manager has cognitive limits.

Although work situations differ markedly in terms of the information processing demands they make on people, there is evidence that overall these demands have been increasing. In considering the problems of information overload, we are mindful of our earlier discussion on heuristics. As we saw in Chapter 1, under conditions of overload, managers resort to heuristic processing strategies. There is consequently a risk of bias.

Let us reconsider the sources of information overload within modern organizational contexts, in order to build up a picture of the strategic information processing now taking place. The problem of information overload is relevant to the effective operation of the internal knowledge markets outlined earlier. Problems of overload are forcing organization theorists to question many of their assumptions. Traditionally, they have assumed that information in organizations is *scarce* and difficult to obtain. This is no longer the case. Consequently, renewed attention is being given to:

- how to enhance the flow of information through cross-unit linkages (Galbraith 1973; Tushman 1977);
- how to facilitate a search for knowledge that is not immediately available (Hansen 1999);
- how to transfer complex knowledge (Zander and Kogut 1995);
- how to reduce message distortions during transmissions (Shannon and Weaver 1949).

In this chapter we have made it clear that the knowledge-based organizational interactions now required of managers, and the evolution towards networked forms of organization, lie at the heart of the information overload problem (Norman 1985). Pettigrew and Fenton (2000) have recently reviewed the literature on new organizational forms, noting that the requirement to leverage intellectual capital within the firm has placed a premium on organizing around the social and relational exchanges that take place within the firm (Nahapiet and Ghoshal 1998) and that inter- and intra-organizational relationships based on the brokering of knowledge have taken over from economic transactions as the primary unit of analysis (Easton and Araujo 1994). As managers deal with the myriad of inter-organizational connections that span owned and affiliated sub-units, joint ventures, strategic partnerships and political, social and professional institutions, the boundaries between organizations and their environments are progressively blurring. The emergence of intra-organizational networks has also had a major impact on knowledge flows within organizations (Hedlund 1994). Dense sets of dispersed, differentiated but interdependent organizational units now form the structure of many organizations (Van Wijk and van den Bosch 2000). These interconnected units act as distributed knowledge systems, decentralized in nature, with a tendency to differentiate on the basis of their resources, capabilities, activities and knowledge (Tsoukas 1996; Galunic and Rodan 1998). In Chapter 2 we noted the autonomous knowledge creation processes that must become established within such organizational forms (Nonaka and Takeuchi 1995). These processes, however, occur in traditional organizations as well. But the knowledge sharing requirements of networked forms of organization are more unique. Each unit pursues its own decisions rather than being guided by the centralized, top-down decisions that characterize multi-divisionalized organizations. Not surprisingly, Van Wijk and van den Bosch (2000: 175) have concluded that 'Understanding the enabling and restricting factors of this knowledge sharing process is of great importance'.

There can be little doubt that the road ahead for those researchers who would seek to meet this challenge will be very steep indeed. One area of research in particular where this is becoming all too apparent is concerned with the analysis of the ways in which actors come to develop and share knowledge of their external competitive environments within the wider marketplace. This work is examined in the next chapter.

4

COMPETITION AND COGNITION

It is generally acknowledged that gaining an adequate understanding of the wider business environment in which the organization is seeking to conduct its affairs is vital to the formulation and implementation of an effective business strategy (see, e.g., Greenley 1989; Hitt *et al.* 1996; Grant 1998; Johnson and Scholes 1999). In this connection, a basic question that has long been central to the strategy field concerns the nature and significance of competition in industries and markets (Abell 1980; Oster 1990), a question that has gained even greater importance in recent years. In Chapter 1 we made the point that organizations are currently operating in a period of hypercompetition (D'Avini 1994). The key challenge this poses for managers is how to manage their businesses in these times of unprecedented disorder. Understanding the ways in which managers think about business competition, therefore, has become a key task. It is also a task to which psychologists can make an important contribution.

In this chapter we consider recent theory and research that has sought to develop insights into the ways in which managers come to develop knowledge of their competitive worlds and represent this knowledge. In recent years a great deal of research attention has been devoted to an examination of the ways in which competitors come to be defined and represented within the minds of

strategic decision makers and those responsible for the implementation of strategy. Little over a decade ago, Porac and Thomas
(1990: 224–5) observed:

> From a cognitive perspective, decision makers act on a
> mental model of the environment. Thus any explanation for
> strategic responses to competitive pressures must ultimately
> take into consideration the mental models of competitive
> strategists ... before competitive strategies can be formu-
> lated, decision makers must have an image of who their rivals
> are and on what dimensions they will compete. Given the
> diverse range of organizational forms and decision makers'
> limited capacity to process complex inter-organizational
> cues, the task of defining 'the competition' is both important
> and problematic.

Building on this fundamental insight, researchers have set out
to systematically explore the structure and content of actors'
mental representations of competition. This work has addressed
two different sets of questions, at different levels of analysis.
First, at an inter-organizational level, researchers have explored
the nature and significance of actors' mental representations of
competition as a basis for gaining a better understanding of the
ways in which the competitive structures of industries (i.e. discernible groupings of competitors) come to be formed and
change over time (see, e.g., Reger and Huff 1993; Porac and
Thomas 1994; Peteraf and Shanley 1997). This body of work is
beginning to shed light on the processes and mechanisms by
which strategic cognition shapes and is shaped by the material
conditions of the market-place, in a dynamic interplay. A second
group of researchers (e.g. Bowman and Johnson 1992; Daniels *et
al.* 1994; Hodgkinson and Johnson 1994) have called into question
some of the key assumptions underpinning this macro approach,
arguing that previous researchers have neglected to consider
individual differences in competitor cognition, and that such
differences may play a central role in the micro-processes of strategy formulation and implementation within firms. As we shall
see, ultimately these differing approaches may actually complement one another. We shall now consider each approach in turn,
beginning with the body of theory and research that has sought

to account for the emergence and evolution of competitive industry structures.

Analysing the structure of business competition: insights from socio-cognitive theory and research

The initial impetus for research into managerial mental models of competition came from a growing dissatisfaction with a body of theory and research centred on the notion of strategic groups. A great volume of work has accumulated which suggests that organizations within an industry do not necessarily compete uniformly with one another. Rather, as explained in Box 4.1, they are organized as a series of *strategic groups*, each group occupying a different location along a variety of *strategic dimensions*. In Figure 4.1, for example, seven such groups have been identified in a strategic groups analysis of the world automobile industry. Here, the strategic dimensions of 'geographical scope' and 'product range' have been employed in order to identify groups of firms following more or less similar approaches to competing within the industry. More generally, as discussed in Johnson and Scholes (1999), a wide range of variables have been used as bases for strategic groups analysis including, for example, 'pricing policy', 'size of the organization', 'number of market segments served', 'utilization of capacity', 'extent of vertical integration' and 'product or service quality'.

A case example, based on research conducted in the European food manufacturing industry (McGee and Segal-Horn 1990) provides a useful illustration of the concepts outlined in Box 4.1. During the 1980s, food manufacturing firms with well-established brands at a national level (national major branders) were able to protect their market positions by virtue of their manufacturing process know-how, marketing skills, local knowledge and brand loyalty on the part of their customers. These isolating mechanisms protected firms following this particular strategy from competitive attacks by players in other strategic groups, such as those pursuing a strategy of weaker branding and supplying own-label products (minor national branders), and those seeking to establish dominance as multinational branders. The former group of players

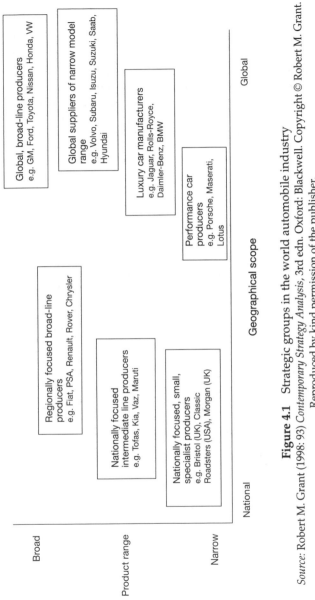

Figure 4.1 Strategic groups in the world automobile industry

Source: Robert M. Grant (1998: 93) *Contemporary Strategy Analysis*, 3rd edn. Oxford: Blackwell. Copyright © Robert M. Grant. Reproduced by kind permission of the publisher.

Box 4.1: Strategic groups theory

Porter (1980: 129) has provided a widely accepted definition of strategic groups:

> A strategic group is the group of firms in an industry following the same or a similar strategy along the strategic dimensions. An industry could have only one strategic group if all the firms followed essentially the same strategy. At the other extreme, each firm could be a different strategic group. Usually, however, there are a small number of strategic groups which capture the essential strategic differences among firms in the industry.

As a tool of strategic analysis, the strategic groups notion is highly attractive, providing an intermediate level of classification between 'the industry', which can often prove too gross for the attainment of meaningful insights, and the individual firm, which is too fine-grained for many purposes. It arose initially in an attempt to account for the differential performance of firms (during the 1960s) in the American home appliance industry (Hunt 1972).

The theory of strategic groups is rooted in a body of work within the field of industrial organization economics, known as the structure → conduct → performance paradigm (Bain 1956; Mason 1957). The main purpose of the economic theory underpinning the notion of strategic groups is to explain variations in the strategic behaviour (conduct) and performance of firms within industries. According to the theory, once strategic groups have formed the various players develop isolating mechanisms (barriers to entry and mobility) that serve to deter new entrants from stepping into the competitive arena and existing players from attempting to switch membership from one group to another (Caves and Porter 1977).

---

sought to protect their positions by being technologically advanced, having low production costs and lower costs overall, together with the ownership of some proprietary processes. The latter group, by contrast, enjoyed considerable consumer brand identification, proprietary process knowledge and enhanced research and development capability, economies of scale, and marketing and organizational skills. The theory of strategic groups predicts that *mobility barriers*, such as those identified in this example, enable significant between-groups performance differences to accrue, over and above differences within groups, due to the fact that these barriers afford stable advantages to particular groups at the expense of other groups within the same industry. Hence the concept of mobility barriers not only provides an explanation for inter-group performance differences, but also a conceptual basis for competitively positioning rival firms (Porter 1981: 615).

Unfortunately, a number of studies have failed to yield significant between-groups performance differences (for reviews see McGee and Thomas 1986; Thomas and Venkatraman 1988). Indeed, in recent years the notion of strategic groups has come under increasingly critical scrutiny. Several researchers have questioned the extent to which secondary financial and accounting information derived from company records or commercially available generic databases, as typically employed by strategic groups researchers, can adequately capture bases of competition (Birnbaum-More and Weiss 1990; Reger 1990a; Reger and Huff 1993; Hodgkinson and Johnson 1994).

A major limitation of this predominantly economic approach is its inability to explain how or why competitive structures in industries come to develop in the first place, and on what basis particular strategies are chosen. Arguably, the most extreme criticisms have come from Hatten and Hatten (1987) and Barney and Hoskisson (1990) who contend that the theoretical base underpinning strategic groups is insufficiently developed to justify the notion, and that in reality strategic groups are merely analytical artefacts of the multivariate data analysis techniques employed to detect them.

In an effort to develop a stronger theoretical basis for the analysis of competitive industry structures and to refine techniques for conducting such analyses, in recent years a growing number of researchers have turned to work in cognitive, social and industrial, work and organizational psychology and related fields. As noted by Hodgkinson (2001a, 2001b) and Lant and Phelps (1999), by and large this work has evolved on a cumulative basis, passing through several key stages of development. We now consider the main elements of this body of work.

The nature and role of categorization processes in competitor definition

We begin with a discussion of *competitor categorization processes*. As we saw in Chapter 1, there are various fundamental limitations to the human information processing system that prevent individuals from undertaking a detailed analysis of all the potentially available information. In keeping with these observations, a number of studies have accumulated over the past 15–20 years which have demonstrated empirically that strategists attend only to a limited sub-set of the many available potential competitors (e.g. Gripsrud and Gronhaug 1985; Porac *et al.* 1987; Hodgkinson and Johnson 1994; P. Johnson *et al.* 1998; Clark and Montgomery 1999; Odorici and Lomi 2001).

Classification is a fundamental cognitive skill which enables information to be organized into manageable units (Eysenck and Keane 1995). Box 4.2 provides an outline summary of the ways in which categorical knowledge might be represented and organized. This has considerable implications for understanding how strategists manage the welter of information impinging on them.

Drawing on the body of theory and evidence outlined in Box 4.2, Porac and his colleagues (Porac *et al.* 1987, 1989; Porac and Thomas 1990, 1994; Porac and Rosa 1996) have argued that strategists' mental representations of competitive industry structures are organized in the form of hierarchical taxonomies (called *categorization schemes*). Within these taxonomies, intermediate-level categories are psychologically more informative compared to those contained in the levels above and below this level of abstraction. They also maintain that strategists assign membership to particular categories on a graded (as opposed to an all-or-nothing) basis, reflecting the extent to which a given exemplar is marked by the various defining characteristics, or features, that determine category membership. These ideas are best illustrated with reference to a specific example. In Box 4.3 we highlight the findings of a study of competitor cognition in a small, rural American town, conducted by Porac *et al.* (1987). Figure 4.2 is also based on data taken from the same study.

The study outlined in Box 4.3 shows that strategists have a general tendency to perceive their own businesses as representative

---

Box 4.2: How is categorical knowledge represented and organized?

A great volume of work has accumulated within the cognitive sciences (see Rosch 1978; Lakeoff 1987) suggesting that categorical knowledge in general is organized in a hierarchical fashion. It has been shown that knowledge represented hierarchically is easier to process, since features that distinguish cognitive sub-categories are stored at relatively high levels of abstraction, thus reducing the burden of information processing. Rosch and her colleagues have shown that these hierarchically organized categories are characterized by indefinite boundary structures and that category exemplars vary in terms of their representativeness (Rosch *et al.* 1976). Certain stimuli are considered to be more prototypical. These prototypes act as the cognitive reference points against which other stimuli are compared (Rosch 1975). Moreover, different levels of abstraction are not equally informative. The level known as the *basic level of inclusion* is generally more informative and consequently is attended to more frequently than other levels. Categories at higher levels of abstraction tend to be characterized by relatively few attributes and these tend to be very general. Consequently they are less informative in nature. Conversely, categories at lower levels of abstraction possess relatively more numerous and more specific attributes. However, these tend to overlap. It is at the basic level of abstraction that categories are optimal in terms of their *information content*, since it is at this level that categories possess the maximum proportion of unique attributes relative to the overlapping attributes of neighbouring categories. For this reason, the basic level is usually found at intermediate levels of abstraction and is said to possess *high cue validity* relative to categories at higher and lower levels of abstraction (Rosch *et al.* 1976).

---

of the categories to which they belong. In the event that no relationships existed between representativeness ratings and one's own category membership, on the basis of chance alone it would be expected that 50 per cent of the ratings reflecting perceptions of own business representativeness would fall below the median rating, and that 50 per cent would lie above it. In fact, only 8 of the

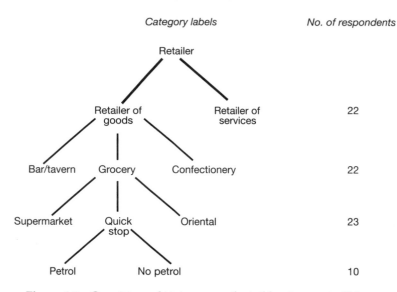

Figure 4.2   Cognitive sub-taxonomy of retail businesses in Urbana-
Champaign, Illinois

Note: at Level 3, respondents listed 25 business categories but only three are
shown. At Level 4, nine categories were uncovered, but again, only three
are shown.

Source: J.F. Porac, H. Thomas and B. Emme (1987) Knowing the competition: the
mental models of retailing strategists, in G. Johnson (ed.) *Business, Strategy and
Retailing.* Chichester: Wiley. Copyright © John Wiley & Sons Ltd. Reproduced
by kind permission of the publisher.

25 ratings were found to fall below the sample median ($\chi^2 = 9.0$,
$P < 0.05$). Similar results were obtained for other levels in the
taxonomy.

If strategists do represent their competitive worlds in the form
of hierarchical cognitive taxonomies, to what extent are the various categories and sub-categories psychologically equivalent to
one another in terms of the power that they have to inform action?
The taxonomy shown in Figure 4.2 provides a convenient basis for
exploring this issue concerning the psychological equivalence of
categories located at varying levels of abstraction. The work of
Rosch *et al.* (1976) would suggest that the various levels within the
taxonomy are not equally informative. On the contrary, one level

Box 4.3: Eliciting shared cognitions at the industry level: the case of the US grocery retail industry

In a study of the US grocery retail industry, Porac and his colleagues set about representing the 'shared' cognitions of their participants at the industry level. Reasoning that managers within the immediate locality would share highly similar views to one another concerning the structure of competition, they aggregated the data elicited from four independent samples. Beginning with the category 'retailer' as the basic starting point (technically known as the 'root beginner category'), participants in the first sample were required to verbalize the various sub-categories that came to mind. These categories were then sorted and coded by the research team (in order to remove any 'redundant terms') before being presented to a second sample, whereupon the participants were required to verbalize the various sub-categories that came to mind in response to the second-level descriptors. As the exercise progressed, fresh samples were employed at each successive level, until the researchers had extracted what they believed to be an adequate representation of the entire competitive arena. The result was the five-level, hierarchical, cognitive taxonomy reproduced (in simplified form) in Figure 4.2. Porac *et al.* then explored the extent to which the competitor categories were graded in structure. A sub-group of participants evaluated the extent to which they considered each of the 25 business categories elicited at Level 3 to be more or less representative of the higher-order (second level) category 'Retailer of goods'. A seven-point Likert scale was employed (1 = 'fits very poorly my idea or image of a retailer of goods', 7 = 'fits very well my idea or image of a retailer of goods'). In keeping with their hypothesis, derived from cognitive categorization theory (Rosch 1975), Porac and his colleagues found evidence to suggest that there were considerable variations in the average ratings (mean and median) of representativeness. For example, the category 'Department store' had a mean rating of 5.9 (median = 6.3), while the mean rating for 'Real estate broker' was only 3.4 (median = 2.8). Rather unexpectedly, they also found that participants generally rated their own business categories as more representative of the super-ordinate category 'retailer of goods' than participants whose businesses fell within the other categories. Notwithstanding the fact that, on average, the category 'Automobile dealers' received one of the lowest ratings over the sample of categories as a whole (mean = 4.7; median = 4.0),

> the one informant whose actual business fell within this particular
> class awarded it the highest possible rating (7). Similarly, the one
> participant in this sample who was a real estate broker awarded the
> highest possible rating to his own business category.
>
> *Source:* Porac *et al.* (1987)

in particular, known as 'the basic level of inclusion', is likely to
provide the greatest information about the environment. As discussed in Box 4.2, typically, basic level categories are found to
reside at intermediate levels. This is because 'middle level'
categories posses higher cue validities in comparison to higher
and lower level categories. Categories located above the basic
level tend to be overly abstract in nature, while those below it
tend to be highly similar, being differentiated only in terms of
one or two minor features. Although it was not rigorously investigated in this particular study, Porac *et al.* provided anecdotal
evidence suggesting that this assertion is an entirely reasonable
proposition. They asked groups of respondents to list as many
attributes as possible that they could recall in relation to each of
the various categories represented in the taxonomy. As might
be expected, participants had great difficulty enumerating
psychologically meaningful attributes in connection with the
higher-level (Level 1 and Level 2) categories. At these levels of
abstraction, only very general attributes were recalled, for
example 'sells things' and 'has customers'. At Level 5, the very
lowest level of abstraction, only the most minor differences
identified the various sub-categories. Thus, for example, as shown
in Figure 4.2, the major factor differentiating the various sub-types
of quick-stop 'convenience marts' is merely the presence or
absence of 'petrol sales'.

In two follow-up investigations, Porac and Thomas (1994) were
able to obtain more extensive evidence in support of the above
arguments. It is now accepted by the majority of theorists and
empirical researchers working in this area that competitor definition categories are organized hierarchically and that category
structures are graded in nature (see e.g. Hodgkinson *et al.* 1991,

1996; Reger and Huff 1993; Hodgkinson and Johnson 1994; Lant and Baum 1995; Hodgkinson *et al.* 1996; Peteraf and Shanley 1997).

Astute readers will have observed that our discussion of competitor categorization processes has, in fact, crossed several different levels of analysis. Drawing on the insights of cognitive categorization theory as a basis for understanding the ways in which strategists as individuals come to define their competitors and represent this knowledge in their minds is one thing – utilizing these insights in order to develop an account of the ways in which groups of firms come to share a common understanding of their competitive worlds and act upon this shared knowledge is an entirely different matter. If individual strategists represent knowledge of their competitive worlds in ways that limit their attention to the extent implied by cognitive categorization theory, what happens when groups of strategists, and other key stakeholders, come together within the wider market-place? How do such potentially idiosyncratic mental representations converge and stabilize to the extent required for discernible competitive industry structures (of the sort implied by Figure 4.2) to emerge? What happens when individuals with radically different mental models enter the scene? Building on the foundations of competitor categorization theory, researchers have addressed these issues, drawing on concepts from a rich variety of theoretical perspectives, interrelating them with one another in an attempt to build a comprehensive 'social constructionist' (Hodgkinson 1997a) or 'socio-cognitive' (Lant 1999; Lant and Phelps 1999) account of the emergence and evolution of competitive groups. We now consider this work in detail.

Competitive enactment and institutional isomorphism

The interrelated notions of enactment and the enacted environment (Weick 1969, 1979a) were introduced in Chapter 1. Drawing on these ideas, together with the insights of Berger and Luckmann (1967), Porac *et al.* (1989) coined the term *competitive enactment* as a basis for understanding the way in which actors from rival firms come to share common conceptions of competition. The idea of competitive enactment was developed in the context of a relatively small-scale, inductive study conducted in the Scottish knitwear industry by Porac and his colleagues. They argued that although individuals' mental models of competition within a given organizational field are idiosyncratic to begin with, they eventually converge over time, through processes of mutual enactment. An analysis of the transcripts of interviews conducted with various top-level executives from rival knitwear producers, using a variant of the taxonomic cognitive mapping technique employed in the US retailing study revealed an overwhelming tendency to disregard as competitors firms located outside the immediate vicinity of Scotland. Despite the fact that Scottish knitwear producers account for a mere 3 per cent of the total amount of knitted outer-wear manufactured on a worldwide basis, only firms within the immediate locality, and who produce a similar range of goods to one another using similar technological processes of production and common channels of distribution, were regarded as serious competition.

According to Porac *et al.* these findings can be accounted for in terms of the processes of enactment outlined in Figure 4.3. These processes have resulted in the emergence of a *group-level mental model* that has come to define the boundaries of the competitive arena. In turn, this has led individual firms to consider a relatively narrow range of strategic options. More generally, Porac and his colleagues (1989: 400) argue that these group-level mental models come about because of a tendency for organizations to imitate one another, both directly and indirectly:

Indirect imitation occurs because strategists from different firms face similar technical/material problems with a finite number of solutions. Belief similarity develops as a result of interpreting the same cues and solving the same problems. Direct imitation occurs because of both formal and informal communications among the set of competitors. Such communications permit the mutual exchange of ideas and concepts by externalizing individual mental models in a publicly observable form. The net result of both indirect and direct imitation is that strategic choices of individual firms take place within the context of many shared beliefs about how and with whom to engage in transactions in the marketplace.

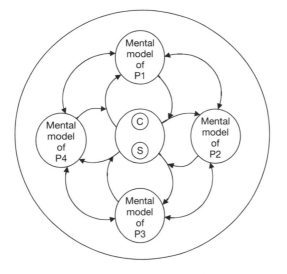

C = customers; S = suppliers; Pn = producers

Figure 4.3 Mutual enactment processes within an industrial sector
Source: J.F. Porac, H. Thomas and C. Baden-Fuller (1989) Competitive groups as cognitive communities: the case of Scottish knitwear manufacturers, *Journal of Management Studies*, 26: 397–416. © Blackwell Publishers Limited. Reproduced by kind permission of the publisher.

More recently, Porac *et al.* (1995) have extended this work in a follow-up investigation conducted in the same industry. This study involved a larger number of participants and utilized comparatively sophisticated research methods, including a structured questionnaire (derived on the basis of taxonomic interviews), and the data were analysed using a variety of multivariate analysis techniques, including network analysis and cluster analysis. The overall findings suggested that a six-category model of organizational forms seems to capture actors' common perceptions of competition within this industry, with several attributes (principally size, technology, product style and geographic location) forming the underlying basis of this commonly perceived structure.

In an attempt to further enrich understanding of competitive enactment processes, Lant and Baum (1995) have introduced the notion of *isomorphism* from institutional theory (Meyer and Rowan 1977; DiMaggio and Powell 1983; Powell and DiMaggio 1991). This is the observed tendency for firms to develop shared beliefs, structures, practices, strategies and networks of relations. According to Lant and Baum, two forms of isomorphism in particular are likely to have a bearing on the formation of competitive structures. The first, *mimetic isomorphism*, arises from the monitoring of firms within the relevant 'competitive set' (Lant and Baum's term for the cognitive analogue of conventional strategic groups), while the second, *normative isomorphism*, stems from a variety of normative sources, such as the parent company (if part of a conglomerate), and agents in the institutional environment who act as transmitters of information, including travel agents, higher education institutions, and industry consultants. In a similar vein to the arguments developed by Porac *et al.*, Lant and Baum contend that these sources of isomorphism provide managers with vital clues about their organization's strategic identity and hence its appropriate strategy.

Taking these insights as their basic point of departure, Lant and Baum predicted that they would find evidence within a sample of $N = 43$ hotel managers in the Manhattan district of New York for the existence of mutually enacted competitive sets, in which rivals with similar characteristics and strategies would tend to identify one another as relevant competitors. They also predicted that the perceptions and attributions of managers within such competitive groups would be more similar than the perceptions and attributions of managers drawn from different groups. Adopting a similar analytic strategy to Porac *et al.* (1995), using a form of network analysis in conjunction with hierarchical cluster analysis, some 14 competitive groupings were identified from a total of 167 hotels. As predicted, managers within each discernible group of hotels tended to regard one another as relevant competitors. Also as predicted, a number of significant differences emerged between the competitive groups in relation to the mean size, price and location (street and avenue) of the hotels, indicating that the aggregation the competitive sets elicited from the individual managers reveals relatively homogeneous groups of hotels. Unfortunately, because this study utilized a cross-sectional design, it was not possible to discern which of the various hypothesized forms of mimetic and normative isomorphism ultimately accounts for the observed pattern of findings. As with the earlier Scottish knitwear study (Porac *et al.* 1989, 1995), which also employed a cross-sectional design, the findings of this research should be regarded as tentative rather than conclusive, opening up the field to further lines of inquiry, with larger samples and greater controls. (For recent studies illustrating several different ways in which this preliminary work might inform future research in this area, see Greve 1998; Odorici and Lomi 2001).

Relational modelling, vicarious learning and social indentification

Building on the insights of competitor categorization theory and the various social constructionist notions outlined above, Peteraf and Shanley (1997) have introduced the notions of *relational modelling* and *vicarious learning* from social learning theory (Bandura 1986; Wood and Bandura 1989), together with the notion of *identity strength* from social identification theory (Tajfel and Turner 1985; Ashforth and Mael 1989), in an attempt to further explain the emergence of strategic groups within industries and how these groups influence the behaviour and outcomes of firms (see Box 4.4). As shown in Figure 4.4, a variety of macro-environmental forces (historical, economic and institutional) condition the development of competitive groups and their identities. However, these forces alone cannot account for structure → conduct → performance relationships, as classically investigated by industrial economists and strategic groups theorists. Ultimately, it is the interaction between a variety of micro- and macro-level factors that needs to be better understood if we are to account for the formation, behaviour and outcomes of such groups.

If the theory outlined in Box 4.4 is correct, strength of identity should be linked to a variety of positive and negative outcomes. On the positive side, stronger group identities will not only result in higher levels of action by group members, and efficiency gains (due to information exchange among group members), but will also increase the positive reputation of the group. On the negative

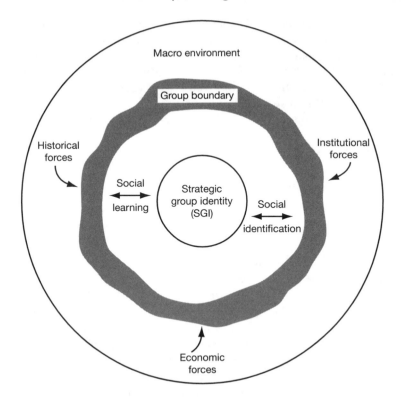

Figure 4.4 Forces generating a strategic group identity (SGI)
Source: M. Peteraf and M. Shanley (1997) Getting to know you: a theory of
strategic group identity. *Strategic Management Journal*, 18 (summer special issue):
165–86. © John Wiley & Sons, Ltd. Reproduced by kind permission of the
publisher.

side, such groups will be characterized by increased resistance
to change and greater inflexibility on the part of individual
members, and stronger group identities will result in myopic
views of the industry domain and its interests. Moreover, strong
group identities are likely to lead the individual firms to sub-
optimize for a variety of reasons, not least the fact that stronger
identities are likely to distort decision makers' perceptions, to the
extent that the perceived benefits of affiliation are likely to exceed
the actual benefits. According to Peteraf and Shanley (1997), these

---

Box 4.4: Peteraf and Shanley's theory of strategic group identity

According to Peteraf and Shanley (1997), managers reflect on their accumulated experiences of inter-organizational interactions, both direct and vicarious, in order to discern which organizations are important for them to observe and emulate and which are of significance in competitive terms, or for reasons of mutual concern. Over time these observations and inferences are encoded into a series of *organizational routines* that guide the future search behaviours of organizations, whether they are looking to solve difficult problems, gather intelligence about competitors or obtain additional resources from cooperative partners. Irrespective of why the information is sought, these routines steer organizations in such a way that they will tend to look to the same group of firms on repeated occasions, which in the long run leads to the development of a relatively stable cognitive entity. The accumulated experience gained through social learning enables organizations to reduce their transaction costs by promoting continued exchange only with those firms found to be reliable interaction partners, predictable in their behaviours and providing tolerable levels of risk. These processes of social learning are a necessary but insufficient condition for the emergence of strategic groups that have real and measurable effects – i.e. groups that will ultimately influence the conduct and performance of their individual members. In addition, social identification must occur; group members must not only perceive the fact that a group exists ('identification of the group'), but also identify with the group. It is the *identity strength* of a strategic group that ultimately determines the extent to which group membership impacts on the conduct and performance of organizations within a given industry. This notion might explain why previous attempts to identify significant differences in organizational performance on the basis of strategic group membership *per se* have yielded inconsistent findings from study to study. Previously hypothesized performance differences will only consistently emerge in situations where strategic groups are characterized by strong identities.

---

conflicting effects can occur simultaneously and it is this that may account for the failure of researchers to accumulate consistent findings concerning performance outcomes in previous studies of strategic groups.

Cognitive inertia

Do these myopic views of the competitive arena have broader effects on organizational behaviour? Population ecology theorists and researchers such as Hannan and Freeman (1977, 1988) have studied the behaviour of mass populations of organizations over many years and have demonstrated that 'inertial forces' often prevent organizations from adapting to major environmental change. Drawing on this work, Porac and Thomas (1990) have argued that a source of such inflexibility might be the cognitive inertia arising from strategists' mental models of the competitive arena. As we have seen, there is a hidden danger when material transactions stabilize to the point where discernible competitive structures and/or industry-wide conceptions of what it takes to compete successfully begin to emerge (cf. Spender 1989): that strategists may become overly dependent on the shared mental model that has come to prevail, so that dramatic changes to the competitive landscape may go undetected (or unheeded) until successful adaptation is no longer possible (see also Levenhagen *et al.* 1993; Abrahamson and Fombrun 1994; Reger and Palmer 1996). Left unchecked, such inertia can threaten the adaptive capabilities of the individual firm or entire sub-populations of firms, to the point of extinction, as demonstrated in the case of the UK residential estate agency industry (see Box 4.5).

Perhaps the dramatic experience of Prudential within this particular industry, with which we began this book, can be explained (in part at least) by the notion of cognitive inertia. Ironically, the overwhelming majority of participants involved in the study summarized in Box 4.5 (drawn from large and small firms alike) continued throughout the entire investigation to view the Prudential, and several other national and quasi-national corporate chains, as the most successful players – despite highly visible, objective evidence that they were in major difficulties and had been for some considerable time: 'When placed in this proper historical context, the results . . . suggest that from the outset of this study the research participants were acting on a mental model which was already out of step with the changing circumstances confronting the industry' (Hodgkinson 1997b: 939).

Box 4.5: Cognitive inertia in the UK residential estate agency industry

The notion that once formed, actors' assessments of competitors become highly resistant to change has recently received strong empirical support through a longitudinal investigation of UK residential estate agents (Hodgkinson 1997b). An initial sample of 208 respondents from 58 firms completed a set of detailed questionnaires at the onset of a recession in the UK property market. The questionnaires were designed to elicit the respondents' perceptions of their own organization and various competitors on a number of key dimensions. A sub-sample of 114 respondents from 41 firms returned a further set of completed questionnaires, 12–18 months later, when the recession had become deeply established. The results of a multidimensional scaling analysis demonstrated that despite a significant downturn in the housing market from the first to the second data collection period, neither the private nor collective mental models of competitive space held by the research participants had changed to any meaningful extent. On the contrary, minimal changes were observed, thus adding empirical weight to theoretical arguments concerning the deleterious role of cognition in ailing industries and markets.

In circumstances where environmental contingencies shift and new forms of competitive strategy emerge to challenge an organization's once protected position, concomitant changes to the way in which strategists view competition would appear to be a fundamental prerequisite for successful adaptation. However, the findings of this study add weight to the considerable body of anecdotal evidence to be found in the popular management literature, which suggests that all too often strategists are unable to reconceptualize the market identity of their businesses in this way (see also Gronhaug and Falkenberg 1989; Reger and Palmer 1996).

Given this state of affairs, perhaps it is little wonder that Prudential continued to remain in the residential estate agency industry until its mounting debts passed the £300 million threshold.

*Challenges to prevailing wisdom: situated learning and the
cognitive life cycle of market domains*

Even if cognitive inertia becomes widespread within a given competitive field, this need not necessarily imply that terminal decline is inevitable. For example, key individuals might challenge the prevailing industry wisdom and competitive orthodoxy to such an extent that new competitive strategies emerge before too much damage occurs. Levenhagen *et al.* (1993) developed a *cognitive life cycle conception* that offers some potentially useful insights into the ways in which established industry structures evolve and change. Insights on this issue have also come from the *situated learning* perspective on strategic groups, recently advanced by Lant and Phelps (1999). Both perspectives provide support for the notion that the actions of key individuals (usually located on the periphery and very often complete outsiders) can act as a catalyst for major change.

In the case of the life cycle conception, a primary task of key *entrepreneurial agents* is to destroy the legitimacy of extant categories of competitor definition, replacing them with a viable alternative. Such 'industry leadership' demands that the 'framemaking entrepreneur' is literally able to 'sell' their vision to the wider community of actors within the competitive arena. Once a sufficiently critical mass of followers has developed, these newer competitive practices become objectified and institutionalized, until further 'frame breaking' activities come to challenge the prevailing orthodoxy.

Through its dynamic emphasis on the importance of both variation and consistency in cognition and action over varying time periods, the situated learning perspective advanced by Lant and Phelps (1999) highlights the importance of multilevel system interaction effects within and between firms and groups of firms, both in the maintenance of market stability and the development of structural change (see also Lant 1999). This perspective challenges a number of the key assumptions that have underpinned much of the previous work on the social construction of competitive structures, as summarized above. Drawing on recent social constructionist accounts of organizational learning (as outlined in Chapter 2), Lant and Phelps have questioned the adequacy of the way in which learning has been portrayed within recent socio-cognitive theory and research on strategic group formation, as a predominantly vicarious process in which referent others are modelled or imitated, exemplified in the recent paper by Peteraf and Shanley (1997). They have also questioned the adequacy of the 'topographic' view of organizations portrayed within the wider body of work on the social construction of competitive industry structures and, indeed, much of the field of organization studies more generally. Two assumptions in particular that are implicit within this view are challenged by Lant and Phelps, drawing on the work of Araujo (1998), Palinscar (1998) and Tsoukas (1992):

- the assumption that knowledge is localized in individual minds or other anthropomorphized entities such as organizations;
- the assumption that organizations are relatively self-contained, bounded entities that learn through key individuals, such as top managers

As we observed in Chapter 2, not all knowledge is so localized. Nor, indeed, are organizations so self-containing. Lant and Phelps contend that the theory of learning and identification portrayed in recent socio-cognitive accounts of the emergence of strategic groups represents an under-situated perspective:

> In contrast, we assume that learning, cognition, and knowledge are inherently situated in a broader social context consisting of actors, artefacts, language, time and space. According to a situated learning perspective, knowledge and its meaning are negotiated and constructed by actors who interact within a community with which they identify and who share the practices of the community . . . Situated learning encompasses meaning (learning as experience), practice (learning as doing), community (learning as becoming), and identity (learning as belonging). Such a view affords a much richer sense of the learning processes that occur within and among organizations than a focus on vicarious learning by top managers.
>
> (Lant and Phelps 1999: 230–1)

This new perspective requires strategic groups theorists to reconsider the nature and role of *mobility barriers* as protective devices that preserve the competitive positions of established industry players (Caves and Porter 1977). Turning conventional wisdom completely on its head, Lant and Phelps (1999) maintain that strategic groups with high mobility barriers will have lower long-term survival chances than groups with lower barriers, due to the fact that these barriers inhibit learning by preventing players with new beliefs and practices from entering the group. Over time, this will result in reduced variation in structures, strategies and beliefs, thus rendering the wider population of firms vulnerable to competency-destroying technological changes of the sort discussed by Tushman and Anderson (1990).

Section summary

A growing body of theory and research has amassed over recent years which suggests that competitive structures within industries develop through a number of interrelated processes of social construction. The fundamental limitations to the human information processing system discussed in Chapter 1 necessitate that managers selectively attend to only a sub-set of all the potentially available competitors from the wider population of organizations as a whole. Research within the cognitive sciences suggests that managers' knowledge of these competitors is organized hierarchically, that intermediate level categories contain the most useful information and that categories of competitor definition are a graded as opposed to an all-or-nothing phenomenon. Recent studies of competitor categorization processes generally support these basic propositions. Organizational strategy researchers have also argued that, through a variety of processes involving social interaction, coupled with the fact that firms within particular competitive fields face similar material and technical problems with a finite number of solutions, managerial mental models of competition converge over time. In turn, these shared mental models come to inform the strategic choices of individual firms, constraining their actions in line with group norms. Researchers have also drawn attention to the dangers of cognitive inertia. Once formed, mental models of competitor definition can serve to filter new information in such a way that individuals and groups become impervious to the need for strategic change, thereby undermining their adaptive capabilities. As we have seen, some empirical evidence has begun to accumulate in support of this notion. More recently, researchers seeking to elucidate the socio-cognitive foundations of strategic groups and related conceptions of competition at the macro-institutional level have begun to debate the nature and significance of a number of related processes concerned with social learning and social identification.

Mapping mental models of competition as a basis for exploring micro-processes of strategizing within and between firms

The body of work reviewed so far has evolved in a highly cumulative fashion. Researchers have filled in the gaps of previous theorizing and have attempted to enrich understanding of the ways in which competitive structures are formed and reformed over time. Despite considerable research, however, there are a number of major gaps in the empirical knowledge base. It is still far too early for researchers to resolve some of the fundamental controversies with which we began this chapter. These include the question as to whether or not strategic groups really do exist (Barney and Hoskisson 1990; Tang and Thomas 1992). In this section, we identify a number of methodological weaknesses associated with the various socio-cognitive studies of strategic groups, in order to show that some of the fundamental assumptions underpinning this work may in fact be unwarranted. We also identify reasons why alternative theoretical conceptions may be required if we are to better understand the nature and significance of strategists' mental models of competition.

Methodological limitations of empirical studies supporting the emerging socio-cognitive theory of competitive industry structures

While many of the theoretical ideas outlined in the preceding section are appealing, closer scrutiny of the accompanying empirical knowledge base reveals a number of major gaps and limitations. Ultimately, a number of large-scale, multilevel, longitudinal studies are required if this emerging body of socio-cognitive theory is to be rigorously tested. Unfortunately, such high quality studies have not been forthcoming. On the contrary, as observed by Hodgkinson (1997a), the vast majority of studies have been relatively small in scale and scope.

All but three studies (Gronhaugh and Falkenberg 1989; Reger and Palmer 1996; Hodgkinson 1997b), have utilized cross-sectional designs and, in the vast majority of cases, just one informant has been recruited from each participating organization (typically the owner-manager, managing director or CEO), as exemplified by the Scottish knitwear study (Porac et al. 1989, 1995) and the study of Manhattan hotels conducted by Lant and Baum (1995). (For additional representative examples, see Dess and Davis 1984; Gripsrud and Gronhaugh 1985; Fombrun and Zajac 1987; Porac et al. 1987; Porac and Thomas 1994). Only one of these studies (Hodgkinson 1997b) has employed a truly prospective longitudinal research design, whereby data is collected on multiple occasions over an extended time period. The Gronhaugh and Falkenberg study employed retrospective recall techniques on an extremely small sample, while the Reger and Palmer study utilized three independent datasets, each gathered over varying time periods, thus introducing a number of confounding factors that limit the inferences which can be drawn in respect of the findings.

As noted by Hodgkinson (1997a, 2001a, 2001b), the use of single-informant, multiple-organization research designs has a number of limitations and drawbacks. Specifically, this approach is predicated upon an implied level of consensus within and between organizations that is highly questionable (Woolridge and Floyd 1989; Floyd and Woolridge 2000). It fails to take into account the possibility that there may be key individual differences in managers' perceptions of competitive environments. To the extent that such differences exist, they may have an important bearing on processes of strategy formulation and implementation. Unfortunately, with the notable exception of Lant (1999) and Lant and Phelps's (1999) recent work, socio-cognitive strategic groups theorists and researchers have neglected to consider such differences, as exemplified by the US grocery retail sector and Scottish knitwear studies (Porac *et al.* 1987, 1989, 1995; Porac and Thomas 1994).

In the case of the US grocery retail study the method of taxonomic mapping employed restricted the analysis to the industry level of aggregation (see Figure 4.2) and while the methods employed in the Scottish knitwear study might have been utilized to investigate the nature and significance of individual and sub-group differences in strategic cognition, instead attention was confined to communal aspects of the data:

> In our analysis of the Scottish knitwear sector we took intra-industry variation as a given. At the same time, however, we ought to distil from interview and secondary data core beliefs that seemed to be repeated by our sources and widely accepted. Our analyses suggest that certain beliefs about competitor and market identity isolate a commonly perceived competitive arena for many of the Scottish managers.
>
> (Porac *et al.* 1989: 405)

In their larger-scale follow-up investigation, while recognizing the importance of differences in perceptions, especially asymmetries in the classification of firms into particular categories of rival, once again Porac *et al.* centred primarily on commonalities, with a view to identifying 'a collectively understood industry model of organizational forms [which] has become part of the macro-cultural belief system of the industry participants' (Porac *et al.* 1995: 221).

In an attempt to address directly Hodgkinson's (1997a) criticisms regarding the small-scale, cross-sectional nature of previous empirical work, Osborne *et al.* (2001) have recently reported the outcomes of a longitudinal study spanning a 20-year time period (1963–82), in which documentary sources (presidents' letters to shareholders) were used to identify cognitive strategic groups (i.e. groups based on managers' mental models of competition) in the US pharmaceutical industry. Previously, Cool and Schendel (1987) investigated strategic groups in this industry using conventional, economic variables, reflecting variations in firm performance. Answering directly Hodgkinson's (1997a) call for studies that seek to establish linkages between actors' mental representations of strategic groups and measures of performance, Osborne *et al.* triangulated the strategic groups identified through their thematic analysis of some 400 documents from 22 firms with the findings of the earlier Cool and Schendel study, covering the same 20-year time period. In total, 37,000 sentences (450,000 words) were content analysed with the aid of computerized software. A series of complex statistical analyses suggested that there was a significant amount of convergence between the cognitive strategic groups identified by Osborne *et al.* and the economic strategic groups identified by Cool and Schendel. This recent study illustrates the fact that there has been a clear strengthening of research methods now being employed in an effort to enrich this field. For example, this study overcomes the sample size limitations of previous cognitive studies, uses a longitudinal research design and concerted efforts have been made to triangulate cognitive findings with economic performance data (all vital prerequisites for ascertaining the validity of the notion of competitive enactment). There are, however, still problems associated with the retrospective use of documentary sources, in that the data they contain may be subject to bias and distortion (see Chapter 7). Moreover, as indicated above, single informant designs yield data that might be unrepresentative of the wider body of strategists within the firm, an issue that we consider in some detail in the remaining sections of this chapter.

The case for studying individual and sub-group mental models of competitor definition: the processual school revisited

In Chapter 3, we developed a number of ideas about organizational memory in the context of decision making within organizations. It is important to note, however, that although individual managers possess cognitive abilities, firms, strictly speaking, do not. In Chapters 5 and 6 we will consider a number of individual-level factors associated with competent performance in modern organizations. At this point we merely seek to highlight the potential importance of such individual differences in competitor cognition, as opposed to cognitive abilities. As we have seen in our discussion of the situated learning perspective on cognitive strategic groups, the potentially significant role that such differences might play in the emergence and subsequent evolution of competitive industry structures is something that has been largely neglected by researchers. That the significance of these differences for understanding the strategic management process has largely been 'assumed away' by cognitive strategic groups researchers is epitomized by the following quotation, taken from a recent paper by Peteraf and Shanley (1997). In this paper, in which they outlined their social identity theory of strategic groups, Peteraf and Shanley questioned the conditions under which it is reasonable to apply a cognitive perspective collectively to an organization:

> When a firm is led by a single top decision maker, as many small firms are, the cognitive processes of the CEO are arguably the same as those of the firm. This is because although the firm may be composed of many individuals, the CEO has full responsibility for scanning the environment and charting a course of action for the firm. Few would dispute that a cognitive analogy from individuals to firms is applicable in such a circumstance. . . . More often, however, a firm is managed by a top management team that exercises collective decision-making. In this case, the team may be characterized as a collective actor with cognitive capabilities if group-level processes (Larson and Christensen 1993) allow team members to reconcile their cognitive differences and make decisions in a relatively unified and consistent manner . . . When the top management team is relatively homogeneous and when there is continuity of management, it is even more reasonable to view the firm as a collective cognitive actor.
>
> (Peteraf and Shanley 1997: 167–8)

However, the issue of consensus in mental models of competitor definition within industries and markets is fundamentally problematic. The extent to which each of the conditions outlined in the above quotation actually hold in the various studies reviewed in the previous section is highly debateable. Given that none of these studies actually assessed the extent of cognitive variation or homogeneity within and between firms, let alone controlled for the various intra-organizational processes alluded to in the quotation, it is impossible to judge the extent to which these key assumptions are justified. Certainly, the situated learning perspective on strategic groups recently advanced by Lant (1999) and Lant and Phelps (1999) openly challenges the adequacy of this viewpoint. There are, however, additional reasons for opening up the analysis of managerial representations of competitive industry structures to the study of individual and sub-group differences.

The main value of the various taxonomic mapping studies of an aggregate nature, discussed earlier, is in terms of their contribution to the competitive analysis of industries through their grounding in managerial thinking. There are, however, important issues of a *processual* nature, which such research has touched upon, but with which it is not been centrally concerned. It is to these issues that we now turn our attention.

Hodgkinson and Johnson (1994) have noted that the processual approach, emphasizing the fact that the development of strategies is perhaps best explained by understanding social, political and cultural processes within organizations (Bower 1972; Pettigrew 1973, 1985; Pfeffer and Salancik 1974; Hedberg and Jonsson 1977; Pfeffer 1981a, 1981b; Johnson 1987; Pettigrew and Whipp 1991), has important implications for the study of competitor cognition. There is clearly a need for cognitive studies of competitive structures to be extended to a variety of additional levels of analysis, particularly the organizational level, functional group level and the individual level. The primary reason for this is that different managers, in different roles, face different *environmental contingencies* in terms of context, function and level of responsibility (Lawrence and Lorsch 1967). Clearly, to the extent that managers' mental models of their business environments are shaped by past experiences and material circumstances we would expect to find differences in the nature and characteristic features of these mental models from one research participant to another.

Moreover, a number of writers have argued that there exist sets of relatively common assumptions related to different managerial contexts. A manager is likely to be influenced by, and interact with, all of these *frames of reference* (Huff 1982). Figure 4.5 represents some of these different sets of assumptions.

These frames of reference exist at the:

- industry level (Grinyer and Spender 1979; Spender 1989);
- organizational level (Sheldon 1980; Pfeffer 1981a; Bartunek 1984; Prahalad and Bettis 1986; Johnson 1987, 1988; Laughlin 1991).

Arguably however, the diversity of frames of reference upon which managers draw goes still wider than the organizational or industry level. For example, there is increasing evidence that *national culture* affects managers' interpretations and responses to strategic issues (Schneider and De Meyer 1991; Calori *et al.* 1992, 1994), and their perceived control of the environment and strategic behaviour (Hofstede 1980; Kagono *et al.* 1985). There are

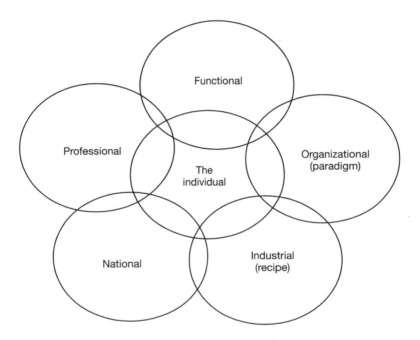

Figure 4.5 Various frames of reference of managers that might have a bearing on mental models of competitor definition
Source: G.P. Hodgkinson and G. Johnson (1994) Exploring the mental models of competitive strategists: the case for a processual approach, *Journal of Management Studies,* 31: 525–51. © Blackwell Publishers Limited. Reproduced by kind permission of the publisher.

also various intra-organizational influences. At the level of functional groups, for example, it has been argued that there are functionally specific belief systems and perceptions of issues (Dearborne and Simon 1958; Handy 1985). It has also been argued that managers' views of the world are shaped, at least in part, by their career backgrounds (e.g. Bouchet 1976; Hambrick and Mason 1984; Gunz and Whitley 1985; Whitley 1987; Gunz 1989). Finally, there are various individual-level frames of reference that might influence the way in which managers perceive their competitive environments (Markus 1977; Markus and Nurius 1986; Markus and Wurf 1987).

To summarize, any manager, or group of managers, draws upon a series of frames of reference to make sense of their world. There is a continual interplay between the individual, the context in which they operate, the frames of reference related to these contexts, and the political and social processes at work. Understanding the process of strategic management is therefore centrally concerned with explaining how diverse frames of reference are reconciled within and between organizations in order to formulate and implement strategies.

Empirical findings concerning the extent of individual and sub-group differences and homogeneity in mental models of competitor definition

A number of studies, conducted across a range of sectors, have attempted to contribute to our understanding of the nature and significance of these diverse influences on managerial mental models of competitive industry structures. Through these studies researchers have debated the extent to which the knowledge structures of individual strategists are highly idiosyncratic in nature, or can be seen to reflect some form of socio-cognitive communality.

To the extent that the theorizing outlined above is correct, we would expect to find evidence of *systematic patterns of difference* in the structure and content of managers' mental models within the same industrial sector, in accordance with their background characteristics and psychological make-up. A growing number of researchers have investigated mental models of competitive structures at the level of the individual participant and have uncovered such differences (see, e.g., Bowman and Johnson 1992; Calori *et al.* 1992, 1994; Daniels *et al.* 1994; Hodgkinson and Johnson 1994; P. Johnson *et al.* 1998). One of the earliest studies of this nature was conducted in the Chicago bank market by Reger (1990a). The key findings are outlined in Box 4.6.

However, it is important to note that following a re-analysis of the same data set (using a different set of statistical techniques) Reger and Huff (1993) observed considerable agreement in terms of the research participants' categories of competitors. On the basis of this re-analysis, they concluded that the findings of their study offer complementary support for the views of Porac and his colleagues (Porac *et al.* 1989; Porac and Thomas 1990) concerning

---

Box 4.6: Individual differences in the mental models of managers in the US banking sector

In her study of competition in the Chicago banking market, Reger (1990a) investigated the mental models of senior managers from a number of rival firms at the individual level, in order to find out whether the participants agreed about the bases of competition. She concluded that there was a surprisingly low level of agreement regarding the important strategic dimensions of the industry. The proposition that key strategic dimensions would be widely shared by strategists was not supported. Somewhat speculatively, Reger argued that sub-groups of strategists might be expected to share more commonality of dimensions than exhibited by the group as a whole. For example, members of the same bank holding company might be expected to share more common dimensions, on the grounds that they interacted more often with each other and were more likely, therefore, to directly discuss competitors' strategies and key strategic dimensions of the industry. She also argued that strategists who shared similar functional or product backgrounds would be more likely to share common dimensions, on the grounds that their training and experience would more than likely be similar. Such factors are likely to shape the cognitive constructive systems of managers in similar ways.

Source: Reger (1990a)

---

the socio-cognitive underpinnings of strategic group formation. Clearly this reinterpretation of the results is somewhat at variance with Reger's (1990a) initial conclusions that strategists have different cognitive frameworks, and serves well to illustrate the fact that the comparative evaluation of data across individuals, in an effort to assess the structure and content of their mental representations of strategic phenomena, is far from straightforward.

Preliminary evidence supporting the hypothesis that there are systematic patterns of difference in the structure and content of managers' mental models within the same industrial sector, in accordance with their background characteristics and psychological make-up, has also been obtained in two other recent studies conducted in the offshore pumps industry (de Chernatony *et al.* 1993; Daniels *et al.* 1994) and the UK grocery retail industry (Hodgkinson and Johnson 1994). Both studies yielded similar results. The findings of the latter study are highlighted in Box 4.7.

Box 4.7: Systematic variation in the structural complexity of managers' mental models

Hodgkinson and Johnson (1994) uncovered evidence suggesting that the degree of detail (*structural complexity*) associated with mental models of competitive structures may vary systematically according to the role requirements of the strategist's job. Managers whose roles require them to have a more detailed grasp of the business environment (e.g. those concerned with the formulation of national merchandising policy at head office) were found to have significantly more elaborate cognitive structures in comparison to their counterparts whose roles do not require them to possess such detailed insights and knowledge concerning the actions of their competitors (e.g. regional area managers concerned with the implementation of policy in the field). Hodgkinson and Johnson contend that these differences have arisen because differing jobs place differing demands upon individuals and sub-groups which, in turn results in differing interpretations of the competitive arena (see also Calori *et al.* 1994).

As in Reger's initial analysis, Hodgkinson and Johnson's (1994) suggested that there was considerable variation among managers in terms of their views of the way in which their industries were structured. However, in keeping with the findings of de Chernatony et al. (1993) and Daniels et al. (1994), the results also indicated that:

• managers within particular organizations share more similar views than managers across organizations;
• managers with common functional and/or role responsibilities are more similar in their views compared to their counterparts with differing functional and/or role responsibilities.

The debate still continues. Another recent study lends support to the idiosyncrasy of strategists' mental models as opposed to there being a socio-cognitive grouping. P. Johnson et al. (1998) reported the findings of a study of 22 managers spanning three organizations operating in the international automotive industry. On the basis of three separate sets of analysis, focusing on the competitors named by the participants, the number of constructs they employed and a content analysis of these constructs, P. Johnson et al. concluded that there was little evidence of industry, organizational or even group-level homogeneity in the knowledge structures that the managers held of their competitive environment:

> When considering the issue of the level to which managers' knowledge structures can be considered commonly held, the findings ... support a high degree of idiosyncrasy and therefore subscribe to the individual level perspective. That is managers failed to demonstrate sufficient homogeneity to group together at the organization level or even the functional level.
>
> (P. Johnson et al. 1998: 140–1)

On the basis of these findings, P. Johnson et al. (1998) question the validity of propositions concerning the idea that managers' knowledge structures demonstrate commonality at the strategic group and organizational level (Porac et al. 1987, 1989; Reger and Huff 1993). They argue instead that managers' knowledge structures are to a large extent idiosyncratic in nature. This pattern of findings also conflicts with the findings of Hodgkinson and Johnson (1994) and Daniels *et al.* (1994), whose work suggests that managers from the same organization and functional position do tend to share similar beliefs. P. Johnson *et al.* attribute such variations to differences in analytic focus. Hodgkinson and Johnson, and Daniels *et al.*, drew their conclusions on the basis of comparisons of the content *and* structure of their participants' cognitive maps, whereas P. Johnson *et al.*'s analysis focused on map content *per se.* Such debates highlight a key problem bedevilling progress in the study of managerial and organizational cognition in general: that of obtaining a body of empirical findings that are sufficiently robust to emerge across a range of situational contexts, using alternative methods of data collection and analysis (Hodgkinson 1997a, 2001a). Nonetheless, we can draw some important conclusions from this body of work.

Section summary

Social constructivist notions such as 'competitive enactment,' 'institutional isomorphism' and the theory of strategic group identity seem to imply that differences in actors' cognitions are of little consequence in accounting for the strategy and performance of organizations; that ultimately it is the commonalities in decision makers' cognitive maps that unite individuals and galvanize collective action – deviations from the 'norm' being little more than 'error variance'. However, when we consider the theoretical arguments concerning the nature and significance of intra- and inter-organizational cognitive diversity in managerial mental models of competition, together with the findings of the growing number of empirical studies across a range of sectors which clearly demonstrate such diversity, it becomes clear that the theoretical notions outlined earlier in this chapter, to say nothing of the ways in which researchers have gone about testing these notions, may well be too simplistic.

Towards fusion: exploring the relative impact of task and institutional influences on managerial mental models of competitive industry structures

In the final analysis, both sets of theory and research outlined in this chapter must be reconciled if we are to develop a truly comprehensive understanding of the nature and significance of managerial mental models of competitive industry structures. To this end, a study conducted recently by Daniels *et al.* (2002) has sought to delineate the relative contributions of 'task and institutional influences' as determinants of managerial representations of competitive industry structures, in an exploration of the UK financial services industry. Building upon both streams of theory and research, Daniels *et al.* have used a specialist form of multiple regression in order to explore the relative contribution of managerial function, level of seniority, organizational membership and the interaction effects of these variables on the overall levels of belief similarity vs. dissimilarity in their sample of participants.

Theories emphasizing the primacy of institutional forces such as 'mimetic adoption' (e.g. Lant and Baum 1995) suggest that managerial mental models within the same industry sector should move towards convergence at the levels of the industry, strategic group and managerial function and level. Theories asserting the primacy of the competitive or task environment (e.g. Hodgkinson and Johnson 1994), on the other hand, predict that a divergence of cognition should emerge between organizations, between management functions and among managers of differing levels of seniority. Interestingly, the overall pattern of findings observed by Daniels *et al.* (2002) suggests that neither task nor institutional explanations are inherently superior in the context of this particular industry setting. While there is some evidence that the institutional environment exerts significant influence (primarily through convergence of mental models among middle managers across the industry as a whole) there is also evidence of significant task influences. In particular, a number of significant differences emerged across organizations, with greater differentiation among senior managers.

This study has brought together these hitherto largely disparate streams of theory and research within a unified framework. In exploring the relative contributions of task and institutional influences on managers' mental models of competition, it has undoubtedly broken new ground. However, it should also be noted that one of us has criticized this work on methodological grounds. Hodgkinson (2002) argues that the way in which Daniels *et al.* elicited and compared the cognitive maps in their study may well have biased the results obtained in favour of the substantive hypotheses under test (for further details of this debate see Chapter 7). Methodological problems notwithstanding, it is clear that Daniels *et al.* (2002) have set a new agenda for future work in this vitally important area of research. It is fitting, therefore, that we should end the chapter by highlighting this work.

Conclusions

In this chapter we have summarized a number of theoretical arguments and empirical findings concerning the importance of managerial mental models of competitive industry structures in strategy formulation and implementation processes. Two major trends are discernible within the literature. One group of scholars (e.g. Porac *et al.* 1989, 1995; Porac and Thomas 1990, 1994; Lant and Baum 1995; Peteraf and Shanley 1997) have focused their attention at the inter-organizational level of analysis, arguing that through related processes of social construction, inter-organizational learning, social identification and institutionalization, actors' mental representations of competition become highly unified over time, leading to the emergence of stable groupings of firms. A second group of scholars (e.g. Daniels *et al.* 1994; Hodgkinson and Johnson 1994; P. Johnson *et al.* 1998) have focused their attention primarily on the search for significant intra- and inter-organizational individual differences in mental representations of competitive structures, arguing that such differences might play a central role in a variety of non-trivial processes associated with strategy formulation and implementation. As we have seen, researchers have recently begun to draw on both strands of work in an effort to better understand the determinants and consequences of competitor cognition.

To the extent that there are substantively meaningful differences among organizational actors in terms of their cognitions of the competitive environment, or for that matter any other issue of major strategic importance, this inevitably raises fundamental questions of a processual nature regarding the optimum composition of executive teams and the way in which the cognitions of senior managers impact on the direction and performance of the organization as a whole. To what extent do homogeneous or heterogeneous cognitions among groups of managers facilitate and/or inhibit successful strategy development and implementation? If the worldviews of senior managers within an organization are largely idiosyncratic in nature, how are coherent strategies formulated and implemented? On the one hand, widely-held cognitions might facilitate organizational performance, through the development of a shared vision, which in turn may provide a basis for unified action. Then again, too much cognitive homogeneity within the executive team may undermine the organization's adaptive capabilities, as the group fails to register salient information that conflicts with its shared worldview – the situation characterized by organizational behaviour scholars as 'group think' (Janis 1982).

The unresolved theoretical issues highlighted in this chapter pose a highly practical dilemma for the field: to what extent should executive teams encourage cognitive diversity and/or homogeneity in their quest to ensure the long-term survival and well-being of their organizations? Fortunately, there are other bodies of work that have attempted to examine cognitive processes in executive teams, which in turn might shed light on these fundamental issues. It is to this work that we now turn.

5

STRATEGIC COGNITION IN TOP MANAGEMENT TEAMS

In Chapter 1, we briefly introduced Herbert Simon's (1947) notion of *bounded rationality*. This concept captures the idea that actors are unable to take decisions in a completely rational manner, due to the fact that they are constrained by fundamental information processing limitations. Nevertheless, they strive for rationality within their cognitive limits. Since they are unable to process all available environmental cues, decision makers must selectively filter information, thereby simplifying reality to a manageable form. As we saw in Chapter 4, this line of reasoning is borne out by recent theory and research concerned with managerial mental models of competitive industry structures. As discussed, the past experiences and background characteristics of strategic decision makers are likely to play a crucial role in this filtration process, giving rise to potentially significant individual and sub-group differences in the structure and content of managerial mental models of competitor definition. As we saw, there is increasing evidence to suggest that there are variations in mental models within and between organizations in the same industrial sector, leading us to question the extent to which it is desirable for top management teams to be selected on the basis of homogeneous or heterogeneous background characteristics.

There are of course many strategic issues and problems that the executive team of an organization has to confront in the process of strategizing, and it would be very wrong to consider the optimum composition of such teams on the basis of research into managerial mental models of competition alone. Ultimately, in order to determine the optimum composition of top management teams with any degree of confidence it is first necessary to gather empirical evidence concerning the interrelationships between team composition on the one hand, and strategic cognition (in respect of a range of issues and problems) and organizational outcomes on the other.

The upper echelons perspective on top management teams

Unfortunately, conducting work of this nature on sufficiently large samples of individual executives and top management teams is easier said than done. The highly sensitive nature of the issues and problems confronting executive teams, to say nothing of the time pressure under which they function, renders access for research purposes highly problematic. For this reason, Hambrick and Mason (1984) developed an approach for studying strategic decision processes in top teams which obviates the need to employ direct methods of cognitive assessment. In view of the obvious practical difficulties associated with attempting to study directly the psychological characteristics of senior executives, they advocated the use of external, observable characteristics as indicators of the givens that members of the top management team bring to bear on their administrative situation. The essence of their theoretical approach, known as *upper echelons theory*, is outlined in Box 5.1.

A diagrammatic representation of Hambrick and Mason's theoretical model, recently updated by Finkelstein and Hambrick (1996), is shown in Figure 5.1. Three clear stages are identified, in an attempt to capture the way in which executives selectively filter strategic information. *Limited field of vision* arises from the fact that decision makers are exposed to a limited sub-set of the available stimuli. The second stage, *selective perception*, occurs due to the fact that, as noted in Box 5.1, only a portion of the stimulus

---

Box 5.1: Hambrick and Mason's upper echelons theory

According to Hambrick and Mason (1984), organizational outcomes such as strategy and effectiveness are ultimately a reflection of the values and 'cognitive base' of 'the dominant coalition' within the firm. By definition, the dominant coalition constitutes the organization's power élite. Accordingly, the cognitions and values of this group of actors ultimately determine its strategic choices. Drawing on a range of psychological and sociological studies, Hambrick and Mason argued that a variety of observable managerial characteristics such as age, socio-economic roots, functional background, executive tenure and education shape the values and beliefs of the individual manager. These characteristics underpin the tendency for executives to perceive only a limited portion of all potentially relevant information in the internal and external environment. Often, they derive idiosyncratic interpretations of reality and assign differential weights to the various potential outcomes.

---

information within the executive's limited field of vision is actually attended to. The third stage, *interpretation*, entails the attachment of meaning to stimuli. Starbuck and Milliken (1988) employ the term 'sense-making' to describe this stage, a concept that was introduced in Chapter 1.

In order for researchers and managers to have faith in any demonstrated link between the demographic characteristics of top teams and the cognitive base from which they generate strategic decisions, it is necessary to understand the assumed causal links between the two. Figure 5.2 illustrates the way in which Wiersema and Bantel (1992) have postulated such theoretical linkages, in a study of top management team demography and corporate strategic change.

According to Wiersema and Bantel, measures of *demographic diversity* – such as age, organizational tenure and tenure of top team membership, education and functional background – are convenient *proxy variables* that reflect those qualities directly associated with the evolution of executive experience (e.g. training, team beliefs and values, interaction patterns with colleagues and the ability to integrate new information). The latter cannot be

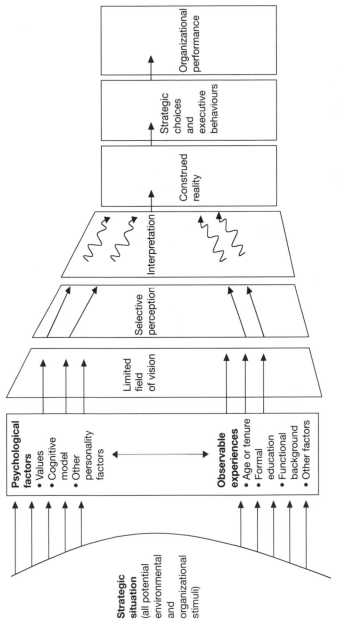

Figure 5.1 Strategic choice under bounded rationality: the executive's constructed reality

Source: adapted from Hambrick and Mason (1984) by S. Finkelstein and D.C. Hambrick (1996: 42). *Strategic Leadership: Top Executives and their Effects on Organizations.* © West Publishing Company. Reproduced by kind permission of the publisher.

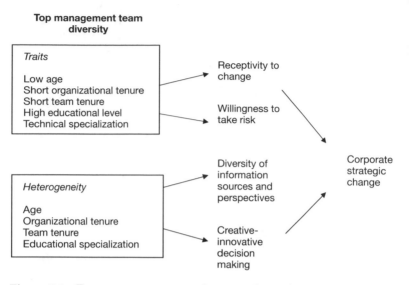

Figure 5.2 Top management team demography and corporate strategic change

Source: reproduced with permission from M.F. Wiersema and K.A. Bantel (1992) Top management team demography and corporate strategic change, *Academy of Management Journal*, 35: 91–121. © *Academy of Management Journal.*

assessed without direct access to the top management team. However, according to Wiersema and Bantel, the former provide convenient substitutes.

The use of the terms 'homogeneity' or 'heterogeneity' to describe the characteristics of top teams is a development of earlier work on *group dynamics* and *organizational clans* (Murray, 1989). Homogeneity/heterogeneity is typically operationalized using aggregate measures of interpersonal similarity along one or more dimensions.

Evidence for the upper echelons perspective

Numerous studies have explored the various correlates of top team demography in an attempt to empirically validate the Hambrick and Mason model. A variety of indicators designed to capture the demographic composition (homogeneity vs. heterogeneity) of top management teams (reviewed in Tsui and Gutek 1999) have been employed as predictor variables in studies investigating links between demography and organizational outcomes. The outcomes investigated in this stream of research have been many and varied, for example:

- innovation (Bantel and Jackson 1989);
- firm performance (Norburn and Birley 1988);
- the nature and extent of strategic change (Wiersema and Bantel 1992);
- bankruptcy (D'Avini 1990);
- corporate illegal activity (Daboub *et al.* 1995; Williams *et al.* 2000);
- firms' competitive moves (Hambrick *et al.* 1996);
- the level of international involvement in diversification strategies (Sambharya 1996).

A detailed consideration of all the available evidence for and against the upper echelons perspective lies beyond the scope of this book. Here, we provide a selective overview of the findings from several of the more salient lines of inquiry. Our intention is to highlight the main achievements and limitations of this whole approach. For a comprehensive overview, see Finkelstein and Hambrick (1996), Lau and Murnighan (1998), Milliken and Martins (1996), Pelled (1996), Pettigrew (1992) and Williams and O'Reilly (1998).

Empirical studies linking top team diversity and organizational performance

In Chapter 2 we discussed the advantages of socio-cognitive complexity in the context of organizational learning. Research suggests that heterogeneous groups should perform better when adaptability, creativity, conflict and a variety of solutions to new problems are sought. Top team demography researchers have argued that more diverse team composition is implicitly linked to more elaborate and complex socio-cognitive structures that constitute a resource for the team to draw upon. Organizational learning is a long-term performance outcome for organizations, but we begin by outlining a study that has examined the link between top team diversity and organizational performance both from a short- and long-term perspective. Murray (1989) argued that the relationship between heterogeneity and organizational (as opposed to team) performance is not simple and set about testing it. He made a distinction between short- and long-term performance measures. Where performance criteria are more long-term it is likely that heterogeneous top management teams will perform best. However, to the extent that homogeneous groups have a shared understanding of how the organization operates, they will have the advantage of shared values and lower costs of communication and coordination. Where shorter-term, efficiency-based measures of organizational performance are used, therefore, homogeneous top teams should outperform their heterogeneous counterparts. The findings from Murray's study are outlined in Box 5.2.

Another significant study exploring the relationship between top team diversity and performance was carried out in the US banking sector by Bantel and Jackson (1989). They examined the extent to which various banking innovations (assessed by means of some 51 scaled items) were correlated with top team diversity, operationalized in terms of age, length of service, education (length and mix) and functional mix. Innovations in this context were operationalized as changes introduced by less than 10 per cent of banks and where cost was a relatively insignificant factor, so as to avoid conflating innovation with organizational size. A significant, positive correlation (accounting for 31 per cent of the explained variance) was found between diversity and output of innovations: greater diversity levels were associated with higher output levels. Demographic diversity still accounted for 11 per cent of the variance, even after controlling for the size of the organization and its geographical location. While age was found to be negatively correlated with top team innnovation in this study ($r = -0.22$, $P < 0.01$), the innovation record was found to be positively correlated with average education level ($r = +0.31$, $P < 0.01$) and the functional mix of the top team ($r = +0.21$, $P < 0.01$).

An interesting supplemental issue arising from this research is the question of whether top team characteristics are more predictive of organizational innovation than the characteristics of the CEO. Bantel and Jackson's (1989) findings suggested that this is

---

Box 5.2: Murray's study of top team diversity and short- and long-term organizational performance

Murray (1989) studied a sample of 84 Fortune 500 firms from the food and oil sectors over the period 1967 to 1981. He constructed group-level indices of homogeneity based on two types of measure:

- the coefficient of variation in temporal measures of age of top team members, and tenure within the firm and the top team;
- measures of the proportion of team members holding different types of university degree or diploma.

He also investigated the functional backgrounds of the participants concerned. Analyses of the link between the various measures of top team homogeneity/heterogeneity and measures of change, competition and performance revealed that the contribution of managers was not constant. Rather, it was tempered by the sector strategic context and the measure of performance chosen. However, managers (as measured by diversity of top team characteristics) made a significant difference to organizational performance. Top team diversity measures accounted for about 25 per cent of the variance in short-term performance measures, but well over 50 per cent of the variance in respect of longer-term performance. Temporal heterogeneity (in respect of measures of age and tenure) was found to be negatively related to short-term measures of performance, but also positively related to long-term performance in the oil sector, while occupational heterogeneity was found to be negatively related to long-term performance.

---

indeed the case. It is highly noteworthy, however, as Sparrow (1994) has observed, that there was virtually no diversity in terms of gender and ethnicity in the top teams of the US banks studied by Bantel and Jackson; hence the impact of these variables could not be investigated. Also, their finding that functional heterogeneity improves long-term innovation performance contradicts Murray's (1989) finding of a negative link between occupational diversity and the long-term market performance of the organization.

One other study which is worthy of comment was undertaken by Üsdiken (1992). Like Bantel and Jackson's (1989) study, this was also conducted in the banking sector. Üsdiken examined the impact of a major shift in the environmental context, the way this affects who gets the top jobs and the resulting demographic characteristics of top teams in the Turkish banking sector. Demographic data were collected on 380 executives (general managers and assistant general managers) at four points in time (1976, 1979, 1982 and 1985). Measures were taken of average age at appointment, length of company service, tenure in the top team and number of years of post-secondary education. The findings revealed that, as environmental uncertainty increased, the top teams enlarged and there was a significant increase in their level of formal education (P < 0.001). The top teams also became younger (P < 0.01), particularly in the smaller banking organizations. However, this study can say little about the reasoning or causality behind such changes in top team diversity. The changes could reflect either a conscious change in selection and assessment decisions or a more general change in the labour pool in the direction observed. However, it is interesting to note that the direction of diversity change reflects the top team characteristics that were associated with higher levels of innovation in the US banking sector (Bantel and Jackson 1989).

Executive succession, managerial learning and strategic reorientation

The topic of top team heterogeneity cannot be considered in isolation from the topic of *top management turnover*. Issues of executive succession, the psychological pressures associated with the perseverance with existing strategy and the role of managerial learning in reorienting or changing a top team have been examined by a number of researchers (e.g. Tushman *et al.* 1985; Virany and Tushman 1986; Lant *et al.* 1992; Virany *et al.* 1992).

Milliken and Lant (1991) point to the psychological pressures within organizations that encourage top team managers to persist with past strategies in times of uncertainty. In Chapter 1 we observed how a number of theoretical concepts and supporting empirical evidence help to explain the tendency for 'the escalation of commitment to a failing course of action', while in Chapter 4 we encountered the related notion of 'cognitive inertia' – the tendency for changes to managerial mental models of strategic issues and problems to lag behind major shifts in the environmental contingencies confronting the organization (see also our discussion of competency traps and progressing organizational simplicity in Chapter 2).

Top management team turnover is one of the most effective ways of breaking down an organization's natural inclination to persist with prior strategies. According to Virany *et al.* (1992), top management change results in the unlearning of old routines and, consequently, may be associated with an increased probability of *strategic reorientation*. Top management teams characterized by greater heterogeneity should also have lower levels of psychological investment in the prevailing strategy and, therefore, be less likely to succumb to the pitfalls of cognitive inertia, escalation of commitment and the like (cf. Milliken and Lant 1991). All other things being equal, greater diversity of perspectives, disagreement about equivocal experiences, more extensive discussion of options, wider learning opportunities and a greater range of possibilities being considered should all follow in top teams characterized by higher turnover levels. Without exception, these are all factors that should be associated with more frequent strategic reorientation.

Following this line of reasoning, Lant *et al.* (1992) examined empirically how past performance, managerial interpretations and top management demographic characteristics influenced the managerial learning process and the likelihood of strategic reorientation in different environmental contexts. They investigated the level of change in 40 firms from two industries (furniture and computer software). The measures of top team heterogeneity were the same as those used by Bantel and Jackson (1989) and Murray (1989). Managerial awareness of environmental change was found to be an extremely significant predictor of the likelihood of strategic reorientation. In terms of staff turnover, only CEO turnover (not other top management turnover) increased the likelihood of reorientation. Organizations with more heterogeneous teams were also more likely to reorient strategy than organizations with less diverse teams.

What is the role of top management in triggering and interpreting strategic issues and defining events that have the potential to influence the organization's current and future strategy?

**Box 5.3: Wiersema and Bantel's study of strategic change
outcomes**

Wiersema and Bantel (1992) selected a random sample of 87 organizations from the 500 largest manufacturing firms in the USA for the
year 1980. They tracked strategic business data for the period
1980–3. Homogeneity/heterogeneity indices for the top management team (chairman, CEO, president, chief operating officer and
the next highest tier) were calculated on the basis of age and organizational tenure. Diversity measures of educational level reflected the
number of years of schooling, and educational specialization was
represented by the discipline focus of the highest obtained university degree. The strategic change measure focused on diversification strategy (the establishment of business positions in different
industries) using a measure of sales diversity across related and
unrelated activities. Control variables were used to cancel out the
effects of prior organizational performance, organizational size, top
management team size and industry structure. Top team diversity
and effective diversification decisions were positively related,
although the benefits of diversity tapered off as heterogeneity
increased, eventually creating negative consequences such as communication strain and conflict.

Wiersema and Bantel (1992) focused on this question (see Box 5.3).
They investigated the role of top teams as *decision making groups*,
exploring the link between the type and variety of top team
members' cognitive perspectives and a strategic outcome
(diversification). The Wiersema and Bantel (1992) study revealed
significant relationships between a range of demographic variables and the strategic outcome of diversification. The main findings of this study are summarized in Table 5.1.

Criticisms of the upper echelons perspective

The upper echelons perspective has not been without criticism. As
with most areas of applied cognition research, there are problems
both of a methodological and conceptual nature. While initial

Table 5.1 Regression analysis of demographic variables of top teams on measures of diversified strategic change

Variable	Standardized regression coefficient	Strategic change team characteristics
Mean team age	−0.18[a]	Youth
Mean team organizational tenure	+0.27[b]	Short organizational tenure
Mean team executive tenure	+0.27[b]	High team tenure
Mean team executive level	+0.45[c]	High educational tenure
Mean team educational level	+0.18[a]	Academic training in the sciences
Educational specialization heterogeneity	+0.40[c]	Heterogeneity of education specialization
R	+0.38	
Adjusted R	+0.32	
F	6.91[c]	

[a] $p < .05$ [b] $p < .01$ [c] $p < .001$

Source: reproduced with permission from M.F. Wiersema and K.A. Bantel (1992) Top management team demography and corporate strategic change, *Academy of Management Journal*, 35: 91–121. © *Academy of Management Journal.*

findings, such as those reviewed above, generally supported Hambrick and Mason's (1984) theoretical predictions concerning the linkages between top management team composition and organizational outcomes, the picture is now exceedingly complex. As Hodgkinson (2001a, 2001b) has observed, a large number of studies (reviewed in Pettigrew 1992; Finkelstein and Hambrick 1996; Milliken and Martins 1996; and Williams and O'Reilly 1998) have yielded inconsistent and contradictory findings. This is particularly the case for studies that have explored the linkage between group demography and organizational performance and the question of whether homogeneous or heterogeneous teams best contribute to team and organizational success. Recent studies investigating the linkage between the degree of top management team functional background diversity and financial performance, for example, have revealed mixed findings. For instance, whereas Roure and Keeley (1990) found that top management team diversity in terms of functional background was predictive of financial performance, no such relationship was observed in a later study by West and Schwenk (1996).

What, then, can we usefully conclude from this stream of research? As observed by Sparrow (1994: 158):

Despite the numerous methodological constraints and difficulties in assuming the underlying causal links, the presence of any statistically significant relationship between specific demographic aspects of top teams (who frequently only represent 0.1% of total organizational membership) and aspects of the organization's performance is remarkable and constitutes strong support for further study of top management teams.

It is indeed remarkable that any link can be demonstrated between top team diversity and significant organizational outcomes. Such findings reinforce the importance of bringing the insights of psychological theory and research to bear on the analysis of the strategic management process. However, the extent to which this research lends support for the managerial and organizational cognition perspective, and the question of what form future studies should take, has been the subject of intense debate and controversy over recent years.

Several writers – most notably Lawrence (1997) and Pettigrew (1992) – have called into question on conceptual grounds the validity of the entire demographic approach as a basis for inferring underlying processes and mechanisms. These arguments are summarized in Box 5.4. They reveal some fundamental limitations in respect of the original line of reasoning that gave rise to the demographic approach as a basis for indirectly studying underlying cognitive processes within executive teams. Recent empirical research conducted by Markoczy (1997) lends considerable credence to the theoretical arguments developed by Pettigrew and Lawrence. There have been surprisingly few studies that have investigated the degree of correlation between *managerial background characteristics and perceptions and beliefs* – i.e. studies that have attempted to look within the black box of organizational

---

Box 5.4: The Pettigrew and Lawrence critique of organizational demography research

Both Pettigrew (1992) and Lawrence (1997) have challenged the use of demography as a proxy for executive cognition and the other intervening processes and constructs that have been hypothesized to mediate the relationships between top management team composition and organizational outcomes. On the basis of a compelling series of arguments, these writers cast doubt upon a key, but dubious, assumption that dates back to a paper by Pfeffer (1993). This paper appeared in the year prior to Hambrick and Mason's (1984) seminal article. In this paper, Pfeffer outlined the case for demography as a potentially important factor that might indirectly influence a range of organizational outcomes via a variety of intervening variables. However, he also added an important caveat: that the fulfilment of the promise of the demographic approach to organizational analysis was dependent on the resolution of several key issues. In the context of top management team research, the primary empirical question that needs to be addressed concerns the extent to which demography (the independent variable) predicts and explains not only variation in the dependent variables (strategy process and organizational performance outcomes), but also the extent to which it predicts or explains managerial cognition (the intervening construct). This is a standard 'black box' criticism. According to Pfeffer an understanding of the intervening construct or process is not necessary or desirable. He argues that to embark on the search for such understanding will invariably lead to an infinite regress from which the researcher cannot logically escape. However, in a carefully constructed theoretical critique of the Pfeffer paper, Lawrence (1997) demonstrated how multiple and potentially conflicting processes might intervene between demography on the one hand and organizational outcomes on the other.

---

demography. At best, the limited work that has been conducted has yielded equivocal findings, as exemplified by studies that have sought to demonstrate systematic linkages between functional background and managerial cognition (see Box 5.5).

Markoczy (1997) has argued that equivocal findings can similarly be listed in respect of the relationships between cognition

---

Box 5.5: The linkage between functional background and managerial cognition

Relatively few studies have directly tested the assumed relationship between individual charactertistics and cognition, and these have yielded contradictory and conflicting findings. An early study by Dearborn and Simon (1958) (upon which Hambrick and Mason 1984 partially derived their original theoretical framework) indicated that managers' views are biased by their functional positions. However, subsequent research has yielded inconsistent findings. A study by Bowman and Daniels (1995), for example, which revisited Dearborn and Simon's research on methodological grounds, confirmed their original claim, whereas other studies by Walsh (1988), Waller *et al.* (1995) and Beyer *et al.* (1997) have not. Moreover, as observed in Chapter 4, several recent studies investigating managerial representations of competitive industry structures have also yielded inconsistent and contradictory findings in respect of the claim that functional position influences cognition (e.g. Daniels *et al.* 1994; Hodgkinson and Johnson 1994; P. Johnson *et al.* 1998).

---

and a number of other background characteristics. Consequently, additional studies are required to further investigate the validity of using external characteristics as substitutes for the direct measurement of perceptions and beliefs. As part of a wider multi-cultural study of managers employed by Hungarian companies which had recently come under foreign ownership, Markoczy (1997) investigated the relationships between functional background, age, hierarchical position and national culture, on the one hand, and actors' causal belief systems with respect to organizational success on the other, arguing that these characteristics have received the strongest support on the basis of previous theory and research within the Hambrick and Mason tradition. Employing a systematic method for eliciting and comparing causal maps devised by Markoczy and Goldberg (1995), partial relationships were observed between three of the four background characteristics investigated (output functional background, age and non-Hungarian nationality) and the measured causal beliefs. The combination of these three factors accounted for just 17.2 per cent of the variance (change in adjusted R^2) in the similarity to one of two empirically derived clusters formed on the basis of the participants' causal maps (see Table 5.2).

Hambrick and Mason (1984) have never denied that demographic characteristics are 'rough surrogates' of managerial cognition. However, on the basis of her findings, Markoczy (1997) argues against the continued use of external characteristics as substitutes for the direct measurement of executive perceptions and beliefs. She argues that none of the individual characteristics previously employed in top management team research constitute

Table 5.2   Results of hierarchical regression analyses in Markoczy's (1997) study. The table explores the relationships between various external characteristics of a sample of managers (N = 91) and proximity (overall similarity) to the centres of two empirically derived clusters. Cluster membership was determined on the basis of a cluster analysis of the participants' causal cognitive maps. Separate regressions were calculated for similarity to cluster centre 1 and cluster centre 2

	Cluster centre 1		Cluster centre 2	
Variable	*β*	*s.e.*	*β*	*s.e.*
Step 1: control variables				
Company A member	.04	.03	.15	.03
Company B member	.15	.03	.32*	.04
Company C member	.07	.03	.23†	.05
R^2	.02		.07	
Adjusted R^2	−.02		.04	
Step 2: independent variables				
Age	−.10	.00	.26*	.00
Non-Hungarian	.36**	.03	−.03	.04
Top level	−.18	.03	−.02	.04
Output function	.19	.03	−.03	.04
ΔR^2	.20**		.06†	
ΔAdjusted R^2	.17		.02	

** p < .001   * p <. 01   † p < .05

Source: reproduced with permission from L. Markoczy (1997) Measuring beliefs: accept no substitutes, *Academy of Management Journal*, 40: 1228–42. © *Academy of Management Journal*.

an acceptable exchange for direct measures of attitudes, beliefs and propensities. To be effective, a proxy measure has to be extremely closely correlated to the object that it is replacing. Markoczy also challenges the convenience argument advanced by Hambrick and Mason and their followers as a basis for using external characteristics in preference to the use of direct methods of cognitive assessment. She argues that researchers can now use a series of more appropriate measures:

> Although not as convenient as external characteristics, beliefs, attitudes and propensities can be measured fairly directly and often through relatively traditional means as well as by the method (causal maps) used in this study. Furthermore, various relevant cognitive aspects on which individuals might differ (e.g. risk aversion) are also measurable, and tools have been developed and used for measuring them.
>
> (Markoczy 1997: 1240)

Indeed, in Chapter 7 we present an overview of a range of techniques (including causal mapping techniques) for revealing actors' mental representations of strategic issues and problems. Meanwhile, does the sustained attack on demographic research imply that researchers should abandon the quest to identify linkages between external characteristics, strategic cognition and organizational outcomes? We would maintain emphatically that such a course of action is not called for. On the contrary, the fact that inconsistent and contradictory findings have emerged points overwhelmingly to a need for further studies in which the search for correlates of executive beliefs is widened in an attempt to better understand the antecedents of managerial cognition (cf. Walsh 1995). Why should such research continue? Two main reasons can be suggested:

- this line of work could have important implications not only for future theory and research, but also for the design of interventions for facilitating processes of strategy formulation and implementation within organizations;
- to the extent that executive beliefs impact on organizational processes and outcomes, knowledge of the various factors that

shape these beliefs might have important implications for the selection and development of top management teams (cf. Wells and Bantel 2000).

Summarizing the research reviewed so far in this chapter, it is clear that Hambrick and Mason's (1984) article has profoundly influenced the nature and direction of research on top management teams for much of the past two decades. Not only did the upper echelons perspective lay the theoretical foundations for much of the research into top management teams that followed, it also made a major contribution to the methods by which such research has been undertaken. However, in response to the various criticisms that have been levelled against the demographic approach, researchers have recently begun to move in one of two broad directions. They have either:

- continued in the demographic tradition but attempted to redress the above criticisms through the introduction of various conceptual refinements and increased statistical controls; or
- incorporated direct methods of cognitive assessment in an attempt to better model the determinants and consequences of executive cognition, both at the individual and team levels of analysis.

In the remaining sections of this chapter we consider each of these developments in turn. We begin by reviewing a number of recent attempts to refine understanding of top team processes through the introduction of new theoretical constructs and increased statistical controls.

Increased statistical controls and conceptual refinements

To a certain extent, upper echelon researchers have always been sensitized to the potential limitations of adopting a basic input-output approach to data collection and analysis. From the outset there have been various methodological enhancements and refinements introduced in an attempt to increase the predictive efficacy of top team demography. As we saw earlier, Murray

(1989), for example, was careful to differentiate short-term and longer-term performance measures in seeking to demonstrate empirical links between top management team heterogeneity and organizational outcomes. Murray hypothesized that a different pattern of relationships would emerge for each type of perform-ance measure employed. Bantel and Jackson (1989) controlled for organizational size and geographical location in their study of top team composition and organizational innovation in the US bank-ing sector. More recently, researchers have utilized increasingly sophisticated research designs, incorporating the use of control variables and contingency factors in order to strengthen their results. These measures have included:

- environmental turbulence (Haleblain and Finkelstein 1993; Keck 1997);
- strategy process variables such as communication and social integration (Smith *et al.* 1994) and decision comprehensiveness and debate (Simons *et al.* 1999);
- the use of longitudinal research designs in conjunction with time series data (Keck and Tushman 1993).

Several new theoretical constructs have also been developed in an effort to refine our understanding of the nature and sig-nificance of demographic variables. For example, Lau and Murnighan (1998) have recently introduced the notion of 'demo-graphic faultlines' as an explanation for sub-group processes of conflict. These are hypothetical dividing lines, the effect of which is to split groups into sub-groups on the basis of one or more key attributes, such as age or educational experience. According to Lau and Murnighan, the formation of conflicting sub-groups becomes much more likely when the demographic characteristics within a group that form a faultline are related to the group's task. Presumably this is because such sub-groups are easier to identify.

Two other potentially useful notions were articulated by Pelled (1996). The concept of *visibility* reflects the extent to which demo-graphic variables are observable by group members. *Job relatedness* reflects the extent to which the variables in question shape per-spectives and skills directly related to tasks. According to Pelled, *affective conflict* within the team is primarily a function of high visibility variables (such as age, gender and race). However, *sub-stantive (task) conflict* is influenced by a variety of job relatedness variables (such as organizational tenure, and educational and functional background). Both of these relationships are mediated by *group longevity*. Turnover in the team is determined by the level of affective conflict. Cognitive task performance, by contrast, is jointly influenced by substantive and affective conflict.

Thus, one response to the various calls for a fundamental re-examination of the validity of the demographic approach has been to continue the refinement of theoretical predictions within the demographic tradition, through the introduction of new constructs and a variety of additional statistical controls, in the hope that stronger, theoretically consistent relationships might emerge. These recent conceptual and empirical developments have undoubtedly extended and, to a certain extent, redirected the demographic approach to the analysis of top management teams. They have also suggested new hypotheses that might account for some of the discrepancies observed in the more traditional upper echelon research. In the final analysis, however, this stream of research is fundamentally limited by the fact that external characteristics continue to be employed as substitutes for managerial cognition. Ultimately, as the work of Markoczy (1997) has demonstrated, external characteristics – however carefully selected – are very poor substitutes indeed.

Recent studies incorporating direct methods of cognitive assessment

An alternative and more satisfactory response to the various criticisms levelled against the conventional upper echelon approach entails the use of direct methods of cognitive assessment, as advocated by Markoczy (1997). Two sorts of investigation have emerged:

- an exploration of the relative influence of a range of factors as determinants of executive perceptions and beliefs (e.g. Sutcliffe and Huber 1998; Chattopadhyay et al. 1999);
- an exploration of the impact of managerial cognition on team

processes and outcomes with a view to refining theoretical models of strategic decision processes within the top team (e.g. Miller *et al.* 1998; Tyler and Steensma 1998).

Exploring the determinants of executives' perceptions and beliefs about strategy

As we saw in Chapter 4, two broad, opposing theoretical arguments prevail concerning the relative importance of firm and industry as determinants of executive perceptions of the environment:

- a variety of social processes are seen to give rise to common perceptions within and among organizational sub-populations inhabiting the same environment (Aldrich and Pfeffer 1976; Huff 1982; DiMaggio and Powell 1983; Porac *et al.* 1989; Spender 1989);
- executive perceptions differ significantly between organizations inhabiting the same environment due to variations in organizational structures and processes (Nelson and Winter 1982; Huber 1991; Daniels *et al.* 1994; Hodgkinson and Johnson 1994; Jablin 1997).

This theoretical discrepancy is a very important issue from a practitioner perspective. As we observed in Chapter 4, commonality of perceptions within industries may or may not be beneficial to the longer-term survival of entire populations and sub-populations of firms, depending on the extent to which such commonalities facilitate inter-organizational coordination and the processes of coalition formation and/or give rise to 'industry blindspots' (Zajac and Bazerman 1991). Under the latter scenario, whole industries may be rendered impervious to the threat of new entrants and innovative competitive practices.

Recently Sutcliffe and Huber (1998) have attempted to shed further empirical light on this unresolved controversy. They have explored the role of firm and industry as determinants of perceptual commonality among executives. In contrast to the studies of mental representations of competitive industry structures reviewed in Chapter 4 – which utilized a variety of cognitive mapping techniques in an effort to capture managers' perceptions of the business environment – Sutcliffe and Huber employed a series of multi-item Likert scales in order to assess executive perceptions of environmental attributes (see Box 5.6). Their conclusions support those of the Daniels *et al.* (2000) study, which was discussed in the previous chapter.

It seems, then, that executive teams do in fact hold more closely associated sets of beliefs and values than can be found across organizations and industries. But what is it that determines these managerial beliefs? The empirical findings of another recent study have shed light on this important question. Chattopadhyay *et al.* (1999) developed and tested two opposing theoretical models. The *functional conditioning model*, reproduced in Figure 5.3, is based on a stream of psychological theory and research evidence that emphasizes the fact that beliefs develop through experiences (Fiske and Taylor 1984; Lord and Foti 1986) by virtue of the feedback and rewards associated with those experiences, which in turn serve to amplify the salience of particular goals and processes (Locke and Latham 1990). According to this view, a combination of functionally-related factors associated with

---

Box 5.6: The role of firm and industry as determinants of perceptual communality among executives

Sutcliffe and Huber (1998) studied a sample of 307 top management team members from 58 organizations drawn from 19 industries. They employed a series of multi-item Likert scales to assess executive perceptions of five *environmental attributes*: instability, munificence, complexity, hostility and controllability. The relative contribution of industry and organizational membership as determinants of participants' environmental perceptions along the five dimensions was investigated by means of a multivariate analysis of variance (MANOVA) in conjunction with a series of univariate analyses of variance (ANOVAs). On the basis of their findings, they concluded that there was evidence of *significant commonality* in environmental perceptions among top managers both within organizations and within industries, but that commonalities of perception existed within top management teams over and above those within industries.

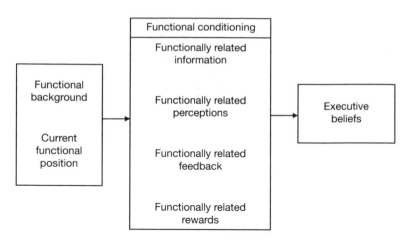

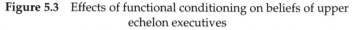

Figure 5.3 Effects of functional conditioning on beliefs of upper
echelon executives

Source: reproduced with permission of the publisher from P. Chattopadhyay,
W.H. Glick, C.C. Miller and G.P. Huber (1999) Determinants of executive beliefs:
comparing functional conditioning and social influence, *Strategic Management
Journal*, 20: 763–89. © John Wiley & Sons, Ltd.

organizational rewards and recognition processes will jointly
serve to condition managerial perceptions and beliefs.

Chattopadhyay *et al.* contend that a possible explanation for the
empirical inconsistencies observed across previous studies of functional conditioning is that researchers may have failed to consider
the impact of one or more key factors that have a bearing on executive belief formation. None of the studies reviewed in Box 5.5, for
example, have considered additional explanatory variables other
than the external characteristics of the individual manager. In an
attempt to redress this limitation (technically known as *model mis-
specification*), they developed an alternative model: the *social influence model*. Reproduced in Figure 5.4, this model takes into account
the overlapping social processes of *communication, socialization* and
social information processing in an attempt to better explain the formation of executive beliefs. Within this model, the functional background similarity and other relational demographic characteristics
of the upper echelon team are hypothesized to moderate the impact
of the beliefs of the wider team on the beliefs of the focal executive.

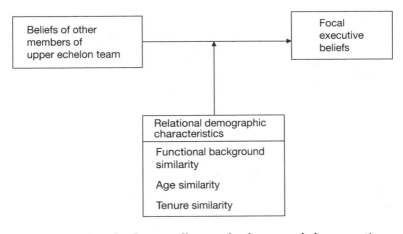

Figure 5.4 Social influence effects on focal upper-echelon executive
beliefs
Source: reproduced with permission of the publisher from P. Chattopadhyay,
W.H. Glick, C.C. Miller and G.P. Huber (1999) Determinants of executive beliefs:
comparing functional conditioning and social influence, *Strategic Management
Journal*, 20: 763–89. © John Wiley & Sons, Ltd.

The model in Figure 5.4 is based on a body of theory and research
within social and organizational psychology that suggests the
beliefs of individual top management team members are likely to
both shape, and be shaped by, a variety of social influence processes including shared *sense-making* and verbal and non-verbal
communication (Salancik and Pfeffer 1978; Gioia 1986; Weick 1995).
The impact of the beliefs of the other members of the upper echelon team on the formation of focal executives' beliefs is unlikely to
be uniform, however, with some individuals exerting differentially greater levels of influence than others. One factor in particular singled out by Chattopadhyay *et al.* is the degree of *demographic
similarity* between the focal executive and the wider team.

Drawing on *referent choice theory* (Kulik and Ambrose 1992) and
similarity-attraction theory (Byrne 1971), Chattopadhyay *et al.* contend that functional background similarity (and similarity on the
other demographic dimensions shown in Figure 5.4) might
moderate the relationship between the beliefs of other members of

the team and the beliefs of the focal executive by influencing the degree to which the various wider team members communicate with the focal executive and one another. These relational demographic characteristics might also affect the extent to which team members attend to one another's behaviour and/or are receptive to one another's views regarding organizational matters.

What does the empirical evidence suggest actually happens? Chattopadhyay *et al.* (1999) measured executives' beliefs concerning the efficacy of a broad set of business strategies and goals in achieving long-term profitability in order to test the relative explanatory power of the alternative theoretical models shown in Figures 5.3 and 5.4. The sampling strategy entailed collecting data from across a diverse range of industries, so as to increase the generalizability of the findings. The sample comprised 371 executives from 58 strategic business units, spanning 26 industries. In addition to measuring executive beliefs and gathering necessary demographic data, the researchers controlled for various contextual features of the research setting that might independently influence the beliefs of individual participants. These factors could give rise to shared beliefs through processes unrelated to those incorporated in the hypothesized social influence model. Specifically, they controlled for the following:

- environmental turbulence;
- environmental munificence;
- degree of strategic business unit autonomy from the parent organization;
- the extent to which the participating organizations were functionally or divisionally structured;
- organizational size;
- organizational effectiveness.

Neither of the two models tested in this study adequately accounted for all of the results obtained. A given variable was found to influence executives' beliefs about some issues, but not others. However, the social influence model gained far greater support than the functional conditioning model. While the results of a series of multiple regression analyses substantially supported the hypotheses associated with the former model, with regard to the latter, just 3 of the 25 effects tested for functional background and 5 of the possible 25 effects tested for current functional position yielded statistically significant standardized beta co-efficients. A series of useful conclusions can be drawn from this study:

- the effects of functional conditioning on executive beliefs, whether in the form of past experiences or current rewards and responsibilities, are minimal;
- the impact of social influence is moderate, but larger by comparison;
- the moderating effect of demographic variables on executive beliefs is considerably more complex than that hypothesized on the basis of previous theory and research.

Another study that has sought to integrate concepts from upper echelons, group process and social cognition theory in an effort to better understand the determinants of strategic cognition in executive teams is that reported by Knight *et al.* (1999). Whereas the aim of the Chattopadhyay *et al.* study was to account for the perceptions and beliefs of the individual executive, like Sutcliffe and Huber (1998), Knight *et al.* were concerned with modelling the determinants of strategic consensus among *groups* of managers. Drawing on a range of conflicting arguments concerning the inter-relationships between top team (demographic) diversity, group processes (interpersonal conflict and agreement seeking) and strategic consensus at the team level, these researchers tested com-petitively the three rival theoretical models outlined in Figure 5.5.

In this study, top management team diversity was operational-ized using measures of functional, age, educational and employ-ment tenure diversity. Strategic consensus was assessed via a 48-item instrument designed to capture respondents' perceptions of a wide range of strategic issues and priorities. Responses within each team were aggregated into a consensus measure by sum-ming the within-team standard deviations calculated in respect of the 48 items (each item had a five-point Likert scale response format) and multiplying the final scores by -1. The effect of this operation was to set the metric for the scale, such that high scores denoted greater levels of team consensus (i.e. high similarity among top management team members' mental models). Con-versely, low scores denoted a lack of consensus within the top

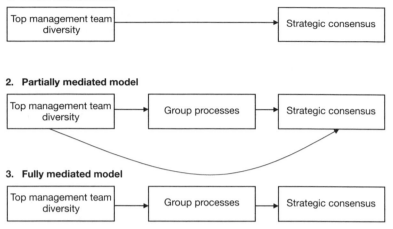

Figure 5.5 Alternative models relating top management team
diversity, group processes and strategic consensus
Source: reproduced with permission of the publisher from D. Knight, C.L. Pearce,
K.G. Smith, J.D. Olian, H.P. Sims, K.A. Smith and P. Flood (1999) Top
management team diversity, group process and strategic consensus, *Strategic
Management Journal*, 20: 445–65. © John Wiley & Sons, Ltd.

management team. The results of a LISREL analysis (Joreskog and
Sorbom 1993) indicated clearly that the partially mediated model
(shown as Model 2 in Figure 5.5) was superior to the others in
terms of the various goodness of fit criteria employed.

As shown in Figure 5.6, the pattern of significant parameter estimates for this model reveals a complex interplay, with two of the
demographic variables (educational and employment tenure
diversity) directly influencing strategic consensus levels (in opposite directions to one another), functional diversity exerting both
a direct and indirect effect (the latter via interpersonal conflict,
which in turn is mediated via agreement seeking), and age diversity exerting an indirect effect only (via agreement seeking). While
agreement seeking was found to directly influence strategic consensus, interpersonal conflict exerted its effects indirectly, via a
negative relationship with agreement seeking.

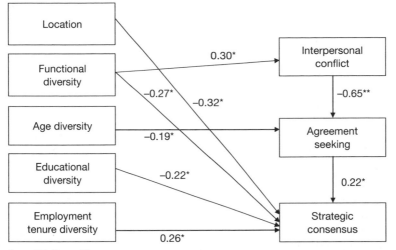

Figure 5.6 Significant parameter estimates associated with the partially mediated model
Source: reproduced with permission of the publisher from D. Knight, C.L. Pearce, K.G. Smith, J.D. Olian, H.P. Sims, K.A. Smith and P. Flood (1999) Top management team diversity, group process and strategic consensus, *Strategic Management Journal*, 20: 445–65. © John Wiley & Sons, Ltd.

Exploring the consequences of executives' perceptions and beliefs

Identifying the determinants of executives' perceptions and beliefs is undoubtedly a useful exercise in its own right, as a basis for theory building and theory testing, but what are the consequences of these perceptions and beliefs in terms of their impact on strategic decision processes and organizational outcomes? Tyler and Steensma (1998) have recently reported the findings of an interesting study shedding light on this question. The purpose was to investigate the *cognitive orientations* that executives use when they individually make assessments that they subsequently bring with them into the wider *decisional arena*. Assessment of technological alliance opportunities was modelled as a function of three major sets of factors:

- executives' perceptions of their companies' emphasis on technology and risk and their perceptions of past successes and failure in alliances;
- various alliance attributes specific to the technology, the firm, the partner and the relationship;
- executive experience (age cohort, educational orientation and work experience).

Using a technique known as *policy capturing* (Slovic and Lichtenstein 1971), participants were required to evaluate a variety of scenarios by means of a wide range of criteria, which *a priori* had been identified by the researchers as likely bases of their decisions. Separate multiple regression analyses were performed on the judgements elicited from each participant in order to identify those criteria which were the most influential in their decision making. The policy capturing exercise was based on 30 scenarios and 17 predictor variables. *Inter alia*, it was hypothesized that older executives would have simpler mental models compared to their younger counterparts and that education, training and functional background would, in differing ways, influence the assessment of potential alliances as depicted in the various scenarios. Education, for example, is likely to engender differing problem solving skills and mental models, while individuals from technical backgrounds are likely to differ from those with non-technical backgrounds in terms of the extent to which they are proactive or reactive in their stance towards alliance formation. *Risk judgements* are also likely to vary as a function of education, training and functional background, non-technical individuals being more risk averse in their assessments of potential technical alliances in comparison to their technically educated, trained and/or experienced counterparts. The findings of this study offered support for several of these predictions. Technically educated executives were found to place greater weight on the opportunities provided by alliances, relative to those with other types of education, and those who perceived their firms to have a technological emphasis and past success in technical alliances were found to focus more on the opportunities of alliances and less on the risks involved, in comparison to those not sharing such perceptions.

This brings us back full circle to the fundamental issue of process with which we started this chapter. If the individual members of executive teams, for whatever reason, have differing mental models and strategic choice preferences in relation to the issues and problems confronting them, what might this imply in terms of the processes by which strategic decisions are enacted? In a series of three interrelated studies, Miller *et al.* (1998) explored the effects of *cognitive diversity* among upper echelon executives on *strategic decision processes*. Two processes were investigated:

- comprehensiveness of strategic decision making;
- extensiveness of strategic planning.

The first two studies comprised single informant designs in which the CEOs of various firms (Study 1) and chief administrators of various hospitals (Study 2) completed questionnaires assessing perceived cognitive diversity (preferences and beliefs), decision comprehensiveness and extensiveness of strategic planning processes. Several control variables (i.e. environmental turbulence and organizational size) were also measured, in an effort to disentangle equivocal findings from previous studies linking diversity to positive and negative outcomes and processes (Bantel and Jackson 1989; Murray 1989; Smith *et al.* 1994). Study 3 employed similar measures, but responses were elicited from a range of top team members and aggregated at the team level, thus addressing methodological limitations associated with Studies 1 and 2 concerning the inadequacy of single informant designs as a basis for investigating team processes. The overall pattern of results from the three studies was largely convergent, suggesting that, contrary to a widely held assumption:

- cognitive diversity in top management teams inhibits rather than promotes decision comprehensiveness;
- cognitive diversity inhibits extensive long-range planning.

Drawing upon previous research which has demonstrated positive links between each of these process variables and organizational performance outcomes (Miller and Cardinal 1994), Miller *et al.* (1998) concluded that cognitive diversity indirectly influences firm performance in a negative fashion, as shown in Figure 5.7.

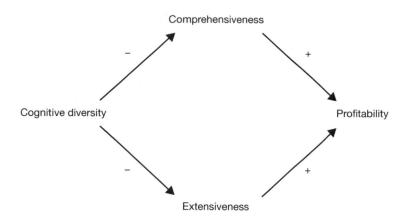

Figure 5.7 Diversity-profitability causal model
Source: reproduced with permission of the publisher from C.C. Miller, L.M. Burke
and W.H. Glick (1998) Cognitive diversity among upper-echelon executives:
implications for strategic decision processes, *Strategic Management Journal*, 19:
39–58. © John Wiley & Sons, Ltd.

One further study is worth mentioning before concluding this
chapter. Papadakis *et al.* (1998) investigated a number of interrelationships between decision process characteristics, top
management team characteristics, the nature of the strategic
decision and a range of broader contextual factors. Their overarching theoretical model is shown in Figure 5.8. The overall
pattern of findings emerging from this research, based on a
multi-method, in-depth series of field interviews, together with
the use of questionnaires and archival data, gathered over a
14-month period, suggests that decision-specific characteristics
have the most influence on decision processes, rather than contextual factors and/or management characteristics. As noted by
Papadakis *et al.*, it will be interesting over the coming years to
ascertain the extent to which these findings, based on an analysis
of 70 strategic decisions within 38 manufacturing firms in Greece,
generalize to other countries, particularly those in which the vast
majority of strategic management research has previously taken
place (the USA, UK and Canada).

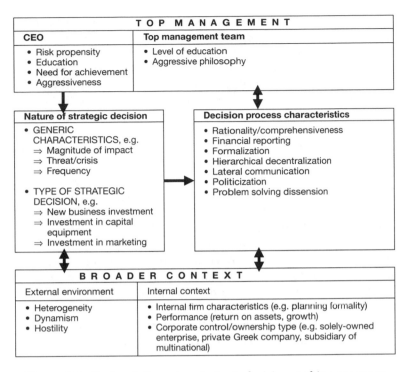

TOP MANAGEMENT	
CEO	**Top management team**
• Risk propensity • Education • Need for achievement • Aggressiveness	• Level of education • Aggressive philosophy

Nature of strategic decision	**Decision process characteristics**

• GENERIC
  CHARACTERISTICS, e.g.
  ⇒ Magnitude of impact
  ⇒ Threat/crisis
  ⇒ Frequency
 	
• TYPE OF STRATEGIC
  DECISION, e.g.
  ⇒ New business investment
  ⇒ Investment in capital
     equipment
  ⇒ Investment in marketing
	• Rationality/comprehensiveness
	• Financial reporting
	• Formalization
	• Hierarchical decentralization
	• Lateral communication
	• Politicization
	• Problem solving dissension

BROADER CONTEXT	
External environment	Internal context

• Heterogeneity
• Dynamism
• Hostility
	• Internal firm characteristics (e.g. planning formality)
	• Performance (return on assets, growth)
	• Corporate control/ownership type (e.g. solely-owned
	  enterprise, private Greek company, subsidiary of
	  multinational)

Figure 5.8 Factors influencing strategic decision-making processes
Source: reproduced with permission of the publisher from V.M. Papadakis,
S. Lioukas and D. Chambers (1998) Strategic decision-making processes: the role
of management and context, *Strategic Management Journal*, 19: 115–47. © John
Wiley & Sons, Ltd.

Summary and conclusions

Research into cognitive processes in top management teams has
advanced considerably over recent years. Increasingly, researchers
are moving away from studies of the input-output variety, characteristic of 1980s and early 1990s, in order to study executive perceptions and beliefs directly, in a concerted attempt to open up the
black box of organizational demography.

We concluded Chapter 4 with a fundamental dilemma for the
field of strategic management: the extent to which executive teams

should encourage cognitive diversity and/or homogeneity in the quest to ensure the long-term survival and well-being of their organizations. Although the theoretical frameworks and empirical evidence reviewed in this chapter have moved us some way towards being able to resolve this dilemma, there is much yet to be done in this research area. Researchers have barely scratched the surface in their quest to understand the causal antecedents and consequences of executive cognition. While the studies surveyed in this chapter represent a useful beginning, more work is now badly needed in order to extend this embryonic line of inquiry.

A wider range of contextual and process variables needs to be considered and more top management team characteristics (particularly personality and individual differences variables such as those discussed in the next chapter) need to be incorporated in future studies. Virtually without exception, each of the many studies reviewed in this chapter has been cross-sectional in nature. As with the research on managerial mental models of competition outlined in Chapter 4, this is unsatisfactory as a basis for studying what is a highly complex series of interrelated, multi-level processes. Clearly, the work required should keep researchers occupied for a considerable period of time to come.

6

MANAGERIAL COMPETENCIES AND INDIVIDUAL LEVEL FACTORS

In the previous chapter we examined the dilemma concerning the extent to which organizations should encourage diversity or homogeneity in top management teams. We noted that research on the causal antecedents and consequences of strategic cognition is only just beginning to emerge. A number of important individual differences and competencies that might ultimately have a bearing on the ways in which executives and other senior managers process strategic information are now being examined. In this chapter we outline some of the latest theory and research relating to several of these factors. Inevitably our coverage of this work must be selective. Our aim is to combine a number of cognitive and behavioural perspectives in order to enhance understanding of the interrelationships between various aspects of strategic cognition and managerial behaviour.

We noted in Chapter 1 that some researchers have argued that the study of behaviour has nothing to offer by way of insight into the nature and significance of managerial and organizational cognition (Spender and Eden 1998). In part, this statement reflects the desire of academics to concretize an emerging field of study and its associated research methods. While understanding this need, we take the opposite view. For industrial, work and organizational psychologists to ignore the behavioural side of cognition would be to throw away half of their traditional expertise. For practising managers too, behaviour lies at the heart of individual and organizational effectiveness. We have talked much about cognitive structures and processes. However, in order for managers to develop rich and powerful cognitive structures they must also possess and apply a series of competencies that enable the effective processing of strategic information – i.e. that enable them to search, encode, structure and recall salient data, bringing it to bear on the problems at hand.

As we have seen, managers now have to absorb, process, make sense of and then disseminate a bewildering flow of information so that the organization can make effective decisions and solve problems. Such are the complexities involved, that in thinking about the strategic issues and problems confronting their organizations, managers must establish rich interconnections between variables, rather than simply pointing to immediate solutions. Increasingly, managers of all levels of seniority are unable to hide behind economic rationality and analysis; they are having to admit that they may be as lost as the rest of us, sailing in uncharted waters, tentatively seeking answers to what are increasingly loaded questions. Ultimately, they need to understand that there are fundamental limits to their power, and 'downsides' to their decisions, while managing the consequences of those decisions (Sparrow 1999a). Not surprisingly, psychologists have argued that the management of cognition is inextricably linked with the management of strategic risk. Why? Because, as observed in Chapter 3, modern managerial role specifications have given rise to concerns about the 'cognitive limits' of managers. Are managers capable of such skilful thought? Perhaps as a consequence of recent questioning about the due diligence required in these roles, calls are emerging for new, more intelligent (in the true sense of the word) approaches to management. But on what sorts of factor might such approaches be based? Intelligence in today's world involves much more than the mere possession of unbiased cognitions and information-rich knowledge. Might the answer lie in developing skills in intuition, creativity and emotional intelligence? In this chapter we show why constructs such as these are gaining increasing legitimacy within the popular and academic management literatures, while also highlighting a number of problems associated with their conceptualization and measurement.

We have already drawn attention to a series of individual competencies that are often understated in the traditional managerial competency literature. We have identified a number of conditions in which managers need competency in such things as transactive memory, schema accuracy, generative learning, dialogue, knowledge elicitation skills, interactive intelligence and sense-making and sense-giving. In this chapter we focus on those facets of individual managerial competency that overlap most with cognitive structures and processes. We do not cover general interpersonal competencies in this book, nor, indeed, the interpersonal competencies of strategic leadership (interested readers should consult the recently published book by Flood *et al.* 2001, which is devoted entirely to these issues). Instead, we attempt to develop conceptual insights with regard to a number of important individual-level factors that have a bearing on the way in which individuals acquire, store, recall, interpret and act upon strategic information, and in so doing, transform such information into knowledge. We also argue that managers cannot avoid having to deal with emotionality in today's world.

Currently, many managers are operating in a context of low trust and face difficult issues of fairness and equity. Indeed, as observed by Herriot (2001), how to engage employees in employment relationships of a form that will enhance both their individual contribution and the organization's performance has become one of the most urgent problems facing contemporary managers. Cool, rational strategic thought is often inappropriate in such a context. As managers try to make sense of this complex and ambiguous world, the quality and appropriateness of their knowledge structures move to centre-stage. These cognitive structures can be remarkably insensitive to important but subtle changes in the strategic environment. We have seen in previous chapters that cognitive inertia is a highly significant risk. In Chapters 2 and 3 we noted that many current changes in organizational form (e.g. involving downsizing and outsourcing) also carry risk, primarily the potential loss of organizational memory.

There is also the problem of information overload. In Chapter 3 we outlined a number of ways in which information load is increasing and noted the individual and organizational problems that can arise. Herein lies a potential major dilemma. On the one hand, strategists need to be able to access and process a considerable volume of information with attention to detail. Often it is in the detail that real insights can occur that will prevent organizations from embarking on courses of action that are destined to failure from the outset and/or will enable them to recognize when hitherto unforeseen problems are beginning to emerge. On the other hand, as we have seen, information overload is a very real problem for many modern managers. Left unchecked, such overload may culminate in 'paralysis by analysis'. Clearly two sorts of competency are required to deal with this paradoxical state of affairs. Analytical skills are needed in order to process detail, while a second, complementary set of skills is also required, enabling individuals to monitor the 'bigger picture' in a more holistic fashion. Understandably, then, academic management scholars and popular writers alike are increasingly drawing attention to tacit and unconscious forms of intelligence and reasoning, in an effort to identify and better understand the competency requirements that will enable individuals to thrive in this unprecedented period of organizational and social change.

Experimental psychologists (Schneider and Shiffrin 1977; Shiffrin and Schneider 1977; Evans 1984, 1989) and social cognition researchers (e.g. Chaiken 1980, 1987; Petty and Cacioppo 1986) have long recognized the importance of this twin imperative of having to process information in detail and cut through that detail in order to perform tasks efficiently. Accordingly, a number of dual-processing theories have emerged in an attempt to account for the ways in which such processing is skilfully accomplished (for reviews see Petty 1995; Evans and Over 1996; Chaiken and Trope 1999). Theorists and empirical researchers are generally agreed that two modes of processing are necessary in order to perform a variety of tasks: a mode that lies largely beyond conscious control, and a deeper form. The former, automatic mode enables individuals to rapidly cut through vast quantities of information, while the latter, controlled mode of processing, entails detailed analysis and is consciously controlled.

Not surprisingly, this general distinction between controlled and automatic processing has found credence as a basis for enriching understanding of the information processing dilemmas confronting individuals involved in the strategic management process. Reger and Palmer (1996), for example, have argued that controlled and automatic processing strategies are central to an understanding of how cognitive inertia comes to develop in managerial assessments of competition. They contend that the reason managers fail to notice significant changes in their business environments is because they tend to monitor competitors' actions automatically, using extant cognitive categories. Similarly, Hodgkinson and his colleagues (Hodgkinson *et al.* 1998; Hodgkinson and Bown 1999; Hodgkinson and Maule 2002; Maule *et al.*, in press) have postulated a dual-process theory of strategic decision making, in which the concepts of Type I (heuristic), and Type II (elaborative) processing are central. Issues of lower salience are given relatively scant attention (using decisional heuristics of the sort discussed in Chapter 1) and are processed largely on an automatic basis, whereas significant issues (determined on the basis of past organizational history, likely impact on the performance of the organizational sub-unit or wider organization to which the focal individual belongs, and their political significance for the individual concerned) are processed in detail, in an analytic fashion.

We now consider a range of factors that have a bearing on the deployment of heuristic and elaborative processing strategies, beginning with a wider consideration of personality and individual differences. Rather than merely seeking to compile an exhaustive list of the many individual differences that might have a bearing on actors' capabilities to acquire strategic competence, we seek to illustrate the ways in which some of these factors might impact on the processing of strategic information.

Locus of control

In Chapter 1 we defined the strategically competent organization in terms of responsiveness to the external environment. It was argued that organizations that develop the capability to process information strategically are more likely to proactively shape their own destiny, whereas strategically incompetent organizations are more likely to react to their environments. A useful construct that has a bearing on this capability has been termed *locus of control*. The locus of control construct reflects the beliefs of individuals about who controls the key events in their lives. It refers to a generalized belief in the external or internal control of reinforcement (Rotter 1966). Individuals with extreme external locus of control beliefs are marked by a strong tendency to attribute the various outcomes in their lives to luck, chance and powerful people or institutions; they believe that uncontrollable forces cause the events in their lives. Individuals with a tendency towards extreme internality, by contrast, trust their capacity to influence the environment and believe that they can control the events in their lives through their own efforts and skill. We introduce this construct at the beginning of this chapter because it stands at the crossroads of cognition and behaviour (Coleman *et al.* 1999).

The locus of control construct originated as an attempt to account for the fact that there are strong individual differences in the control of reinforcement. According to Rotter (1954), these differences are the product of an interaction between the individual and their meaningful environment over time; dispositional tendencies, and past learning experiences and reinforcement histories combine to yield generalized control expectancies. There is growing evidence that locus of control beliefs are related to a variety of important work attitudes and outcomes such as work motivation and organizational commitment (Spector 1982; Luthans *et al.* 1987; Furnham *et al.* 1994; Kinicki and Vecchio 1994) and in recent years this construct has been the subject of a number of investigations within the field of strategic management. In particular, researchers have analysed relationships between the locus of control beliefs of CEOs and various strategic, structural and performance variables associated with their firms (see, e.g., Miller *et al.* 1982; Miller 1983; Miller and Toulouse 1986; Boone 1988; Govindarajan 1988; Boone and de Brabander 1993, 1997; Boone *et al.* 1996, 2000). *Inter alia*, these studies have revealed significant correlations between CEO internality and the tendency for firms to engage in strategic planning (often for a period of several years hence), to seek information about the business environment and to lead rather than follow competitors. Moreover, business organizations led by internally-oriented CEOs are more likely to inhabit dynamic and hostile environments, and to consult specialist technical staff in decision making (Miller *et al.* 1982; Miller 1983; Miller and Toulouse 1986).

Clearly, to the extent that locus of control beliefs are influenced by actors' past experiences of success and failure to attain mastery of the business environment, we would expect to find that this variable has a bearing on the way in which actors process strategic information and represent this information in their mental models. On the basis of a highly detailed review of the literature on top executives, Finkelstein and Hambrick (1996) have identified how this might occur. Locus of control beliefs influence an individual's field of vision, selective perception and interpretation of information in a variety of ways: for example, 'internals' devote greater effort to environmental scanning, using a wider array of sources, and are aware of a greater proportion of the information that they scan in comparison to their external counterparts. Building on this insight, it is reasonable to speculate that these differences will be reflected in the structure and content of actors' mental models of strategic issues and problems, the mental models of internally-oriented individuals being relatively enriched in comparison to those of externally-oriented individuals. Clearly, this hypothesis is worthy of investigation in future work.

Before concluding this discussion of locus of control it is worth noting that the way in which this construct has been operationalized in psychological investigations of strategic management (as in the wider field of psychology more generally) is highly controversial. Strategic management researchers have tended to employ the well-known I-E scale (Rotter 1966). Unfortunately, however, there are several limitations associated with this instrument, which Spector (1982, 1988) and Hodgkinson (1992), among others, have argued render it unsuitable for use in organizational research. First, as Phares (1976) has observed, the I-E scale is only a rough measure of the construct and researchers need to develop their own, domain-specific scales (cf. Adler and Weiss 1988: 315). In line with this recommendation, a number of scales have been devised over the years for use in domains as varied as physical and mental health (Wallston *et al.* 1976; Lau and Ware 1981; Wallston and Wallston 1982; Wood and Latak 1982), politics (Davis 1983), economic psychology (Furnham 1986), work settings (Spector 1988) and careers (Trice *et al.* 1989). A second limitation of the I-E scale is its tendency to correlate with social desirability response set (Spector 1982). Given that none of the studies investigating CEO locus of control have controlled for this response set, it is possible that some, or indeed all, of the relationships previously observed between strategy-making, structure and environment are a function of respondents attempting to present themselves in a socially desirable manner.

In an attempt to redress these limitations, Hodgkinson (1992) devised a domain-specific instrument for use in the context of strategic management. The strategic locus of control scale comprises a total of 16 items, balanced in terms of the number of internally and externally worded items. Responses to all 16 items are summed in order to derive an overall score, higher values denoting greater externality. Construct validation studies conducted on two samples, comprising 94 owner-managers of small, local businesses and 208 residential estate agents demonstrated that this instrument exhibits acceptable reliability (internal consistency), assessed by coefficient alpha, and convergent and discriminant validity with respect to the Marlowe-Crowne social desirability scale (Crowne and Marlowe 1964) and the original I-E and Spector (1988) work locus of control scales. Responses to all three locus of control instruments were positively intercorrelated with one another. In keeping with previous research (reviewed in Joe 1971), the I-E scale correlated significantly with the Marlow-Crowne scale. However, neither the strategic locus of control scale nor Spector's instrument was contaminated by social desirability. As predicted, Hodgkinson's strategic locus of control scale was found to correlate negatively with various measures of organizational structure, strategy and environment, as previously employed by Miller and his colleagues (Miller *et al.* 1982; Miller 1983; Miller and Toulouse 1986). Finally, and again as predicted, the strategic locus of control scale was also found to correlate negatively with several measures of environmental scanning behaviour and organizational performance.

In response to this work, Boone and de Brabander (1993) have argued that the development of the strategic locus of control scale was not necessary and that researchers should continue to adopt the I-E scale, on the grounds that it is a true measure of personality, whereas Hodgkinson's scale merely reflects the organizational circumstances confronting the CEO. They cite evidence from a number of psycho-physiological studies to suggest that there may be key differences in the cerebral functioning of internally- and externally-oriented individuals. In reply, Hodgkinson (1993) has argued that this misrepresents the true nature of his scale and the locus of control construct in general. According to Hodgkinson, as conceived by Rotter (1954), and commonly understood by subsequent researchers, the locus of control construct does not reflect an immutable personality trait (cf. Rotter 1975). Rather, as noted above, control expectancies are formed as a function of dispositional factors *and* environmental influences, which combine to determine generalized beliefs concerning the control of reinforcement. While such beliefs are generalizable, they are also likely to vary across situational contexts, hence the logic for developing domain-specific scales comprising a mixture of specific and general items. In keeping with this rationale, Hodgkinson's (1992) scale actually contains a balanced mix of items, reflecting firm-specific strategic control expectancies (e.g. 'my company is able to influence the basis upon which it competes with other firms') and general strategic control expectances (e.g. 'many of the problems experienced by businesses can be avoided through careful planning and analysis'). Hence, rather than merely capturing firm-specific circumstances, the summed responses to the 16 items reflect individual differences along a domain-specific continuum representing respondents' generalized strategic control expectancies. Nevertheless, Boone and de Brabander and their associates have continued to advocate and use the original Rotter I-E scale in their subsequent work (see, e.g., Boone and de Brabander 1997; Boone *et al.* 1996, 2000). Consequently, their findings may represent an overstatement of the link between CEO control expectancies and organizational behaviour and performance.

For the sake of completeness, one other study worthy of brief mention with regard to this issue of measurement is that conducted in Finland, recently reported by Littunen and Storhammar

(2000). Using a sample of small business entrepreneurs, these researchers attempted to compare directly the relative impact of strategic control expectancies (assessed by Hodgkinson's 1992 strategic locus of control scale) and locus of control beliefs in general (assessed by means of a modified version of the original I-E scale) on a variety of variables reflecting firms' decision processes, strategy and performance. With the exception of Hodgkinson's (1992) original work, this is the only study to have attempted a direct comparison of the relative merits of strategic control expectancies versus general control expectancies as a basis for investigating locus of control in business management research. Littunen and Storhammar assessed general control expectancies by means of a 12-item instrument, which in turn was based on a factor analytic investigation of the Rotter I-E scale conducted by Levenson (1981). Three scales, reflecting 'chance,' 'powerful others' and 'internal attribution' were utilized by Littunen and Storhammar. Each scale comprised four items, each item having a 5-point response format. A number of significant relationships emerged between the various indicators of locus of control and the other variables investigated. Littunen and Storhammar interpreted their findings as offering broad support for Hodgkinson's arguments concerning the need to refine the conceptualization and measurement of the locus of control construct. Unfortunately, however, this study is beset by a number of limitations, not least the fact that, with the notable exception of Hodgkinson's scale (alpha = 0.70), all the locus of control indicators employed had very poor scale reliabilities. Reliabilities for the chance (alpha = 0.49), powerful others (alpha = 0.48) and internal attribution (alpha = 0.47) scales all fell below the 0.50–0.70 threshold regarded by Nunnally (1978) as the margin of acceptability for such instruments. Doubtless this debate will continue.

The extent to which it is uniformly desirable for organizations to select strategists on the basis of internal locus of control beliefs and/or to foster such beliefs is another open question that also requires careful investigation. Clearly, a key danger associated with excessive internality is that individuals or groups might develop *illusions of control*, along the lines highlighted in Chapter 1. Hence, it may be advisable to select individuals with intermediate levels of internal-external strategic control expectancies throughout the top team or, indeed, the wider organization as a whole. Alternatively, a strategy of building teams comprising individuals with mixed control expectancies might prove more helpful in the longer run.

Need for achievement and flexibility

Two other factors that are likely to have a bearing on the way actors process strategic information and, hence, the structure and content of their mental representations of strategic issues and problems are 'need for achievement' (*n-ach*) (McClelland 1961) and flexibility (Gough 1960). As with locus of control, Miller and his associates (e.g. Miller and Toulouse 1986) have found significant correlations between differing *n-ach* and flexibility levels among CEOs and perceptions of strategy, structure and environment. Extrapolating from this work on CEOs to strategic decision makers in general, we hypothesize that the greater is an individuals *n-ach*, the more likely they are to scan their business environment for strategic information and to assimilate this within an enriched mental model of the strategic situation. By definition, high *n-ach* individuals are more goal-directed in comparison to their low *n-ach* counterparts, being driven by a desire to fulfil their expectations. It follows, therefore, that high *n-ach* individuals are more likely to actively seek out and reflect on information that they perceive to be of strategic significance. Hence, such individuals are likely to be characterized by superior strategic competence, as viewed within the confines of our information processing perspective. The *n-ach* construct has been incorporated in the overarching theoretical model of strategic decision process recently proposed by Papadakis *et al.* (1998). We briefly considered this model at the end of Chapter 5 (see Figure 5.8).

High flexibility – roughly akin to openness to experience within the Big Five Framework (McCrae and Costa 1987; Digman 1990) – is also likely to have a bearing on the strategic competence of individuals. As highlighted in the introduction to this chapter and discussed further in the next section, psychologists have identified a number of ways in which individuals characteristically process information. Theoretically, high flexibility levels should enable the individual to rapidly switch from one processing strategy or style to another, thereby capitalizing on the benefits and avoiding the attendant weaknesses associated with each approach.

Individual differences in the processing of information

Another factor that is likely to have a bearing on the formation of actors' mental representations of strategic issues and problems is the characteristic manner in which information is gathered and assimilated. A number of individual differences in the processing of information have been identified, including, for example, differences in cognitive style (Streufert and Nogami 1989; Hayes and Allinson 1994), learning style (e.g. Kolb 1976; Honey and Mumford 1982), learning strategy (e.g. Warr and Allan 1998) and decision making style (Scott and Bruce 1995). We shall confine our attention to a brief discussion of the ways in which these sorts of variables can have an impact on the capabilities of the individual to process strategic information appropriately or otherwise, centring largely on the notion of cognitive style.

Messick (1984) defined *cognitive style* as a consistent individual difference in preferred ways of gathering, organizing, processing and evaluating information. Cognitive style characterizes the way individuals arrive at judgements or conclusions based on their observations (Hunt *et al.* 1989). It differs from *cognitive ability*, which refers to mastery of content and an individual's capacity to perform. Cognitive style is concerned more with what an individual will do in a given type of situation – i.e. it describes the manner, form and nature of performance as opposed to the level of performance (Messick 1984). Sternberg's (1988) triarchic model of intelligence, for example, focuses on how intelligence is directed (cognitive style) rather than on how much intelligence a person has (cognitive ability). Many researchers also distinguish cognitive style, a factor that yields consistent behaviour across a wide variety of situations, and *cognitive strategies* or *coping behaviours,* which represent a conscious decision made by an individual to cope with a particular task (Robertson 1985; Kirton 1989).

The main contribution of the cognitive style construct lies in its ability to bring together notions of information processing theory and personality (Hayes and Allinson 1994; Sternberg and Grigorenko 1997; Riding and Rayner 1998). It has been used to study decision making behaviour, conflict, strategy development and group processes. It initially found favour among educational psychologists, but has also been discussed in relation to a number of topics covered in this book, such as organizational learning, the development of shared mental models and the quality of sense-making (see, e.g., Hayes and Allinson 1998). It has also been implicated as an important factor in decision processes (Tversky and Kahneman 1981; Gul 1984; Ruble and Cosier 1990), the assessment of risk (Henderson and Nutt 1980), strategic problem formulation (Ramaprasad and Mitroff 1984; Cowan 1987), organizational design (Mitroff and Kilmann 1975; Ramakrishna and Schilhavy 1986); organizational change (Slocum 1978; Hamilton 1988) and strategic renewal (Hurst *et al.* 1989).

March (1991) argues that an increase in the competence of any activity – information processing included – increases the likelihood of rewards associated with engaging in that activity, thus further increasing competency. The danger, however, as we saw in Chapter 2, is that this can blind the manager to information that might signal a need for change in the skills and knowledge required, leading, at the collective level, to a degrading of the organizational knowledge base (see 'Competency traps and progressing organizational simplicity' pp. 66–9).

Streufert and Nogami (1989) argue that managers need to be able to apply a range of different approaches to the processing of information, be capable of differentiating between different styles and strategies, and be capable of selecting and applying strategies contingent upon the demands of the situation.

There are at least three levels at which psychologists have attempted to model stylistic differences relating to cognition:

- *cognitive style* is concerned with individual differences in the processing of information;
- *decision making style* is concerned with differences in the characteristic manner in which individuals engage in decision processes;

- *decision making behaviour* is concerned with the way in which individuals actually approach particular decision situations.

While individual managers might well have dominant or preferred decision making styles, their actual decision making behaviours are influenced also by the demands of the situation and/or the task at hand. Given the high degree of overlap between these various constructs, there has been much debate concerning how best to operationalize them, how they might relate to each other and the extent to which they are in fact similar and hence redundant.

Numerous dimensions of cognitive style have been identified over the years, including:

- field-dependence versus field-independence (Witkin 1962);
- serialists versus holists (Pask and Scott 1972);
- levellers versus sharpeners (Gardner *et al.* 1959);
- reflection versus impulsivity (Kagan 1965);
- convergers versus divergers (Guilford 1967);
- adaptors versus innovators (Kirton 1976);
- local versus global thinking styles (Sternberg and Grigorenko 1997).

Unfortunately, as Riding and Rayner (1998) have observed, many of the available labels in the literature have emerged from single studies which have not been supported by subsequent empirical research. A series of reviews in the area have tried to gain some clarity (see, e.g., Struefert and Nogami 1989; Hayes and Allinson 1994; Kirton 1994; Riding and Rayner 1998; Sadler-Smith 1998). As with locus of control and need for achievement, cognitive style influences the way managers scan the environment for new information, organize and interpret this information and incorporate their interpretations into the mental models that guide their actions (Hayes and Allinson 1998). It is an important factor underlying the development of strategic competency, in that those individuals who process information in ways that fail to recognize important changes to their situation may also fail to update their knowledge and skills. This failure to adapt may have drastic implications for their individual careers and also for the organization as a whole.

On the basis of their review of the cognitive style literature, Hayes and Allinson (1994) concluded that a single, overarching dimension underpins the various facets of cognitive style identified by previous researchers, which they refer to as 'the analysis-intuition dimension' (see Box 6.1). The 'intuition' pole is used to describe what is often called 'right brain' thinking – i.e. immediate judgements based on feeling and the adoption of a global perspective; while the 'analysis' pole is used to describe 'left brain' thinking – i.e. judgements based on mental reasoning and a focus on detail (Allinson and Hayes 1996: 122).

There is conflicting evidence concerning the construct validity of the CSI, the instrument devised by Allinson and Hayes (1996) in an attempt to capture these stylistic differences. Allinson and Hayes's claims, regarding the uni-dimensional structure of this instrument, are based on factor analyses of item parcels, spanning seven independent sub-samples comprising groups of construction managers, management students, brewery managers, teachers, business and economics students, miscellaneous managers and workshop participants. A replication study involving a sample of 1050 participants, comprising personnel specialists, owner-managers, local government employees and business and management students yielded a similar single factor solution (Sadler-Smith et al. 2000). More recently Hodgkinson and Sadler-Smith (in press) have re-examined the factor structure of the CSI, arguing that the single factor solutions observed in previous studies may have been an artefact of the way the researchers formed the item parcels. Whereas in previous studies mixed parcels, comprising analytic and intuitive items combined, were employed as the basis of the factor analyses, Hodgkinson and Sadler-Smith formed separate parcels of items from the analytic and intuitive domains and submitted these to a series of exploratory and confirmatory factor analysis procedures. Three rival models were evaluated: the original unitarist conception of style (Model 1), as hypothesized by Allinson and Hayes (1996); an uncorrelated two-factor model, reflecting separate uni-polar sub-scales for the analysis and intuition components (Model 2); and a two-factor model in which the analytic and intuitive components were hypothesized to inter-correlate with one another (Model 3). The findings strongly supported Model 3. Neither of

Box 6.1: The cognitive style index: a globalized measure of cognitive style?

Allinson and Hayes (1996) developed a measure called the cognitive style index (CSI), a 38-item instrument which purports to measure stylistic preferences in the processing of information along a single underlying dimension, characterized as analysis versus intuition. This instrument, designed for use in large-scale survey work in organizational field settings, has been employed in a number of studies, including educational studies concerning the management of student-supervisor relationships (Armstrong *et al.* 1997) and the learning preferences of students (Sadler-Smith 1999a, 1999b). It has also been used in a variety of studies in workplace settings, including studies of entrepreneurial behaviour (Allinson *et al.* 2000), gender differences in cognitive style and stylistic variations on the basis of job level (Allinson and Hayes 1996; Sadler-Smith *et al.* 2000) and the impact of cognitive style on leader-member relations (Allinson *et al.* 2001).

Three alternative answers can be given to each of the 38 questions: 'true,' 'uncertain' or 'false'. Seventeen items reflect an intuitive style (e.g. 'I prefer chaotic action to orderly inaction') and 21 items reflect an analytic style (e.g. 'I always pay attention to detail before reaching a conclusion'). Both the initial research underpinning its development, and subsequent studies, have demonstrated that the CSI exhibits good reliability in respect of internal consistency, as measured by Cronbach's Alpha (e.g. Allinson and Hayes 1996; Sadler-Smith *et al.* 2000) and in respect of test-retest reliability (Allinson and Hayes 1996; Armstrong *et al.* 1997).

Allinson and Hayes (1996) report that scores on the CSI correlate as expected with a series of personality inventories, including the Myers-Briggs Type Indicator (Myers 1962), suggesting a link between personality and cognitive style. However, it is difficult to be certain about the links between cognitive style and personality. For example, CSI scores have been found to vary across job level (Allinson and Hayes 1996; Sadler-Smith *et al.* 2000). Senior managers are more intuitive than their junior colleagues, but it is unclear whether this simply reflects a difference in preferred strategy or a difference in underlying cognitive style. These differences may have arisen because managers with a particular style have been selected for senior positions, or, alternatively, may lend support to the proposition that managers can modify their approach to information processing. There are also significant variations in CSI scores with nationality. Allinson and Hayes (2000) argue that cross-cultural variations in cognitive style may represent a fundamental obstacle to productive working relationships between managers from different cultures. Results from a mixed sample of managers and students from ten countries revealed that the most intuitive groups were the Anglo, North European and European Latins, while the most analytic groups were found to be in the Far East, the developing countries and the Arab nations. However, another recent cross-national study, in which the samples were closely matched in respect of a number of key background characteristics, failed to observe any statistically significant differences across Egyptian, Greek and UK participants (Savvas *et al.* 2001). Unfortunately, the participants in this later study were all drawn from undergraduate business and management populations. Further work is now needed in order to replicate and extend these findings using experienced managers.

the other models was supported. On the basis of their findings, Hodgkinson and Sadler-Smith proposed a revised scoring procedure for the CSI, entailing the derivation of separate scores for the analytic and intuitive components.

Drawing on the work of Epstein and his colleagues (e.g. Epstein 1990, 1991, 1998; Epstein *et al.* 1996), Hodgkinson and Sadler-Smith have explained their findings in terms of a dual processing model, known as the *cognitive-experiential self theory*. This theory asserts that analytic and intuitive processing are in fact two independent processes, each served by separate cognitive systems. Further research is now needed to investigate the extent to which utilizing the revised scoring procedure increases the predictive power of the CSI. Future studies might explore the empirical relationships between the constituent components of the CSI and other multidimensional, uni-polar measures designed to tap individual differences in analytic and intuitive processing. One instrument that might be fruitfully employed in such work is the rational-experiential inventory (REI) devised by Epstein *et al.* (1996). Based on cognitive-experiential self theory, the REI comprises two orthogonal scales, a 'need for cognition' scale (modified from the work of Cacioppo and Petty 1982) and a 'faith in intuition' scale. The former is designed to capture individual differences in rational-analytic processing, the latter being a measure of heuristic processing based on the operation of an organized, adaptive system known as the experiential system. According to Epstein *et al.* this system functions independently of the rational system underpinning the analytic mode of processing. Responses to these orthogonal scales have been shown previously to differentially correlate with a variety of measures of personality, achievement, interpersonal relations and emotional adjustment (Epstein *et al.* 1996). To the extent that the revised scoring procedure for the CSI was found to yield the appropriate pattern of correlations with this instrument (i.e. convergent and discriminant validity), this would provide further powerful evidence of construct validity in favour of both instruments, together with additional empirical support for this dualistic conception of information processing styles.

Interestingly, Bennett and Anthony (2001) have recently reported a study of boardroom activity in which the processing styles of internal and external board members were investigated using a set of measures based on earlier work by Anthony and Daake (1994). Of particular interest is the fact that analytic intuitive processing styles were operationalized using separate multi-item indicators, rather than a uni-dimensional, bipolar measure. Both scales had acceptable reliabilities, the alpha for the 9-item analysis measure being 0.89, while the 5-item intuition measure had an alpha of 0.76. As with the Epstein instrument, these measures could usefully be incorporated in a future construct validation exercise involving a range of measures for the assessment of analysis and intuition. Other instruments that might be incorporated include the various mental self-government (MSG) scales (Sternberg and Wagner 1991; Sternberg 1997) and Scott and Bruce's (1995) general decision making style (GDMS) questionnaire.

One other instrument worthy of mention is the cognitive styles analysis (CSA) devised by Riding (1991a, 1991b). The CSA is a computer-presented test that identifies an individual's position on two orthogonal dimensions of cognitive style: the wholist-analytic (WA) and verbalizer-imager (VI) dimensions. It consists of four sub-tests: Sub-test 1 (verbal processing) is a test of the verbal-imagery dimension in which participants are required to judge whether a number of statements relating to visual appearance are true or false; Sub-test 2 (visual processing) is a test of the verbal-imagery dimension in which participants are required to judge whether a number of statements relating to conceptual categorization are true or false; Sub-test 3 (wholist processing) is a test of the wholist-analytical dimension in which participants are required to judge as true or false the similarity of pairs of geometrical shapes; Sub-test 4 (analytical processing) is a test of the wholist-analytical dimension in which participants are required to judge as true or false whether a simple shape is contained in a simultaneously-presented complex geometrical shape. Participants' median response times for the items correctly answered in each of these sub-tests are combined and used to indicate, by means of the verbal-imagery ratio (Sub-tests 1 and 2) and wholist-analytic ratio (Sub-tests 3 and 4), an individual's position on each of the two dimensions. A high score on the WA dimension indicates an analytic style and vice versa. A high score on the VI dimension indicates an imagery style and vice versa. Hence, by combining scores on these two dimensions it is possible to classify individuals into one of four stylistic types.

In future work it will be most interesting to discover the extent to which the CSA and the various paper-pencil tests highlighted above are intercorrelated with one another. To the extent that the CSA and these other instruments are in fact tapping the same or similar constructs we would expect scores associated with each to be significantly intercorrelated. The recent work of Sadler-Smith *et al.* (2000) has begun to shed some light on this issue. In their aforementioned construct validation study of the CSI, correlations between both dimensions of the CSA and the CSI (conventionally scored, so as to yield a single analysis-intuition score) were found to be low and non-significant.

Over the years there has been a proliferation of alternative constructs and assessment instruments, each purporting to capture individual differences in cognitive style (for reviews see Streufert and Nogami 1989; Hayes and Allinson 1994; Riding and Rayner 1998). Hodgkinson and Sadler-Smith (in press) note that, overall, there are two rival theoretical traditions prevailing within the literature. One group of scholars argue that cognitive style is best conceived within complex, multidimensional frameworks.

211

The work of Jung (1923) has proven particularly influential in this regard and has led to the development of a variety of multi-dimensional instruments concerned with the assessment of cognitive style (and the associated construct of learning style) such as the well-known and widely used Myers-Briggs Type Indicator (MBTI) (Myers 1962), the cognitive style instrument (Whetten et al. 1994), the Keegan Type Indicator (Keegan 1982), and the learning style inventory (Kolb 1976). The CSI, by contrast, is based on an alternative, unitarist conception of style in which it is hypothesized that all aspects of style are embodied within a single, overarching system (see also Robey and Taggart 1981; Nickerson et al. 1985; Miller 1987, 1991). However, the recent studies by Hodgkinson and Sadler-Smith (in press), underpinned by the rational-experiential self theory of Epstein et al. call into question the validity of this unitarist assumption, in respect of the CSI at least. From a practical, interventionist perspective, the two-factor model identified by Hodgkinson and Sadler-Smith is clearly superior. In the final analysis intuitive *and* analytic approaches to the processing of information are required if individuals are to prosper in contemporary organizations.

Surely the ultimate skill, which increasingly needs to be fostered, must be the ability to adapt the ways in which information is processed, switching back and forth from 'habits of mind to active thinking' as appropriate to each particular situation. Louis and Sutton (1991) have aptly coined the phrase 'switching cognitive gears' to characterize this vital competence, arguing that effectiveness may be as much a function of an individual's capacity to sense when such a switch is required as to process information in one mode or another. Our analysis has thus returned full circle, to the importance of cognitive versatility. Unfortunately, however, as originally conceived, the CSI precludes the development of such versatility, since, by definition, movement in either direction along the analytic-intuitive dimension implies an increased capability to adopt one information processing strategy at the expense of the other. The revised scoring procedure developed by Hodgkinson and Sadler-Smith (in press) should help to overcome this limitation.

In summary just as there are many competing measures of locus of control, we find many competing measures of decision-making style, learning style and cognitive style. Managers are seeking convenient and reliable and valid ways of measuring these various constructs, each seeking to capture individual differences that have a bearing on the processing of information and, ultimately, the structure and content of actors' mental representations of strategic issues and problems.

Are the many dimensions indirectly tapped by commonly available measures significantly different from each other? A recent study by Leonard *et al.* (1999), albeit based on student populations, has examined this issue. A number of inventories that assess different aspects of cognitive style were investigated, including the MBTI, Witkin's (1962) Embedded Figures Test, a measure of field dependence (characterized by an inability to separate an object or phenomenon from its environment) versus field independence (the opposite tendency), and Kolb's (1984) learning styles inventory, an instrument designed to assess stylistic preferences in relation to the acquisition and use of information in learning situations. The findings indicated that cognitive style is indeed a complex variable with multiple dimensions, thus casting further doubts on the validity and utility of unitarist conceptions of the construct (see Table 6.1).

Despite conceptual and empirical differences in terms of how best to measure cognitive style, a number of potentially useful practical interventions based on an assessment and understanding of this construct have been suggested, as shown in Table 6.2.

Intuitive and creative cognition

We have touched upon the role of intuition at several points in this book. In the previous section we outlined its importance as a major dimension of the manager's underlying cognitive style. In Chapter 2 we discussed the nature of implicit knowledge and noted that while discussing the sociology of science, Polanyi (1967) drew attention to the importance of non-conscious predispositions, aptly summed up by his widely quoted maxim that 'we know more than we know we say'. Polanyi (1958) distinguished between objective knowledge and tacit knowledge and in Chapter 2 we noted that tacit knowledge is not just knowledge that is

213

Table 6.1 Significant relationships between measures of decision making style, decision making behaviour and cognitive style

	E	I	S	N	T	F	J	P	FD	FI
Concrete experience						X				X
Abstract conceptualization				X					X	
Active experimentation	X									
Reflective observation		X								
Directive decision making			X							
Behavioural decision making						X				
Analytical decision making				X						
Conceptual decision making	X									
Field dependence				X						
Field independence			X							

Key: E = extravert, I = introvert, S = sensing, N = intuitive, T = thinking, F = feeling, J = judging, P = perceiving, FD = field dependence, FI = field independence.

Source: reproduced by kind permission of the publisher from N.H. Leonard, R.W. Scholl and B. Kowalski (1999) Information processing style and decision making, *Journal of Organizational Behavior*, 20: 407–20. © John Wiley & Sons, Ltd.

harder to communicate, but is knowledge of a different kind. We highlighted its importance in organizational learning. In discussing the work of Nonaka we considered the importance of intuition in knowledge creation processes. We saw how the use of metaphor can facilitate intuitive understanding and the transfer of knowledge from tacit to explicit forms, as well as the reconversion of explicit knowledge into tacit, intuitive understanding. At this point, we turn to examine in more detail the role of intuition and intuitive and creative cognition in the strategic management process. As we do so it becomes immediately apparent that there is a much broader managerial skills and competencies agenda, which cuts across the information processing and decision making perspectives outlined in Chapter 1.

Intuition and cognitive maps

Many managerial and organizational cognition researchers have argued that intuition is an important source of sense-making

Table 6.2 Interventions to facilitate individual and collective learning in organizations

Focus of organization intervention	Examples
Improving the level of individual and job	• Using selection, placement and transfer decisions to match cognitive style with the sort of attention managers have to deploy, e.g. executive jobs that require multi-channel attention to permit the rapid tracking of large amounts of complex data; selecting managers not subject to cognitive narrowing • Career counselling, where perceptions of cognitive style may be used to influence job preferences and convey the consequences for satisfaction and performance • Modifying the information processing demands of the job by providing buffers against information load factors such as uncertainty and complexity • Modifying the cognitive style of the individual in order to improve person-job fit by promoting stylistic versatility through training
Improving the effectiveness of training interventions	• Increasing the quantity of training • Improving the quality of training by matching the learning style orientation of learning activities to the style of trainees • Improving the quality of training by matching the learning style of trainees to that of the trainer or mentor
Managing group composition to promote effective learning	• Increasing awareness of communication difficulties that arise from different cognitive styles to improve the quality of information sharing • Ensuring that managers in key 'gatekeeping' roles who acquire critical information are prepared to modify their mental models • Minimizing diversity and bringing together people with similar cognitive styles in line with an appropriate cognitive climate

Source: derived from interventions discussed by Hayes and Allinson (1998)

(e.g. Jenkins and Johnson 1997a). Indeed, a number of studies have stressed the importance of combining intuitive insight with normative approaches to decision making (Einhorn 1972; Showers and Chakrin 1981; Blattberg and Hoch 1990; Kleinmuntz 1990; Spangler 1991; Papadakis and Barwise 1998). A number of researchers argue that in managerial environments in which large unstructured decisions have to be made, the effectiveness of the group decision in terms of meeting objectives or generating learning is heavily dependent on the cognitive ability of individuals to judge the situation. Our previous discussions of bounded rationality, selective information search and contrasting cognitive styles are all relevant to this issue; so too is our discussion in Chapter 3 on complementary knowledge structures and the role of transactive memory and distributed knowledge. We suggest that intuitive aspects of the manager's individual schema should be considered in this team context.

Despite there being a consensus on the importance of intuition, cognitive scientists still differ in their interpretation of the role that it plays in decision making, and more importantly its underlying nature. Intuition has been variously portrayed as:

- an innate problem solving ability, visualizing causes of a situation (Swink 1995);
- a way for managers to use their heads rather than formulae (Kleinmuntz 1990);
- a combination of facts and experiences (Agor 1989);
- a means of complex data processing (Payne *et al.* 1988);
- an ability to appraise a situation holistically and pull patterns together (Showers and Chakrin 1981);
- an unconscious and preliminary perception of coherence (pattern, meaning, structure) that guides thought and inquiry towards a hunch or hypothesis about the nature of that coherence (Bowers *et al.* 1990);
- a questioning outlook on certain types of data and situations – i.e. judging when normative analysis breaks down (Blattberg and Hoch 1990);
- soft and personal information; 'gut-feel' (Molloy and Schwenk 1995).

For Weick (1995: 88), intuition is simply 'compressed expertise in which people arrive at an answer without understanding all the steps that led up to it'. For others also, intuition enables managers to jump between the inputs to a decision and the decision itself, with or without a conscious process of cognition. We need to understand the role that intuition plays as a core decision making element (Huff 1997) and the way in which cognitive constructs can be juxtaposed in new and creative ways (Daniels and Henry 1998). An example of how this is currently being attempted is provided in Box 6.2. (Various approaches for analysing cognitive maps, including those highlighted in Box 6.2 are examined in more detail in Chapter 7.)

We discussed the issue of information sampling behaviours and the limitations that these might bring to the development of team mental models in Chapter 3. Intuitive elements of cognitive maps are seen here as 'unshared information'. Clarke and Mackaness (2001) have approached the link between individual intuition and the content of cognitive maps from a management science perspective on decision making. This suggests that combinations of hard and soft information produce more efficient and more effective decisions. Rather than supporting the view of Agor (1989), that managers use intuition when they are faced with insufficient facts and complex alternatives, and to simplify a given decision situation, the exploratory study outlined in Box 6.2 suggested that:

Senior managers do not appear to use more complex and more coherent decision schemas compared to less senior executives ... Senior managers seem to opt to use simpler cognitive explanations, putting greater reliance on key constructs and a higher proportion of non-factual information ... Intuition seems, therefore, to come more into play as a means of 'going beyond' the rational data and information, by using experiences to 'cut through' to the essence of a situation, helping to make sense of it, and as a test of its validity. Viewed in this way, we begin to see how cognitive and intuitive constructs might interplay within the decision schema of an individual manager and the potential implications for group decision-making.

(Clarke and Mackaness 2001: 166)

Box 6.2: Managerial intuition in retail superstore investment decisions

Relatively little is known about the role that cognitive constructs play in distilling the essence of a situation, or indeed the relationship between such constructs and intuition. Recent research by Clarke and Mackaness (2001) has used the structure and content of executives' causal cognitive maps to isolate the intuitive elements of their individual decision schemata. Answering the call by Hodgkinson and Johnson (1994) for more sophisticated techniques to link structural representations of competitors with managers' causal logics regarding competition, they captured the key elements of 'intuition' used by three senior electrical retail managers in new store investment and construction decisions. Collective group interviews defined common decision goals. Prototyping techniques from artificial intelligence studies were used to identify selected stores. Individual cognitive mapping interviews were then carried out. Links between the individuals' concepts were given different status levels, including causal (direct influences), connotative (implied associated influences) and temporal (change over time) links. A series of propositions relating intuition to cognitive maps were developed in an attempt to construct a definition of intuition as a core decision making element. First, because of their relative remoteness from the day-to-day business, one might expect the cause maps of CEOs to be less factually based and thus more intuitive than those of functional managers. Within the particular organization investigated, a total of 53 per cent of the information used by the managing director was non-factual compared to 40 per cent for the retail estates manager. The findings suggested that the use of non-factual information was positively associated with level of experience rather than position in the hierarchy. A second proposition investigated by Clarke and Mackaness was that the maps of senior managers would be more structurally complex, coherent and explanatory than those of other managers because of a greater understanding of the situation. Such complexity is typically measured in terms of the ratio of links to the nodes in a map, the degree of clustering or grouping of nodes, and/or the average length of the concept chains. Although the findings did reveal a clear relationship between level of seniority and average chain length, contrary to the proposition investigated, chain lengths were found to be *shorter* with increasing seniority. Senior managers approach problems by attempting to simplify rather than use complex frames of reference. They delicately trade-off depth for the benefits of breadth. A third proposition investigated by Clarke and Mackaness was that senior managers would perceive unique influences on strategic decisions which those in more junior positions would fail to notice. Respondents had about one third of their constructs in common. There were a number of partially common constructs, and then a clear set of individual (interpreted as intuitive) constructs not 'seen' by others. The senior executives brought a substantial proportion of these individual constructs to bear on their decisions.

Source: Clarke and Mackaness (2001)

Intuition and the intelligent unconscious

In order to understand the importance of this form of knowledge in terms of individual managerial competency, psychologists are resuscitating the idea of the *intelligent unconscious* by exploring the nature of the 'implicit' or 'tacit' cognitive system. The majority of managers today believe that the rules of the past are no longer a guide to the future. We have therefore seen renewed attention being given to more subjective, intangible, implicit cognitive skills, and a return to the analysis of 'telling' individual differences that may help managers cut through chaotic environments, including:

- the investigation of less tractable areas of human cognition, such as intuition (Claxton 1998) and creative processes that help managers adapt to sudden crises and major adjustments (Finke *et al.* 1992; Finke and Bettle 1996; Rickards and Moger 1999);
- the management of emotions in organizations and the role of emotional intelligence (Goleman 1995; Ryback 1998).

Historical interest in intuition – which is now seen by psychologists as an alternative, competing and inductive *way of knowing* – has waxed and waned in relation to the level of discomfort felt with the more rational, deductive and analytic forms of knowing that tend to accompany a scientific and technological world (Davis-Floyd and Arvidson 1997). Intuition is knowledge derived from inward illumination and insight. It is an inseparable twin of *creativity*, which involves the production of novel ideas that are useful and appropriate to the situation (Amabile 1983). The statement that something is creative actually represents a subjective judgement which is based on the perceived novelty of an individual's or group's behaviour. Intuition is also often considered alongside *innovation*, of which creativity is again a vital element. At the individual level, innovation is an intentional attempt to bring about benefits from change. A number of important questions are now being asked:

- What do these abilities really look like?
- What can we learn from intuitive and creative strategists?
- To what extent do factors such as intuition drive the 'intelligent unconscious'?
- Can these abilities help managers cope with information overload, or manage a way through it?
- Is there an identifiable set of cognitive processes that are associated with intuitive or creative analyses and, if so, how might we move towards a more solid assessment, and training and/or development of such competencies?

The answers to such questions are slowly emerging. Intuition has been portrayed as knowledge derived from the inward light of the mind – a beam of light cast upon a chaotic confusion. The construct has literally been demonized (Inglis 1987). Socrates referred to the concept of 'daemon', which is a force, a presence, a voice, a passion, an urge of certitude that impels people to action. It could take the form of the Muses, which inspired poets, artists, writers and composers, or the eureka effect that serves scientists and mathematicians. But in the scientific nineteenth century, such knowledge was subjugated to scientific inquiry. By then, the English word 'demon' was interpreted as an evil influence. The current interest in intuition does not, however, just reflect a period of low institutional trust and technological society discomfort. Interest in intuition in the managerial process has ranged from the popular acclaim of innovative entrepreneurs to the study of creative problem solving techniques, and the development of product and process innovations and technological breakthroughs within research and development-led organizations (Glaser 1995). There are also very practical reasons why it is forming the basis of scientific study. As computers are used to provide expert knowledge systems for an ever-widening range of professions, the field of knowledge engineering has developed (Harbort 1997). The aim of knowledge engineers is to enable computers to be programmed to act and think like human experts (i.e. to draw upon the unique role that human intuition plays). Ultimately, this is an impossible task, as humans may consciously perceive intuitions at a series of progressive levels that we can assume are not replicable in computers (Vaughan 1979) – i.e. physical (bodily awareness); emotional (feelings); mental (images, ideas and thoughts); and spiritual (mystical experiences). Nevertheless, this body of work has directed attention towards cognitive aspects of intuition, especially in relation to decision making.

The role of intuitive decision making

There has long been a debate as to whether analytical expert judgements are better than intuitive ones, especially in situations of uncertainty. For Simon (1987: 63) there is nothing unique about intuition, which he saw simply as 'analysis frozen into habit'. Intuition, insight and inspiration are just different forms of analysis, rather than being driven by special mechanisms of creativity or discovery (Spender 1998). Linking back to Chapter 2 and the introduction of the idea of competent mindlessness, we noted that consideration has been given to decision making based on processes that do not take rational elements into account and that are driven by automatic processing (Csikszentmihalyi and Csikszentmihalyi 1988). In conceptualizing these parallel forms of reasoning, cognitive psychologists tend to adhere to *phylogenetic theory* (Spender 1998). This argues that conscious systems of cognition are built upon and emerge from a deeper, implicit system. Having evolved later in life, the conscious system is of a higher order – i.e. there should be less difference between managers' implicit competencies or capabilities, but more difference between their higher order, conscious cognitive capabilities. As we shall see, the emotional intelligence movement questions this assumption.

The implications of this assumed different range of competencies are only just beginning to be considered. Studies comparing the accuracy of an individual's intuitive judgement versus the application of some external, rational, rule-based analysis of the problem, unsurprisingly find rational analysis to be more accurate than intuition. However, when Hammond *et al.* (1997) compared the use of intuitive versus rational judgements *within* individuals (a group of expert highway engineers) they found that intuitive reasoning performed as well as, or better than, rational analysis. A reliance on analytical reasoning was more likely to produce extreme errors or failures, which was not the case with intuitive reasoning. Intuition was found to be the best strategy when:

- information presented to the manager required a reliance on perceptual processes to interpret it (i.e. the information was carried in media that require the manager to *sense* it by relying unduly on vision, hearing etc.);
- cues were multiple and appeared in parallel rather than a simple, linear sequence;
- many of the cues were redundant or irrelevant.

Our discussion of information overload in Chapter 3 suggested that these are the very conditions under many contemporary strategists are having to work. Certainly research on executive decision making shows that intuition now plays a significant role (see Box 6.3).

Although psychologists worry about their ability to assess the competency of effective intuitive decision making, some frameworks do exist (Agor 1991; Cappon 1994; Lank and Lank 1995). Practical applications are found in firms like Bell Atlantic, which lists intuition as an important quality in its job descriptions, and the US Marine Corps, which stresses the role of intuition as a central part of victorious decision making in command and control situations. We recognize, of course, that to some the latter might not be such a positive endorsement of the construct!

Intuition and insight

Recent theory and research has examined intuition in this more balanced light. Primary process cognition theory (Kris 1952) proposed that creative people could alternate between primary

Box 6.3: Taking the mystery out of intuitive decision making among executives

In our discussion of cognitive style it was noted that senior managers have been found to use more intuitive strategies. Qualitative research also supports this. Burke and Miller (1999) examined the use of intuitive decision making in major projects and programme developments managed by 60 senior executives. Thematic content analysis showed that 47 per cent of executives claimed to use intuitive decision making often, and a further 37 per cent occasionally. Their intuitive skills were seen as being learnable. The use of these skills expedited decisions that had to be made in the absence of data, made decisions more adaptive and multi-purpose, introduced qualities such as fairness into judgements, and avoided the need for rework. There were five types of intuitive decision that the executives made:

- *Experience-based,* in which mental maps were generated from years of experience and perceived relevant situations – decisions based on accumulated successes and failures.
- *Affect (feelings and emotions) based,* in which gut feelings were employed – emotions triggered by the presentation of information.
- *Cognitive,* entailing the proactive use of trained intuitive skills, tools and techniques.
- *Subconscious mental processing,* entailing automatic processing, leading to appropriate paths in the absence of information.
- *Value-based,* involving personal introspection to generate decisions compatible with a personal moral code or organizational culture.

Reliance on intuition was triggered by a number of things. Most notable were the non-verbal cues from other people – a glance that would lead to a reconsideration of the situation. Intuitive decisions were used in four situations:

- personnel or people-related judgements;
- rapid or unexpected decisions;
- uncertainty-pervaded or novel situations;
- situations lacking explicit informational cues.

Of particular interest is the fact that the attribute of being an effective intuitive decision maker carried remarkable 'positive currency'. Those managers who had a track record of effective intuitive

> decisions were also seen as being confident, open-minded, flexible, experienced, willing to take risks, fair and unbiased, reflective, insightful and creative!

process thought (found in states such as dreaming and reverie, as well as abnormal states such as psychosis and hypnosis) and secondary process thought (abstract, logical, reality-orientated, conscious). Creative inspiration involves a regression to primary cognition. Certainly, creative people have been found to report more fantasy activity and remember dreams better. They are also more easily hypnotized (Martindale 1999). The view that intuitive knowledge is derived from information that seeps into conscious awareness without the mediation of logic and rational processing is now being challenged. Intuitive 'knowing' is likely to have several origins, as seen in ideas about species memory, direct apprehensions and traditional neurological processing. A distinction should also be made between what proves to be valid intuitive knowledge and what actually are no more than speculative impulses, projections and biased perspectives. Davis-Floyd and Arvidson (1997) have analysed intuition drawing upon research from the fields of cultural anthropology, philosophy, neuropsychology and transpersonal psychology. Studies of differing levels of consciousness suggest that there is evidence to support the view that valid intuitions may indeed come through the senses first, but at a subliminal or non-conscious level of processing and storage, prior to entering conscious awareness.

Understanding intuition in such a way that we might be able to identify and assess those managers who possess this particular competency or competency set is no easy task. If we move beyond the personality predispositions indicated by such instruments as the MBTI, towards the range of skills and competencies needed to be an effective intuitivist, we can very quickly identify a broad set of abilities needed. Phenomenological approaches to the study of intuition attempt to identify and describe the characteristics that shape the transformation and reorganization of an individual's field of consciousness at the intuitive moment (Arvidson 1997). This stream of work has helped to describe some of the most important intuitive processes, focusing on the shifts of attention that can be detected in the stream of conscious-ness. Bastick (1982) differentiates sudden insight types of intuition into:

- eureka experiences (sudden insights into a solution preceded by a period of inattention to the problem, or 'recentering');
- 'clicking-in' experiences (insights preceded by a period of concentration in an attempt to solve the problem, also known as 'drifting').

A series of shifts in attention have to occur for these intuitions to take place (see Box 6.4). Although the processes that precede these intuitions are different, the shifts in attention at the moment of intuition are the same.

Conversations with other people form a critical part of the process that allows intuitions to occur (Arvidson 1997). This form of intelligence operates at the unconscious level and reflects a combination of innate factors and learning. It is seen as a rapid form of intelligence that has a large processing capacity.

All too often, we have assumed that explicit, articulate think-ing is the most powerful form of cognition. 'Ways of knowing' that are hazy have been denigrated. This conventional view is now under attack. Claxton (1997, 1998) asks: 'how do we know, without knowing why?' Intuition (often referred to as 'inklings' or 'glimmerings' of understanding) is defined as a sense in which vision and immediate knowledge are identical. Intuitions are often of a fleeting quality, faintly grasped by the individual, easily dissolved and lost in the next moment. An intuition may 'arrive' in several different ways: 'it may arrive abruptly "like a bolt from the blue", or it may emerge into consciousness much more slowly. It may be absolutely clear-cut, already formulated in all essential details, or it may be much more hazy: a hunch, an inkling or a glimmering of something that cannot yet be articu-lated' (Claxton 1998: 217). Without being able to articulate clearly the reason or justification, the individual finds that an answer to a question, a solution to a problem or a suggested course of action comes to their mind with an aura or conviction of 'rightness', plausibility or fruitfulness.

Psychologists have investigated the way in which people develop 'hunches' and convert them into explicit knowledge and

---

Box 6.4: Shifts in attention that occur with intuitions

According to Gurwitsch (1966), four shifts in attention can occur during the course of intuition. In each case, what is an otherwise standard cognitive process can be seen to involve a particular twist when an intuitive insight is involved:

- *Serial shifting*, which includes formal analysis on the basis of shifting attention from one theme to a related theme and back again. Intuitions involve this, but can also be triggered by 'jumping over' intermediate steps.
- *Elucidation*, in which vague lines of reference are progressively clarified as the theme of thought is reorientated in a more meaningful way. Rather than the focal theme remaining the same, but being given more meaning by changing the relevant context for the theme, it is the theme itself that changes as a new theme that was previously absent is presented, thereby giving meaning to the contextual rules that had been established.
- *Singling-out*, in which something that was previously a constituent of the theme becomes the theme itself. Rather than just narrowing down or selecting one of the constituents of the theme, by shifting attention to the constituent part a new set of internal and contextual relationships are perceived.
- *Synthesis*, (zooming out) in which the theme is reorganized so that what was previously part of the context which the manager drew upon to give meaning to the theme becomes a new and central constituent. A new theme has been created, because nothing remains as it was. In the replacement of the old theme with the new theme, relationships become reorganized, taking on new meaning.

'know-how'. This meta-ability is called *implicit learning* or *intuitive expertise*. When people are asked to perform a complex practical task, their expertise in the task develops well before their ability to articulate, explain or even consciously detect the patterns of information they have picked up (Lewicki *et al.* 1992; Reber 1993). We act intuitively before we act rationally. In the early stages of implicit learning, people 'guess' even before they develop 'hunches' and these guesses often have more validity than they are given credit for. Managers, therefore, undervalue their intuitions and place more weight on systematic thinking, often in situations where research tells us that systematic analysis is not the best tool for the job. Far from being a fuzzy and inferior way of knowing, intuition is actually the functional basis of informed choice, even after conscious understanding has been developed. Karmiloff-Smith (1992) uses the anecdote of the Rubik cube to explain this. Children are remarkably good at solving the puzzle of rotating and aligning the colours of the mini-cubes by using a strategy of playing and then unknowingly picking up the perceptual-motor patterns that emerge. Adults, on the other hand, in trying to adopt an intellectual approach and figure out the solution to what is actually far too complex a problem to solve in such a fashion, underperform. Implicit learning requires the manager to tolerate a temporary state of confusion. Complex, counter-intuitive predicaments are best mastered in this unconscious state, rather than through the generation of conscious hypotheses. Those who persist in operating intuitively maintain higher levels of skilled performance. Those who fall back on conscious rationality see decrements in their performance.

Studies have examined whether new insights occur rapidly and without much warning (rapid perceptual framing) (Metcalfe and Weibe 1987) or after predictable increments of prior knowledge (Weisberg 1995). *Meta-cognitive monitoring techniques* have been used to track participants' feelings of being warm or cold in relation to solving problems. For non-insightful problems they feel progressively warmer, whereas insightful problem solutions come on with little warning. We need to further enrich our understanding of what happens during intuitions if we are to identify how some managers are more sensitive than others to the way that intuitions 'pop' into their minds.

Intuitions are characterized in two ways: the ability of the manager to gain fast access to faint stimuli; and the ability to slowly incubate a creative solution. We consider the second usage in considerable detail below (see 'Creative Cognition'). In order to explain the first, Claxton (1998: 219) quotes Linford Christie's insistence that in order to win a 100-metres race: 'one must learn to go on the "b" of bang! If you wait till you've consciously heard the gunshot, you've already lost the race'. The fleeting and ephemeral nature of this fast access type of intuition has a physical reflection in the phenomenon of 'sub-threshold priming'. Such intuitions result when a stimulus triggers some neural or bio-chemical activation (researchers are unclear exactly what the physical representation is), which may have nothing to do with the territory of the intuition. Often, this activation is not enough to be consciously recognized. However, an associated concept is already primed, and as the neural activation spreads out from the 'epicentre' the small amount of stimulation it receives is enough for it to 'pop into the mind'. It becomes sufficient to influence the 'guess' that is produced, or to bias the global assessment of a situation that the individual makes. (Witness, for example, the goalkeeper who has a remarkably good record of guessing the right direction of penalty kicks.)

Creative cognition

Clearly, imagination serves as a source of ideas for strategic managers, but this does not just involve the generation of new ideas. Much innovation is essentially akin to 'theft' – the ideas were already around, but the manager finds a new 'recombina-tion' formula that creates the new insight. Creativity is a complex competency to understand. In fact, intuition and creativity are strongly influenced by the ability of the manager to 'incubate' and to draw upon the 'creative value of patience and reverie – of daring to wait and drift' (Claxton 1998: 217). For example, studies into award-winning Nobel prize laureates show that the vast majority place intuition at the heart of their success. The creative cognition approach provides an explicit account of the relevant cognitive processes and structures that lead to such insights by identifying measurable cognitive operations. Creativity is seen as the product of many types of mental process, each of which helps to set the scene for subsequent insight and discovery (see Box 6.5, for an example of one particular process).

As discussed in Box 6.6, Finke and Bettle (1996) have given attention to 'pre-inventive' structures (see also Finke *et al.* 1992). These are used and exploited by managers when they engage in creative search and exploration. Unlike schemata, pre-inventive structures are largely uninterpreted at the time they are initially

228

Box 6.5: Preverbal imagery and perception: Janusian thinking and percept genesis

Rothenberg (1991) tested the relationship between Janusian and homospatial processes and creativity. The Roman god Janus 'had faces that simultaneously looked in diametrically opposite directions' (Rothenberg 1991: 183). In the same vein, humans can use homospatial processes whereby they actively conceive of two or more discrete entities or elements occupying the same mental space (Rothenberg and Hausman 2000). This type of conception can lead to the articulation of new identities. Writers and artists, when exposed to superimposed images, generate more creative metaphors than when using more traditional associational, analogue or gestalt reasoning. Similarly, the process of percept genesis in creative perception and imagery has been studied (Smith 1990; Smith and Van der Meer 1997). Creative people are found to be extraordinarily open to subjective impressions, alternatives and insights (Martindale *et al.* 1996). Even when presented with brief and ambiguous stimuli they can generate positive interpretations and share impressions with others.

---

formed and remain so for a considerable time. Consequently, they are particularly useful for associating novel, incongruous, ambiguous and/or divergent but implicitly meaningful information. The previous section on intuition and insight summarizes some of the key processes that take place with the rapid or incubated *perceptual framing* that forms part of creative cognition. If psychologists are ever able to reliably assess such mental processes, organizations will be able to consider recruiting, selecting and developing more intuitive and creative managers in a serious way.

Key debates on creativity

Creativity is commonly defined as a mental process (West and Farr 1990), or more appropriately a collection and combination of such processes. A number of themes have come to dominate recent developments in cognitive theories of creativity (see Dacey and Lennon 1998), the most notable of which are:

Box 6.6: The Geneplore model of creative functioning:
pre-inventive structures

Creative thinking is characterized by the combination and employment of different sets of generative and exploratory processes:

Generative processes	*Exploratory processes*
Retrieval of existing structures from memory attributes	Search for novel or desired mental structures
Formation of simple associations among these structures, or combinations of them	Search for metaphorical implications of structures
Mental synthesis of new structures	Search for potential functions of structures
Mental transformation of existing structures into new forms	Evaluation of structures from different perspectives or contexts
Analogical transfer of information from one domain to another	Interpretations of structures to represent solutions to problems
Categorical reduction into more productive constituents	Search for practical or conceptual limitations of structures

These processes are used to build pre-inventive structures. Unlike schemata, these structures are not complete. They hold untested but promising ideas that bear the hallmark of creativity. Examples of pre-inventive structures can include symbolic visual patterns and diagrams, three-dimensional representations, exemplar novel categories, mental models of conceptual or physical systems and verbal combinations and associations. The generation of pre-inventive structures and the use of pre-inventive generative and exploratory cognitive processes in the context of constraining factors, lead to a focusing and expansion of concepts (schemata). There is considerable overlap, therefore, between creative and non-creative cognition as these processes (albeit in different blends) are used to focus or expand non-creative schemata as well as creative ones.

Source: Finke and Bettle (1996)

- The link between creativity and problem solving and the level of coincidence or disjointedness in their underlying processes.
- Ways in which problem solvers can strategically control mental processes (Mayer 1995) and regulate and monitor 'metacognitions' and 'metacognitive knowledge' – i.e. one's knowledge of and attention to one's own thought processes (Pesut 1990). The role of self-monitoring, self-evaluation and self-reinforcement as conscious attempts to implement methods of thinking to generate creative associations falls into this category of research, as does the emerging focus on the concept of emotional intelligence, discussed later in this chapter.
- The role of creative metaphors, analogies, linguistic meaning and mental models as mechanisms that help individuals shift from one understanding of a concept to a new or different understanding/meaning (Chi 1997; Gibbs 1997; Markman *et al.* 1997; Perkins 1997).

One of the major debates currently underway concerns the question whether creativity is a unitary concept, or whether it comes in many different forms. In part, the answer to this question depends on how the whole process is considered. We have so far broken the process down into separate elements associated with insight and intuition, creative cognition and subsequent innovative behaviour. There are different psychological dynamics underpinning each element of the creative process, in terms of cognition and of the motivations associated with each element (Unsworth 2001). Another way in which this issue has been addressed, however, has been to consider whether the creative process looks the same or operates in the same way across different domains of knowledge. Reinforcing the discussion of intuitive decision making, there is considerable evidence that rather than being a generic skill that one can master, creativity tends to be restricted to particular tasks or domains. Creative performance is tied to expertise in a particular field. This expertise enables the person to retrieve relevant information and recognize its significance. Unsworth (2001), for example, argues that it is a mistake to view creativity as a unitary concept and to focus so much on the final outcome of (successful) creativity. The former ignores the fine grain understanding of the different types of creativity that organizations might need, while the latter tends to ignore the less successful but nonetheless still creative processes that managers use. Unsworth considers the different ways in which people become engaged in the creative process. Four different types of creativity are identified within the confines of a 2 × 2 framework:

- the type of driver for engagement in the creative process (which may be internal and self-determined choice or external – i.e. the situation requires it);
- the problem type to which the creativity is directed (which may be closed or presented to the individual, or open, whereby it is discovered by the individual).

A related issue concerns the link between creativity and other competencies. The 'mental ability' approach to creativity has explored links between creativity and intelligence, thinking styles and problem solving, and has led to the development of idea generation techniques, creativity training and attempts to assess and select for creativity. There are two implicit questions that continue to generate debates within this stream of research:

- Are creativity and intelligence the same or not?
- If not, does creativity involve a special type of thinking or is it a recombination of traditional mental abilities?

The answer to these questions still splits cognitive psychologists. Nevertheless, West and Farr (1990) argue that there is a general consensus in the research literature that there is only a weak relationship between general intelligence and creativity among people with high IQs, that the achievement of research scientists is unrelated to general intelligence, and that being gifted is 'domain-specific' – i.e. the psychological requirements vary from one occupational setting to another.

Are creativity and intelligence the same or not? Early work on thinking styles indicated that divergent thinking and creativity were synonymous, portraying creativity as the antithesis of rational, logical thought. Subsequently, however, it became clear that tests of divergent thinking were little better than IQ tests at predicting real-world creative achievement, and that creativity implied 'appropriate' solutions. It is now appreciated that creativity involves divergent *and* convergent thinking. Similarly, different styles of equally creative thought, such as adaptive and innovative styles, have begun to emerge (Kirton 1976).

Sternberg and O'Hara (1999) have reviewed the evidence in respect of five possible answers to the question of whether or not creativity and intelligence are one and the same construct: (1) creativity is a sub-set of intelligence; (2) intelligence is a sub-set of creativity; (3) creativity and intelligence are overlapping; (4) they are essentially the same thing; or (5) they bear no relationship to each other at all. Box 6.7 summarizes some of the evidence in respect of this debate, highlighting in particular the nature of individuals' implicit theories of intelligence and creativity. The overall conclusion of Sternberg and O'Hara is that at the very least creativity involves several aspects of intelligence:

- *synthetic intelligence*, to come up with ideas;
- *analytical intelligence*, to evaluate the quality of ideas;
- *practical intelligence*, to formulate ways of effectively communicating ideas and persuading others of their value.

Beyond this basic conclusion, all five possible relationships have been proposed and there is some evidence to support each. This is still very much an open question.

The opposing school of thought does not suggest that creativity and intelligence are totally unrelated. Rather, it emphasizes the role of unique processes within creativity. This school (e.g. Getzels and Jackson 1962; Wallach and Kogan 1965) argues that:

- Creativity is a special form of thinking, involving cognitive processes such as the unconscious incubation of ideas, conscious illumination and insight and the perception of new connections between the elements of problems.
- Creativity involves additional abilities beyond simple rationality. For example, problem finding or generation (the ability to identify the key problem in a given domain), questioning and information elicitation are as important as problem solving, and are reflective of motivation, not cognition (Csikszentmihalyi 1988);
- Such insightful thinking requires a highly selective set of cognitive processes, including: the selective encoding of only those

---

Box 6.7: Implicit theories of creativity and intelligence

Sternberg (1985) has become associated with the 'overlapping circles' model of creativity and intelligence. He asked lay people and specialists in physics, philosophy, art and business about their implicit theories (folk conceptions) of intelligence and creativity. Creativity involved eight components and intelligence six:

Creativity	*Intelligence*
Non-entrenchment, seeing things in novel ways	Practical problem solving ability
	Verbal ability
Integration and intellectuality	Intellectual balance and integration
Aesthetic taste and imagination	
Decisional skills and flexibility	Goal orientation and attainment
Perspicacity (acuteness of perception, discernment, understanding)	Contextual intelligence, i.e. intelligence in the everyday environment
Drive for accomplishment and recognition	Fluid thought
Inquisitiveness	
Intuition	

On the basis of this analysis, Sternberg came to the conclusion that the two concepts do share a degree of overlap.

Source: Sternberg (1985)

---

bits of information likely to be useful later; a recognition of which bits to combine; and the relation or comparison of new information to existing knowledge (Sternberg and Davidson 1985; Sternberg 1988). This art of making the appropriate 'selections' is seen to lie at the heart of creative ability.

Cognitive psychologists are still at odds over the link between creative problem solving and problem solving in general. The balance of evidence seems to be moving towards the view that the cognitive processes involved in creativity are far more commonplace and generic than previously assumed. The study of creative cognition is an extension of its parent discipline, cognitive psychology. Researchers have adapted its concepts, theories and methods and developed them through the experimental study of explicitly *generative* human cognitive functioning (Ward *et al.* 1999). Rather than supporting the commonly held view that creativity is limited to a small class of gifted people, and that cognitive processes are used in radically different ways by creative people, this research demonstrates that human 'capacity for creative thought is the rule rather than the exception' (Ward *et al.* 1999: 189).

Implications

In the light of the above discussions concerning intuition, insight and creative cognition, we contend that there is an urgent need to fundamentally reconsider what it means to be intelligent in a modern organization, and what it takes to be an effective initiator and/or implementor of strategic change. We must question what intelligence in modern organizations really looks like and consider the extent to which the new styles of intelligence and supporting cognitive skills are amenable to development, and/or are something that is better selected for (or deselected out of) the organization. According to Finke *et al.* (1992: 6) such skills are readily transferable from one situation to another, thus suggesting that managers can indeed learn how to think in ways that maximize the opportunity for creative insight:

> There is no reason that [the] cognitive strategies that promote creativity in one domain could not be extended to other domains as long as . . . the person could recognise when an idea in the new domain was truly important . . . creative people share a basic understanding of how to go about being creative; they can then extend their creative skills into other areas as long as they know something about the relevant issues, methods, and values and are sufficiently motivated to do so.

Simon (1987) argues that while intuitive skill is based on years of experience and training, it can also be developed as well as selected for. The implications of the shift towards developing greater reliance on the intelligent unconscious within organizations are considerable. As we unpack the concepts of intuition and creative cognition, psychologists will have to look for ways to make them more amenable to investigation, and therefore ultimately to assessment. In turn, this will undoubtedly influence the ways in which we go about selecting, educating, and training and developing the managers and strategists of the future.

Sense-making and sense-giving

Another means of gaining insight into better ways of developing strategic competence is to analyse the evolutionary strategic thought processes of strategists over extended time periods. Recently, cognitive scientists working in the strategic management field have begun to conduct such investigations. An example of this can be seen in the work of Lindell *et al.* (1998). They were interested in the phenomenon of *dynamic stability* – defined as the sensitivity of cognitions to situational change. Longitudinal studies such as this can further our understanding of the dynamic interplay between managerial cognition and managerial action and behaviour. The findings of this research show how simple analyses of the cognitive structures of strategist – and changes to these cognitive structures – can be misleading. Lindell *et al.* used textual analysis, focusing in particular on the use of sentences to convey meaning, to track the thought processes of an individual strategic manager in a Swedish university hospital over a three-year period. They were able to examine the timing, appearance and disappearance of key issues or organizing constructs in the strategist's mind. Reflecting the processual leadership school of thought articulated by Pettigrew (1985) they found that the strategist was particularly adept at introducing new concepts and redefining the meaning of concepts already in use. This behaviour constituted a deliberate attempt on the part of the strategist to influence the sense-making of other members of the organization, particularly middle-level managers, and redefine their shared conception of organizational reality. Although the strategist had often developed new concepts through his own thought processes, these were not always communicated clearly. Indeed, the basic belief and value structures of the strategist about

236

issues such as centralization, the role of leadership and the functionality of the organization remained stable throughout the whole period. These constructs appeared to have been formed early on in the strategist's career, and seemed to reflect his personality and education. However, he was able to use two key competencies:

- *Sense-making*, defined as the introduction of new concepts and the redefinition of concepts already in use by involved parties, an attempt to develop meaningful frameworks for understanding the nature of strategic change.
- *Sense-giving (sometimes called 'thought leadership)'*, defined as the process through which managers attempt to influence the sense-making of others around them towards a preferred redefinition of organizational reality. Our discussion of mental models of competition in Chapter 4 touched upon the importance of such thought leadership at the inter-organizational level, where we highlighted the work of Lant and Phelps (1999) and Levenhagen *et al.* (1993) on situated learning and the cognitive life cycle of market domains respectively.

The work of Lindell *et al.* (1998), as one of the few longitudinal studies of individual managerial cognition, has provided us with some insights into the processes of individual sense-making, which must necessarily precede sense-giving. They found that there was a continuous mental adaptation to both the internal and external forces at work. However, a skeletal framework of strong and stable beliefs, values and assumptions prevailed, around which beliefs and opinions about specific situations changed more easily. Hence, the cognitions of the individual manager in his capacity as a stategic leader changed in relation to the local situation, rather than in relation to fundamental management issues.

Gioia and Chittipeddi (1991) identified the processes of sensemaking and sense-giving as being crucial to the success of top managers in initiating strategic change. These cognitive competencies are likely to underpin a number of behavioural competencies. Certainly, the process of sense-giving forms one of the central features of Senge's (1990a) work on the process of generative learning and the leadership competencies needed to manage in a learning organization (see Chapter 2).

Based upon a longitudinal study conducted at the organizational level, Pettigrew and Fenton (2000: 297–9) have recently drawn attention to a number of political process skills that strategic leaders can use to give sense to others. Chief among these are 'simplification routines' deployed in an effort to strike an appropriate balance in terms of the level of complexity/simplicity that they create in the minds of the recipients of their messages. Strategic leaders have to 'convey clear, simple and evocative messages' that link the future to key concerns in the present. They have to create 'zones of relative comfort' for others, because in an era of relentless and continuous change, managers need some areas of stability before they can engage with new ideas. Linking the future to elements of the past (whether the past is reinterpreted or reduced to an essential core) is a powerful way of doing this. There are of course significant dangers associated with the deployment of such simplification tactics, not least those of falling into competency traps and the associated problem of 'progressing organizational simplicity' (Miller 1993) (see Chapter 2). Clearly this is a very difficult balance to strike.

In introducing the notion of thought leadership as a strategic competence, we do not wish to imply the endorsement of an overly simplistic top-down view of strategizing. On the contrary, we view sense-making and sense-giving as fundamentally intertwined, multi-directional processes, pervading all organizational levels, strategies being the product of a negotiated order, as discussed in Chapter 1. Indeed, an interesting avenue for future research would be to investigate the extent to which there are fundamental differences in the ways in which such thought leadership is attempted (and countered) across varying organizational levels. Another potentially fruitful line of inquiry would be to investigate the extent to which the various individual differences variables discussed in this chapter have a bearing on this key competence. A third line of inquiry might investigate the degree of linkage between differing approaches to leadership, or leadership style, and the way in which sense-making and sense-giving are accomplished. Presumably, in seeking to adapt the mental representations of others, there are strong differences in the extent to which those attempting such thought leadership merely seek to impose their own ideas on others, as opposed to engaging in dialogue. The latter requires a wider range of supporting behavioural competencies, not least empathy, as discussed in the next section.

The work reviewed in this section implies that the mental structures of organizational actors function in a holistic way and, in fact, comprise a mixture of thoughts, values and emotions. As we have seen, increasingly, managers are having to think and act far more holistically in order to deal with the wide range of potentially conflicting contingencies confronting the organization, hence the growth of interest in intuition as a strategic competence. Thinking and acting are intertwined processes, but even though strategic managers may have rather stable belief structures, the concepts that they use may be flexible enough, as a skeletal framework, to allow substantial sensitivity to situations and the development of new understandings. Empirical studies of strategic change and the ways leaders think support this view that managers use thematic sets of values, assumptions, beliefs, ideas and thoughts about key concepts to manage change within their organizations (Hellgren and Melin 1993). The combination of stable belief structures and continual adaptation of, and sensitivity to, situations lies at the heart of the competencies of sense-making and sense-giving. Lindell *et al.* (1998) note that cognitive structures are considered to be pure knowledge structures; but they are of course constructed by human beings who have hopes, emotions and values (see Sims and Lorenzi (1992) who similarly argue that *affect* and *emotion* influence cognitions and behaviour). This brings us to the final set of individual competencies that we wish to highlight: the competencies associated with *emotional attunement*.

The emotionally-attuned manager

The relationship between IQ and broad measures of life success is weak, and small in relation to other characteristics brought to life (Hernstein and Murray 1994). The validity of IQ tests in predicting executive or management competencies is low – leaders have to have a baseline level of intelligence to be effective and tend to be more intelligent than the average group member, but they are not invariably the most intelligent within the group (Bahn 1979). Ultimately, strategic success depends upon a number of attributes that lie beyond the rational side of management. As noted earlier, strategy within an already large number of contemporary organizations is much more of an emotive affair than of old. The world has been turned upside down for many managers trying to make judgements and implement change (Sparrow 2000). As processes of globalization, downsizing and restructuring herald deep shifts in the pattern of work and society, and influence the perceptions that employees and their managers have of work, the problems associated with increased levels of emotionality at work have become an important issue. Research on a series of deep emotional issues has become the focus of academic attention, including:

- breach of the implicit or psychological contract (Rosseau 1995; Morrison and Robinson 1997) and the human resource management consequences of this (Sparrow and Cooper 1998);
- the endemic lack of trust and change in the nature of trust within organizations (Kramer and Tyler 1996; Herriot 2001);
- the perception of fairness (or lack of it) and the role of organizational justice in managing accountability for events that have a negative impact on material and/or psychological well-being (Folger and Cropanzano 1998);
- the need for much better retrospective sense-making and the ongoing creation of reality in a complex and ambiguous organizational world (Weick 1995);
- the need for organizations and their managers to make the knowledge and experience of individuals and groups more explicit and understandable (J. Sparrow 1998).

Briner (1999) has pointed out that until recently two parallel schools of thought informed the way in which we viewed the topic of strategic management, the actions of managers, and the skills and competencies we assumed they needed. The first – and still dominating – school of thought was rational and precise. According to this view, 'cool strategic thinking is not to be sullied by messy feelings. Efficient thought and behaviour tame emotion and good organizations manage feelings, design them out or remove them' (Fineman 1996: 545). This school of thought is characterized by an approach that argues 'let's keep emotion out of this and deal with things rationally' (Cooper 1998). A second school of thought, however, has explicitly acknowledged the role of emotionality in organizational life. This school has addressed the nature and significance of stress, satisfaction and trust within the workplace, together with a consideration of the changing nature of the psychological contract and its attendant consequences for the workforce. Emotion at work is being discussed in both positive and negative ways. Positive discussion centres on the fact that organizations can and must generate feelings of excitement and high personal engagement, and positively influence behaviour (what psychologists refer to as 'emotional contagion') among their employees; while negative discussion centres on the fact that much organizational strategy today seems to be making people more angry, resentful, anxious and/or depressed (Herriot 2001).

There is still a divide in management thinking between the rational and the emotional, but a new orthodoxy is emerging (Cassell 1999) which argues that emotions cannot be separated from the managerial thought process and the process of strategic change. Both the cognitive and social processes that surround strategic decision making are influenced by emotion (Daniels 1999). Specifically, the quality of the mental models that managers develop is influenced by their emotional state. As exemplified by our earlier discussion of the Janis and Mann (1977) conflict theory of decision making (see Chapter 1), it has long been recognized that perceptions of stress and environmental threats undermine the quality of information processing and hence the ability of individuals to monitor effectively key events that signal a need for adaptation (see also Argyris 1999). The attentional narrowing and defensive distortions that accompany high stress levels can only serve to fuel cognitive bias and inertia (Hodgkinson and Wright, in press).

If managers live in a more emotional world, then the very content of their thought processes becomes more emotional too. For most managers, change is seen as a complex and intensely emotional psychosocial drama. The ability to trust one's own and others' emotions has become a key competency requirement of modern organizations. When organizations adopt strategies that

241

purposefully place individuals in organizational units characterized by cognitive climates inimical to their own cognitive style (in
an attempt to stimulate innovation and change, or to challenge
strategic myopia) the resulting conflict and misunderstandings, to
say nothing of the defensive routines that will almost invariably
ensue, make this competency all the more important. Throughout
this book we have argued that the management literature has
given too much attention to the hyper-rational, objective view of
intelligence, which focuses on the role of a rather limited set of
cognitive attributes and language to describe the way the mind
registers and stores information. The ability to be aware of one's
own mental processes has, however, become a key focus for more
subjective definitions of intelligent behaviour.

Before concluding this chapter, therefore, we briefly consider the
notion of 'emotional intelligence' (EI). This has also been referred
to as 'emotional quotient' (EQ), 'personal intelligence', 'social intelligence' and 'interpersonal intelligence' (Goleman 1995; Cooper
1997, 1998; Cooper and Sawaf 1997; Ryback 1998), reflecting this
shift in focus. It is a notion that has arisen out of the search for a set
of measurable tendencies, which in addition to IQ, can serve as
predictors of academic, occupational and life success. It draws
upon research that has focused on intelligent behaviour in natural
situations, or practical intelligence (Wagner and Sternberg 1985;
Sternberg and Wagner 1993; Sternberg et al. 1995; Neisser et al.
1996). The designation 'emotional intelligence' is justified on the
grounds that it requires the processing of specific emotional information within the manager, and because some level of competence
in the skills associated with this notion is necessary for adequate
social functioning (Salovey and Mayer 1990).

EI is a label that can be applied to a set of competencies that deal
with the recognition, regulation and expression of moods and
emotions (Fox and Spector 2000). These competencies tend to be
related to the experience of moods and emotions (one's own and
those of others) and the use of these to successfully navigate the
social environment. Given that EI comprises a series of emotion-
handling competencies, this suggests that some aspects of it are
indirectly assessible through their reflection in a variety of behavioural competencies such as self-awareness, emotional management, empathy and personal style. Empathy is one of the central

competencies to have featured under the EI umbrella. In this context, the term 'empathy' itself is used in two ways (Davis 1996):

- *Cognitive empathy (role-taking):* when one person attempts to understand another by imagining the other's perspective – i.e. the ability to understand the other person's psychological point of view, including their likely reactions to one's own behaviour. This ability to predict the responses of other social actors is believed to facilitate the ability to manoeuvre through complicated social settings.
- *Affective reactivity:* the emotional outcomes experienced by the observer in response to the distressed emotional displays of another person.

For our purposes it is important to note that EI is linked to the previous discussion of the intelligent unconscious, because it shares many attributes in common. In particular, it:

- Creates positive mood states, which in turn increase the retrieval of more extensive sets of related and positively-toned material from memory, more inclusive categorizations and more unusual associations with neutral words. These are all cognitive processes that are associated with problem solving, innovation and creativity (Isen 1984; Forgas and Bower 1987; Isen *et al.* 1987).
- Operates at a pre-conscious level and is seen to share many common neurological processes with intuition and creativity (Goleman 1995).
- Serves as a source of energy, drive and feelings that subsequently act as a wellspring for intuitive and creative wisdom and guide people to unexpected possibilities (Cooper 1998; Ryback 1998).

But what is the evidence that is used to support the existence of this meta-ability in real organizational settings? Is this just another catchy-sounding construct that will appeal to leaders convinced that it is something they surely possess, or is it a psychologically valid construct? If a valid construct, is it something that can realistically be assessed at the individual level? Most research on EI has been conducted outside the work context.

However, industrial, work and organizational psychologists are now attempting to assess EI using traditional competency identification techniques (Dulewicz and Higgs 1998). The notion is appealing because it offers the potential to explain aspects of success at work that are overlooked by more traditional tests of intelligence and attainment. As noted earlier, interest in EI has developed due to the inability of alternative constructs to explain performance outcomes. Potentially, EI can provide self-awareness of one's own cognitions. Such *meta-ability/meta-cognition* determines how well people use the other skills they have, including their intellect. EI draws upon 'the ability to sense, understand and effectively apply the power and acumen of emotions as a source of human energy, information, trust, creativity, connection and influence' (Cooper 1998: 48).

Goleman's (1995) popularist work on EI has gained most prominence. He drew attention to the need to explore the extent to which there is both intelligence 'in' the emotions, and the way in which intelligence can be brought 'to' emotions. EI represents a collection of traits and abilities, defined as: 'the ability to motivate oneself and persist in the place of frustrations; to control impulse and delay gratification; to regulate one's moods and keep distress from swamping the ability to think; to emphasize and to hope' (Goleman 1995: 34).

Considering whether EI can be assessed, Dulewicz and Higgs (1998) note conflicting views. It may just be seen as a marketing concept and not a scientific term, and we may only meaningfully speak of EQ as long as we don't claim to be able to measure it precisely. The difficulty in terms of assessment techniques is that many of its behavioural reflections, such as empathy, are best seen (and therefore assessed) through the eyes of others.

In the final analysis, that the EI notion has considerable predictive efficacy is evidenced by the recent study of Dulewicz and Higgs (1998) who conducted a longitudinal study linking managerial competency data from managers assessed in 1988/9 with subsequent career advancement and current level of seniority. Traditional competency measures were found to be predictive of career success. However, they reassigned 40 competency measures across three components: *emotional intelligence* (sensitivity, resilience, influence and adaptability, decisiveness and adaptability, energy and leadership); *rational and intellectual intelligence* (analysis and judgement, planning and organizing, strategic perspective and creativity and risk-taking); and *management process effectiveness* (supervision, oral communication, business sense, and initiative and independence). Process competencies, rational and intellectual competencies, and EI competencies accounted for 16, 11 and 9 per cent respectively of subsequent managerial advancement (see also Dulewicz and Herbert 1999).

Concluding remarks

In this chapter we have identified and discussed a range of factors and competencies that have a likely bearing on the way in which individuals process strategic information and knowledge. In addition to a consideration of factors that determine the extent to which individuals are motivated to search for relevant information and integrate this into their cognitive structures, considerable attention has been devoted to the processes of creativity and intuition, and the role of affect in the strategic management process.

It is important to note that the creative cognition perspective does not refute the proposition that individual differences account for higher levels of creative outcomes at extreme levels of accomplishment (Simontin 1994; Eysenck 1995). Such individual differences can be understood through variations and combinations of specific cognitive processes, the intensity of their application, the richness or flexibility of the stored cognitive structures and the capacity of memory systems (see Simontin 1997 and Ward *et al.* 1997 for a contrasting view on this). It also acknowledges that from a managerial perspective, other factors in addition help to explain whether a particular product will eventually be adjudged to be creative, such as the level of intrinsic motivation, the timeliness of the idea, and the value that national cultures place on innovation (Runco and Chand 1995; Sternberg and Lubart 1996) and that creativity is as much a cultural and social phenomenon as an individual one. Without social validation, a new product may be novel and inventive but not necessarily creative (Csikszentmihalyi 1999). However, despite the need for this social validation, this chapter has provided insights into what lies beneath individual competency in this area and has made it clear that creative solutions seem to emerge from generic and more commonplace cognitive processes.

We have also argued that managers cannot avoid having to deal with emotionality in today's world. In analysing problems they work in a context of low trust and face a variety of difficult interpersonal issues relating to fairness and equity. As we have seen, cool, rational strategic thought is often not appropriate in such a context. In any event, they are incapable of it. As managers try to make sense of this complex and ambiguous world, the quality and appropriateness of their knowledge structures comes to the fore. Our analysis overall has highlighted a number of significant problems: these cognitive structures can be remarkably insensitive to important but subtle changes in the strategic environment. In other words, cognitive inertia is a significant risk. Moreover, many current changes in organizational form, such as downsizing and outsourcing, also carry risk, primarily through the potential loss of organizational memory. However, the most significant issue is the problem of information overload. Our analysis has indicated a number of ways in which information load is increasing. Returning to the question we posed at the start of this chapter: does the answer to the problems that we have identified lie in developing intuitive skills, creativity and emotional intelligence? The potential contributions that they can make seem only too self-evident, – but are these facets of the 'intelligent unconscious' valid, practical and assessable? These are exceedingly complex issues. Undoubtedly, they will form a major focus of research activity over many future years.

7

KNOWLEDGE ELICITATION TECHNIQUES AND METHODS FOR INTERVENTION

It takes more than 64 words to describe the noun 'knowledge' in the *Oxford English Dictionary and Thesaurus* and another 112 to describe the adjectives and verbs of 'knowledgeable', 'knowing' and 'known'.[1] Given the complexity involved, how have researchers set about the task of investigating organizational actors' mental representations of strategic knowledge? How close or distant are we from understanding what really goes on in the mind of the strategist?

The purpose of this chapter is to provide an overview of a range of tools and techniques that have underpinned the development of psychological research and organizational interventions in the field of strategic management. Within a remarkably short time period, the field has witnessed a dramatic proliferation in the range of procedures being applied in an effort to 'map' the mental representations of decision makers (see, e.g., Huff 1990; Fiol and Huff 1992; Walsh 1995; Eden and Spender 1998; Hodgkinson

---

1 We are indebted to Yvonne Shayegan for this observation, which is taken from a written analysis entitled 'What is knowledge', which she conducted as part of a consulting assignment with a large oil producing organization.

2001a; Huff and Jenkins 2002). From a researcher's point of view, the aim of these developments has been to try and better understand the nature and significance of managerial and organizational cognition in processes of strategy formulation and implementation, as exemplified by the many studies reviewed in earlier chapters. From a practitioner standpoint, the ultimate purpose of this body of theory and research is to enhance the practice of strategic management.

One way in which psychological knowledge might contribute to the enhancement of practice is through the application of cognitive mapping techniques and related procedures, as a basis for intervening in the strategy process. Two problems in particular have been highlighted in earlier chapters that might benefit from such intervention work: cognitive bias and cognitive inertia. The effect of forcing strategists to confront their 'taken for granted' operating assumptions, or 'theories in use' (Argyris 1999), should be that mental models of the sort that constrain reliable inquiry into organizational processes will be challenged. To the extent that such interventions are 'successful', the risk of debacles unfolding, of the sort epitomized by the Prudential case outlined in Chapter 1, should hopefully be minimized.

In its most general sense, the term cognitive mapping can be applied to any research method used as a basis for eliciting actors' knowledge and beliefs in a systematic fashion. Given the sheer scale of developments over recent years, it is not possible to provide comprehensive coverage of the many methods presently available for mapping strategic knowledge. Rather, our aim is to selectively highlight particular tools and techniques in order to illustrate the sorts of insight that can be generated from the application of cognitive mapping techniques in general. This will enable us to consider a number of non-trivial methodological issues confronting researchers and practitioners seeking to better understand and/or enhance the strategic management process from a psychological standpoint. A consideration of these issues is vital if we are to fully appreciate the strengths and limitations of the existing empirical knowledge base underpinning this field, and evaluate the claims of those seeking to utilize cognitive mapping and related procedures for the purposes of intervention in organizational decision making. Readers seeking a comprehensive treatment of the issues raised in this chapter should also consult Fiol and Huff (1992), Hodgkinson (2001a), Huff (1990), Walsh (1995) and J. Sparrow (1998).

The chapter is organized as follows. Following this introduction, we provide an overview of the varieties of knowledge that pervade organizational life. This is necessary in order to contextualize the various tools and techniques that we evaluate in detail in later sections. In the next section we commence our review in earnest, with a consideration of causal cognitive mapping procedures. Next we highlight various qualitative and quantitative methods for revealing dimensional and hierarchical relationships among conceptual stimuli. Given their widespread prominence as a method for intervening in the strategy process, the next section is devoted to a consideration of scenario planning techniques. In the final section, 'Concluding remarks', we draw together a number of methodological issues arising from the chapter as a whole, which are of general concern to both researchers and practitioners alike, who, for whatever reason, might wish to map strategic knowledge.

Varieties of knowledge

In attempting to capture the complexity of knowledge, and in clarifying the popular usage of terms such as mental models, scripts, schemata and cognitive maps in the strategic management literature, we have to return to some basic psychology. In Chapter 3 we noted that in order to understand knowledge we need to be clear about the different kinds of mental material that managers deal with, such as facts, skills and conscious and unconscious experiences. We have to appreciate the different forms of thought employed, and consider the varying ways in which these different kinds of mental material are processed. In this connection, J. Sparrow (1998) has identified five different kinds of mental material:

- *Semantic understanding:* labels and concepts (largely developed through education, but also derived from experience) used to imbue meaning. Personal construct theory (Kelly 1955) represents one attempt to account for the way in which individuals construe meaning in order to make inferences about the world. According to personal construct theorists, the labels we construct as individuals not only enable us to make sense of our past, but also help to guide our future actions.

- *Episodic memories:* experiences memorized as a sequence of events. Particulars about space and time in the episode are encoded and can subsequently be linked to, and recalled by, the use of particular sensory cues that formed part of the experience (Tulving 1972). Episodic memories are often stored in the form of scripts, which are basic routines or sequences of events (Schank 1982).
- *Skills:* actions used to guide and execute the performance of a task. The direction of these actions becomes increasingly automatized with increased levels of skill (Anderson 1983). The verbal knowledge that is initially used to articulate a particular skill – rules and deliberations – comes under less conscious control as expertise develops.
- *Tacit feel:* expertise that has never become part of verbal knowledge and is a product of pure experiential learning. Variously called 'inarticulate knowledge' (Polanyi 1958), 'tacit knowledge' (Berry and Broadbent 1984), implicit learning, latent learning, implicit memory or tacit feel (Hintzman 1990). The nature and significance of this type of knowledge was considered in some detail in Chapter 2 and revisited in Chapter 6.
- *Unconscious interpretations:* non-conscious processing of information about our perceptions and ourselves. This type of processing may occur in relation to the unconscious symbols (Piaget 1951) that we use to assimilate knowledge. These icons may themselves become fragmented (parts become deleted, replaced or lose their form) as we unconsciously play out ideas (Freud 1900). Used in particular to deal with complex emotional information, and evidenced in patterns of thinking driven by excess, rigidity/impulsivity, transformation and denial.

Managers, then, work with several alternative kinds of mental material. They also use different forms of thought to configure this material in more or less useful ways. The manner in which they put such information together (i.e. 'forms of thought') affects the way in which it can be used in subsequent decisions (J. Sparrow 1989). It also makes subsequent processing more, or less, easy. J. Sparrow (1998) has identified two main forms of thought:

- *Propositional:* in order to establish linkage between ideas, objects or events, propositional codes (generated when the event is first experienced) are used to connect them. The creation of such linkages establishes what may be called 'channels of move-ment' or 'systems of constructs' (Kelly 1955, 1969; Fransella and Bannister 1977). Perceptions and decisions are processed through a network of 'action pathways' that can serve both to limit the manager and/or open up their thought process to new 'pathways of freedom'.

- *Imagistic:* almost a century ago, Betts (1909) argued that images can be coded and represented in line with each of the various senses through which they are initially detected. Accordingly, images may be classified as visual, auditory, cutaneous (repre-senting a sense of touch), kinaesthetic (representing bodily movements), gustatory (representing taste), olfactory (repre-senting smell) or organic (representing mood, states and feel-ings). These images may be more evocative than words and can trigger a wide range of associations. Imagistic thought is assumed to be associated with more artistic and creative forms of thinking.

The mental models employed by managers are thus not unitary representations (cf. Johnson-Laird and Bara 1984). Rather, they are the product of multiple representations of knowledge (Bibby 1992). These models are constructed online, drawing on different forms of representation, in order to assist in the task of reasoning. Reasoning, however, is not the only type of thinking employed by managers and other organizational actors. According to J. Sparrow (1998), three different types of thinking pervade organizational life; if organizations are to truly understand the perspectives of their participants then they have to consider the nature and significance of each type:

- *Reasoning:* going beyond the information given through the use of rational processing (Galotti 1989). Different patterns of reasoning can yield different explanations. Causal thinking, for example, yields linear sequences. Systems thinking, by contrast, yields complex patterns of interaction, while dipolar thinking takes account of the interdependence of polar opposites, and contextual thinking recognizes cultural and historical contexts of interpretations (Reason and Rowan 1981).

- *Autistic:* non-directed thoughts, cut off from the outside world. Such thoughts are used automatically and intuitively to sense views about people and situations. Daydreaming, for example, falls within this category. Daydreams can be placed along a continuum ranging from planful/anticipatory through to pure daydreaming (Fournier and Guiry 1993) and the prevailing tone of particular instances of daydreaming have been linked to particular mood states (Valkenburg and Vandervoort 1995). Autistic thinking is assumed to generate new linkages, of varying radicality, between elements of knowledge – as for example found in aggressive daydreams on the trip home from work after a conflictual day at the office.

- *Mood:* pervasive states that colour the interpretation of, and deliberation on, events. Moods – and their associated emotions – may be a more integrated part of cognition, as noted in Chapter 6. Three mood-cognition linkages have been observed: a 'pervasive' effect, whereby pleasant items are processed more efficiently and actively than unpleasant ones, and word recall is in descending order of unpleasantness; a 'mood congruent' effect, such that powers of memory may be superior when the material to be learned is congruent with the learners' current mood state; and 'mood-state dependence effects', whereby people recall items or events when the mood they were in on some previous occasion is the same as their current mood (Matlin 1994).

Another useful distinction, that was highlighted in Chapter 3, is the distinction between procedural knowledge (knowledge of how to do things), declarative knowledge (describing what something is) and causal knowledge (describing why things happen) (Zack 1999). As Shadbolt and Milton (1999) have observed, procedural knowledge is commonly confused with tacit knowledge. While it is certainly true some forms of tacit knowledge are concerned with how to do things (i.e. procedural knowledge), not all forms of procedural knowledge are tacit; nor are all forms of tacit knowledge procedural. Thus, for example, it is possible to articulate how to cook a meal, but not how to ride a unicycle.

We have incorporated this discussion of the varieties of knowledge, not to compile an exhaustive taxonomy, but in order to reinforce further the fact the processes of knowledge elicitation and knowledge representation are exceedingly complex. At the very least, as summarized in Figure 7.1, it appears that several different types of thinking interact with several different types of mental material and several different thought forms, in a variety of ways.

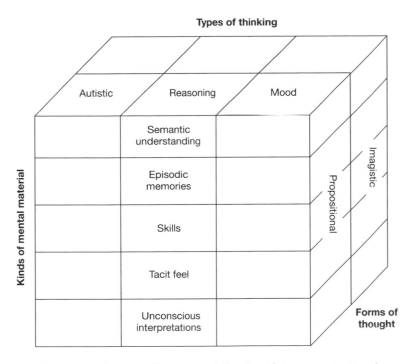

Figure 7.1 An overall framework for classifying organizational knowledge, based on kinds of mental material, forms of thought, and types of thinking

Source: reproduced by kind permission of the publisher from J. Sparrow (1998) *Knowledge in Organizations: Access to Thinking At Work.* London: Sage. © John Sparrow.

253

The general implications of this analysis are that a wide range of procedures is needed if we are to capture strategic knowledge in its many forms. Here, however, we shall confine our attention to just two broad classes of cognitive mapping procedure: causal mapping techniques and techniques designed to reveal dimensional and hierarchical relationships among conceptual stimuli.

Causal cognitive mapping techniques

Causal mapping techniques fall within a general class of procedures that Huff (1990: 16) has categorized as methods for revealing understanding of 'influence, causality and system dynamics'. As implied by their name, these techniques are designed to capture actors' causal belief systems. An emphasis on action, focusing on the perceived interrelationships between a given situation and its antecedents and likely consequences, renders this approach to cognitive mapping particularly attractive for descriptive research purposes and as a basis for intervening prescriptively in the strategic management process.

Over the past two decades or so, causal mapping techniques have been employed in order to investigate a wide range of organizational phenomena from a cognitive perspective (for representative examples, see Bougon *et al.* 1977; Roos and Hall 1980; Hall 1984; Salancik and Porac 1986; Weick and Bougon 1986; Narayanan and Fahey 1990; Jenkins and Johnson 1997a, 1997b; Budhwar 2000; Hodgkinson and Maule 2002; Budhwar and Sparrow in press). These procedures have been employed fruitfully not only in order to investigate individual thinking (Cosette and Audet 1992) but also in an effort to represent the collective logics of organizations and wider communities as a whole (e.g. Roberts 1976).

Methods for eliciting and representing causal maps

Despite the widespread popularity of these techniques there is currently no consensus within the literature concerning the most appropriate way to elicit actors' causal belief systems. In its earliest form, causal mapping involved the coding of documentary sources (Axelrod 1976). In recent years, however, causal mapping procedures have been adapted to study actors' cognitions in a relatively direct fashion, through the medium of face-to-face interviews and/or structured questionnaires and related approaches. Some scholars continue to employ causal mapping procedures primarily as a method of content analysis, drawing on documentary sources of evidence as the basis of data collection (Stubbart and Ramaprasad 1988; Barr et al. 1992; Barr and Huff 1997), while others utilize these techniques as a means for content analysing interview transcripts (Calori et al. 1992, 1994; Jenkins and Johnson 1997a, 1997b). A growing number of researchers and practising management consultants, however, are employing one or more variants of causal mapping directly, as a means of eliciting actors' cognitions in situ, in an attempt to gain insights into the nature and significance of cognitive processes in organizational decision making (e.g. Markoczy 1995, 1997; Swan 1997; Swan and Newell 1998), and/or prescriptively as a basis for intervention through 'action research' (Cropper et al. 1990; Eden et al. 1992; Eden and Huxham 1996; Eden and Ackermann 1998).

In cases where causal cognitive mapping procedures are used for consultation purposes, dynamic media are usually employed (e.g. interactive computer software, laminated magnetic symbols or self-adhesive labels in conjunction with whiteboards) to help individuals and groups reflect critically, in a systematic fashion, on the emerging strategic conversation. Typically, this process is steered through the use of a facilitator (for representative examples see Eden and Ackermann 1998; Eden and Radford 1990). In this context, maps are developed iteratively, over an extended period (often two to three days), primarily as a vehicle for recording and reflecting on the decision making process. Where such mapping is not used for consultation, data is usually gathered on a one-off basis using interviews and/or a range of standardized self-report data collection procedures.

In their most basic form, cause maps can be depicted graphically using the medium of the influence diagram (Diffenbach 1982). Variables are depicted as nodes in a network, interconnected by a series of arrowheaded pathways, terminating on the dependent variable(s); the arrowheads depict the directions of causality.

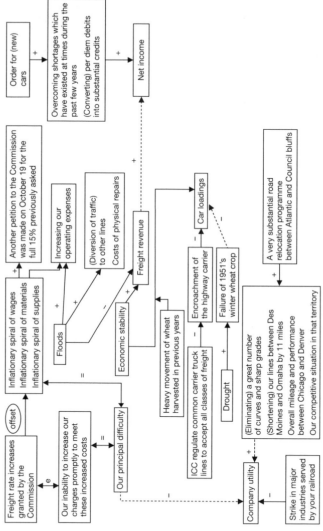

Figure 7.2 Cause map of the Rock Island Railroad Company in 1951

Source: P.S. Barr, J.L. Stimpert and A.S. Huff (1992) Cognitive change, strategic action, and organizational renewal, *Strategic Management Journal*, 13: 15–36. © John Wiley & Sons, Ltd. Reproduced by kind permission of the publisher.

Figure 7.2 shows an example of a cause map, taken from a study of US railroad companies conducted by Barr *et al.* (1992). Here, perceived positive causal relationships in which increases in one variable are thought to cause an increase in one or more other variables, are depicted by means of plus signs that accompany the arrowheaded pathways linking the variables in question. Conversely, perceived negative causal relationships, in which increases in one variable are thought to cause decreases in one or more other variables, are depicted by means of arrowheaded pathways, accompanied by minus signs.

The cognitive map shown in Figure 7.2 is one of several derived by Barr *et al.* in an investigation of the impact of environmental change on organizational performance. Drawing on documentary sources of evidence, they examined the views of top managers from two US railroad companies (the C&NW and the Rock Island), both facing deregulation over an extended time period. This study revealed that the executives of both companies recognized the threats deregulation posed to their businesses (as evidenced by changes in their mental models), but only one of the organizations concerned was able to understand how to realign its business strategy to respond effectively to these environmental changes. Not surprisingly, it was this organization that ultimately survived over the longer term. Barr *et al.* contend that although the mental models of the executives of both companies changed over time, only the C&NW, the surviving company, exhibited a true process of learning, in marked contrast to the Rock Island Company. While the former is still viable to this day, the latter sought bankruptcy protection in the mid-1970s and was wound up accordingly.

Cause maps can be far more complex than that illustrated in Figure 7.2. Increasingly sophisticated variants of this technique are available in which a range of different types of relationship between variables are evaluated – i.e. in addition to basic positive and negative causality. The research participant whose cognitive map is depicted in Figure 7.3, for example, has differentially weighted the paths identified on the basis of their varying belief strengths concerning each particular causal assertion.

As noted above, there is a considerable range of ways in which causal maps can be derived. The map shown in Figure 7.2, for

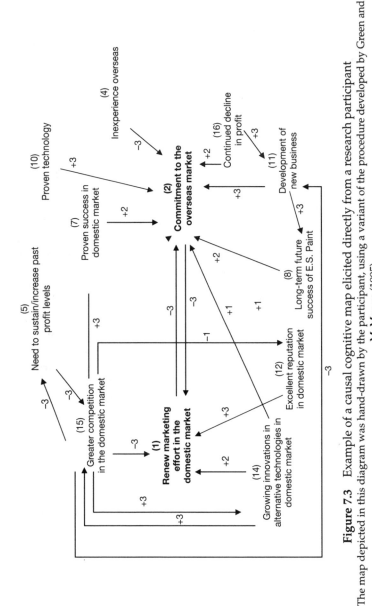

Figure 7.3 Example of a causal cognitive map elicited directly from a research participant

The map depicted in this diagram was hand-drawn by the participant, using a variant of the procedure developed by Green and McManus (1995)

Source: G.P. Hodgkinson and A.J. Maule (2002) The individual in the strategy process: insights from behavioural decision research and cognitive mapping, in A.S. Huff and M. Jenkins (eds) *Mapping Strategic Knowledge.* London: Sage. © Sage Publications Ltd.

example, was derived indirectly through documentary sources, whereas the map depicted in Figure 7.3 was elicited directly from the participant, using a semi-structured questionnaire under laboratory conditions. Each of these approaches is characterized by particular strengths and weaknesses. From a research point of view, the main strength of the documentary approach lies in the fact that it is 'non-intrusive'. This enables investigators to access strategic knowledge without unduly influencing the thought processes of the participant – a primary weakness of direct elicitation procedures, when used in a research context. On the other hand, a major limitation of the documentary approach is the fact that documents are often prepared for particular audiences. Consequently, they are likely to represent a biased source of information. An advantage of direct elicitation procedures is that they enable the researcher to focus the discussion on issues of concern to the investigation. However, there is a danger that participants may be led to think in unnatural ways and that the resulting maps are merely an artefact of the elicitation procedure(s) employed. Such 'reactivity' is likely to be less of a problem in the context of intervention work, where the aim is to challenge actors' beliefs and taken-for-granted assumptions.

An intermediate approach between documentary methods and highly structured direct elicitation methods, entails use of the face-to-face interview in order to elicit the relevant background information, which in turn is coded independently by multiple trained assessors in order to derive a causal map (see, e.g., Calori *et al.* 1992, 1994; Jenkins and Johnson 1997a, 1997b; Maule *et al.* in press). While this approach has much to commend it, as in the case of the documentary approach, often the process of coding the data can be very cumbersome. In sum, the choice of elicitation procedure in causal mapping applications is far from straightforward (see also Box 7.1).

Memory errors in causal mapping

Drawing on work on different types of memory error (see Box 7.2), Hodgkinson *et al.* (2000) have argued that hand-drawn maps may underestimate the true complexity of actors' mental representations, including only a sub-set of those variables actually used to

---

Box 7.1: Hand-drawn versus pairwise comparison procedures for the direct elicitation of causal cognitive maps

Clearly there is much work yet to be done to unravel the complexities surrounding the question as to which elicitation procedures are more or less appropriate for particular purposes of application in respect of causal maps. A recent study by Hodgkinson *et al.* (2000) helped shed light on this problem. It investigated the relative efficacy of two rather different procedures for the direct elicitation of causal cognitive maps: a structured questionnaire-based approach, entailing pairwise evaluations of causal relationships, and a relatively direct approach involving the production of influence diagrams drawn by hand. The relative merits of the two approaches were evaluated by means of a counterbalanced within-participants experimental design. Managers' causal belief systems regarding a strategic investment decision were elicited using both approaches and compared by means of various structural measures, each designed to capture the extent to which the resulting maps were psychometrically comparable across the differing task conditions. In addition, participants' reactions to the mapping tasks were investigated using a series of Likert scale items. As predicted, the pairwise approach yielded relatively elaborate maps, but the participants found the task to be more difficult, less engaging and less representative of the ways they thought about the decision problem in comparison to the freehand approach. On the basis of a task analysis, the researchers argued that each approach places fundamentally differing demands on the participant in respect of the underlying memory mechanisms involved. Whereas the pairwise method is heavily dependent upon recognition mechanisms, freehand mapping is predominated by recall. Consequently, both approaches are likely to yield inaccurate representations of individuals' mental models, but with fundamentally different types of error.

Source: Hodgkinson *et al.* (2000)

---

make the decision. However, what is included in these maps is highly likely to have been incorporated in the actors' mental representation at the time of the decision. The pairwise comparisons technique, by contrast, is likely to include more of the

---

Box 7.2: Two types of memory error

In discussing differences between recognition and retrieval, Baddeley (1990) identified two kinds of memory error. The first, errors of commission or false positives, occurs when people report something that was not present. In the context of the Hodgkinson *et al.* (2000) study outlined in Box 7.1, this would involve participants reporting a causal relation that was *not* part of their original representation of the problem. The second type, errors of omission or false negatives/misses, occurs when people fail to remember something that *was* present. In the context of the Hodgkinson *et al.* study, this would involve participants failing to report a causal relation that was actually part of their original mental representation of the problem. Baddeley has argued that recognition involves fewer errors of omission but more errors of commission.

Source: Baddeley (1990)

---

variables that were present in the actor's mental representation, but also additional variables that were not. Hence, participants would be expected to be particularly vulnerable to commission errors that reflect more stable and enduring aspects of their mental models (cf. Daniels *et al.* 1995).

Baddeley's (1990) explanation of memory errors has important implications for deciding which mapping technique to use in any particular situation. It suggests that researchers should assess the likely impact of these two different kinds of error on their overall objectives, and choose the method that minimizes the potential for such errors to undermine these objectives. For example, in the context of a prescriptive application of mapping that aimed to develop a richer and more elaborate understanding of a decision problem, the costs of omission errors would be higher than those resulting from errors of commission, given that the primary aim is to elaborate an actors' understanding of the problem. Commission errors provide a source of new information to elaborate the actor's mental model of the problem. In contrast, an alternative application might involve identifying the extent to which particular groups of senior managers have common or shared understandings of a complex strategic problem. Here, the costs of commission errors may be higher, given that they may lead to an overestimation of consensus and a failure to recognize the need to address important differences in actors' understandings of the problem (cf. Daniels *et al.* 1994; Hodgkinson and Johnson 1994).

The general implications arising from the findings of the Hodgkinson *et al.* (2000) study are that in future, researchers employing causal mapping techniques should not assume that relatively direct, less time-consuming methods for eliciting participants' cognitions are psychometrically comparable to their more cumbersome and time-consuming counterparts. Rather, the choice of elicitation procedure needs to be carefully justified, taking into account the nature of the specific research question and the substantive knowledge domain under investigation.

Comparing causal maps

While relatively simple causal maps can be conveniently summarized visually, this medium is not so convenient in situations where the purpose is to investigate the properties of much larger maps or to compare maps across large numbers of participants or over several points in time. Under these circumstances it is more appropriate to employ the various specialist coding procedures (e.g. Wrightson 1976; Huff *et al.* 1990) and numerical measures, based on the mathematics of graph theory (Axelrod 1976; Langfield-Smith and Wirth 1992), that have been derived for the qualitative and quantitative analysis of causal maps. Fortunately, there have been a number of recent developments in terms of software and associated algorithms that can be readily implemented in order to facilitate such analyses (Eden *et al.* 1992; Laukkanen 1994; Markoczy and Goldberg 1995; Wang 1996). One such development is highlighted in Box 7.3.

The primary advantage of the Markoczy-Goldberg procedure, highlighted in Box 7.3, lies in the fact that participants' judgements are elicited on a systematic basis using a common language format. This greatly facilitates the analysis of the resulting maps, obviating the need for cumbersome, post hoc coding procedures – unlike the ideographic procedures devised by Laukkanen (1994)

Box 7.3: A technique for eliciting and comparing causal cognitive maps

Markoczy and Goldberg (1995) have devised a systematic method for eliciting and comparing causal maps. Building on the earlier work of Langfield-Smith and Wirth (1992), Markoczy and Goldberg (1995: 30) advocate the following five-stage procedure for use in situations where there is a requirement to investigate the linkages between cognition and other characteristics of the participant:

1 Develop a *pool* of constructs by conducting and analyzing interviews with managers and a review of relevant literature – this is done prior to the study so that each subject selects constructs from the same pool.
2 Have each subject select a fixed number of constructs by identifying items from a constant pool of constructs.
3 Construct the causal map of each individual subject by having her/him assess the influence of each of her/his selected constructs on her/his other selected constructs.
4 Calculate distance ratios between causal maps using a generalized version of Langfield-Smith and Wirth's (1992) formula.
5 Perform a variety of statistical tests on the distance ratios to identify what characteristics account for similarities in thinking.

The distance ratio (DR) formula assesses the overall degree of similarity versus dissimilarity between a given pair of maps. DRs range between zero and unity inclusive, values of zero indicating that a given pair of maps are identical in all respects, values of 1 indicating total dissimilarity. The distances derived from this procedure can be meaningfully employed to investigate patterns of similarity and difference among sub-groups of participants, in addition to conducting correlational analyses. To conduct such analyses, it is first necessary to empirically derive multiple clusters of participants using cluster analysis. Once the centre of each cluster has been identified, distances between the centres and each individual map can be calculated. In turn, these distances form the basis for performing standard statistical analyses. Markoczy (1997) adopted this approach in a recent investigation of the validity of using external, individual characteristics as a proxy for executive cognition. This study was reviewed in considerable detail in Chapter 5.

Source: Markoczy and Goldberg (1995); Markoczy (1997)

---

and Eden *et al.* (1992) which are highly labour intensive by comparison (Hodgkinson 2001a).

Goldberg (1996) has devised a set of computer programs, known collectively as 'the distrat/askmap suite of programs', which perform various tasks associated with the Markoczy-Goldberg approach. Although these programs are available to researchers on a non-commercial basis, as observed by Hodgkinson (2001a) the various algorithms are not in a form that readily facilitate the transfer of input and output data to and from other systems, especially of the larger, fully integrated, interactive variety. Nevertheless, the Markoczy-Goldberg approach to comparative causal mapping represents a significant methodological breakthrough which stands to greatly enrich the quality of future investigations that require the systematic comparison of causal cognitive maps in the search for empirical correlates of strategic cognition, as for example in the case of research into cognitive processes in top management teams (see Chapter 5).

Causal mapping techniques as a basis for organizational intervention

As noted earlier, causal mapping techniques and related procedures are increasingly being used as a tool of intervention for facilitating strategy development in private and public sector organizations (Eden 1990, 1993; Morecroft 1994; Eden and Ackermann 1998). However, to date there have been virtually no studies demonstrating their efficacy for use in this context. To the extent that cognitive biases of the sort identified by behavioural decision researchers, under laboratory conditions, can be attenuated by recourse to causal mapping, this would provide tangible evidence that potentially there are indeed positive benefits to be gained from the use of these techniques in practical settings.

Following this line of reasoning, Hodgkinson *et al.* (1999) investigated the efficacy of one particular variant of causal cognitive mapping as a basis for attenuating the framing bias, a factor known to reduce the quality of decision making in a broad range of situations, and which previous studies have implicated as a contributor to the well documented escalation of commitment phenomenon in the context of strategic reinvestment decisions (Bateman and Zeithaml 1989a). As discussed in Chapter 1, this bias arises when trivial changes to the way in which a decision problem is presented, emphasizing either the potential gains or potential losses, lead to reversals of preference, with decision makers being risk averse when gains are highlighted and risk-seeking when losses are highlighted (Kahneman and Tversky 1984). To overcome this bias, decision makers are encouraged to adopt procedures 'that will transform equivalent versions of any problem into the same canonical representation' (Kahneman and Tversky 1984: 344) in order to bring about the normatively desirable state of affairs whereby individuals' preferences conform to the basic axioms of rational choice. In other words, decision makers need to develop more elaborate models of problems, taking into account the potential gains and losses involved, so as to ensure that trivial features of the decision context do not unduly influence choice behaviour.

Hodgkinson *et al.* (1999) conducted two studies, using elaborated decision scenarios under relatively controlled, experimental conditions. In Study 1, final-year business and management studies undergraduate students were allocated at random to one of four treatment groups: positively vs. negatively framed decision scenarios, with pre-choice versus post-choice mapping task orders. Participants were required to complete a cognitive mapping exercise either before or after making a decision on the basis of the information presented. As predicted, participants allocated to the post-choice mapping conditions succumbed to the framing bias, whereas those allocated to the pre-choice mapping conditions did not. Study 2 adopted a similar approach in an organizational field setting, but employed a sample of senior managers and a decision scenario that closely mirrored a strategic dilemma confronting the organization in question at the time of the investigation. In both cases, the application of causal mapping *prior* to choice eliminated the framing bias, providing supporting evidence for its efficacy as an intervention technique for use in practical settings.

These studies represent but the vital first steps in attempting to demonstrate the practical benefits to be gained from the use of cognitive mapping as a basis for intervening in processes of strategic decision making. As with any new line of inquiry, the findings raise more questions than they resolve. At the time of writing, work is underway to explore the structure and content of participants' cognitive maps, with a view to better understanding the ways in which the framing bias impacts on individuals' mental representations of strategic issues and problems, and the means by which causal mapping attenuates this bias (for further details see Hodgkinson and Maule 2002).

Doubtless more sophisticated research designs are required, involving the use of control groups and the direct comparison of multiple interventions one with another before the value added contribution of cognitive mapping procedures *per se* is truly ascertained. Additional studies are required not only to address these fundamental concerns, but also to determine the extent to which causal mapping will enable strategic decision makers to overcome other cognitive biases, identified by behavioural decision researchers and strategy scholars, as reviewed in Chapter 1 (see also Schwenk 1995; Das and Teng 1999; Maule and Hodgkinson 2002).

In summary, causal mapping techniques are a highly versatile collection of procedures that have been adapted in a variety of ways over the years, both for research purposes and as methods of intervention. Another class of procedures that have proven equally versatile are methods for revealing the 'dimensions of categories and hierarchies among concepts' (Huff 1990: 21) and it is to these techniques that we now turn.

Mapping techniques for revealing dimensional and hierarchical relationships among conceptual stimuli

There are a great many procedures falling within this class. Here we confine our attention to just three. First, we consider qualitative methods based on hierarchical taxonomic interview techniques, following which we discuss two quantitative procedures: scaling and clustering methods based on direct judgements of (dis)similarities between concepts, and repertory grid techniques.

The procedures reviewed have formed the bedrock of research into managerial mental representations of competitive industry structures, outlined in Chapter 4. We revisit some of this work here in order to illustrate the comparative strengths and weaknesses of each particular technique.

Hierarchichal taxonomic interview techniques

These techniques are predicated on the work of experimental cognitive psychologists (reviewed in Chapter 4) which suggests that knowledge stored hierarchically is easier to process and store in long-term memory (Rosch et al. 1976). Drawing on this and the related work of Kempton (1978), Porac et al. (1987, 1989, 1995), Porac and Thomas (1994) and Hodgkinson and Johnson (1994) have devised a set of interview procedures for eliciting and representing hierarchical taxonomic mental models of competitive industry structures. One such procedure, known as the 'top-down, between subjects' approach (Porac and Thomas 1987), was discussed in Chapter 4, but it is worth briefly restating its main features in order to compare later variants, designed to capture individual-level cognitive taxonomies.

The purpose of the top-down, between-subjects variant is to derive an aggregate taxonomy representing the collective cognitions of multiple sub-groups of research participants. An initial sample of participants is required to identify the various sub-categories of business stemming from a starting category, known as the 'root beginner', provided by the interviewer. The data elicited from this sample are then pooled and sorted by an independent panel of judges in order to remove redundant sub-categories. Following this, further samples of participants are used to identify successive levels within the taxonomy, until no further meaningful sub-categories can be identified (for further details, see Chapter 4, Figure 4.2 and Box 4.3). Throughout, the emergent findings are recorded on a portable whiteboard, so that the participant is free to correct or modify their responses as the session progresses. A major limitation is that each successive group of respondents is forced to consider the responses of previous sub-groups in order to generate additional levels in the resulting taxonomy. From an anthropological perspective, considerable caution is required when categories elicited from one individual or sub-group are subsequently imposed on another (Buckley and Chapman 1997). Potentially, the resulting aggregate taxonomy may bear no relation to the 'private' views of the individual participants.

Other variants of this technique, known as 'within-subjects assessments' (Porac and Thomas 1987) enable the researcher to explore the complete taxonomies of individual respondents. One such approach, known as the 'top-down, within-subjects assessment procedure' was employed by Porac *et al.* (1989, 1995) in the Scottish knitwear industry study, discussed in Chapter 4. Using this approach, participants identify the sub-categories emanating from a root beginner supplied by the researcher. Further sub-categories are elicited at successively lower levels, until no further meaningful distinctions can be drawn. Analysis proceeds on a 'depth-first' or breadth-first' basis, but in either case the end result is a complete taxonomy which represents the cognitive structure of the individual respondent. Again, the entire process is recorded on a portable whiteboard, so that participants can moderate their responses, as appropriate. However, as with the top-down, between subjects variant of this technique, the fact that the root beginner is supplied by the researcher means that care must be taken when drawing inferences from the data. A great deal hinges on the adequacy of the procedure by which the starting category was identified at the outset.

One approach to taxonomic interviewing which circumvents the 'native category problem' (Buckley and Chapman 1997) associated with the above variants, is known as the 'self-entry, within-subjects assessment' procedure (Porac and Thomas 1987). As in the case of the top-down, within-subjects assessment procedure, this approach enables the researcher to elicit a complete taxonomy from each respondent. However, rather than providing participants with a common root beginner and proceeding in a top-down fashion, participants are required to generate their own starting category. In order to identify this, they are asked to discuss the nature of their business and what class of business they are in. Following this they are asked to identify any related classes and sub-classes of business. The process is continued upwards, until the participant is unable to generalize usefully any further;

laterally, until all related classes of business have been recorded; and downwards until no further useful distinctions can be made. Having generated the taxonomy, the respondent is asked to indicate which category best describes their own business (the 'organizational self-identity category') and to locate the categories that constitute their major and secondary sources of competitive threat. Once again, the whole process is recorded, using the medium of the portable whiteboard, to permit maximum flexibility.

The self-entry, within-subjects assessment procedure was employed by Hodgkinson and Johnson (1994) in their study of individual and sub-group differences of managerial mental models of competitor definition in the UK grocery retail industry.

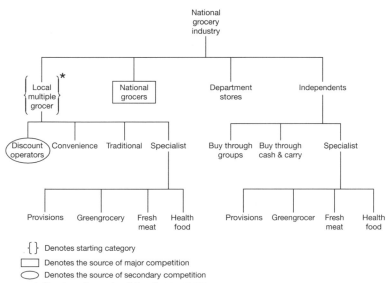

Figure 7.4 Example of a cognitive taxonomy elicited from the CEO of a UK grocery retail organization, using the self-entry, within-subjects assessment procedure

Source: reproduced by kind permission of the publisher from G.P. Hodgkinson and G. Johnson (1994) Exploring the mental models of competitive strategists: the case for a processual approach, *Journal of Management Studies*, 31: 525–51.
© Blackwell Publishers Limited.

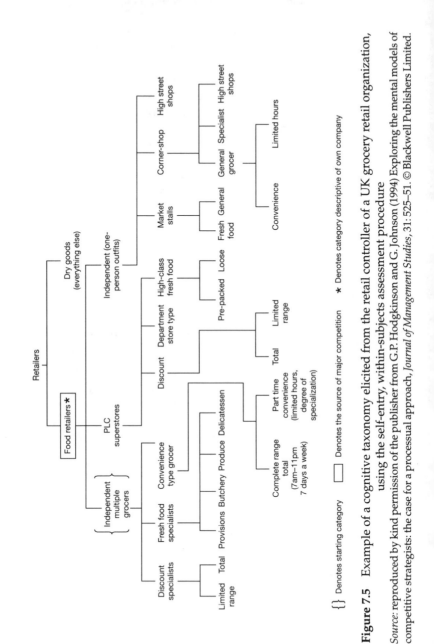

Figure 7.5 Example of a cognitive taxonomy elicited from the retail controller of a UK grocery retail organization, using the self-entry, within-subjects assessment procedure

Source: reproduced by kind permission of the publisher from G.P. Hodgkinson and G. Johnson (1994) Exploring the mental models of competitive strategists: the case for a processual approach, *Journal of Management Studies*, 31: 525–51. © Blackwell Publishers Limited.

As can be seen from Figures 7.4 and 7.5, considerable variations can emerge from one manager to another, in terms of the richness of the resulting taxonomies (as defined by the number of levels and terminal categories). As noted in Chapter 4 (Box 4.7), the overall pattern of findings emerging from this study suggested that the taxonomic mental models of managers whose roles required them to posses a relatively detailed knowledge of the overall market-place were significantly richer than their counterparts whose roles required less detailed insights.

Similarity-based scaling and clustering techniques

Whereas the cognitive maps resulting from taxonomic interview procedures (all variants) are based purely on the *qualitative judgements* of the research participants, each of the following methods involve *quantitative judgements* and the use of relatively complex multivariate analysis techniques to gain insights into the underlying structure of the data. A detailed consideration of multivariate analysis techniques lies beyond the scope of this book. Here, we can only provide a brief conceptual overview of each procedure, with sample outputs. Interested readers requiring further information should consult the accompanying references, each of which will provide the necessary technical background. More generally, Tabachnik and Fidell (1996) have produced a highly accessible overview of multivariate analysis techniques as a whole.

We begin with a consideration of similarity-based scaling and clustering methods. These techniques for eliciting and representing actors' cognitions of strategic issues and problems centre on the analysis of participants' judgements of the (dis)similarities of conceptual stimuli. Such stimuli might include various contrasting strategic issues, a portfolio of strategic business units or a range of competing brands or business competitors. Judgements of (dis)similarities can be elicited directly in pairwise fashion from the participants, using an m-point rating scale. The resulting data are then averaged across the sample as a whole, separately for each pair of stimuli in turn, to derive a 'proximities matrix' which can be submitted to a variety of multivariate analysis techniques in order to investigate its structural properties.[2]

Table 7.1 presents an example of a proximities matrix from a study of consumers' mental models of competing retail stores and product brands (Hodgkinson *et al.* 1991). Participants were required to evaluate a number of competing stores and brands using a six-point rating scale, with responses ranging from 1 (very dissimilar) to 6 (very similar). The raw data associated with this study were reverse-scored, prior to aggregation.

An analogy is helpful at this juncture. Think of proximities data of the form contained in Table 7.1 as the psychological equivalent to a table of distances in a road atlas. Smaller values (distances) within the table represent greater levels of similarity between the stimuli in question. Thus, *The Sun* and *The People* ($d = 1.55$) are relatively similar in comparison to *The Sun* and *Financial Times* ($d = 6.00$), the latter being highly dissimilar to one another.

Two techniques that have proven to be useful for the analysis of proximities matrices are multidimensional scaling (MDS) and hierarchical cluster analysis. MDS refers to a collection of procedures whose primary goal is to capture the information contained within proximities matrices in the form of a spatial representation comprising as few dimensions as possible, without unduly distorting the data (Kruskal and Wish 1978). MDS techniques seek to construct 'maps' which preserve the relative distances between stimuli. Stimulus elements located closer together within the map are more closely related (i.e. relatively similar) to one another in comparison to their 'distant' counterparts. Whereas geographical distances are usually represented in two dimensions (north–south and east–west), perceptual maps based on conceptual stimuli may require a greater number of dimensions in order to represent adequately the underlying structure of the participants' judgements; typically MDS solutions range from two to four dimensions.

---

2 There are of course additional ways in which the structural properties of direct similarities data can be investigated, beyond the use of techniques for revealing dimensional and hierarchical relationships. One class of procedures, known as 'block modeling', has been employed widely in the analysis of social networks (see, e.g., Krackhardt 1987, 1990; Wasserman and Faust 1994). Increasingly, block modelling procedures and related techniques are being used by researchers with an interest in the socio-cognitive analysis of strategic groups (e.g. Lant and Baum 1995; Porac *et al.* 1995; Odorici and Lomi 2001).

Table 7.1 Mean ratings of overall similarity-dissimilarity for various pairs of competing newspapers

	1	2	3	4	5	6	7	8	9	10	11	12	13	14	15
1 The Sun															
2 Daily Mirror	1.9														
3 Daily Star	1.7	2.0													
4 Today	3.0	2.7	3.6												
5 Daily Express	3.3	3.0	3.3	2.1											
6 Daily Mail	3.4	3.1	3.2	1.6	1.6										
7 The Independent	5.8	5.2	5.4	4.8	4.7	4.3									
8 The Guardian	5.8	5.3	5.5	4.8	4.8	1.9	2.1								
9 The Times	5.6	5.4	5.9	4.6	4.4	4.3	2.1	2.2							
10 The Daily Telegraph	5.5	5.3	5.4	4.6	4.2	4.1	1.8	2.7	1.8						
11 Financial Times	6.0	5.8	5.7	5.4	5.4	5.1	2.6	3.0	2.4	2.5					
12 News of the World	1.1	2.3	1.8	3.0	3.6	3.5	5.6	5.7	5.8	5.5	6.0				
13 The Observer	5.8	5.4	5.5	4.3	4.2	4.2	1.6	2.0	1.9	2.3	2.6	5.5			
14 The People	1.5	2.3	1.8	2.8	3.1	3.5	5.4	5.6	5.6	5.4	5.9	1.6	5.4		
15 Yorkshire Post	4.2	3.7	3.9	3.7	3.6	3.4	4.1	4.3	4.7	4.9	5.2	4.1	4.8	4.2	
16 Sheffield Star	3.8	3.0	2.7	3.5	3.8	3.6	4.9	4.9	5.3	5.0	5.7	3.7	5.2	3.1	2.5

Source: reproduced by kind permission of the publisher from G.P. Hodgkinson, J. Padmore and A.E. Tomes (1991) Mapping consumers' cognitive structures: a comparison of similarity trees with multidimensional scaling and cluster analysis, *European Journal of Marketing*, 25(7): 41–60. © MCB University Press Limited.

Figure 7.6 presents an example of a two-dimensional cognitive map of local and national newspapers derived from the proximities data shown in Table 7.1. The first dimension has been labelled 'general quality' in order to reflect the fact that those newspapers targeted at the top end of the market (*The Guardian*, *Financial Times* etc.) tend to be separated out from those targeted at the lower end (*The Sun*, *News of the World*, *Daily Star* etc.). The former are renowned for their in-depth coverage of newsworthy and topical events, together with high standards of journalism; the latter tend to be associated with sensationalism – i.e. the so-called 'gutter press'.

The second dimension, labelled 'awareness,' reflects the tendency for the *Sheffield Star* and *Yorkshire Post* to separate from the rest of

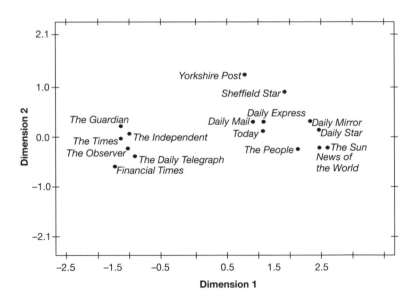

Figure 7.6 MDS representation of various competing newspapers
Source: reproduced by kind permission of the publisher from G.P. Hodgkinson, J. Padmore and A.E. Tomes (1991) Mapping consumers' cognitive structures: a comparison of similarity trees with multidimensional scaling and cluster analysis, *European Journal of Marketing*, 25(7): 41–60. © MCB University Press Limited.

the newspapers, as they have relatively small circulation sizes and are confined to a particular locality of the UK.

Hierarchical clustering techniques also seek to provide a pictorial representation of the information contained within proximities matrices, but in the form of a hierarchical tree diagram. In this case, concepts that are judged to be more similar to one another are grouped together within common branches of the tree, while dissimilar concepts are allocated to different branches. One particular form of hierarchical clustering procedure that has been found to be especially useful in the analysis of pairwise similarities judgements of conceptual stimuli (of the form presented in Table 7.1) is known as *additive similarity tree* (ADDTREE) analysis (Sattath and Tversky 1977). Figure 7.7 presents the results of an ADDTREE analysis applied to the dataset of Table 7.1.

It can be seen that the newspapers fall into three clear groupings: a group comprising the tabloid press (*The Sun, News of the World, The People, Daily Star, Daily Mirror, Daily Express, Daily Mail* and *Today*); a group comprising a range of relatively high-quality national newspapers (*The Times, The Daily Telegraph, The Independent, The Observer, The Guardian,* and *Financial Times*); and a group comprising the two regional newspapers (*Yorkshire Post* and *Sheffield Star*).

We recommend that readers interested in the details of the underlying theory and supporting software for MDS, ADDTREE and related clustering techniques should consult Kruskal and Wish (1978), Corter (1996) and Aldenderfer and Blashfield (1984) respectively.

It should be noted that while the use of direct (dis)similarities judgements of the sort highlighted in Table 7.1 has a long and distinguished history in psychology and management research, there are several potential problems associated with this approach. First, given the abstract nature of the rating scales employed, it is not clear on what basis the various judgements have been derived. The fact that a given pair of stimuli are judged to be more or less similar or dissimilar to one another is not very informative. In what ways are the stimuli in question (dis)similar?

Tversky (1977) has demonstrated that globalized (dis)similarity judgements of many conceptual stimuli (of the sort shown in Table 7.1) are often better represented using non-spatial modelling

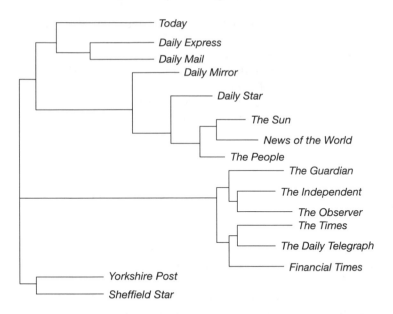

Note that the relative lengths of the branches (i.e. the horizontal path lines from the root of the tree, terminating at the stimuli) denote the extent to which the various stimuli and groups of stimuli are similar/dissimilar to one another. The shorter the total horizontal distance (branch-length) between stimuli, the greater their degree of overall similarity and *vice versa*.

Figure 7.7   Representation of various competing newspapers derived through the application of ADDTREE

Source: reproduced by kind permission of the publisher from G.P. Hodgkinson, J. Padmore and A.E. Tomes (1991) Mapping consumers' cognitive structures: a comparison of similarity trees with multidimensional scaling and cluster analysis, *European Journal of Marketing*, 25(7): 41–60. © MCB University Press Limited.

techniques, based on an alternative to the basic Euclidean distances model underpinning many standard MDS and clustering procedures. In fact, this alternative, known as the *contrast model*, in which such judgements are modelled as a combination of common and distinctive features, underpins the ADDTREE algorithm employed by Hodgkinson *et al.* (1991, 1996), as illustrated in Figure 7.7. A second, related procedure, beyond the scope of this book, known as EXTREE (Corter and Tversky 1986), is also underpinned by a feature-based model. This technique has also been successfully employed by Hodgkinson and his colleagues in the analysis of consumers' mental representations of competition (see Hodgkinson *et al.* 1991, 1996).

Another major drawback associated with the pairwise comparisons rating technique illustrated above is that the number of judgements participants are required to perform increases dramatically as a function of the number of stimuli employed within a given study. Even with moderate numbers of stimuli, the number of pairwise comparisons becomes quite large, thus placing a considerable burden on all but the most dedicated of research participants. Not surprisingly, participants often find this laborious procedure rather tedious to perform. There is a substantial body of psychological theory and research (reviewed in Farjoun and Lai 1997) demonstrating that when individuals are required to evaluate conceptual stimuli in this way, all too often the judgements are flawed. Similarity judgements have been found to be both context sensitive and asymmetric, for example, and when faced with numerous complex judgements, individuals tend to use heuristics in order to simplify the processing of information (Tversky 1977; Tversky and Gati 1978).

Repertory grid and related techniques

An alternative approach is to require participants to evaluate separately in turn each stimulus using a variety of bipolar rating scales associated with a range of attributes. A group of interrelated procedures, known collectively as *repertory grid techniques* have proven highly popular in this connection.

These techniques originated in the field of clinical psychology, based on the notions of *personal construct theory* (Kelly 1955). This theory is based on the fundamental premise that individuals behave in a manner akin to natural scientists as they go about their everyday business, formulating hypotheses about their worlds, which they then seek to 'validate' through observation. To the extent that their hypotheses are confirmed, individuals' personal construct systems remain intact. In the event that their hypotheses are falsified, however, individuals will set about the task of revising their construct systems.

The primary strength of the repertory grid technique lies in its inherent flexibility, both from the point of view of data collection and analysis (Slater 1976, 1977; Fransella and Bannister 1977; Smith and Stewart 1977; Dunn and Ginsberg 1986; Ginsberg 1989; Reger 1990b) and in recent years this approach has come to enjoy considerable success in applied studies of social cognition, in a wide variety of domains well beyond its clinical roots and ideographic origins (e.g. Forgas 1976, 1978; Forgas *et al.* 1980; Stewart *et al.* 1981; Smith and Gibson 1988).

In its original form, each participant is required to draw up their own list of stimuli/elements (e.g. various competing firms in a market domain), which in turn are used to elicit bipolar dimensions/constructs (e.g. the attributes differentiating competing firms). The elements are randomized by the researcher and presented to the participant in triads (i.e. three elements are presented at any one time). The participant is required to explain the ways in which any two of the three elements so presented are similar to one another but different from the third. This exercise is continued until it becomes evident that all possible constructs have been elicited. The constructs elicited in this way are used as a basis for forming a series of bipolar rating scales, which the participant is required to use in order to evaluate each of the various elements in turn. The end result is an n × m matrix (or 'grid') containing the participant's complete set of evaluative judgements. These matrices (one for each participant) form the basis for conducting subsequent statistical analyses (usually involving the application of one or more multivariate techniques) in order to represent the participants' cognitive maps of the phenomenon under investigation.

In the field of strategic management, repertory grid techniques have been employed successfully in several studies of competitive industry structures. Reger (1990a), for example, employed a repertory grid approach to elicit the construct systems of her participants in the US banking industry. Daniels *et al.* (1994) also adopted a variant of the technique in their study of firms supplying pumps to the North Sea offshore oil industry, and in their later study exploring the relative influences of task and institutional environments on the formation of managerial mental models of competition in the UK financial services industry (Daniels *et al.* 2002).

(See also Walton 1986; Reger and Huff 1993; Reger and Palmer 1996.)

A major problem in the use of repertory grid procedures, as employed in their conventional, ideographic form (i.e. when participants are free to choose their own elements and constructs) is the question of how the resulting cognitive maps should be subsequently compared with one another. This is especially problematic in the context of large-scale, hypothetico-deductive research (i.e. in situations where the researcher wishes to test a range of hypotheses using standard statistical procedures). If participants have based their judgements on different elements and constructs, how can the resulting maps be meaningfully compared with one another? This was the problem confronting Daniels *et al.* (1994, 2002) in their recent studies of managerial mental models of competition.

In an attempt to circumvent this problem, Daniels *et al.* have devised a procedure whereby participants are required to rate the similarity of one another's maps (derived using cluster analysis and related multivariate procedures) to their own, personal mental model prevailing at the time the similarity rating tasks are performed. In their study of the UK financial services industry, for example, Daniels *et al.* (2002) required their participants to judge the degree of similarity between their maps using two 5-point Likert-type scales, comprising a dissimilarity scale (1 = 'The same as my view of the competitive environment', 5 = 'Not at all similar to my view of the competitive environment') and a comprehension scale (1 = 'I can easily understand the logic underlying this map', 5 = 'I cannot understand any logic underlying this map'). Responses to these two scales were combined in order to derive an overall similarity score. The overall scores for each map were then averaged across the various raters in an attempt to increase 'measurement accuracy'. This approach, as a basis for comparing cognitive maps, has been extensively criticized by Hodgkinson (2001a, 2002) on the grounds that the resulting ratings are likely to result in highly biased data in favour of the substantive research hypotheses under test.

The use of globalized similarities rating scales is problematic because it is not clear on what basis the judgements elicited have been derived, and because such judgements are far from objective, as demonstrated by Tversky (1977) and Tversky and Gati (1978). These and other limitations discussed in Hodgkinson (2001a, 2002) render the use of similarities rating scales unsuitable for objective hypothesis testing of the sort attempted by Daniels *et al.* Ultimately, if cognitive maps are to be compared systematically, as noted by Markoczy and Goldberg (1995), the maps to be subjected to the comparison process also need to be elicited on a systematic basis (for a counter-view to Hodgkinson's criticisms see Daniels and Johnson 2002).

In a development paralleling the Markoczy-Goldberg advance in the systematic elicitation and comparison of causal maps, Hodgkinson (1997b) devised a procedure for systematically eliciting and comparing dimensional representations of competitor categories in his longitudinal study of the UK residential estate agency industry, reviewed earlier (see Box 4.5). This procedure utilizes a 'three-way scaling' (Arabie *et al.* 1987) or, equivalently, 'weighted multidimensional scaling' (Schiffman *et al.* 1981) approach to compare maps elicited via a modified repertory grid technique. In this system, which entails a substantial departure from Kelly's (1955) personal construct theory, both the elements and the constructs are supplied by the researcher, on the basis of a careful preliminary investigation involving the use of industry insiders and the consultation of relevant documentary sources to ensure comprehensiveness in terms of the coverage of the domain to be mapped, and that the rating tasks are meaningful for the individual participants (cf. Markoczy and Goldberg 1995). The elements comprise a personalized list of named competitors, elicited in response to a series of standardized category titles, each depicting a different type of competitor. Participants are required to evaluate in turn each of the competitors contained within their individual, personalized lists (including their own firm) using the various bipolar rating scales (constructs) supplied by the researcher on the basis of the preliminary industry study. Using a procedure for the analysis of 'profile proximities' as set out in Kruskal and Wish (1978: 70–3), the data derived can be formed into a series of Euclidean distance matrices, which in turn form the basis of a three-way scaling exercise.

Proximities matrices are derived by comparing in turn the average profile of ratings across the various attributes for each pairwise combination of stimuli. For each combination a distance score is derived, reflecting the extent to which the attribute profiles are similar or dissimilar. The more closely a given pair of profiles resemble one another, the smaller the distance score derived for the pair of stimuli in question. Conversely, the greater the dissimilarity between the profiles, the greater the accompanying distance score. Datasets which have been transformed in this way are amenable to analysis by a variety of MDS and clustering techniques in much the same way as proximities matrices based on direct pairwise comparisons of overall (dis)similarity (for technical details see Kruskal and Wish 1978: 70–3).

Adopting this approach, Hodgkinson (1997b) found that a two-dimensional group space configuration ('quality' × 'market power') meaningfully represented the aggregated judgements of 206 participants, drawn from 58 organizations (see Figure 7.8). Participants were required to assess 20 competitor categories using a total of 21 bipolar rating scales. A follow-up investigation of a sub-sample of 114 of the original participants from 41 of the organizations was conducted some 12–18 months later. It revealed that neither the group space configuration nor the 'source weight' (Arabie et al. 1987) vectors, reflecting individual differences in the relative salience of the underlying dimensions of the group space configuration, differed significantly, despite a highly significant downturn in the domestic housing market from Time 1 to Time 2. Hodgkinson interpreted these findings as offering strong support for the cognitive inertia hypothesis (i.e. the notion that once formed, actors' assessments of competitors become highly resistant to change, often to the detriment of the individuals and organizations concerned) (see also Reger and Palmer 1996).

As noted by Hodgkinson (2001a, 2002), with a little imagination on the part of future researchers, this procedure could be adapted to facilitate the rigorous investigation of actors' mental representations of a range of strategic issues and problems. As with the Markoczy-Goldberg procedure, the fact that participants' judgements are elicited on a systematic basis, the stimuli to be rated and the bipolar rating scales forming the bases of the judgements both being presented in a common language format, greatly facilitates the analysis of the resulting maps, obviating the need for cumbersome, *post hoc* coding procedures. As with several of the taxonomic

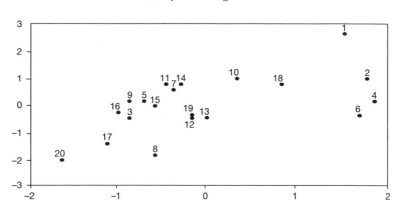

Note: dimensions revealed via application of a three-way multidimensional scaling analysis of profile proximities matrices based on the full sample of respondents at Time 1. This solution accounts for approximately 84.6% of the variance in the original input proximities matrices. In total 21 matrices were scaled, each matrix reflecting the aggregate judgements of N = 206 participants averaged over one particular bipolar attribute rating scale.

Key
1 My Business
2 My major competitor
3 A solicitor agent
4 An estate agent owned by a building society
5 A traditional estate agent
6 An estate agent owned by an insurance company
7 An estate agent offering a professional service
8 An estate agent with a poor reputation
9 An estate agent with chartered surveyor status
10 An estate agent specializing in exclusive property
11 An estate agent specializing in commercial and industrial property
12 An estate agent specializing in residential property
13 A secondary competitor
14 An estate agent with a good reputation
15 A diversified estate agent
16 An independent estate agent
17 An inferior competitor
18 A very successful estate agent
19 A moderately successful estate agent
20 An unsuccessful estate agent

Figure 7.8   Two-dimensional representation of 20 estate agency categories

Source: reproduced by kind permission of the publisher from G.P. Hodgkinson (1997a) Cognitive inertia in a turbulent market: the case of UK residential estate agents, *Journal of Management Studies*, 34: 921–45. © Blackwell Publishers Limited.

interview procedures reviewed earlier, however, considerable care is required in order to ensure that the categorical stimuli and attributes presented to the participants have been carefully selected, so as to minimize the problems identified by Buckley and Chapman (1997), albeit in a rather different context.

In summary, as with causal mapping procedures, researchers have devised a highly flexible collection of methods for the investigation of similarity and association between concepts. Each of these techniques is characterized by their own strengths and limitations. Of the quantitative techniques reviewed in this section, arguably those techniques that obviate the need for the direct pairwise comparison of stimuli (using globalized rating scales of overall (dis)similarity) are the least burdensome. Fortunately, proximity data representing the overall similarity/dissimilarity of stimuli can be derived indirectly from data that has been collected using the less cumbersome bipolar rating scale procedures. As we have seen, datasets which have been transformed in this way are amenable to analysis by a variety of MDS and clustering techniques in much the same way as proximities matrices based on direct pairwise comparisons of inter-stimulus (dis)similarity.

Scenario-based intervention procedures

In Chapter 5 we observed the fact that business history is littered with organizations that have become extinct because they were unable to adapt successfully to major environmental shifts. One explanation for this is the 'cognitive inertia' often found among key individuals and groups in situations where there is clearly an urgent requirement for actors to radically alter their thinking and behaviour. As we have seen, in an effort to reduce the amount of cognitive activity required, experience, captured in long-term memory, can be influential in determining an individual's responses to current situations or stimuli. Actions that worked in the past are routinely applied to the present, so as to free up mental capacity. While such top-down processing is ordinarily functional, a danger is that actors may become overly dependent on their extant mental models of the situations they face, to the extent that they fail to notice the need for change until the key environmental stimuli signalling this requirement have become so widespread and/or significant in other ways, that their organization's capacity for successful adaptation has been seriously undermined.

How can we facilitate individual and collective 'learning' to minimize the potentially catastrophic impact of cognitive bias and inertia? As noted earlier, ultimately what is required is the development of intervention techniques that will enable individuals and groups to explore the largely taken-for-granted operating assumptions and beliefs that drive their day-to-day behaviour, in order that they are able to change and reframe their mental representations so that they register the nature and significance of new events or situations and are able to ensure that the strategic capabilities of the organization are realigned accordingly.

One technique in particular that has increasingly been advocated over recent years for this purpose is the method of scenario planning (Schoemaker 1995; Van der Heijden 1996; Fahay and Randall 1998; Wright and Goodwin 1999; Goodwin and Wright 2001). While there are a variety of approaches to scenario planning, there are several discernible key features common to each which render this technique in general potentially useful for facilitating organizational learning and strategic renewal:

- systematic yet highly flexible;
- highly participative, involving extensive data gathering and reflection, both at an individual and collective level;
- scenario planning techniques force strategists to explicitly confront the changing world and consider its implications for the current strategy;
- not an attempt to predict the future – rather, scenario planning techniques involve the use of speculation and human judgement in an attempt to gain fresh insights and 'bound' future uncertainties.

In contrast to traditional strategic planning techniques, which seek to forecast the future in probabilistic terms in an attempt to plan for a predetermined future, scenario planning techniques seek to develop a series of stylized portraits of the future, capturing what may or may not happen and thereby providing a basis for developing a strategy for dealing with the various contingencies so identified, thus directly incorporating uncertainty in the analysis (van der Heijden 1994). According to van der Heijden (1996: 41) the benefits stemming from the application of scenario methods are twofold:

- in the longer term, development of a more robust organizational system, better able to withstand the unexpected shocks that will come its way;
- in the shorter term, increased adaptability by more skilful observation of the business environment.

A brief illustration of this technique in action, as recently applied by an organization contemplating its technological future, will help to clarify the nature and potential benefits of scenario planning approaches (see Box 7.4). However, we must emphasize the fact that this illustration represents but one form of scenario planning. For details of additional approaches and further illustrative examples, see Fahey and Randall (1998).

As noted above, the object of a scenario planning exercise is to 'bound' the future uncertainties facing an organization. In the case outlined in Box 7.4, Schoemaker and Mavaddat (2000) commenced their exercise by gathering and developing a master list of 74 fundamental drivers (social, political, technological and economic forces) that would likely determine the longer-term shape of the newspaper industry. Working with the senior management team of the organization concerned, these key drivers were rated in terms of their overall importance (relative to the other forces identified) in terms of shaping the future, and were classified into *Trends* (i.e. forces that were deemed to be highly predictable in terms of their overall direction and impact within the timeframe under consideration) and *Key Uncertainties* (i.e. forces that were deemed to be unpredictable). Having screened for obvious redundancy (in terms of their similarity in content and meaning) the various forces were classified in terms of their overall importance and predictability and the results (compiled by means of a survey) were depicted graphically and in tabular form, as shown in Figure 7.9 and Table 7.2 respectively. In turn, this material was employed by a number of teams, comprising a mixture of company personnel and outside advisers, in order to develop a series of scenarios depicting a range of

---

Box 7.4: Scenario planning for disruptive technologies

In the early 1990s, Knight-Ridder's Philadelphia Newspapers Inc., publisher of *The Philadelphia Inquirer* and *The Daily News*, upgraded its printing presses to the tune of $300 million. This long-term investment decision predated the explosion of the World Wide Web, 'the mental landscape' of Knight-Ridder's managers clearly lacking a vivid image of the Web and the impact that this new technology would have on the newspaper industry over future years. Shortly after the new presses had been ordered, the potential ramifications of the Web became all too apparent: would newspapers still exist in 10–20 years' time? Scenario planning was designed to address this kind of dilemma. Through its use, Schoemaker and Mavaddat were able to assist the senior managers of Philadelphia Newspapers Inc. in their strategic sense-making and subsequent deliberations, by amplifying a number of weak signals in the wider technological environment that might otherwise have gone undetected until it was too late for the organization to successfully adapt. When, in 1999, the Xerox organization announced that it was to offer Pressline – a new service that would enable the electronic delivery of newspapers to hotels and other locales – the fact that the management of Philadelphia Newspapers Inc. had been forced to consider a wide range of issues as a result of undertaking a scenario building exercise meant that they were able to interpret the relevance of this announcement through a series of multiple lenses.

Source: Schoemaker and Mavaddat (2000)

---

plausible futures. A 2 × 2 'scenario framework' (traditional versus new business model × minor versus major changes in the use of information by consumers) was developed to generate four major 'scenario blueprints': (a) Business as usual . . . with a twist; (b) Unbundling of information and advertising; (c) Consumers in control; and (d) Cybermedia. The scenarios were each written from the perspective of a historian in the year 2007. They each addressed the following issues (under the differing assumptions as postulated by the respective blueprint):

- a snapshot of what the world would be like in 2007 under that scenario;

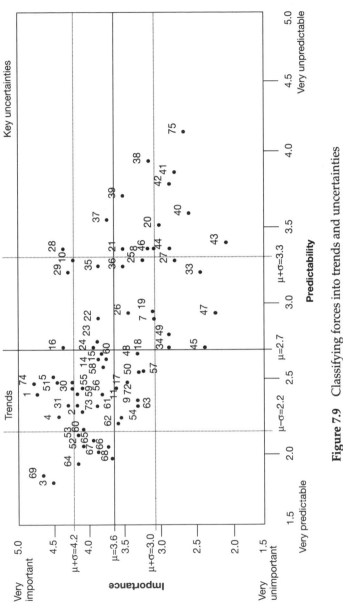

Figure 7.9 Classifying forces into trends and uncertainties

Source: reproduced by kind permission of the publisher from P.J.H. Schoemaker and V.M. Mavaddat (2000) Scenario planning for disruptive technologies, in G.S. Day and P.J.H. Schoemaker with R.E. Gunther (eds) *Wharton on Managing Emerging Technologies*. New York: Wiley. © John Wiley & Sons, Inc.

Table 7.2   Key uncertainties and trends

Key uncertainties

U_1 (F10 + F20). How will the future media companies make money: from selling content and advertising to transactions and commerce?

U_2 (F23 + F24). How will the emergence of highly targeted, interactive and measurable media affect advertising strategies?

U_3 (F28). To what extent will suppliers eliminate intermediaries such as real estate brokers, car dealers etc.?

U_4 (F29). What new intermediaries will emerge?

U_5 (F35). To what extent will privacy of individuals be protected?

U_6 (F37). To what extent will media cross-ownership rules be relaxed?

U_7 How will people prefer to access and use information?

U_8 Who will be the future providers of information?

U_9 (F14, 15, 16, 17, 18). How will the newspaper industry's key classified and retail advertising categories be affected by technological change?

U_{10} To what extent will new revenue sources emerge?

U_{11} (F36). To what extent will environmental regulation of newsprint emerge?

U_{12} (F38). To what extent will anti-trust regulations and legislation change?

U_{13} (F39). To what extent will postal deregulation occur?

Trends

T_1 (F1). Technological change is heating up competition in news and information industries.

T_3 (F3). Information is becoming a commodity product.

T_6 (F30). One-to-one marketing will continue to proliferate aided by an increased use of data.

T_7 (F31). Businesses are placing products in the hands of consumers through new and different channels.

Table 7.2   Continued

Trends

T_{10} (F52). Consuming on the go: consumer multi-tasking, looking for short cuts, consuming on the go.

T_{12} (F54). Telecommuting increasing, which may change reading habits and shopping.

T_{15} (F59). Privacy is becoming a major issue for people, as technology advances have led to increasing incursions into the domain of personal information.

T_{20} (F67). Minority populations are growing and concentrating in certain geographic areas.

T_{23} (F70). Technology has enabled a 'global' economy, where information crosses country boundaries as well as regional boundaries and can be accessed instantaneously, anywhere, at any time.

Source: reproduced by kind permission of the publisher from P.J.H. Schoemaker and V.M. Mavaddat (2000) Scenario planning for disruptive technologies, in G.S. Day and P.J.H. Schoemaker with R.E. Gunther (eds) *Wharton on Managing Emerging Technologies*. New York: Wiley. © John Wiley and Sons, Inc.

- a description of the key events and linkages among them that led to the evolution of that particular world over the ten-year period of 1997–2007;
- a discussion about the strategic implications of the scenarios for the newspaper business model of 1997;
- an illustrative vignette describing a typical 'day in the life' of a key advertiser who needs to make decisions about advertising strategy, or a typical consumer needing information.

Table 7.3 presents several of the key themes associated with each of the four blueprint scenarios. For further details, see Schoemaker and Mavaddat (2000).

Before concluding this discussion, it is important to note that scenario planning is not without its critics. Two problems in particular have been highlighted that the would-be user would be well advised to consider. First, scenario planning is a practitioner-derived method with very little supporting evidence, other than

Table 7.3 Scenario themes

	Scenario A	Scenario B	Scenario C	Scenario D
Consumer markets	Consumers have multiple options across media to access information	Consumers are willing to pay for products that meet unique needs	Consumers are highly dependent on affinity groups, buying clubs etc.	Consumers have numerous choices across multiple media
	Consumers won't pay for content	Highly targeted marketing proliferates	Information sources radically change; new commercial entities emerge	Strong demand for local and tailored information
Technology	Changes the nature of advertising, even in traditional media	Bandwidth challenges resolved	Internet takes off rapidly	New printers allow home printing of custom newspapers
	Bandwidth challenges continue	Intelligent agents abound	Customized delivery dominates, both doorstep and electronic	Inexpensive portable Internet appliances abound
		e-commerce proliferates	e-commerce takes off	
Industry players	Content providers create fierce competition	Niche marketing is a large opportunity	Product companies compete with news providers to create information/ entertainment that customers demand	Hypercompetition is the norm
	Industry consolidation		Custom publishing is an attractive business	

Business models	Heightened economic pressure due to competition	High quality journalism is important	Media companies have multiple revenue streams	Print media are struggling
	Media displace old ones where they're more cost effective	New business models emerge with less focus on advertising	Disintermediation wipes away much of classified ads base	Classified revenue is gravely threatened
Legal issues	Privacy concerns continue; no major changes	Environmental movement progresses	Privacy issues remain important, but unresolved	
	Anti-trust and cross ownership issues still important; no major changes	Privacy regulations pose distribution challenges		
		Libel and slander charges increasing against media companies		

Source: reproduced by kind permission of the publisher, from P.J.H. Schoemaker and V.M. Mavaddat (2000) Scenario planning for disruptive technologies, in G.S. Day and P.J.H. Schoemaker with R.E. Gunther (eds) *Wharton on Managing Emerging Technologies.* New York: Wiley. © John Wiley and Sons, Inc.

basic anecdotal evidence, for its efficacy (though for a notable exception in this respect see Schoemaker 1993). Second, as noted by Mintzberg (1994), accounts of the use of scenarios in the (limited) extant literature have been restricted to 'success stories' such as the case example highlighted in Box 7.4 and Pierre Wack's highly acclaimed account of scenario planning in the Royal Dutch Shell organization (Wack 1985a, 1985b), which enabled the company to anticipate the dramatic shift in the world market for petroleum that occurred in 1973. However, Hodgkinson and Wright (in press), drawing on their experience of a 'failed' intervention in a private sector organization, have highlighted a number of boundary conditions – circumstances in which scenario planning techniques are unlikely to succeed. For a variety of reasons, participants may be unwilling, or unable, to confront the future in the manner that scenario techniques require. It is not always possible to identify viable alternatives to the present course of action, even in situations where major strategic change is clearly warranted. Faced with the unacceptably high levels of decisional stress that such a state of affairs generates, a series of defensive routines are likely to come into play, as predicted by the conflict theory of decision making (Janis and Mann 1977) discussed in Chapter 1.

Concluding remarks

In this chapter we have presented a systematic review of a variety of techniques that have been employed over the years in an effort to capture strategic thinking in a systematic fashion, with a view to better understanding the nature and significance of managerial and organizational cognition in the strategy process and/or for intervening in this process. Regardless of which particular procedures are utilized, and for whatever purpose, ultimately it must be ensured that the techniques yield reliable and valid data. However, as Hodgkinson (2001a) has observed, all too often procedures have been adopted by researchers and practitioners which have yet to be screened in terms of their basic psychometric properties. Virtually none of the procedures reviewed in this chapter, for example, have been subjected to standard tests for ascertaining the extent to which the resulting data are reliable and valid. Such fundamental work is vital if we are to disentangle method effects from substantively meaningful findings. Basic requirements for establishing the psychometric efficacy of assessment procedures for mapping strategic knowledge have been outlined in Hodgkinson (2001a).

The question as to what extent such procedures yield genuine insights into the extant mental models of research participants and/or lead them to generate responses 'online' is an exceedingly complex issue that requires urgent attention. Scholars in the field of attitude measurement have long recognized that actors' beliefs elicited in research settings are the product of a complex interplay between the stimulus materials presented and a combination of computational and retrieval processes (see, e.g., Sandelands and Larsen 1985; Feldman and Lynch 1988). Any attempt to elicit actors' mental representations of organizational phenomena must involve elements of recognition and recall and a combination of computational and retrieval processes, with some elements of the participants' response being constructed online. As noted earlier, for research purposes, where the aim is to try and understand the nature and significance of managerial and organizational cognition in the process of strategizing, as distinct from intervention work, where the aim is to challenge extant mental models and taken for granted assumptions, it is vital that such reactivity is minimized.

One way in which such method effects might be minimized in future research is through the adoption of multiple procedures, each placing different cognitive demands on the research participant. This would greatly increase the degree of confidence that could be placed in a given set of findings, providing of course that the diverse methods so employed gave rise to convergent findings (Eysenck and Keane 1995: 24). In the absence of such convergence, researchers would need to further investigate the properties of the methods adopted, so as to disentangle method effects from substantive findings relating to the phenomena under investigation.

In sum, there is a considerable way to go before we will be in a position to fully understand the interaction between the methods employed to identify actors' mental representations of strategic issues and problems, and the data gathered using these procedures. Wherever possible, therefore, it is highly desirable to utilize a range of assessment procedures in research settings.

From a practitioner standpoint, there is also an urgent need for further research in order to establish the extent to which cognitive mapping (and related procedures such as scenario planning) are genuinely capable of enhancing the quality of strategic decision processes, yielding tangible benefits for organizations. As noted above, the ultimate purpose of these techniques, when used in the context of intervention work, is to challenge the otherwise taken-for-granted beliefs and assumptions of key decision makers, with a view to overcoming a number of fundamental limitations of human information processing. As Hodgkinson (2001a) has observed, it is a matter of great concern that virtually no attempts have been made to rigorously evaluate the efficacy of scenario planning and causal mapping techniques, as methods of intervention, given the widespread popularity of these related procedures for use in this prescriptive fashion.

There are of course limits in terms of the extent to which the various methods of assessment and intervention can yield insights into, and improvements in, the strategic management process. In Chapter 1 we drew attention to Janis and Mann's (1977) conflict theory of decision making. This work highlights the fact the psychological stress of having to confront head-on fundamental problems of a strategic nature may prove too painful to bear for many individuals. Under these circumstances, a series of defensive-avoidance strategies come into play. Unfortunately, the majority, if not all, of these psychological defences are deeply rooted and well beyond conscious awareness (Kets de Vries 1980; Kets de Vries and Miller 1984), and, as the work of Argyris (1999) and Brown and Starkey (2000) has shown, these defences can severely undermine the capacity of organizations to learn from their past mistakes. In the last section of this chapter, we observed the fact that documented cases of failed interventions have been rare. At this point in time, it is not possible to specify under what circumstances cognitive mapping and related procedures are likely to succeed or fail. What is clear, however, is that confronted with extreme, unconscious defensive reactions, of the sort documented by Kets de Vries (1980) and Kets de Vries and Miller

(1984), it is most unlikely that these techniques alone will prove effective as a basis for organizational intervention (Hodgkinson and Wright in press).

In Chapter 2, drawing on the work of Nonaka (1991, 1994), we highlighted the distinction between explicit knowledge and tacit knowledge, arguing that both forms are vital to the processes of organizational learning. The extent to which the various methods surveyed in this chapter can render tacit knowledge explicit – a fundamental prerequisite for the 'knowledge creating company' – is also debatable. As we have seen, many of the processes under-pinning the development, storage, recall and transfer of tacit knowledge are beyond conscious awareness and, as such, may not be accessible through such direct methods of assessment (J. Sparrow 1998).

As we saw in Chapter 6, a number of non-conscious processes lie at the heart of creativity and innovation. The question of how precisely the 'tacit mental material' associated with these pro-cesses might be openly accessed for research and/or intervention purposes is very much at the leading edge of our field. Our dis-cussion of individual-level competencies provided some indi-cations of how this might be accomplished; but we also noted the very real challenges that have yet to be confronted, in terms of ensuring the reliability and validity of the various assessment techniques currently being developed. Beyond the procedures briefly highlighted in Chapter 6, J. Sparrow (1998) has identified a number of developments that are currently taking place in an attempt not only to elicit tacit mental material, but also as a means of gaining access to unconscious forms of interpretation, includ-ing psychodynamic material of the sort alluded to above. Unfor-tunately, consideration of these developments lies beyond the scope of this book. Interested readers should consult J. Sparrow (1998). Once again, however, we would emphasize the consider-able challenges that lie ahead in terms of establishing the reliability and validity of these procedures.

In the final analysis, the rigorous testing of the many theoretical developments currently taking place within the psychology of strategic management is being hampered by a lack of procedures suitable for the mass assessment of managerial and organizational cognition. Few of the techniques surveyed in this chapter yield data in a form amenable to large-scale, multilevel hypothesis testing of the sort required to enable research on the psychology of strategic management to mature beyond its present embryonic status. Fortunately, however, a number of developments are presently occurring, which, over the longer term, should help to rectify this state of affairs.

8

CONCLUSIONS AND FUTURE DIRECTIONS

As noted in the opening chapter, in many ways, the psychology of strategic management is still in its infancy. Nevertheless, the rate and pace at which this new body of work has developed over the past 10–15 years has been such that we have only been able to provide only a selective overview of some of the main issues and themes in strategic management which are currently capturing the attention of managerial and organizational cognition researchers, in order to illustrate some of the potential insights to be gained from the adoption of a psychological approach. In this, our final chapter, we briefly revisit some of the major issues arising from the book as a whole, in order to identify what we consider to be the most pressing priorities for future research.

We have two aims in mind. First, we seek to offer some meta-conclusions – i.e. conclusions on our conclusions. We have surveyed a large volume of theory and research in this book, deriving our principal conclusions in respect of each major theme as we have gone along. At this stage, however, we need to reintegrate this body of work in order to gain an overall sense of the extent to which we have fulfilled the objectives that we set ourselves at the outset. Accordingly, we pull together some of the main conclusions that cut across the key themes that we have variously addressed at different points along the way. In particular, we revisit the notion of strategic competence, considering afresh its utility both for academics and practitioners, in the light of the considerable volume of theory and research reviewed throughout the book as a whole. Second, we present some of the most likely and important directions of future research and scholarship. In so doing, we introduce more theory and research in order to highlight some of the very latest developments that are beginning to form the foci of new work on the psychology of strategic management.

We defined strategic competence as 'the ability of organizations (or more precisely their members) to acquire, store, recall, interpret and act upon information of relevance to the longer-term survival and well-being of the organization' (pp. xiv–xv). Strategic competence, as we have defined it, is a multi-level phenomenon. In part, this competence resides within individuals, comprising the cognitions and behaviours required in order to be best equipped to deal with what is becoming an increasingly complex and turbulent business world. Other aspects of this competence, however, reside among intra- and inter-organizational collectives. As we have seen, the effective management of the processes of dialogue and interaction that create collective memory and learning is central, as is the design of appropriate systems and structures, i.e. systems and structures of a form that enable both a matching and stretching of individuals, and organizational collectives, in terms of their ability to procure and utilize strategic information. In short, we have argued that the strategically competent organization and the learning organization are one and the same entity. Our ultimate goal has been to discover the extent to which the notion of the learning organization and the associated concept of organizational learning might usefully be translated into 'actionable knowledge' (Argyris 1999), i.e. knowledge that is both valid and applicable to the world of practice. Such knowledge is typically encoded in the form of a series of propositions, 'if-then' statements that will automatically follow if particular actions are adopted.

Just how far have we progressed in the development of knowledge that is actionable? At the individual level of analysis, we have made considerable progress, but there are also some clear limitations. Analysis and understanding of the cognitive processes and related behavioural competencies required by all levels of employee, whether they be strategic leaders or individuals who need to influence the strategic thoughts of their colleagues from less formal positions of power, has now begun to approach a relatively sophisticated level. For example, as discussed in Chapter 6, some very useful insights are emerging into the nature and role of individual differences in strategic cognition. Notwithstanding the measurement problems we identified regarding the assessment of the various factors highlighted (particularly in respect of intuition and other forms of non-conscious cognition) there is every prospect that this work will start to add real value to the world of practice in the near future, informing, for example, the design and implementation of assessment and development centres.

At the organizational level of analysis also we have developed some useful insights into the problems posed by new forms of work and organizational design. In particular, we have begun to understand the processes by which knowledge flows to and from individuals – through the deeper institutional structures that exist within organizations that form a central part of the strategic management process. We are also starting to better understand how individuals interact with the knowledge-embedded artefacts that surround them. In addition, through this body of new work, we are beginning to identify a number of potentially dysfunctional consequences that can arise from modern work practices.

We have also identified a number of tools and techniques that have been deployed in an effort to challenge the deeply held assumptions and beliefs of key organizational actors, with a view to facilitating organizational learning and strategic renewal (see Chapters 4 and 7). What is becoming clear is that cognitive mapping and related procedures such as scenario planning are highly effective as a basis for initiating debate and dialogue, through the identification of patterns of belief similarity and difference among groups of organizational actors. These techniques can be deployed in order to surface the likely underestimated strategic risks faced by organizations that might result from errors of judgement and the negative effect of these on performance of employees (cf. Sparrow and West 2002). All in all, considerable progress has been made over a remarkably short time period.

Clearly, industrial, work and organizational psychologists have much to contribute both to an understanding of the strategic management process and to the development of interventions for enhancing this process. In summing up the remarkable achievements of this embryonic area of study, however, it also needs to be acknowledged that the necessary scientific work that will enable the psychology of strategic management to mature into a full-blown field in its own right has barely begun. The scant research attention given to ascertaining the reliability and validity of cognitive mapping techniques and related procedures, for example, means that the extent to which they are truly effective as a basis for fostering strategic competence is far from clear (Hodgkinson 2001a). The potential territory for exploration that we hope this book has opened up is vast, and the research agenda that beckons very exciting indeed. By far the greatest challenge is to demonstrate the link between organizational effectiveness and the various elements of strategic competence that we have identified at the individual and collective levels of analysis.

Validating key components of strategic competence at the individual level

We have argued that the study of effective behaviour at the individual level provides some useful insights into the nature of strategic competence. Recent research has begun to unpack a number of individual differences that lie at the crossroads of cognition and behaviour. In our early chapters, we drew attention to a number of individual-level phenomena that are likely to have a direct bearing on strategic competence, such as information sampling, schema accuracy, generative learning, knowledge elicitation skills and interactive intelligence. Later in the book, we highlighted the importance of dual-processing strategies as a means of enabling managers to skilfully alternate the ways in which they process information, switching back and forth between automatic and controlled modes as and when required. In turn, this led into a discussion of a wide range of individual differences, including locus of control, need for achievement, flexibility, cognitive style, insight and intuition, and creativity and intelligence that each, in differing ways, have a bearing on one or the other mode of processing.

One area of fruitful investigation in future will be to ascertain the degree of linkage between the various relevant individual differences that we have identified and the structure and content of actors' mental representations of strategic issues and problems. We have signalled a number of areas where such linkage is most likely to be demonstrated. First, we can consider the environmental scanning behaviours that influence the formation of actors' mental representations of strategic issues and problems. Strategic competence requires the formation of rich cognitive maps, which in turn require (and enable) high levels of responsiveness to the external environment. In Chapter 6, we drew attention to two individual differences that are likely to be associated with more effective scanning behaviours: locus of control and need for achievement. The capability to process information strategically is associated with proactive attempts to shape the organization's own destiny. Not surprisingly, research has linked the locus of control of CEOs to a number of strategic, structural and performance variables associated with their firms. The way that locus of control influences an individual's field of vision, selective perception and the interpretation of information is now becoming clear (Finkelstein and Hambrick 1996). We argued that it is likely that locus of control differences may also be linked to the structure and content of individuals' mental models, but this conjecture, remains unproven. Similarly, individual differences in *n-ach* are likely to be associated with variations in the structure and content of actors' mental representations of strategic issues and problems, again mediated as a function of differences in environmental scanning behaviour. As we have seen, high *n-ach* individuals and those characterized by relatively internal locus of control beliefs are more likely to attempt to proactively assimilate information in their respective quests to attain their goals, and to gain and maintain mastery over their environments. In both cases, enriched mental models are a fundamental prerequisite.

Cognitive style, learning style, learning strategy and decision making style all impact on the capability of individuals to gather strategic information, organize it, process it appropriately, assimilate it and then evaluate it. We argued that these individual differences determine the way in which the individual arrives at judgements or conclusions based upon their observations. These factors explain the manner, form and nature of performance, as opposed to the capacity to perform (or level of performance) – the latter being accounted for more by the individual's cognitive ability. Cognitive style has proven a particularly useful construct because it has been linked to a number of topics covered in this book, such as organizational learning, the development of shared mental models, the quality of sense-making, decision making and the assessment of risk, and strategic problem formation (see, e.g. Hurst *et al.* 1989; Hayes and Allinson 1998).

However, as discussed in Chapter 6, at the present time many of the individual-level constructs that we have identified as potentially important factors in the attainment of strategic competence are beset by problems of conceptualization and measurement. There is a continuing debate concerning locus of control, for example, in terms of whether this construct is best operationalized using domain-specific or general measurement scales (e.g. Hodgkinson 1992, 1993; Boone and De Brabander 1993; Littunen and Storhammar 2000). The way in which cognitive style, decision making style, learning style, emotional attunement and various of the other constructs identified in Chapter 6 might be best operationalized are similarly the subject of ongoing debates. There has been a proliferation of related measures for the assessment of cognitive style, for instance, and the likely false assumption that these measures are all essentially tapping the same underlying phenomenon (cf. Hayes and Allinson 1994). The reality is probably more complex. As we have seen, there is a continuing debate about the structural nature of cognitive style. In keeping with our dual-processing conception of the strategically competent decision maker, there has been an increasing weight of evidence to support our contention that the analysis and intuition components of cognitive style are in fact separate phenomena, served by fundamentally different cognitive systems (Epstein *et al.* 1996). It also seems highly likely that there is a range of other individual differences closely related to, but separate from, cognitive style. Further research is now needed to clarify which of these best account for the ways in which organizational decision makers process and accommodate and assimilate pertinent information within their mental representations of strategic issues and problems.

There is an emerging consensus that analysis and intuition yield knowledge of a different kind. A central premise of this book is that in an increasingly complex and uncertain world, the capacity to draw upon and elicit intuitions is becoming an important element of strategic competency. We saw the importance of such intuitive processing in relation to organizational learning and knowledge creation in Chapters 2 and 3. Yet again, however, a major barrier to the use of intuition in the workplace has been the lack of available psychometrically sound instruments, suitable for its assessment. To a certain extent, recent advances in instrumentation such as the development of the CSI (Allinson and Hayes 1996) and the CSA (Riding 1991a, 1991b) have ameliorated this situation, although there is still considerable controversy surrounding the conceptualization and measurement of intuition in workplace and other settings. Not surprisingly, its operationalization for research purposes has proven equally problematic. If this construct is to realize its full potential, we need to clarify precisely which of the many competing definitions are the most useful, both from a theoretical standpoint and for the purposes of practical intervention. There is also an urgent need to clarify the interrelationships between the various instruments presently available that purport to measure this construct, before we embark on the development and validation of yet more new measures.

Creativity seems to be an inseparable twin of intuition and insight. It too is slowly being unpacked as a cognitive process. The role of a number of generative and exploratory processes that take place in the mind of the individual is being revealed and understood, as is the functioning of pre-inventive mental structures. It is also apparent that while creativity draws upon some generic cognitive processes, it is not a generic skill that can be mastered. Rather, it seems to take on particular forms across different domains of knowledge. Here also, there are a number of nontrivial conceptual and methodological issues that need to be confronted if the insights arising from this work are to be rendered actionable in the form of interventions for facilitating the strategic management process. The same is true of a number of the other individual-level constructs that we have identified at varying points, not least the notions of transactive memory and emotional attunement. In the case of transactive memory and emotional attunement, however, these difficulties are further compounded, by virtue of the relational connotations implied by these constructs.

In sum, there are two pressing concerns that need to be addressed in future research in respect of the wide range of individual-level factors that we consider to have a major bearing on the attainment of strategic competence:

- the need to clarify the conceptual nature of these factors, and to refine the measurement techniques currently in use as a basis for operationalizing them;
- the need to demonstrate empirical linkages between these factors and the structure and content of individual's mental representations of strategic issues and problems.

There is an urgent need to reconsider what it means to be intelligent in the modern organization, and an effective initiator and implementer of strategic change. Undoubtedly, psychologists face a considerable challenge over the immediate years to come. They will be called upon to make more amenable to assessment the various complex individual-level factors that we have identified. In some cases, this will necessitate the development of more inventive and non-traditional methods of assessment, while ensuring that these new forms possess traditional psychometric qualities such as reliability and validity.

Psychologists will also be called upon to clarify which of the various individual-level characteristics associated with strategic competence are best selected for, and/or are capable of being acquired through training and development. If we wish to foster higher levels of strategic competence, we must ensure that interventions designed with this aim in mind are appropriately informed by psychologically sound research. Undoubtedly, much can be done to foster strategic competency among individuals, but we need to better understand why particular interventions are more or less effective.

The strategic up-side of selective processing

At varying points throughout this book we have drawn attention to the potential dangers associated with the selective processing of strategic information. As we saw in Chapter 1, such processing is necessary due to several fundamental capacity limitations associated with the human information processing system, not least limitations of attention span and working memory. Simon (1947) coined the term 'bounded rationality' in an effort to convey the idea that organizational decision makers strive to behave rationally within the restrictions imposed by their limited capacity information processing systems. The field of behavioural decision making has subsequently illuminated the ways in which such bounded rationality is attained – i.e. through the deployment of heuristics – as well as identifying a number of attendant biases that can arise as a result of such selective processing. While generally acknowledging that there are some potential benefits to be gained, researchers in the field of strategic management (e.g. Barnes 1984; Schwenk 1984, 1995; Das and Teng 1999), like many of their counterparts in the behavioural decision making field, have tended to concentrate on the 'down-side' of heuristic processing, seeking prima facie evidence of cognitive bias through the analysis of actual strategic decisions and laboratory simulations. As we have seen, a number of studies have confirmed that various of the biases identified by behavioural decision researchers would indeed appear to occur in the context of strategic decision making, and, accordingly, work has commenced in an effort to eliminate, or at least attenuate, such biases in this context (Hodgkinson *et al.* 1999; Hodgkinson and Maule 2002; Maule and Hodgkinson 2002).

Recently, however, some sections of the behavioural decision-making community have begun to re-evaluate a number of the premises upon which much of the early work in their field was founded. In particular, Gigerenzer and his colleagues (e.g. Gigerenzer *et al.* 1999) have questioned the extent to which mainstream behavioural decision research, such as that highlighted in Chapter 1, is ecologically valid. They have argued that many of the experimental studies demonstrating the irrationality of human judgement are based on tasks involving probabilistic reasoning and other forms of abstract judgement that are far removed from the real-world environments to which humankind has readily adapted over many years:

> bounded rationality is often characterized as a view that takes into account the cognitive limitations of thinking humans – an incomplete and potentially misleading characterization. If we want to understand how real human minds work, we must look not only at how our reasoning is 'limited' compared to that of supernatural beings, but also at how our minds are adapted to real-world environments. This two-sided conception of bounded rationality should inform our choice of criteria by which to evaluate the performance of heuristics.
>
> (Gigerenzer and Todd 1999: 21)

Based on a fundamentally different conception of bounded rationality, ecological rationality (i.e. 'rationality that is defined by its fit with reality' – Gigerenzer and Todd 1999: 5), Gigerenezer and his colleagues have identified a whole new class of heuristics known as fast and frugal heuristics. These make minimal computational demands on the decision maker, do not involve probabilities and utilities and are deployed in situations that require individuals to draw inferences with limited time and knowledge. According to Gigerenzer and his colleagues, these fast and frugal heuristics complement satisficing heuristics (i.e. heuristics for searching through available alternatives). The latter are deployed in choice situations where the decision maker does not know much about the possibilities ahead of time. In general, individuals are said to behave in an ecologically rational manner when the heuristics they deploy are matched to the structure of the environment they inhabit. Gigerenzer and his colleagues contend that satisficing heuristics, as originally conceived by Simon (1947), and fast and frugal heuristics are both adaptively matched to the real-life environment of the decision maker and, hence, ecologically valid. Both forms of heuristic underpinning ecological rationality are 'simple heuristics that make us smart' (Gigerenzer et al. 1999).

A dramatic illustration of the power of fast and frugal heuristic processing has been provided by Gigerenzer and Todd (1999: 3–5).

Conclusions

Apparently, some 19 separate cues are routinely monitored by staff at the San Diego Medical Centre, University of California, upon admitting heart-attack patients; clearly, the information from each of these cues must somehow be evaluated and then combined in order to arrive at a final conclusion as to whether or not the patient is in imminent danger of cardiac arrest and hence in need of emergency treatment. However, Breiman *et al.* (1993) have devised a simple three-stage decision tree, involving basic dichotomous (yes/no) questions in respect of: (1) minimum systolic blood pressure over the initial 24-hour period (>91?); (2) the age of the patient (>62.5?); and (3) whether or not sinus tachycardia is present. In the event that the patient's blood pressure falls below 91, they are immediately classified as a high-risk case; otherwise, the clinician needs to move on to the second question. Should the answer to this prove negative the patient is classified as a low-risk case; otherwise, an answer to the third question is required, the presence of sinus tachycardia being indicative of high risk. Simple it may be, yet this basic strategy for making what are literally life and death decisions has been found to outperform a number of rather complex statistical classification methods that process and combine all of the available predictors! We observed an analogous situation in Chapter 3, when we considered the notion of 'swarm intelligence' – the application of simple foraging rules within colonies of ants, which has served as a useful model for organization theorists and researchers seeking to gain insights from the field of complexity theory, the science of complex systems (Bonabeau and Meyer 2001).

The work of Gigerenzer and colleagues is beginning to reshape the way in which behavioural decision researchers view bounded rationality, re-emphasizing the 'up-side' of limited information search and informing the design of artificial systems to aid decision making. The fast and frugal heuristic discussed above, for example, could be readily built into emergency-room equipment.

This new line of work is of immense potential significance to the strategic management field. At the very least it should cause us to reconsider afresh the essentially negative message emanating from studies of strategic decisions that have been informed by conventional theory and research from the field of behavioural decision making. While these are very early days indeed for this new body of work, to the extent that we were able to identify such fast and frugal heuristics in the context of real-life strategic decision making, this would greatly further understanding of the 'up-side' of selective information processing, while enhancing our capabilities to design interventions for facilitating the strategic management process. In the meantime, there are still some positive messages to be derived from the work we have reviewed on the cognitive limitations of managers and other organizational actors.

As we saw in Chapter 1, the managerial and organizational cognition perspective highlights a number of potential weaknesses in the way individuals and groups handle information, weaknesses which can (and frequently do) undermine the strategy process. In drawing attention to these dangers, however, we did not wish to imply that selective attention and limited information search are invariably dysfunctional. As with the recent work of Gigerenzer and his colleagues, the work on intuition reviewed in Chapter 6 suggests that there are a number of positive benefits to be gained from the adoption of 'fast and frugal' processing strategies. In the absence of such filtering techniques, we would be greatly over-whelmed by the sheer complexity of the world. Indeed, there are a number of studies indicating that strategies which are simple, coherent and easily understood may lead to better performance than those which are sophisticated and highly complex (Pettigrew and Whipp 1991; Pettigrew and Fenton 2000). Towards the end of Chapter 6 we discussed the competencies of sense-making and sense-giving in this context, and introduced the concept of 'simplification routines'. A simplified view of the world may help unite organization members – undoubtedly a key factor in successful strategy implementation. (But note also the attendant dangers of competency traps and progressing organizational sim-plicity, as discussed in Chapter 2 and revisited at various points in later chapters.) This discussion signals a fundamental tension within the strategic management process: increasingly, actors must be open enough to consider new and innovative ideas and approaches, but also be single-minded enough to provide the commitment and focus needed to implement such ideas.

Another important research task that has yet to be completed is to integrate this work which has examined the political skills and tactics that appear to underpin the process of sense-giving/ thought leadership at the organizational level, with the voluminous work on individual cognition and leadership behaviours. Once again, we need to confront a number of non-trivial conceptual and measurement issues. In particular, there is a need to unpack the concept of strategic thought leadership in ways that will render it amenable to reliable and valid assessment.

Understanding the implications of new forms of work organization

As we have seen, a number of new organizational forms have begun to emerge in response to the unprecedented changes that are presently occurring in the modern workplace. In Chapter 3 we drew attention to the need to better understand the psychological implications of these new organizational forms, especially in terms of the job demands that they are placing on the individuals and groups working within them. There were several ways in which this became apparent.

In discussing team cognition we highlighted the need to manage the interrelationship between the various activities of group members and to concentrate attention on – and develop a clear understanding of – which cognitions need to be shared. Theoretical ideas abound in this area, but, as yet, there has been very little empirical research. Depending on the structural solutions adopted by particular organizations, and the co-ordination and control demands that these create, very different individual and collective competency requirements might come to light. Moreover, the trade-offs made in respect of organizational design might also impact on the range of psychological issues that have to be managed (Sparrow 1998b).

In Chapter 3 we highlighted the increasingly commonplace problem of information overload. Clearly, the ability to control and manage the quantity and quality of information that flows through the 'intra-organizational information market' is a key element of strategic competence. The number of strategically significant informational interactions that now have to be managed appears to be increasing markedly, following several major developments in information and communication technologies and fundamental changes to the design of organizations. These developments have taken place in the context of a rapidly evolving knowledge-driven economy, in which the brokering of information across internal and external markets is *the* major commodity traded, thus making the need to understand the complexities of organizational learning and the different forms of knowledge that reside within organizations all the more crucial.

We began by highlighting the need to manage at least four types of knowledge and learning within organizations, spanning two orthogonal dimensions: explicit versus tacit; and individual versus collective. As we explored the nature of knowledge management, we also saw that there are in fact multiple ways of knowing within organizations, and that organizational knowledge resides not only within the minds of individuals, but also within collectives and within organizational artefacts. Currently, however, our tool-kit for rendering accessible these different forms of knowledge is limited. As noted earlier, far too few of the procedures presently available for mapping the various forms of strategic knowledge that reside within the individual have been subjected to any form of reliability and validity analysis. Moreover, as we have seen, moving beyond the analysis of individual-level knowledge structures, in an attempt to decode collective knowledge within and between organizational institutions, presents a striking set of challenges, both in research terms and from a practitioner point of view. Organizations face significant hurdles in attempting to create sufficient levels of knowledge convergence or cognitive consensus, and we need to better understand the processes at work. Attempting to uncover the ways in which individual, collective and system-embedded behaviours and characteristics impact on knowledge convergence/divergence and cognitive consensus/dissensus will continue to foster cross-disciplinary work over many years to come.

Researchers appear to have underestimated the role of distributed knowledge and we now urgently need to understand the impact that different knowledge management strategies and systems are having on the development of strategic competence. In some cases there may be a fundamental mismatch in terms of the requirements imposed by the new working practices we have highlighted, involving decentralized and distributed decision making and new patterns of communication, and the level of readiness and individual competence on the part of the members of 'the wider team' to accept the increased responsibilities associated with these practices.

We have seen too that strategic competence involves the ability to transfer tacit knowledge between individuals, collectives and systems. There is the additional challenge now, that in many cases such transfer of tacit knowledge has to take place in the absence of face-to-face contact – contact that is so important for individual creative insight. Alternative mechanisms for the transfer of tacit knowledge, above and beyond individual-to-individual inter-action and exposure, are now being sought. The role of organizational memory has been highlighted as a useful guiding process for this transfer and as a basic safety check. However, there are many examples of organizations that are likely to be ill-equipped to meet the challenges posed by major changes in the economy and wider technological environment that might soon engulf them. In the process appointing young executive teams, while simultaneously purging their middle ranks of older and experienced individuals, these organizations have unwittingly dismantled their corporate memories. This represents a major strategic risk. On the other hand, as we have argued in Chapters 1 to 4, there are also considerable dangers associated with an over-reliance on past rules and procedures, not least the dangers of cognitive inertia, competency traps and progressing organizational simplicity, defensive avoidance, and the escalation of commitment to a failing course of action.

In Chapter 3 we called for more case studies on the successful decoding of organizational memory, in order that we might assess the extent to which this notion is of practical utility. Once more, we need to understand the trade-off between competing managerial strategies, in that the development of information rich knowledge management systems may seem attractive on the surface but might in fact serve to blind the organization to the value and power of the creation of ongoing dialogues between people. Given the current state of knowledge, it would seem that there is a delicate balance that needs to be struck; organizations need to establish systems and procedures that at least access some deeper levels of organizational memory, while at the same time avoiding the potential pitfalls of overly elaborate systems and procedures.

Competence, trust and the paradoxical need to trust *in* competence

The pursuit of new organizational designs and knowledge management systems is but one response to the many challenges confronting modern organizations *en route* to strategic competence. As became apparent in Chapter 2, the recent convergence of ideas from the fields of educational sociology and developmental psychology has led to a growth of interest in the notion of 'communities of practice' – a notion that had also gained considerable credence within the fields of management and organization studies. The learning taking place within such communities can be facilitated by (and arguably incorporated into) knowledge management systems. However, this need not necessitate the use of advanced information and communication technologies. Simply relying on technologies in an attempt to broaden access to and disseminate organizational knowledge would be a misguided strategy. As we have seen, one of the potential dangers in adopting technical solutions is that it can result in the creation of new, hitherto unforeseen, barriers to employee participation, in the form of 'electronic fences' (Newell *et al.* 2001). Clearly, in order for effective learning to occur there is a requirement to stretch the legitimate limits to participation that exist within the organization. By necessity, groups located on the periphery of learning communities must be readily incorporated, which in turn requires the conscious management of each individual's ZPD, providing them with a licence to perform.

Discussion of the importance of communities of learning is not just idealistic rhetoric. Many organizations, especially those pursuing global strategies, now appreciate that the rapid transfer of knowledge across business units can only be achieved through the pursuit of such broadened networks – be they called 'communities of practice', 'communities of interest' or 'global expertise networks'. However, it is clear that organizations responding in this way face a watershed. There will come a point at which managers will have to hand over control and direction to the communities/ networks themselves. They will have to trust in the competence of their devolved units, allowing communities within the organization to develop their own identities, professional skills and career paths. This requires a major act of faith and is a high-trust change strategy for organizations to pursue. Undoubtedly, for many managers it will prove a hard pill to swallow in a business climate that has tended to emphasize executive leadership and command and control behaviours. Rather like an untrained skier careering down a mountain, at the first sign of loss of balance the natural tendency is to lean back into the mountain, rather than to lean out into the abyss – yet this is the surest way to create a fall. The difficulties of keeping one's nerve in the pursuit of strategic competence in these highly turbulent times should not be underestimated.

It is highly likely that those organizations that have spent several years attending to issues of basic management competency (which is a necessary precursor for self-directed learning to prove fruitful), and those highly entrepreneurial start-up ventures that have rapidly arisen over recent years, will be the ones most open to changing their perceptions about the nature of strategic competence and new approaches to strategizing. For those organizations, high levels of trust, commitment and responsiveness within the existing workforce are required in order to ensure that the transition to strategic competence progresses smoothly. It is also clear that in order to foster these enabling conditions, sophisticated human resource management strategies are required, and that human resource management issues will need to be given enduring attention. We have not addressed strategic human resource management requirements in detail in this book, and merely signal now the importance of adopting a strategic approach to the management of people for successfully embedding the sorts of managerial competencies, policies, practices and organizational designs that we have outlined.

Clearly, an important area for future research will be to examine the preconditions that are needed in order to make organizations more receptive to the pursuit of strategic competence. In much the same way that human resource specialists have argued that there is little point in unleashing a sophisticated performance manage-ment system into the hands of an incompetent managerial work-force, many of the elements of strategic competence that we have outlined, if taken or adopted in isolation, could prove to be highly dysfunctional. Returning to some of the earliest messages that emerged about how best to forge strategic change in respect of the way that people are managed (Sparrow and Pettigrew 1988), organizations will have to create multiple pressure points for change, and manage the requirements that we have highlighted, as part of an integrated and mutually reinforcing package.

The scale of personal and organizational change required to develop strategic competence should not be underestimated. Indeed, as the experiences of the design engineering teams dis-cussed in Chapter 2 has shown, communities of practice can soon fall into disuse, and organizations can quickly learn to forget, through processes of silence and solitude. If organizations find it difficult to maintain their own (largely internal) communities of practice, they will struggle even more when they attempt to foster the transfer of knowledge across organizational boundaries – as in the case of firms involved in strategic partnerships, alliances and joint ventures. We shall return to this issue later, when we consider emerging work on globalization and international management.

Understanding the nature and significance of emotion

While the bulk of this book has centred on managerial and organizational cognition, future work needs to give greater promi-nence to the nature and significance of affective variables in the strategy process. In particular, as noted by Daniels (1998, 1999), the recent upsurge of interest in cognitive processes in strategic management has neglected to consider the potential impact of emotions on strategic cognition (see also Langley *et al.* 1995; Walsh 1995). Since a number of studies in laboratory (e.g. Dalgleish and Watts 1990; MacCleod 1991; Matt *et al.* 1992) and organizational field settings (e.g. Burke *et al.* 1993; Spector and O'Connell 1994; Williams *et al.* 1996) have demonstrated significant linkages between affect and cognition, it follows that affective processes could account for much of the variance in actors' strategic perceptions and beliefs. On the basis of this reasoning, Daniels (1998) has conducted an exploratory investigation of the relationships between trait negative affectivity and perceptions of the strategic environment, as assessed by means of a series of Likert scale items designed to tap the perceived performance, growth, complexity and competitiveness of participants' organizations relative to industry norms. The results of this study, based on two samples, suggest that this is a fruitful line of investigation worthy of longer-term follow-up, with several of the relationships tested yielding highly significant correlations, even after controlling for other variables such as age, gender, the number of organizational levels from the CEO, tenure in current position and organizational size. These findings are sufficiently strong to suggest that future studies of cognitive processes in executive teams, along the lines of those reviewed in Chapter 5, would benefit from the incorporation of this variable, as would studies seeking to elucidate the antecedents of actors' mental representations of specific strategic issues and problems, such as competition.

Meanwhile, in a separate development, Elsbach and Barr (1999) have begun investigating the effects of mood on the use of structured decision protocols under laboratory conditions. Their findings suggest that in situations where the use of such protocols is the usual method adopted, individuals in moderately negative, as opposed to moderately positive, mood states are more likely to execute all the steps of the protocol, in the correct sequence, and rely on the outcome of the protocol as the primary basis of the decision. As demonstrated by the more recent work of Finucane *et al.* (2000), in the final analysis, judgements of the risks and benefits associated with particular hazards may ultimately be determined by the operation of an 'affect heuristic'. Hence, the incorporation of affective variables in future studies of strategic decision processes may not only enhance understanding of strategic management, but also clarify our understanding of the role of affect in judgement and decision making more generally.

Refining the assessment of actors' mental representations and the modelling of the strategic management process

At various points in our analysis we have highlighted a number of non-trivial methodological problems which are hampering the development of the psychology of strategic management into a mature field in its own right. If research on the psychology of strategic management is to progress beyond present levels we must develop the capability to disentangle the myriad of potential cause and effect relationships that have a bearing on the strategic management process. Nowhere is this more apparent than in respect of the mass of research that has been concerned with actors' mental representations of competitive industry structures and the analysis of cognitive processes in top management teams, as reviewed in Chapters 4 and 5 (see also Chapter 7). In this section, we briefly revisit this work in order to consider the longer-term development of possible strategies for increasing the methodological rigour of psychological research in the strategy field in general.

As we saw in Chapter 4, the adoption of a cognitive perspective on strategic management shifts the focus of analysis away from the objective characteristics of firms, industries and markets, to consider the subjective and the inter-subjective worlds of individuals and groups. In so doing, the cognitive perspective challenges two of the core assumptions of neo-classical economics – namely, that all firms have equal access to information about the market-place, and that they will invariably respond to such information in similar ways. It is clear that the core assumption that business environments are objective entities waiting to be discovered through the application of analytical procedures and techniques, implicit within much of the mainstream literature on competitive strategy and strategic planning, does not stand up to theoretical and empirical scrutiny. Rather, competitive industry structures are socially constructed through processes of inter-action and learning. However, we have barely begun to scratch the surface in terms of discovering precisely how such structures come to be created and recreated over time. Very few of the methods employed for the assessment of actors' mental models of competition have been subjected to some form of basic reliability and/or validity analysis (Hodgkinson 2001a, 2002) and in the top teams area, it is only very recently that we have started to progress beyond the use of demographic variables as a proxy for the assessment of actors' assumptions and beliefs. Ultimately, in both of these areas we need to be able to assess cognition in a form that will enable the modelling of multilevel processes over time. Unfortunately, as we saw in Chapter 7, far too few of the techniques presently available for mapping strategic knowledge yield data of a form suitable for these purposes. With the notable exceptions of the technique devised by Markoczy and Goldberg (1995) for the systematic elicitation and comparison of causal maps, policy capturing methods, such as that employed by Tyler and Steensma (1995, 1998) in their studies of technological alliances, and three-way scaling procedures, such as the one employed by Hodgkinson (1997b) in his study of competitor cognition in the UK estate agency industry, virtually none of the techniques presently available for mapping strategic knowledge yield data in a form suitable for the comparison of large numbers of maps on a systematic basis. One major methodological challenge, therefore, is the need to develop additional procedures which are suitable for the mass assessment of actors' mental representations of strategic issues and problems.

Arguably, however, the greatest methodological challenge confronting researchers is the need to secure access to sufficiently large samples of individual participants and organizations for statistically robust findings to be generated. As with virtually any newly developing line of inquiry, the overwhelming majority of studies used to support the development of theory in relation to the psychology of strategic management in general have been relatively small-scale, exploratory studies, characterized by poor or non-existent controls, thereby rendering problematic the extent to which alternative explanations for key findings can be ruled out. A partial solution to this problem in future work might involve the greater use of experimental techniques. As Hodgkinson (2001b) has recently observed, despite the obvious advantages of the experimental method, this approach has been greatly under-utilized in the field of strategic management (see also Schwenk 1982, 1995; Hodgkinson and Maule 2002). Two recently published papers by Clark and Montgomery (1999) and Kilduff *et al.* (2000) illustrate how use of the experimental method might be extended beyond the study of heuristics and biases in strategic decision making (as outlined in our opening chapter) in future work, in order to further understanding both of the socio-cognitive processes underpinning the development of competitive structures in industries and markets, and as a basis for illuminating the nature and significance of cognitive processes in top management teams.

Clark and Montgomery (1999, Study 2) employed MARKSTRAT2 (Larreche and Gatignon 1990), a business game designed to simulate processes of competition, as part of a wider investigation into competitor categorization processes. The overall findings complement and add to various insights derived from previous studies into competitor categorization processes (as reviewed in Chapter 4) showing, for example, that managers may name too few competitors, that they should focus more on competitors as defined by customers (using demand-based as opposed to supply-based attributes), that they should be aware of perceptual asymmetries (e.g. the tendency for small firms to 'look up to' larger firms but not the converse), that they should periodically revisit how they identify competitors and that they should identify potential competitors for tracking purposes.

More recently, Kilduff *et al.* (2000) employed a variant of the MARKSTRAT simulation as a vehicle to examine the linkages between demographic and cognitive team diversity, and the reciprocal effects of diversity and firm performance. The findings indicated that high-performing teams were marked by a tendency to preserve multiple interpretations of reality at the outset, with greater clarity emerging towards the end of the team's life cycle. While cognitive diversity in teams affected (and was affected by) changes in firm performance, contrary to the researchers' expectations – but by no means inconsistent with several other recent studies conducted outside the confines of the laboratory (e.g. Markoczy 1997) – demographic diversity had no noticeable effects on cognitive diversity. There are, of course, a variety of possible explanations for this negative finding, not least the possibility that the particular simulation package (MARKSTRAT) and/or the particular measures of demographic and cognitive diversity employed may be insensitive to the detection of such relationships (cf. our earlier discussion in Chapter 5 on demographic faultlines as initiated by Lau and Murnighan 1998, and Pelled's 1996 intervening process theory). Nevertheless, these findings demonstrate that laboratory simulations provide a useful basis for ensuring that results obtained through less rigorous procedures, such as observational field studies and interviews, can be replicated under controlled conditions.

In the final analysis, however, laboratory experiments are no match for the gathering of large-scale, high-quality datasets in the field. Ultimately, future investigations need to be based on the adoption of multilevel approaches to the mapping of strategic knowledge, *in situ*. Fortunately, as noted in Chapter 7, a number of recent methodological advances have occurred in the quantitative assessment of managerial and organizational cognition that have created the potential for such larger-scale theory testing, using longitudinal research designs of a form that will permit researchers to systematically disentangle cause-effect relationships in field settings. Our call for the development of additional procedures notwithstanding, there is no reason why, suitably adapted, methods such as those outlined in Chapter 7 could not be used in conjunction with LISREL (Joreskog and Sorbom 1993) and/or other structural equation modelling procedures, such as EQS (Bentler 1989) and AMOS (Arbuckle 1997), now commonplace within the better-established sub-fields of industrial, work and organizational psychology (James and James 1989; Kelloway 1996). These procedures, and related techniques for the modelling of multilevel datasets (Bryk and Raudenbush 1992; Goldstein 1995; Kreft and de Leeuw 1998), are ideally suited for rigorously testing the various socio-cognitive explanations for the emergence of competitive industry structures reviewed in Chapter 4. These methods could also be fruitfully employed to evaluate competing models leading to further understanding of the causal antecedents and consequences of executive cognition in top management teams, as explored in Chapter 5.

Previous studies investigating the correlates of executive cognition have focused almost exclusively on the external characteristics of the individuals concerned, such as age and educational and functional background. There are encouraging signs, however, that this work is approaching new levels of sophistication, with recent studies incorporating a range of measures to control for key characteristics of the organization and its environment. While these developments are to be welcomed, there is a compelling need to balance the incorporation of such contextual features in the modelling process with a consideration of a number of psychological variables that might also mediate or moderate executive cognition. An obvious starting point for increasing the degree of psychological sophistication in the study of executive cognition would be to incorporate some of the variables that we identified in Chapter 6 as having a likely impact on the structure and content of actors' mental representations of strategic issues and problems: *n-ach*, for example, and cognitive style and locus of control. In view of the theory and research reviewed in Chapter 6, there is reason to believe that these variables will be associated with differences in terms of the complexity levels of individuals' mental representations of strategic issues and problems. Accordingly, these variables might account for some of the discrepant findings that have emerged from recent studies seeking to identify the correlates of executive cognition, as reviewed in Chapter 5.

From a prescriptive standpoint, the extent to which greater levels of complexity in the mental models of executives facilitate or inhibit the longer-term performance of the wider organization is an entirely different matter, which also warrants significant research attention. Arguably, greater levels of complexity, particularly when distributed among several members of the executive team, might foster creativity and innovation, while minimizing the dangers of group-level myopia and cognitive inertia. On the other hand, overly complex mental representations of the organization and its environment might inhibit successful adaptation. Calori *et al.* (1994) were careful not to suggest that cognitive maps characterized by greater levels of complexity would automatically lead CEOs to superior performance, arguing that CEOs' cognitive complexity levels should match the complexity levels of the environment. More recent work by Wells and Bantel (2000), which has considered this issue at the team level, suggests that the attainment of high levels of team-level cognitive complexity is a fundamental prerequisite for competitive success among companies operating in environments characterized by complexity, scarcity and unpredictable change. According to Wells and Bantel, high levels of cognitive differentiation and cognitive integration are both required in these settings in order to foster competitive variety, innovation and competitive speed of response – all vital to the longer-term survival of the organization. The extent to which the tentative findings emerging from this research and the earlier study by Calori *et al.* generalize to other organizations and industry settings, needs to be rigorously evaluated through a series of larger-scale investigations. To the extent that the findings of these preliminary studies are confirmed, this would clearly have important implications for the selection and development of executive teams, not least the need to ensure that teams are balanced in terms of their membership so as to ensure optimum levels of cognitive complexity (both with respect to cognitive differentiation and cognitive integration) at the team level. The extent to which strategic thinking can be systematically developed at the individual and/or team level through the use of cognitive mapping procedures and related techniques such as scenarios is another issue that warrants urgent attention. In the absence of rigorous research evidence it is difficult to specify the extent to which it is desirable for organizations to select for, and/or develop, this particular attribute in CEOs and senior managers, or indeed how such selection and/or development might be accomplished.

Exploring strategic management processes beyond the top team

Before leaving this discussion of top teams it is worth pausing briefly to reconsider the topographic assumptions that have underpinned this stream of work, and much of the other work we have surveyed in this book. As observed in Chapter 4, the very latest theorizing in relation to the development of competitive industry structures has challenged the view that the locus of strategizing resides exclusively within the upper echelons of the organization. At various points we have implied that much strategizing takes place within the lower reaches of the organization.

For instance, our discussion of communities of practice in Chapter 2 suggested that many individuals beyond the top play a crucial role in organizational learning and strategic renewal, as did our discussion of sense-giving/thought leadership in Chapter 6. The work of Floyd and Woolridge gives added support to this claim. In a series of articles spanning the past decade they have explored the significance of middle management in the strategy process (e.g. Woolridge and Floyd 1990; Floyd and Woolridge 1992, 1994, 1997), culminating in a recent monograph (Floyd and Woolridge 2000), in which they have comprehensively set out the case for conducting strategy process research from what they term a 'middle-level perspective':

> The top management perspective that has dominated the field has emphasized the deliberate side of strategy. As markets have become more dynamic and complex, however, the limitations of this approach have become increasingly apparent. Firms that rely on centralized decision making have had difficulty responding to continuous change . . . the central assertion . . . is that much of what separates the performance of firms occurs not at the top but in the middle of organizations, and this is especially true in the present business climate. This proposition is consistent with the decentralization of strategic responsibilities adopted by an increasing number of top-level executives. In research and consulting, we have encountered firms in industries as diverse as insurance, pharmaceuticals and chewing gum that expect strategic thinking and initiative from middle-level managers.
>
> (Floyd and Woolridge 2000: 153–7)

In another recent development, Floyd and Lane (2000) have extended this analysis in an attempt to map out the complexities of 'strategizing throughout the organization'. They have focused on the various role conflicts occurring between top-, middle- and operating-level managers in processes of strategic renewal, arising from 'dissensus' in managers' perceptions of the need for change. According to Floyd and Lane, such conflict can occur within as well as between the various managerial levels.

If the analysis of cognitive processes in top management teams *per se* has proven to be technically challenging, the problems posed by these latest theoretical advances look set to test researchers' methodological ingenuity to the full. The next couple of decades look set to be just as exciting as the previous two, if not more so, for scholars working in this vital area of research.

If the problems identified in this and the previous section are to be addressed on a satisfactory basis, researchers will need to collaborate with one another in large-scale, multidisciplinary teams, in some cases spanning several institutions. While this type of collaboration is undoubtedly a highly labour-intensive process in comparison with conventional approaches to the conduct and management of applied psychological research, the potential benefits must surely outweigh the transaction costs involved.

Further cross-fertilization with adjacent fields of study

As the psychology of strategic management develops into an established area of research in its own right, it is vital that researchers continue to draw upon the insights of adjacent fields of study, for two reasons:

- in order to ensure that we avoid the costly dangers of needless duplication that can so easily occur when scholars from adjacent fields address common problems, however complex, from their separate disciplinary perspectives;
- in order that we continue to realize the genuine synergies that can occur from such cross-fertilization.

Providing that we continue to develop this emerging field as an interdisciplinary endeavour, we will undoubtedly witness even greater levels of synergistic convergence in academic thinking across a number of different research communities in the years to come, which can only work to the mutual benefit of all parties concerned. We envisage such cross-disciplinary collaboration proceeding simultaneously in two directions: first, from the outside in (i.e. psychologists from outside the strategic management field bringing to bear the insights of their core discipline on a range of specific strategic issues and problems); second, from the inside out, requiring that those working within the strategy field remain ever-vigilant to developments that are taking place within adjacent sub-fields of management, such as marketing, human resource management and international business, with a view to spotting opportunities for extended dialogue and cooperation.

When we stand back from the considerable volume of research that we have surveyed in this book, it becomes apparent that much of this work has been tantamount to little more than a limited 'dabbling' in issues strategic. Moreover, in many cases the psychological insights involved have been fairly minimal to say the least. There has been a concentration of some issue specific, cross-disciplinary research with a strong psychological flavour, for example around the issue of the development of competitive industry structures as outlined in Chapter 4, and the analysis of cognitive processes in top management teams as discussed in Chapter 5. However, there are many strategic issues currently facing modern organizations, such new forms of work organization, the virtualization of organizations and work processes, and the changing boundaries between organizations, their customers and suppliers, where very little of the work surveyed has drawn directly upon psychologically informed theories, methods or perspectives. As we have seen, much of the current thinking in respect of these issues and problems has been shaped by work from other fields, such as organizational sociology and economics, and there is now a real opportunity for industrial, work and organizational psychologists to enrich understanding of these vital topics, through cross-disciplinary collaboration, working from the outside in.

However, as the psychology of strategic management – particularly the managerial and organizational cognition approach – continues to mature, we shall also see its knowledge base and methods being applied to, and used to cross-inform, other emerging fields of study, working from the inside out. This will prove most attractive to these other emerging fields because scholars working in these new areas are more open to methodological experimentation than are their peers working in better-established fields. We now highlight a number of areas in which the psychology of strategic management is currently developing along these lines. In particular, we consider a series of developments that are occurring at the interface between the strategy field and the field of international management.

Conclusions

An obvious area for such a cross-fertilization of ideas, under-pinned by sound psychological theory and research, is at the interface with the sub-specialty of international human resource management. We use this example in order to highlight the ways in which work emerging from the psychology of strategic management has begun to inform the thinking of human resource management scholars with an interest in internationalization strategies and globalization. In turn, this new work has begun to further enrich mainstream strategic management research concerned with the psychological analysis of top management teams.

The vast bulk of top team demographic research has assumed that uncertainty is uniformly high in all sectors – indeed, a central premise of this book has been that most sectors are pervaded by such uncertainty. Global strategies are, however, characterized by particularly intense levels of uncertainty (Weick and Van Orden 1990). Social psychologists argue that this gives rise to 'weak situations' in which the influence of individual differences is likely to override group and organizational norms. Moreover, globalization efforts are being hampered by problems of infor-mation overload, managerial complexity in the form of conflicts and paradoxes, domestic myopia and potentially expanded socio-cognitive diversity in the form of national culture differences (Sanders and Carpenter 1998). It is most surprising, therefore, that a recent review of leading international management journals found that studies of top team behaviour were 'notably absent' from the literature on globalization (Lohrke and Bruton 1997: 41).

There have been a small number of studies within the top team demography tradition that have examined the link between the mix of backgrounds and expertise found on the board and the firm's global strategic posture. For example, global strategic posture has been found to be positively related to top manage-ment team heterogeneity – employed as a proxy for diversity of networks (Kim and Mauborgne 1991; Athanassiou and Nigh 1999) – and to top team size (Sanders and Carpenter 1998). Carpenter and Fredrickson (2001) examined a number of important inter-action effects between global posture and top team make-up. Educational heterogeneity was found to be persistently correlated positively with global posture, but functional and tenure hetero-geneity effects were both moderated by levels of uncertainty.

Flood *et al.* (1997) examined the link between demographic characteristics and 'pioneering' behaviour (the capacity to seize unmet customer needs and develop new products ahead of rivals) in US and Irish top management teams. There were no country differences, but significant relationships emerged with respect to age, firm size and incentivization through share options. Finally, the level of international experience of top team members has been linked to the strategic behaviours of small- and medium-sized enterprises (Reuber and Fischer 1997) and the international diversification strategies of US firms (Sambharya 1996).

It is to be hoped that some of the methodological refinements highlighted in Chapter 5 will find their way into the future cross-boundary research that will be conducted at the interface between these new fields. The need to examine what lies within the black box of top team demography becomes all the more essential in the context of international strategic management because differences in national culture (especially on dimensions such as tolerance for uncertainty) suggest that the actual behaviours, cognitions and perceptions of international top teams are likely to vary substantially (Barkema and Vermeulen 1997).

Another fruitful area of overlap that is beginning to be exploited by scholars from adjacent fields is in relation to work on organizational learning and international management. Expatriates have long been presented as a vehicle for knowledge transfer in transnational organizations (Bartlett and Ghoshal 1995), yet to date there has been surprisingly little empirical study of this phenomenon. A notable exception is the recent work of Bonache and Brewster (2001), who applied knowledge transfer theory to the topic of expatriation and conducted a case study in a Spanish company. Clearly, further studies along similar lines, spanning a range of sectors and countries are now badly needed.

One issue that has attracted considerable attention is the importance of organizational learning to the success of international joint ventures (Schuler 2001) and mergers and acquisitions (Schuler and Jackson 2001). This has been posited at a theoretical level and investigated empirically (Barkema *et al.* 1996; Glaister and Buckley 1996; Inkpen 1996; Pilkington 1996). As Schuler and Jackson (2001) have observed, the factors that have driven merger and acquisition strategy over the past decade or so are forecast to intensify. The value of global mergers and acquisitions exceeded $3.5 trillion for the first time in 2000. There is evidence that firms are factoring-in human resource costs (with metrics such as price-per-engineer) in order to value the cost of deals. For example, Broadcom paid $18 million per engineer to buy chip-maker SiByte in November 2000 (Schuler and Jackson 2001). The ability to negotiate quick deals, learn rapidly and apply previous experience from deal-making (called 'combination management') is being championed as a core strategic competence. What might such a competency really entail? Perhaps reflecting the increased attention being given to the acquisition and retention of talent through such strategies, recent work has begun to examine international strategy in the context of organizational learning and adaptation. Vermeulen and Barkema (2001) point out that much research on mergers and acquisitions has demonstrated the limited performance gains associated with international acquisition strategies (Hitt *et al.* 1996). In particular, serious problems with senior management behaviour have been highlighted, including tendencies to pursue personal goals that do not necessarily coincide with the interests of shareholders (Morck *et al.* 1990), to imitate others that have made acquisitions (Haunschild 1993), and to overvalue their ability to manage acquired businesses (Hayward and Hambrick 1997). Acquisitions present a series of managerial challenges, including differences in organizational culture and managerial style, the need to absorb new product lines and varying dominant logics. Despite such critical examination, senior managers continue to make acquisitions at a high rate, and with increasing global reach (Vermeulen and Barkema 2001).

However, there may be a hidden but positive side to the pursuit of acquisitions. In Chapter 2 we introduced the concept of progressing organizational simplicity, whereby repeated use of a knowledge base can lead to the tendency of organizations to become rigid, narrow and simple (Miller 1993). Vermeulen and Barkema (2001) examined the proposition that acquisitions might revitalize the organization through exposure to manageable levels of shock, which in turn might enhance the prospects of longer-term survival. The organizational learning gains might outstrip the short-term downsides of acquisitions; differences between managerial teams can create the opportunity for synergies and learning (Krishnan *et al.* 1997), and added value might be created through processes of corporate renewal (Haspeslagh and Jemison 1991). Vermeulen and Barkema (2001) argued that firms that expand through greenfield investments (setting up a subsidiary from scratch) do not exploit their knowledge base as effectively as those that expand through acquisition (the takeover of an existing company). To test this proposition, they examined data on the expansion patterns of 25 of the largest Dutch non-financial firms (excluding Royal Dutch Shell, Unilever, Philips and Akzo, on the grounds that they form a unique group in terms of their breadth of activities, scope and size) over a period of three decades, and studied survival rates and increases in the viability of subsequent ventures. There were 1349 new affiliations formed, of which 61 per cent were with overseas entities. The researchers traced how long these subsidiaries persisted. When linked to official reports of success or failure, it was clear that official successes had a survival rate 22.5 times higher than the survival rate of failures, in both related and unrelated sectors. The impact on survival rates was tested against the number of preceding greenfield investments and acquisitions in familiar and unfamiliar markets, while controlling for multinational and product diversity.

Summarizing the underlying theory, work that links international expansion strategy to the topic of organizational learning presents the following picture. Firms that expand through greenfield investments are inclined to adopt habitual ways of organizing and managing (Hedberg 1981; Levinthal and March 1993), concentrate on those aspects of their repertoire that appeared most successful in old situations, replicate them and transfer them into the new subsidiary (Miller *et al.* 1996), install similar technical systems, pursue similar competitive actions and organization designs (Miller and Chen 1996; Miller *et al.* 1997), and hire people into the new site that fit the existing culture (O'Reilly *et al.* 1991). This increasing routinization of the old entity and the resulting narrowness of mental models can lead to a failure to perceive and respond to new important stimuli (Starbuck and Hedberg 1977; Prahalad and Bettis 1986; Abrahamson and Fombrun 1994). Greenfield investments in unfamiliar markets constitute an exception to this state of affairs, in that they can result in the bringing of new information, incentives to trigger searches for the creation of new knowledge and the hiring of outsiders (Chatman and Jehn 1994; Miller and Chen 1996; Barkema and Vermeulen 1998). However, acquisitions – whether in related markets or not – can serve as powerful forces of cognitive change. The conflicts they engender unfreeze cognitive maps, structures and processes (Hambrick *et al.* 1996; Krishnan *et al.* 1997), preserve healthy levels of doubt, diversity and debate (Miller 1993), increase the cognitive abilities of organization members (Calori *et al.* 1994), create new knowledge from the combination of existing forms of knowledge (Kogut and Zander 1992, 1993), and inculcate practices that lead to the creation of new knowledge (Bantel and Jackson 1989; Abrahamson and Fombrun 1994). In terms of organizational change, globalization and increased competition have forced firms to pursue a strategy of 'continued renewal', brought about by 'rhythmically' replacing old technologies with new ones. Such strategies necessitate that firms initiate periods of creative destruction at regular and over relatively short-term intervals, in order to advance the creation of new knowledge and foster long-term survivability. Acquisitions may form an important vehicle for enhancing the success of later ventures, be they further acquisitions or greenfield investments.

In the context of specific firms, the link between organizational learning and acquisition behaviour is likely to be far more subtle, and certainly not as black or white as portrayed by the above research. We need empirical evidence to test out many of the above propositions. In order to deliver longer-term viability, the short-term negativities and dysfunctional consequences associated with mergers and acquisitions have to be managed much more effectively. Nor can it be assumed that organizational learning automatically follows from the system shocks postulated above. As Chapter 2 demonstrated, it would be most unwise to assume that the pursuit of a strategy to foster such learning automatically yields long-term benefits or that the strategically competent organization manages individual and collective cognition, and explicit and tacit knowledge, only through immense care and attention. Nonetheless, there is an excellent opportunity to import insights from the organizational learning and knowledge management literatures, and in particular from the organizational strategy literature on top team cognition and collective cognition, into the international strategy field, and there are several academic communities now ready and willing to talk to each other.

Validating the notion of strategic competence at the organizational level

The last issue that we need to address is the question of how best to validate the notion of the strategically competent organization at the organizational level of analysis. We saw in Chapter 2 that there has been considerable recent criticism of the learning organization, with an increasingly sceptical academic audience viewing it as idealistic rhetoric, dangerously out of line with the practical realities of organizational life. Easterby-Smith and Araujo (1999) drew attention to the need to build empirical support for the relevance of organizational learning, a goal that we wholeheartedly support. However, while this is an easy call to make, it is one that will prove remarkably difficult to respond to. We have argued for improved methodologies to open up the black box of organizational demography in respect of the linkages between, for example, top team cognition and organizational performance, and hinted at some of the ways in which this might be achieved in Chapters 5 and 7. We consider here a separate, but additional, set of challenges concerning the question of how to validate a phenomenon that exists across at least three levels of analysis: individual cognition and behaviour; collective learning and memory; and organizational institutions, systems and artefacts.

In supporting a call for the validation of such broad issues as those that we have touched upon in our exploration of strategic competence, researchers will face a very difficult set of challenges indeed. There is some benefit to be gained from an examination of attempts to validate similar, highly complex, multilevel notions in other areas of research in order that some of the already well-rehearsed methodological debates and arguments that have occurred in those contexts might be pre-empted in the present arena. To this end, we now briefly draw on some parallels from the field of human resource management. Sparrow and Marchington (1998) have argued that human resource management is becoming an increasingly difficult to attain ideal, and a goal that is constrained within the prison of political economy and global economic forces. They have also noted that there is often a temptation to reduce new fields of study to collections or packages of policy and practice, and then examine their linkage to organizational performance. Certainly one could fillet this book and garner a fairly long list of preferable approaches to management associated with the acquisition, storage, recall and interpretation of information in an attempt to distil a list of prescriptive insights. We would, however, strongly advise against such attempts, for they would run the risk of oversimplifying our notion of strategic competence to a mere (albeit highly comprehensive) list of activities.

Parallels can be drawn with the discourse that has taken place over recent years on how best to demonstrate the effectiveness of 'bundles' of high performance human resource management practices. This has led to a major debate about methodology (see the opposing arguments of Huselid 1995 and Wright and Snell 1998). Sparrow (1999b) has pointed out that such attempts at what might be called 'field of study validation' naturally challenge researchers in the field in question, and provide pause for thought about the methodologies they adopt for such purposes. To a certain extent, the arguments he made against designing simplistic validation studies to validate bundles of human resource management policies also resonate with our present concerns to validate the strategic competency notion. There are undoubtedly difficult choices to be made about the best financial performance measures to represent organizational 'effectiveness'. Moreover, most 'raw' organizational performance measures have been subjected to situational manipulation – especially when return on assets has been a major focus; but they may not be truly reflective of the inner strength of the organization. There are four levels at which we could measure the strategic competence-organizational effectiveness fit:

- the presence of the guiding principles behind the practice;
- the presence of the actual practice as compared against the presence of different practices;
- the products of those practices (the competencies or behaviours that the practices promote);

- the quality of the practice-process (effective execution or not of the practice).

No consensus exists concerning the level of specificity that should be incorporated into measures or items chosen to reflect the presence of strategic competence. In addition, simply measuring 'inputs' (such as the policies, practices and managerial attributes associated with strategic competence) and 'outputs' (such as broad organizational performance) is likely to 'mask' the sophisticated set of linkages that exist in reality between strategic competence and performance. Any research methodology has to first cope with 'time shift' issues. Investments may be made in the policies that foster strategic competence and these may build up to a critical mass over time, but any positive influences might not take hold until at least two or three years (possibly longer) into the process. Even with time-lagged performance measures, or longitudinal case studies, there are problems in attempting to reveal the underlying nature of such complex causal processes. There is also the issue of organizational politics and power that muddies the identification of simple causal links. Many policies and programmes are run 'politically', with clear 'front-runner' policies introduced with the intention of mobilizing attitudes and changes in behaviour (i.e. there is a clear logic to the sequencing of the policies, but they do not act as a composite bundle; nor do they operate across standardized periods of time). Ultimately, the link between strategic competence and organizational performance depends upon the centrality of people and knowledge-based competition to core business processes. In the same way that organizations vary in terms of 'human asset intensity' (Colf 1997), they are likely to vary in the extent to which a lack of strategic competence will lead to immediate performance declines. Linking effective strategic competence to performance in low-human asset intensive sectors is likely to prove a harder and more sophisticated task than doing so in sectors in which people represent a higher proportion of the costs or add value to the core business process through their operational skills, error detection and/or knowledge capabilities.

Validation studies will probably need to combine a mixture of qualitative and quantitative approaches. Qualitative research needs to be directed at further refining the important 'boxes' that should be incorporated in future larger-scale investigations. However, it will ultimately require quantitative studies to determine the underlying causal mechanisms at work.

At this stage in the development of the psychology of strategic management it would be fair to say that there is little evidence that the competencies alluded to throughout this book cause harm or dysfunctional effects within the organization, but there is a clear logic behind the argument that they can bring process benefits to the ways in which individuals, teams and organizations cope with an uncertain environment. Accordingly, we feel that it is worth persevering with the pursuit of strategic competence. However, this pursuit has to be a measured goal, for various reasons. First, there are obviously some fundamental limits to the capabilities of managers, and as a general principle the creation of organizational designs and business processes that can only be reliably delivered by a very small élite of highly-capable individuals is a very high-risk strategy, not least because of the risk of major strategic error by those who operate on the edge of their competency limits, but also because of the limited diversity in terms of other important attributes, such as societal value-sets, that such a small cadre of actors bring to bear. Second, the task demands inherent in many current high-information load environments are simply dysfunctional. Some of the organizational designs and principles that are currently being espoused (e.g. 'modular self-regulating groups', 'intra-organizational information markets') may sound good on paper and appear to fit the highly technological environments in which they have evolved, but may ultimately prove devilishly difficult to manage effectively. Third, the pace at which organizations develop such competence will be driven in part by labour market conditions. We maintain that organizations at the forefront of knowledge-based competition will have little alternative but to pursue some of the policies and practices we have outlined. The intellectual property associated with employees will probably gravitate towards those organizations that at least attempt to create this form of competency (Cappelli 1999). Organizations that are perceived as being more proactive in this area (i.e. have an employee brand) may well be more able to attract higher calibre applicants, and be more selective about the calibre of people who work for them. Others, however, will not have such talent at their disposal.

Final reflections

For far too long now, senior managers have tended to view industrial, work and organizational psychologists as a purely operational-level, technically competent group of professionals with little or nothing to offer at the strategic level (Hodgkinson 2001a). Accordingly, the vast majority of practising psychologists have not been incorporated routinely in the strategy process in any capacity whatsoever, being neither directly involved through appropriate consultation on substantive issues, nor indirectly in a supportive and/or advisory role (Anderson 1998; Hodgkinson and Herriot 2002). However, as the work surveyed in this book so aptly demonstrates, this has been much to the mutual detriment of both groups. Arguably, had the Prudential Assurance Company and various other UK residential estate agents been in a position to avail themselves of the considerable volume of theory and research on the psychology of strategic management that has amassed over the past 15 years or so, perhaps the unfortunate events with which we began this book might never have occurred.

REFERENCES

Abell, D.F. (1980) *Defining the Business: The Starting Point of Strategic Planning.* Englewood Cliffs, NJ: Prentice-Hall.

Abrahamson, E. and Fombrun, C.J. (1994) Macrocultures: determinants and consequences, *Academy of Management Review,* 19: 728–55.

Ackermann, M.A. and Malone, T.W. (1990) Answer garden: a tool for growing organizational memory. *Proceedings of the ACM Conference on Office Information Systems.* Boston: MIT.

Ackoff, R.L. (1983) Beyond prediction and preparation, *Journal of Management Studies,* 20: 59–69.

Adler, P.S and Cole, R.E. (1993) NUMMI vs. Uddevalla – Rejoinder, *Sloan Management Review,* 34(3): 45–9.

Adler, S. and Weiss, H.M. (1988) Recent developments in the study of personality and organizational behavior, in C.L. Cooper and I.T. Robertson (eds) *International Review of Industrial and Organizational Psychology, Volume 3.* Chichester: Wiley.

Agor, W.H. (1989) The logic of intuition, in W.H. Agor (ed.) *Intuition in Organizations.* Newbury Park, CA: Sage.

Agor, W.H. (1991) How intuition can be used to enhance productivity in organizations, *Journal of Creative Behavior,* 25(1): 11–19.

Aldenderfer, M.S. and Blashfield, R.K. (1984) Cluster Analysis. *Sage University Paper Series on Quantitative Applications in the Social Sciences,* 07–044. Newbury Park, CA: Sage.

Aldrich, H. and Pfeffer, J. (1976) Environments of organizations, *Annual Review of Sociology,* 2: 71–105.

Allinson, C.W. and Hayes, J. (1996) The Cognitive Style Index: a measure of intuition-analysis for organizational research, *Journal of Management Studies*, 33(1): 119–35.

Allinson, C.W. and Hayes, J. (2000) Cross-national differences in cognitive style: implications for management, *International Journal of Human Resource Management*, 11: 161–70.

Allinson, C.W., Chell, E. and Hayes, J. (2000) Intuition and entrepreneurial behaviour, *European Journal of Work and Organizational Psychology*, 9: 31–43.

Allinson, C.W., Armstrong, S. and Hayes, J. (2001) The effects of cognitive style on leader-member exchange: a study of manager-subordinate dyads, *Journal of Occupational and Organizational Psychology*, 74: 201–20.

Amabile, T.M. (1983) The social psychology of creativity: a componential conceptualisation, *Journal of Personality and Social Psychology*, 45: 357–76.

Anderson, C.R. (1977) Locus of control, coping behaviours and performance in a stress setting: a longitudinal study, *Journal of Applied Psychology*, 62: 446–51.

Anderson, J.R. (1983) *The Architecture of Cognition*. Cambridge, MA: Harvard University Press.

Anderson, J.R. (1990) *Cognitive Psychology and its Implications*, 3rd edn. New York: Freeman.

Anderson, N. (1998) The practitioner-researcher divide in work and organizational psychology, *The Occupational Psychologist*, 34: 7–16.

Anderson, N., Herriot, P. and Hodgkinson, G.P. (2001) The practitioner-researcher divide in industrial, work and organizational (IWO) psychology: where are we now and where do we go from here? *Journal of Occupational and Organizational Psychology*, 74: 391–411.

Andrews, K.R. (1971) *The Concept of Corporate Strategy*. Homewood, IL: Irwin.

Ansoff, H.I. (1965) *Corporate Strategy*. New York: McGraw-Hill.

Anthony, W. and Daake, D. (1994) Measurement of analysis and tacit knowledge in decision making. Unpublished working paper, Florida State University.

Arabie, P., Carroll, J.S. and DeSarbo, W.S. (1987) Three-way scaling and clustering. *Sage University Paper Series on Quantitative Applications in the Social Sciences*, 07–065. Newbury Park, CA: Sage.

Araujo, L. (1998) Knowing and learning as networking, *Management Learning*, 29: 317–36.

Arbuckle, J.L. (1997) *AMOS Users' Guide Version 3.6*. Chicago: Small-Waters.

References

Argote, L., Beckman, S.L. and Epple, D. (1990) The persistence and transfer of learning in industrial settings, *Management Science*, 36: 140–54.

Argyris, C. (1977) Double loop learning in organizations, *Harvard Business Review*, 55(5): 115–25.

Argyris, C. (1999) *On Organizational Learning*, 2nd edn. Oxford: Blackwell.

Argyris, C. and Schön, D.A. (1978) *Organizational Learning: A Theory of Action Perspective*. Reading, MA: Addison-Wesley.

Armstrong, S., Allinson, C.W. and Hayes, J. (1997) The implications of cognitive style for the management of student-supervisor relations, *Educational Psychology*, 17(1 & 2): 209–18.

Arvedson, L. (1993) Coming to grips with learning (in) organisations, *European Forum for Management Development*, 1: 5–10.

Arvidson, P.S. (1997) Looking intuit: a phenomenological exploration of intuition and attention, in R. Davis-Floyd and P.S. Arvidson (eds) *Intuition: The Inside Story and Interdisciplinary Perspectives*. London: Routledge.

Ashforth, B. and Mael, F. (1989) Social identity theory and the organization, *Academy of Management Review*, 14: 20–39.

Athanassiou, N. and Nigh, D. (1999) The impact of U.S. Company internationalization on top management team advice networks, *Strategic Management Journal*, 20: 83–92.

Axelrod, R.M. (1976) The mathematics of cognitive maps, in R.M. Axelrod (ed.) *Structure of Decision: The Cognitive Maps of Political Elites*. Princeton NJ: Princeton University Press.

Ayas, K. (1999) Project design for learning and innovation, in M. Easterby-Smith, J. Burgoyne and L. Araujo (eds) *Organizational Learning and the Learning Organization: Developments in Theory and Practice*. London: Sage.

Baddeley, A.D. (1990) *Human Memory*. Hove: Lawrence Erlbaum Associates.

Bahn, C. (1979) Can intelligence tests predict executive competency? *Personnel*, July–August, 52–8.

Bain, J.S. (1956) *Barriers to New Competition*. Cambridge, MA: Harvard University Press.

Balle, M. (1994) *Managing With Systems Thinking*. London: McGraw-Hill.

Bandura, A. (1986) *Social Foundations of Thought and Action*. Englewood Cliffs, NJ: Prentice-Hall.

Bantel, K. and Jackson, S.E. (1989) Top management and innovation in banking: does the composition of top teams make a difference? *Strategic Management Journal*, 10: 107–24.

Barkema, H.G. and Vermeulen, F. (1997) What differences in the cultural backgrounds of partners are detrimental for international joint ventures? *Journal of International Business Studies*, 29: 845–64.

Barkema, H.G. and Vermeulen, F. (1998) International expansion through start-up or acquisition: a learning perspective, *Academy of Management Journal*, 41: 7–26.

Barkema, H.G., Bell, J.H.J. and Pennings, J.M. (1996) Foreign entry, cultural barriers, and learning, *Strategic Management Journal*, 17: 151–66.

Barnard, C.I. (1938) *The Functions of the Executive*. Cambridge, MA: Harvard University Press.

Barnes, J.H. (1984) Cognitive biases and their impact on strategic planning, *Strategic Management Journal*, 5: 129–37.

Barney, J.B. and Hoskisson, R.E. (1990) Strategic groups: untested assertions and research proposals, *Managerial and Decision Economics*, 11: 187–98.

Barr, P.S. (1998) Adapting to unfamiliar environmental events: a look at the evolution of interpretation and its role in strategic change, *Organization Science*, 9: 644–69.

Barr, P.S. and Huff, A.S. (1997) Seeing isn't believing: understanding diversity in the timing of strategic response, *Journal of Management Studies*, 34: 337–70.

Barr, P.S., Stimpert, J.L. and Huff, A.S. (1992) Cognitive change, strategic action, and organizational renewal, *Strategic Management Journal*, 13: 15–36.

Bartlett, C.A. and Ghoshal, S. (1993) Beyond the M-form: toward a managerial theory of the firm, *Strategic Management Journal*, 14 (special issue): 23–46.

Bartlett, C.A. and Ghoshal, S. (1995) *Transnational Management*, 2nd edn. Boston: Irwin.

Bartlett, F.C. (1932) *Remembering: A Study in Experimental and Social Psychology*. London: Cambridge University Press.

Bartunek, J.M. (1984) Changing interpretive schemes and organizational restructuring: the example of a religious order, *Administrative Science Quarterly*, 29: 355–72.

Bastick, A. (1982) *Intuition: How We Think and Act*. New York: Wiley.

Bateman T.S. and Zeithaml, C.P. (1989a) The psychological context of strategic decisions: a model and convergent experimental findings, *Strategic Management Journal*, 10: 59–74.

Bateman T.S. and Zeithaml, C.P. (1989b) The psychological context of strategic decisions: a test of relevance to practitioners, *Strategic Management Journal*, 10: 587–92.

Bazerman, M.H. (1984) The relevance of Kahneman and Tversky's

References

concept of framing to organizational behavior, *Journal of Management*, 10: 333–43.

Bazerman, M.H. (1998) *Judgement in Managerial Decision Making*, 4th edn. New York: Wiley.

Beckman, T.J. (1999) The current state of knowledge management, in J. Leibowitz (ed.) *Knowledge Management Handbook*. Boca Raton: CRC Press.

Bennett, R.H. and Anthony, W.P. (2001) Understanding the role of intuition-tacit knowledge and analysis-explicit knowledge in bank board deliberations, in T.K. Lant and Z. Shapira (eds) (2001) *Organizational Cognition: Computation and Interpretation*. Mahwah, NJ: Lawrence Erlbaum Associates.

Bentler, P.M. (1989) *EQS: Structural Equations Program Manual*. Los Angeles, CA: BDMP Statistical Software.

Berger, P.L. and Luckmann, T. (1967) *The Social Construction of Reality*. New York: Doubleday Anchor.

Berry, D.C. and Broadbent, D.E. (1984) On the relationship between task performance and associated verbalisable knowledge, *Quarterly Journal of Experimental Psychology*, 36A(2): 209–31.

Bettman, J.R. and Weitz, B.A. (1983) Attributions in the boardroom: causal reasoning in corporate annual reports, *Administrative Science Quarterly*, 28: 165–83.

Betts, G.H. (1909) *The Distribution and Functions of Mental Imagery*. New York: Teachers' College, Columbia University.

Beyer, J., Chattopadhyay, P., George, E. *et al.* (1997) The selective perception of managers revisited, *Academy of Management Journal*, 40: 716–37.

Bibby, P.A. (1992) Mental models, instructions and internalisation, in Y. Rogers, A. Rutherford and P.A. Bibby (eds) *Models In The Mind: Theory, Perspective and Application*. London: Academic Press.

Bierly, P.E. and Spender, J-C. (1995) The culture of high reliability organizations: the case of the nuclear submarine, *Journal of Management*, 21: 639–56.

Birnbaum-More, P.H. and Weiss, A.R. (1990) Discovering the basis of competition in 12 industries: computerized content analysis of interview data from the US and Europe, in A.S. Huff (ed.) *Mapping Strategic Thought*, pp. 53–69. Chichester: John Wiley.

Blackler, F., Crump, N. and McDonald, S. (1999a) Organizational learning and organizational forgetting, in M. Easterby-Smith, J. Burgoyne and L. Araujo (eds) *Organizational Learning and the Learning Organization: Developments in Theory and Practice*. London: Sage.

Blackler, F., Crump, N. and McDonald, S. (1999b) Managing experts and competing through innovation: an activity theoretical analysis, *Organization*, 6(1): 5–31.

Blattberg, R.C. and Hoch, S.J. (1990) Database models and managerial intuition: 50 percent model and 50 percent manager, *Management Science*, 36(8): 887–99.

Bonabeau, E. and Meyer, C. (2001) Swarm intelligence: a whole new way to think about business, *Harvard Business Review*, 79(5): 106–14.

Bonache, J. and Brewster, C. (2001) Knowledge transfer and the management of expatriation, *Thunderbird International Business Review*, 43(1): 145–68.

Bood, R.P. (1998) Charting organizational learning: a comparison of multiple mapping techniques, in C. Eden and J-C. Spender (eds) *Managerial and Organizational Cognition: Theory, Methods and Research*. London: Sage.

Boone, C. (1988) The influence of the locus of control of top managers on company strategy, structure and performance, in P.V. Abeele (ed.) *Psychology in Micro and Macro Economics: Proceedings of the 13th Annual Colloquium of the International Association for Research in Economic Psychology*, 1.

Boone, C. and De Brabander, B. (1993) Generalised versus specific locus of control expectancies of chief executive officers, *Strategic Management Journal*, 14: 619–25.

Boone, C. and De Brabander, B. (1997) Self-reports and CEO locus of control research: A note, *Organization Studies*, 18: 949–71.

Boone, C., De Brabander, B. and van Witteloostuijn, A. (1996) CEO locus of control and small firm performance: an integrative framework and empirical test, *Journal of Management Studies*, 33: 667–99.

Boone, C., De Brabander, B. and Hellemans, J. (2000) Research note: CEO locus of control and small firm performance. *Organization Studies*, 21: 641–46.

Bouchet, J.L. (1976) Diversification: composition of the top management team and performance of the firm. *EGOS Conference on the Sociology of the Business Enterprise*, Oxford, 15–18 December.

Bougon, M.G. (1992) Congregate cognitive maps: a unified dynamic theory of organization and strategy, *Journal of Management Studies*, 29: 369–89.

Bougon, M.G., Weick, K.E. and Binkhorst, D. (1977) Cognition in organizations: an analysis of the Utrecht Jazz Orchestra. *Administrative Science Quarterly*, 22: 606–39.

Bower, J.L. (1972) *Managing the Resource Allocation Process: A Study of Corporate Planning and Investment*. Homewood, IL: Irwin.

Bowers, C.A., Jentsch, F., Salas, E. and Braun, C.C. (1998) Analyzing communication sequences for team training needs assessment, *Human Factors*, 40: 672–9.

Bowers, K.S., Regher, G., Balthazard, C. and Parker, K. (1990) Intuition in the context of discovery, *Cognitive Psychology*, 22: 72–110.

Bowman, C. and Daniels, K. (1995) The influence of functional experience on perception of strategic priorities, *British Journal of Management*, 6: 157–67.

Bowman, C. and Johnson, G. (1992) Surfacing competitive strategies, *European Management Journal*, 10: 210–19.

Breiman, L., Friedman, J.H., Oshen, R.A. and Stone, C.J. (1993) *Classification and Regression Trees*. New York: Chapman & Hall.

Briner, R.B. (1999) Feeling and smiling, *The Psychologist*, 12(1): 16–19.

Broadbent, D.E. (1958) *Perception and Communication*. London: Pergamon Press.

Brooks, L., Kimble, C. and Hildreth, P. (2001) Understanding managerial cognition: a structurational approach, in T.K. Lant and Z. Shapira (eds) *Organizational Cognition: Computation and Interpretation*. London: Lawrence Erlbaum Associates.

Brown, A.D. and Starkey, K. (2000) Organizational identity and learning: a psychodynamic perspective, *Academy of Management Review*, 25: 102–20.

Brown, J.S. and Duguid, P. (1991) Organizational learning and communities-of-practice: towards a unified view of working, learning and innovating, *Organization Science*, 2(1): 40–57.

Brown, N.R., Shevell, S.K. and Rips, L.J. (1986) Public memories and their personal context, in D.C. Rubin (ed.) *Autobiographical Memory*. Cambridge: Cambridge University Press.

Brown, S. and Eisenhardt, K.M. (1997) The art of continuous change: linking complexity theory and time-paced evolution in relentlessly shifting organizations, *Administrative Science Quarterly*, 42: 1–34.

Brown, S. and Eisenhardt, K.M. (1998) *Competing on the Edge: Strategy as Structured Chaos*. Boston, MA: Harvard Business School Press.

Bryk, A.S. and Raudenbush, S.W. (1992) *Hierarchical Linear Models: Applications and Data Analysis Methods*. Newbury Park, CA: Sage.

Buckley, P.J. and Chapman, M. (1997) The use of native categories in management research, *British Journal of Management*, 8: 283–99.

Budhwar, P.S. (2000) Strategic integration and devolvement of human resource management in the UK manufacturing sector, *British Journal of Management*, 11: 285–302.

Budhwar, P.S. and Sparrow, P.R. (in press) Strategic HRM through the cultural looking glass: mapping cognition of British and Indian HRM managers, *Organization Studies*.

Bukszar, E. and Connolly, T. (1988) Hindsight bias and strategic choice: some problems in learning from experience, *Academy of Management Journal*, 31: 628–41.

Burke, L.A. and Miller, M.K. (1999) Taking the mystery out of intuitive decision making, *Academy of Management Executive*, 12: 22–42.

Burke, M.J.A., Brief, A.P. and George, J.M. (1993) The role of negative affectivity in understanding relations between self reports of stressors and strains: a comment on the applied psychology literature, *Journal of Applied Psychology*, 78: 402–12.

Butler, P., Hall, T.W., Hanna, A.M. *et al.* (1997) A revolution in interaction, *McKinsey Quarterly*, 1: 5–24.

Byrne, D. (1971) *The Attraction Paradigm*. New York: Academic Press.

Cacioppo, J.T. and Petty, R.E. (1982) The need for cognition, *Journal of Personality and Social Psychology*, 42: 116–31.

Calori, R., Johnson, G. and Sarnin, P. (1992) French and British top managers' understanding of the structure and dynamics of their industries: a cognitive analysis and comparison, *British Journal of Management*, 3: 61–78.

Calori, R., Johnson, G. and Sarnin, P. (1994) CEOs' cognitive maps and the scope of the organization, *Strategic Management Journal*, 15: 437–57.

Cangelosi, V. and Dill, W.R. (1965) Organizational learning: observations toward a theory, *Administrative Science Quarterly*, 10(2): 175–203.

Cannon-Bowers, J.A. and Salas, E. (eds) (1998) *Making Decisions Under Stress: Implications for Individual and Team Training*. Washington: American Psychological Association.

Cannon-Bowers, J.A. and Salas, E. (2001) Reflections on shared cognition, *Journal of Organizational Behavior*, 22: 195–202.

Cannon-Bowers, J.A., Salas, E. and Converse, S. (1993) Shared mental models in expert team decision making, in N.J. Castellan (ed.) *Individual and Group Decision Making*. Hillsdale, NJ: Lawrence Erlbaum Associates.

Cappelli, P. (1999) *The New Deal At Work: Managing The Market-Driven Workforce*. Boston, MA: Harvard Business School Press.

Cappon, D. (1994) *Intuition and Management: Research and Application*. Westport, CT: Quorum Books.

Carpenter, M.A. and Fredrickson, J.W. (2001) Top management teams, global strategic posture, and the moderating role of uncertainty, *Academy of Management Journal*, 44(3): 533–45.

Cartwright, S. and Cooper, C.L. (1990) The impact of mergers and acquisitions on people at work: existing research and issues, *British Journal of Management*, 1: 65–76.

Cartwright, S. and Cooper, C.L. (1993) The psychological impact of merger and acquisition on the individual: a study of building society managers, *Human Relations*, 46: 327–47.

Cassell, C. (1999) Exploring feelings in the workplace: emotion at work, *The Psychologist*, special issue, 12(1): 15.

Caves, R.E. and Porter, M.E. (1977) From entry barriers to mobility barriers: conjectural decisions and contrived deterrence to new competition, *Quarterly Journal of Economics*, 91: 421–34.

Chaffee, E.E. (1985) Three models of strategy, *Academy of Management Review*, 10: 89–98.

Chaiken, S. (1980) Heuristic versus systematic information processing and the use of source versus message cues in persuasion, *Journal of Personality and Social Psychology*, 39: 752–6.

Chaiken, S. (1987) The heuristic model of persuasion, in M. Zanna, J. Olsen and C.P. Herman (eds) *Social Influence: The Ontario Symposium – Volume 5*. Hillsdale, NJ: Lawrence Erlbaum Associates.

Chaiken, S. and Trope, Y. (eds) (1999) *Dual-Process Theories in Social Psychology*. New York: The Guilford Press.

Chatman, J.A. and Jehn, K.A. (1994) Assessing the relationship between industry characteristics and organizational culture: how different can you be? *Academy of Management Journal*, 37: 522–53.

Chattopadhyay, P., Glick, W.H., Miller, C.C. and Huber, G.P. (1999) Determinants of executive beliefs: comparing functional conditioning and social influence, *Strategic Management Journal*, 20: 763–89.

Checkland, P.B. and Scholes, J. (1990) *Soft Systems Methodology in Action*. Chichester: Wiley.

Chi, M.T.H. (1997) Creativity: shifting across ontological categories flexibly, in T. Ward, S. Smith and J. Vaid (eds) *Creative Thought: An Investigation of Conceptual Structures and Processes*. Washington: American Psychological Association.

Christensen, C.R., Andrews, K.R., Bower, J.L., Hamermesh, G. and Porter, M.E. (1982) *Business Policy: Text and Cases*, 5th edn. Homewood, IL: Irwin.

Clapham, S.E. and Schwenk, C.R. (1991) Self-serving attributions, managerial cognition and company performance, *Strategic Management Journal*, 12: 219–29.

Clark, B.H. and Montgomery, D.B. (1999) Managerial identification of competitors, *Journal of Marketing*, 63: 67–83.

Clark, P.A. and Staunton, N. (1989) *Innovation in Technology and Organization*. London: Routledge.

Clarke, I. and Mackaness, W. (2001) Management 'intuition': an interpretative account of structure and content of decision schemas using cognitive maps, *Journal of Management Studies*, 38(2): 147–72.

Claxton, G. (1997) *Hare Brain, Tortoise Mind: Why Intelligence Increases When You Think Less*. London: Fourth Estate.

Claxton, G. (1998) Investigating human intuition: knowing without knowing why, *The Psychologist*, 11(5): 217–20.

Coleman, D.F., Irving, G.P. and Cooper, C.L. (1999) Another look at the locus of control – organisational commitment relationship: it depends on the form of commitment, *Journal of Organizational Behavior*, 20: 995–1001.

Colf, R.W. (1997) Human assets and management dilemmas: coping with the hazards on the road to resource-based theory, *Academy of Management Review*, 22(2): 374–402.

Collins, H. (1993) The structure of knowledge, *Social Research*, 60: 95–116.

Cooke, N.J., Salas, E., Cannon-Bowers, J.A. and Stout, R.J. (2000) Measuring team knowledge, *Human Factors*, 42: 151–73.

Cool, K.O. and Schendel, D. (1987) Strategic group formation and performance: the case of the U.S. pharmaceutical industry, 1963–1982, *Management Science*, 33: 1102–24.

Cooper, R.K. (1997) Applying emotional intelligence in the workplace, *Training and Development*, 51(12): 31–8.

Cooper, R.K. (1998) Sentimental value, *People Management*, 2nd April: 48–50.

Cooper, R.K. and Sawaf, A. (1997) *Executive EQ: Emotional Intelligence in Leadership and Organizations*. New York: Grosner Putnam.

Coopey, J. (1995) The learning organization: power politics and ideology, *Management Learning*, 26(2): 193–214.

Corner, P.D., Kinicki, A.J. and Keats, B.W. (1994) Integrating organizational and individual information processing perspectives on choice, *Organization Science*, 5: 294–308.

Corter, J.E. (1996) Tree models of similarity and association, *Sage University Paper Series on Quantitative Applications in the Social Sciences*, 07–112. Thousand Oaks, CA: Sage.

Corter, J.E. and Tversky, A. (1986) Extended similarity trees, *Psychometrika*, 51: 429–51.

Cosette, P. and Audet, M. (1992) Mapping of an idiosyncratic schema, *Journal of Management Studies*, 29: 309–48.

Cowan, D.A. (1987) The effect of decision styles and levels of experience on executives' representations of organizational problem situations, *Proceedings of the Annual Meeting of the Decision Science Institute*, 2: 1130–2.

Craik, K. (1943) *The Nature of Explanation*. Cambridge: Cambridge University Press.

Cropper, S., Eden, C. and Ackermann, F. (1990) Keeping sense of accounts using computer-based cognitive maps, *Social Science Computer Review*, 8: 345–66.

Cross, R. (1998) *Knowledge and Knowledge Management in Organizations: A Literature Review*. Boston, MA: Boston University School of Management Systems Research Center.

Crowne, D.P. and Marlowe, D. (1964) *The Approval Motive: Studies in Evaluative Dependence*. New York: Wiley.

Csikszentmihalyi, M. (1988) Society, culture and person: a systems view of creativity, in R.J. Sternberg (ed.) *The Nature of Creativity: Contemporary Psychological Perspectives*. Cambridge: Cambridge University Press.

Csikszentmihalyi, M. (1999) Implications of a systems perspective for the study of creativity, in R.J. Sternberg (ed.) *Handbook of Creativity*. Cambridge: Cambridge University Press.

Csikszentmihalyi, M. and Csikszentmihalyi, I.S. (eds) (1988) *Optimal Experience: Psychological Studies of Flow in Consciousness*. New York: Cambridge University Press.

Cyert, R.M. and March, J.G. (1963) *A Behavioral Theory of the Firm*. Englewood Cliffs, NJ: Prentice-Hall.

D'Avini, R.A. (1990) Top managerial prestige and organizational bankruptcy, *Organization Science*, 1: 121–42.

D'Avini, R.A.I. (1994) *Hypercompetition*. New York: Free Press.

Daboub, A.J., Rasheed, A.M.A., Priem, R.L. and Gray, D.A. (1995) Top management team characteristics and corporate illegal activity, *Academy of Management Review*, 20: 138–70.

Dacey, J.S. and Lennon, K.H. (1998) *Understanding Creativity: The Interplay of Biological, Psychological and Social Factors*. San Francisco: Jossey-Bass.

Daft, R.L. (1995) *Organization Theory And Design*, 5th edn. St. Paul, MN: West Publishing.

Daft, R.L. and Lengel, R.H. (1984) Information richness: a new approach to managerial behaviour and organization design, in L.L. Cummings and B.M. Staw (eds) *Research in Organizational Behaviour*, vol. 6. Greenwich, CT: JAI Press.

Daft, R.L. and Lewin, A.Y. (1993) Where are the theories for the 'new' organizational forms? An editorial essay, *Organization Science*, 4(4): i–vi.

Daft, R.L. and Weick, K.E. (1984) Toward a model of organizations as interpretation systems, *Academy of Management Review*, 9(2): 284–95.

Dalgleish, T. and Watts, F.N. (1990) Biases of attention and memory in disorders of anxiety and depression, *Clinical Psychology Review*, 10: 589–604.

Daniels, K. (1998) Towards integrating emotions into strategic management research: trait affect and perceptions of the strategic environment, *British Journal of Management*, 9: 163–8.

Daniels, K. (1999) Affect and strategic decision making, *The Psychologist*, 12(1): 24–7.

Daniels, K. and Henry, J. (1998) Strategy: a cognitive perspective, in S. Segal-Horn (ed.) *The Strategy Reader*. London: Macmillan.

Daniels, K. and Johnson, G. (2002) On trees and triviality traps: locating the debate on the contribution of cognitive mapping to organizational research, *Organization Studies*, 23: 73–81.

Daniels, K., Johnson, G. and de Chernatony, L. (1994) Differences in managerial cognitions of competition, *British Journal of Management*, 5: S21–9.

Daniels, K., de Chernatony, L. and Johnson, G. (1995) Validating a method for mapping managers' mental models of competitive industry structures, *Human Relations*, 48(8): 975–91.

Daniels, K., Johnson, G. and de Chernatony, L. (2002) Task and institutional influences on managers' mental models of competition, *Organization Studies*, 23: 31–62.

Das, T.K. and Teng, B.-S. (1999) Cognitive biases and strategic decision processes, *Journal of Management Studies*, 36: 757–78.

Davenport, T.H. and Prusak, L. (1998) *Working Knowledge: How Organisations Manage What They Know*. Boston, MA: Harvard Business School Press.

Davis, J. (1983) Does authority generalize? Locus of control perceptions in Anglo-American and Mexican-American adolescents, *Political Psychology*, 4: 101–20.

Davis, M.H. (1996) *Empathy: A Social Psychological Approach*. Boulder, CO: Westview Press.

Davis-Floyd R. and Arvidson, P.S. (eds) (1997) *Intuition: The Inside Story and Interdisciplinary Perspectives*. London: Routledge.

de Chernatony, L., Daniels, K. and Johnson, G. (1993) A cognitive perspective on managers' perceptions of competition, *Journal of Marketing Management*, 9: 973–81.

de Geus, A. (1988) Planning as learning, *Harvard Business Review*, March–April: 70–4.

Dearborn, D.C. and Simon, H.A. (1958) Selective perception: a note on the departmental identification of executives, *Sociometry*, 21: 140–4.

Decker, S. and Maurer, F. (1999) Editorial: organisational memory and knowledge management, *International Journal of Human-Computer Studies*, 51: 511–16.

Dess, G.G. and Davis, P.S. (1984) Porter's (1980) generic strategies as determinants of strategic group membership and organizational performance, *Academy of Management Journal*, 27: 467–88.

References

DiBella, A.J., Nevis, E.C and Gould, J.M. (1996) Understanding organizational learning capability, *Journal of Management Studies*, 33(3): 361–79.

Dierkes, M., Antal, A.B., Child, J. and Nonaka, I. (eds) (2001) *Handbook of Organizational Learning and Knowledge*. Oxford: Oxford University Press.

Diffenbach, J. (1982) Influence diagrams for complex strategic issues, *Strategic Management Journal*, 3: 133–46.

Digman, J.N. (1990) Personality structure: emergence of the five factor model, *Annual Review of Psychology*, 41: 417–40.

DiMaggio, P.J. and Powell, W.W. (1983) The iron cage revisited: institutional isomorphism and collective rationality in organizational fields, *American Sociological Review*, 48: 147–60.

Dixon, N. (1994) *The Organizational Learning Cycle: How We Can Learn Collectively*. London: McGraw-Hill.

Dixon, N. (1999) Learning across organization boundaries, in M. Easterby-Smith, J. Burgoyne and L. Araujo (eds) *Organizational Learning and the Learning Organization: Developments in Theory and Practice*. London: Sage.

Douglas, M. (1986) *How Institutions Think*. Syracuse, NY: Syracuse University Press.

Drott, M.C. (2001) Personal knowledge, corporate information: the challenges for competitive intelligence, *Business Horizons*, 44(2): 31–7.

Dulewicz, V. and Herbert, P.J. (1999) Predicting advancement to senior management from competencies and personality data: a seven-year follow-up study, *British Journal of Management*, 10: 13–22.

Dulewicz, V. and Higgs, M. (1998) Emotional intelligence: can it be measured reliably and validly using competency data? *Competency*, 6(1): 28–37.

Duncan, R. and Weiss, A. (1979) Organizational learning: implications for organizational design, in B. Staw (ed.) *Research in Organizational Behavior*. Greenwich, CT: JAI Press.

Dunn, W.N. and Ginsberg, A. (1986) A sociocognitive network approach to organizational analysis, *Human Relations*, 40: 955–76.

Dutton, J.E. and Dukerich, J.M. (1991) Keeping an eye on the mirror: image and identity in organizational adaptation, *Academy of Management Journal*, 34: 517–54.

Dutton, J. and Jackson, S. (1987) Categorizing strategic issues: links to organizational action, *Academy of Management Review*, 12: 76–90.

Dworman, G.O., Kimbrough, S.O., Kirk, S.E. and Oliver, J.R. (1997) On relevance and two aspects of the organizational memory problem. Working paper, http://opim.wharton.upenn.edu,~dnorman,mypapers/orgmems5.pdf.

Easterby-Smith, M. (1997) Disciplines of organizational learning: contributions and critiques, *Human Relations*, 50(9), 1085–113.

Easterby-Smith, M. and Araujo, L. (1999) Organizational learning: current debates and opportunities, in M. Easterby-Smith, J. Burgoyne and L. Araujo (eds) *Organizational Learning and the Learning Organization: Developments in Theory and Practice*. London: Sage.

Easton, G. and Araujo, L. (1994) Market exchange, social structures and time, *European Journal of Marketing*, 28(3): 72–84.

Eden, C. (1990) Strategic thinking with computers, *Long Range Planning*, 23: 35–43.

Eden, C. (1992) Strategic management as a social process, *Journal of Management Studies*, 29: 799–811.

Eden, C. (1993) Strategy development and implementation: cognitive mapping for group support, in J. Hendry and G. Johnson with J. Newton (eds) *Strategic Thinking: Leadership and the Management of Change*. Chichester: Wiley.

Eden, C. and Ackermann, F. (1998) *Making Strategy: The Journey of Strategic Management*. London: Sage.

Eden, C. and Huxham, C. (1996) Action research for the study of organizations, in S.R. Clegg, C. Hardy and W.R. Nord (eds) *Handbook of Organization Studies*. London: Sage.

Eden, C. and Radford, J. (eds) (1990) *Tackling Strategic Problems: The Role of Group Decision Support*. London: Sage.

Eden, C. and Spender, J-C. (eds) (1998) *Managerial and Organizational Cognition: Theory, Methods and Research*. London: Sage.

Eden, C., Ackermann, F. and Cropper, S. (1992) The analysis of cause maps, *Journal of Management Studies*, 29: 309–24.

Einhorn, H.J. (1972) Expert measurement and mechanical combination, *Organizational Behavior and Human Performance*, 7: 86–106.

Eisenhardt, K.M. and Zbaracki, M.J. (1992) Strategic decision making, *Strategic Management Journal*, 13: 737–70.

El Sawy, D.A., Gomes, G.M. and Gonzales, M.V. (1986) Preserving institutional memory: the management of history as an organizational resource, *Academy of Management Best Paper Proceedings*, 37: 118–22.

Elkjaer, B. (1999) In search of a social learning theory, in M. Easterby-Smith, J. Burgoyne and L. Araujo (eds) *Organizational Learning and the Learning Organization: Developments in Theory and Practice*. London: Sage.

Elsbach, K.D. and Barr, P.S. (1999) The effects of mood on individuals' use of structured decision protocols, *Organization Science*, 10: 181–98.

Engestrom, Y. (1987) *Learning By Expanding: An Activity Theoretical Approach to Developmental Research*. Helsinki: Orientat Consultit.

References

Engestrom, Y. (1991) Organizational forgetting: an activity theoretical perspective, in D. Middleton and D. Edwards (eds) *Collective Remembering*. London: Sage.

Engestrom, Y. (1993) Developmental studies of work as a test bench for activity theory: the case of primary care in medical practice, in S. Chaiklin and J. Lave (eds) *Understanding Practice: Perspectives on Activity and Context*. Cambridge: Cambridge University Press.

Epstein, S. (1990) Cognitive-experiential self-theory, in L. Pervin (ed.) *Handbook of Personality Theory and Research*. New York: Guilford Press.

Epstein, S. (1991) Cognitive-experiential self-theory: an integrative theory of personality, in R. Curtis (ed.) *The Relational Self: Convergences in Psychoanalysis and Social Psychology*. New York: Guilford Press.

Epstein, S. (1998) Emotions and psychology from the perspective of cognitive-experiential self-theory, in W.F. Flack and J.D. Laird (eds) *Emotions in Psychopathology: Theory and Research Series in Affective Science*. New York: Oxford University Press.

Epstein, S., Pacini, R., Denes-Raj, V. and Heir, H. (1996) Individual differences in intuitive-experiential and analytical-rational thinking styles, *Journal of Personality and Social Psychology*, 71: 390–405.

Evans, J. St. B.T. (1984) Heuristic and analytic processes in reasoning, *British Journal of Psychology*, 75: 451–68.

Evans, J. St. B.T. (1989) *Biases in Human Reasoning: Causes and Consequences*. Hove: Lawrence Erlbaum Associates.

Evans, J. St. B.T. and Over, D.E. (1996) *Rationality and Reasoning*. Hove: Psychology Press.

Evans, P. and Doz, Y. (1992) A paradigm for human resource and organizational development in complex multinationals, in V. Pucik, N.M. Tichy and C.V. Bartlett (eds) *Globalizing Management*. New York: Wiley.

Eysenck, H.J. (1995) *Genius: The Natural History of Creativity*. Cambridge: Cambridge University Press.

Eysenck, M.W. and Keane, M.T. (1995) *Cognitive Psychology: A Student's Handbook*, 3rd edn. Hove: Psychology Press.

Fahey, L. and Randall, R.M. (eds) (1998) *Learning from the Future: Competitive Foresight Scenarios*. New York: Wiley.

Farjoun, M. and Lai, L. (1997) Similarity judgments in strategy formulation: role, process and implications, *Strategic Management Journal*, 18: 255–73.

Feldman, J.M. and Lynch, J.G. (1988) Self-generated validity and other effects of measurement on belief, attitude, intention and behavior, *Journal of Applied Psychology*, 73: 421–35.

Fenton, E.M. and Pettigrew, A. (2000) Theoretical perspectives on new forms of organizing, in A.M. Pettigrew and E.M. Fenton (eds) *The Innovating Organization*. London: Sage.

Field, L. and Ford, B. (1995) *Managing Organizational Learning: From Rhetoric to Reality*. Melbourne: Longman.

Fineman, S. (1996) Emotion and organizing, in S.R. Clegg, C. Hardy and W.R. Nord (eds) *Handbook of Organization Studies*. London: Sage.

Finke, R.A. and Bettle, J. (1996) *Chaotic Cognition: Principles and Applications*. Mahwah, NJ: Lawrence Erlbaum.

Finke, R.A., Ward, T.B. and Smith, S.M. (1992) *Creative Cognition: Theory, Research and Application*. Cambridge, MA: MIT Press.

Finkelstein, S. and Hambrick, D.C. (1996) *Strategic Leadership: Top Executives and Their Effects on Organizations*. St Paul, MN: West.

Finucane, M.L., Alhakami, A., Slovic, P. and Johnson, S. (2000) The affect heuristic in judgments of risks and benefits, *Journal of Behavioral Decision Making*, 13: 1–17.

Fiol, C.M. (1994) Consensus, diversity, and learning in organizations, *Organization Science*, 5(3): 403–20.

Fiol, C.M. and Huff, A.S. (1992) Maps for managers: where are we? Where do we go from here?, *Journal of Management Studies*, 29: 267–85.

Fiol, C.M. and Lyles, M.A. (1985) Organizational learning, *Academy of Management Review*, 10: 803–13.

Fischhoff, B. (1975) Hindsight and foresight: the effect of outcome knowledge on judgement under uncertainty, *Journal of Experimental Psychology: Human Perception and Performance*, 1: 288–99.

Fischhoff, B., Slovic, P. and Liechtenstein, S. (1977) Knowing with certainty: the appropriateness of extreme confidence, *Journal of Experimental Psychology: Human Perception and Performance*, 3: 552–64.

Fisher, D. (1993) *Communication in Organizations*, 2nd edn. Minneapolis, MN: West Publishing.

Fiske, S.T. and Taylor, S.E. (1984) *Social Cognition*. Reading, MA: Addison-Wesley.

Flood, P.C., Dromgoole, T., Carroll, S.J. and Gorman, L. (eds) (2000) *Managing Strategy Implementation*. Oxford: Blackwell.

Flood, P.C., Fong, C.-M., Smith, K.G. *et al.* (1997) Top management teams and pioneering: a resource-based view, *International Journal of Human Resource Management*, 8(3): 291–306.

Flood, P.C., MacCurtain, S. and West, M.A. (2001) *Effective Top Management Teams: An International Perspective*. Stillorgan, Co. Dublin, Ireland: Blackhall Publishing.

Floyd, S.W. and Lane, P.J. (2000) Strategizing throughout the organization: managing role conflict in strategic renewal, *Academy of Management Review*, 25: 154–77.

References

Floyd, S.W. and Woolridge, B. (1992) Middle management involvement in strategy and its association with strategic type, *Strategic Management Journal*, 13: 153–67.

Floyd, S.W. and Woolridge, B. (1994) Dinosaurs or dynamos? Recognizing middle management's strategic role, *Academy of Management Executive*, 8(4): 47–57.

Floyd, S.W. and Woolridge, B. (1997) Middle management's strategic influence and organizational performance, *Journal of Management Studies*, 34: 465–85.

Floyd, S.W. and Woolridge, B. (2000) *Building Strategy from the Middle: Reconceptualizing Strategy Process*. Thousand Oaks, CA: Sage.

Folger, R. and Cropanzano, R. (1998) *Organizational Justice and Human Resource Management*. London: Sage.

Fombrun, C.J. and Zajac, E.J. (1987) Structural and perceptual influences on intra-industry stratification, *Academy of Management Journal*, 30: 33–50.

Forbes, D.P. and Milliken, F.J. (1999) Cognition and corporate governance: understanding boards of directors as strategic decision-making groups, *Academy of Management Review*, 24: 489–505.

Forgas, J.P. (1976) The perception of social episodes: categorical and dimensional representation in two cultural milieus, *Journal of Personality and Social Psychology*, 34: 199–209.

Forgas, J.P. (1978) Social episodes and social structure in an academic setting: the social environment of an intact group, *Journal of Experimental Social Psychology*, 14: 434–48.

Forgas, J.P. and Bower, G.H. (1987) Affect in social and personal judgements, in K. Fiedler and J. Forgas (eds) *Affect, Cognition and Social Behaviour*. Toronto: Hogrefe International.

Forgas, J.P., Brown, L.B. and Menyhart, J. (1980) Dimensions of aggression: the perception of aggressive episodes, *British Journal of Social and Clinical Psychology*, 19: 215–27.

Fournier, S. and Guiry, M. (1993) An emerald green Jaguar, a house in Nantucket, and an African safari: wishlists and consumption dreams in materialistic society, *Advances in Consumer Research*, 20: 352–8.

Fox, S. and Spector, P.E. (2000) Relations of emotional intelligence, practical intelligence, and trait affectivity with interview outcomes: it's not all just 'G', *Journal of Organizational Behavior*, 21: 203–20.

Fransella, F. and Bannister, D. (1977) *A Manual For Repertory Grid Technique*. London: Academic Press.

Freire, P. (1994) *The Pedagogy Of The Oppressed*. New York: Continuum Publishing.

Frese, M., Chell, E. and Klandt, H. (eds) (2000) Psychological approaches to entrepreneurship, *European Journal of Work and Organizational Psychology*, 9(1): 3–101.

Freud, S. (1900) *The Interpretation of Dreams: Standard Edition*, vols 4/5. London: Hogarth.

Fulk, J. and DeSanctis, G. (1995) Electronic communication and changing organizational forms, *Organization Science*, 6: 338–49.

Furnham, A. (1986) Economic Locus of Control, *Human Relations*, 39: 29–43.

Furnham, A., Brewin, C.R. and O'Kelly, H. (1994) Cognitive style and attitudes to work, *Human Relations*, 47: 1509–21.

Galbraith, J.R. (1973) *Designing Complex Organizations*. Reading, MA: Addison-Wesley.

Gallupe, B. (2001) Knowledge management systems: surveying the landscape. *International Journal of Management Reviews*, 3(1): 61–77.

Galotti, K.M. (1989) Approaches to studying formal and everyday reasoning, *Psychological Bulletin*, 105(3): 331–51.

Galunic, D.C. and Rodin, S. (1998) Resource recombinations in the firm: knowledge structures and the potential for Schumpeterian innovation, *Strategic Management Journal*, 19(12): 1193–201.

Gardner, R.W., Holzman, P., Klein, G., Linton, H. and Spence, D. (1959) Cognitive control: a study of individual differences in cognitive behaviour, *Psychological Issues*, 1: monograph 4.

Garvin, D.A. (1993) Building a learning organization, *Harvard Business Review*, 71(4): 78–84.

Getzels, J.W. and Jackson, P.W. (1962) *Creativity and Intelligence: Explorations with Gifted Students*. New York: Wiley.

Ghoshal, S. and Bartlett, C.A. (1990) The multinational corporation as a differentiated interorganizational network, *Academy of Management Review*, 15: 603–25.

Gibbs, R. (1997) How language affects the embodied nature of creative cognition, in T. Ward, S. Smith and J. Vaid (eds) *Creative Thought: An Investigation of Conceptual Structures and Processes*. Washington: American Psychological Association.

Gibson, C.B. (2001) From knowledge accumulation to accommodation: cycles of collective cognition in work groups, *Journal of Organizational Behavior*, 22: 121–34.

Gigerenzer, G. and Todd, P.M. (1999) Fast and frugal heuristics: the adaptive toolbox, in G. Gigerenzer, P.M. Todd and the ABC Research Group (eds) *Simple Heuristics That Make Us Smart*. New York: Oxford University Press.

Gigerenzer, G., Todd, P.M. and the ABC Research Group (eds) (1999)

Simple Heuristics That Make Us Smart. New York: Oxford University Press.

Gigone, D. and Hastie, R. (1993) The common knowledge effect: information sharing and group judgement, *Journal of Personality and Social Psychology*, 65: 959–74.

Ginsberg, A. (1989) Construing the business portfolio: a cognitive model of diversification, *Journal of Management Studies*, 26: 417–38.

Ginsberg, A. (1990) Connecting diversification to performance: a sociocognitive approach, *Academy of Management Review*, 15(3): 514–35.

Gioia, D.A. (1986) Conclusion: the state of the art in organizational social cognition – a personal view, in H.P. Sims and D.A. Gioia (eds) *The Thinking Organization: Dynamics of Organizational Social Cognition*. San Francisco: Jossey-Bass.

Gioia, D.A. and Chittipeddi, K. (1991) Sensemaking and sensegiving in strategic initiation, *Strategic Management Journal*, 12: 433–48.

Gioia, D.A. and Thomas, J.B. (1996) Identity, image, and issue interpretation: sensemaking during strategic change in academia, *Administrative Science Quarterly*, 41: 370–403.

Glaister, K.W. and Buckley, P.J. (1996) Strategic motives for international alliance formation, *Journal of Management Studies*, 33: 301–32.

Glaser, M. (1995) Measuring intuition, *Research-Technology Management*, 38(2): 43–6.

Goldberg, J. (1996) The Distrat/Askmap Suite of Programs for Cause Map Analysis: A User's Guide. Unpublished manuscript available from Cranfield University Computer Centre, Cranfield University, UK.

Golden, B. (1992) The past is past – or is it? The use of retrospective accounts as indicators of past strategy, *Academy of Management Journal*, 35: 848–60.

Goldstein, H. (1995) *Multilevel Statistical Models*. London: Edward Arnold.

Goleman, D. (1995) *Emotional Intelligence: Why It Can Matter More Than IQ*. London: Bloomsbury.

Goodwin, P. and Wright, G. (2001) Enhancing strategy evaluation in scenario planning: a role for decision analysis, *Journal of Management Studies*, 36(1): 1–16.

Gough, H. (1960) *California Psychological Inventory*. Palo Alto, CA: Consulting Psychologists Press.

Govindarajan, V. (1988) A contingency approach to strategy implementation at the business unit level: integrating administrative mechanisms with strategy, *Academy of Management Journal*, 31: 828–53.

Grant, R.M. (1996) Toward a knowledge-based theory of the firm, *Strategic Management Journal*, 17: 109–22.

Grant, R.M. (1998) *Contemporary Strategy Analysis*, 3rd edn. Oxford: Blackwell.

Green, D.W. and McManus, I.C. (1995) Cognitive structural models: the perception of risk and prevention in coronary heart disease, *British Journal of Psychology*, 86: 321–36.

Greenley, G. (1989) *Strategic Management*. London: Prentice-Hall.

Greve, H.R. (1998) Managerial cognition and the memetic adoption of market positions: what you see is what you do, *Strategic Management Journal*, 19: 967–88.

Grinyer, P.H. and Spender, J.C. (1979) Recipes, crises and adaptation in mature businesses, *International Studies of Management and Organisations*, IX: 113–23.

Gripsrud, G. and Gronhaug, K. (1985) Structure and strategy in grocery retailing: a sociometric approach, *Journal of Industrial Economics*, XXXIII: 339–47.

Gronhaug, K. and Falkenberg, J.S. (1989) Exploring strategy perceptions in changing environments, *Journal of Management Studies*, 26: 349–59.

Gronhaug, K. and Falkenberg, J.S. (1998) Success attributions within and across organizations, in C. Eden and J-C. Spender (eds) *Managerial and Organizational Cognition: Theory, Methods and Research*. London: Sage.

Guilford, J.P. (1967) *The Nature of Human Intelligence*. New York: McGraw-Hill.

Gul, F.A. (1984) The joint and moderating role of personality and cognitive style on decision-making, *The Accounting Review*, 59: 264–77.

Gunz, H.P. (1989) *Careers and Corporate Cultures: Managerial Mobility in Large Corporations*. Oxford: Blackwell.

Gunz, H.P. and Whitley, R.D. (1985) Managerial cultures and industrial strategies in British firms, *Organization Studies*, 6: 247–73.

Gurwitsch, A. (1966) *Studies in Phenomenology and Psychology*, Evanston, IL: Northwestern University Press.

Haleblain, J. and Finkelstein, S. (1993) Top management team size, CEO dominance and firm performance: the moderating roles of environmental turbulence and discretion, *Academy of Management Journal*, 36: 844–63.

Hall, R.I. (1984) The natural logic of management policy making: its implications for the survival of an organization, *Management Science*, 30: 905–27.

Hambrick, D.C. and Mason, P. (1984) Upper echelons: the organization as a reflection of its top managers, *Academy of Management Review*, 9: 193–206.

Hambrick, D.C., Cho, T.S. and Chen, M-J. (1996) The influence of top management team heterogeneity on firms' competitive moves, *Administrative Science Quarterly*, 41: 659–84.

Hamilton, E.E. (1988) The facilitation of organizational change: an empirical study of factors predicting change agents' effectiveness, *Journal for the Applied Behavioral Sciences*, 24: 37–59.

Hammond, K.R., Hamm, R.M., Grassia, J. and Person, T. (1997) Direct comparison of the efficacy of intuitive and analytical cognition in expert judgement, in W.M. Goldstein and R.M. Hogarth (eds) *Research on Judgment and Decision Making: Currents, Connections and Controversies*. Cambridge: Cambridge University Press.

Handy, C.B. (1985) *Understanding Organizations*. Harmondsworth: Penguin.

Handy, C.B. (1989) *The Age of Unreason*. London: Business Books.

Hannan, M. and Freeman, J. (1977) The population ecology of organizations, *American Journal of Sociology*, 82: 929–64.

Hannan, M. and Freeman, J. (1988) *Organizational Ecology*. Cambridge, MA: Harvard University Press.

Hansen, M.T. (1999) The search-transfer problem: the role of weak ties in sharing knowledge across organization subunits, *Administrative Science Quarterly*, 44: 82–111.

Hansen, M.T. and Haas, M.R. (2001) Competing for attention in knowledge markets: electronic document dissemination in a management consulting company, *Administrative Science Quarterly*, 46(1): 1–28.

Hansen, M.T., Nohria, N. and Tierney, T. (1999) What's your strategy for managing knowledge? *Harvard Business Review*, 77(2): 106–16.

Harbort, B. (1997) Thought, action and intuition in action-orientated professions, in R. Davis-Floyd and P.S. Arvidson (eds) *Intuition: The Inside Story and Interdisciplinary Perspectives*. London: Routledge.

Harris, S.G. (1994) Organizational culture and individual sensemaking: a schema-based perspective, *Organization Science*, 5: 309–21.

Haspeslagh, G. and Jemison, D.B. (1991) *Managing Acquisitions: Creating Value Through Corporate Renewal*. New York: Free Press.

Hatten, K.J. and Hatten, M.L. (1987) Strategic groups, asymmetrical mobility barriers and contestability, *Strategic Management Journal*, 8: 329–42.

Haunschild, P.R. (1993) Interorganizational imitation: the impact of interlocks on corporate acquisition activity, *Administrative Science Quarterly*, 38: 564–92.

Hayes, J. and Allinson, C.W. (1994) Cognitive style and its relevance for management practice, *British Journal of Management*, 5: 53–71.

Hayes, J. and Allinson, C.W. (1998) Cognitive style and the theory and practice of individual and collective learning in organizations, *Human Relations*, 51(7): 847–71.

Hayward, M.L.A. and Hambrick, D.C. (1997) Explaining the premium paid for large acquisitions: evidence of CEO hubris, *Administrative Science Quarterly*, 42: 103–27.

Hedberg, B. (1981) How organizations learn and unlearn, in P.C. Nystrom and W.H. Starbuck (eds) *Handbook of Organizational Design*. Oxford: Oxford University Press.

Hedberg, B. and Jonsson, S. (1977) Strategy making as a discontinuous process, *International Studies of Management and Organizations*, VII: 88–109.

Hedlund, G. (1994) A model of knowledge management and the N-form corporation, *Strategic Management Journal*, 15: 73–90.

Heimann, C.F.L. (1993) Understanding the *Challenger* disaster: organizational structure and the design of reliable systems, *American Political Science Review*, 87(2): 421–35.

Hellgren, B. and Melin, L. (1993) The role of strategists' way-of-thinking in strategic change processes, in J. Hendry and G. Johnson with J. Newton (eds) *Strategic Thinking: Leadership and the Management of Change*. Chichester: Wiley.

Henderson, J. and Nutt, P.C. (1980) The influence of decision style on decision making behavior, *Management Science*, 26: 371–86.

Hernstein, R.J. and Murray, C. (1994) *The Bell Curve: Intelligence and Class Structure in American life*. New York: Free Press.

Herriot, P. (2001) *The Employment Relationship: A Psychological Perspective*. London: Routledge.

Hicks, M., Wright, P. and Pocock, S. (1999) A distributed cognition perspective on civil aircraft failure management system design, *Engineering Psychology and Cognitive Ergonomics*, 3: 101–10.

Hintzman, D.L. (1990) Human learning and memory: connections and dissociations, *Annual Review of Psychology*, 41: 109–39.

Hitt, M.A., Ireland, R.D. and Hoskisson, R.E. (1996) *Strategic Management: Competitiveness and Globalization*, 2nd edn. St Paul, MN: West.

Hitt, M.A., Hoskisson, R.E., Johnson, R.A. and Moesel, D.D. (1996) The market for corporate control and firm innovation, *Academy of Management Journal*, 39: 1084–119.

Hodgkinson, G.P. (1992) Development and validation of the strategic locus of control scale, *Strategic Management Journal*, 13: 311–17.

Hodgkinson, G.P. (1993) Doubts about the conceptual and empirical status of context-free and firm-specific control expectancies: a reply to Boone and De Brabander, *Strategic Management Journal*, 14: 627–31.

Hodgkinson, G.P. (1997a) Cognitive inertia in a turbulent market: the case of UK residential estate agents, *Journal of Management Studies*, 34(6): (special issue) 921–45.

Hodgkinson, G.P. (1997b) The cognitive analysis of competitive structures: a review and critique, *Human Relations*, 50: 625–54.

Hodgkinson, G.P. (2001a) The psychology of strategic management: diversity and cognition revisited, in C.L. Cooper and I.T. Robertson (eds) *International Review of Industrial and Organizational Psychology*, vol. 16. Chichester: Wiley.

Hodgkinson, G.P. (2001b) Cognitive processes in strategic management: some emerging trends and future directions, in N. Anderson, D.S. Ones, H.K. Sinangil and C. Viswesvaran (eds) *Handbook of Industrial, Work and Organizational Psychology, Volume 2: Organizational Psychology*. London: Sage.

Hodgkinson, G.P. (ed.) (2001c) Facing the future: the nature and purpose of management research re-assessed, *British Journal of Management*, 12 (special issue): 51–80.

Hodgkinson, G.P. (2002) Comparing managers' mental models of competition: why self-report measures of belief similarity won't do, *Organization Studies*, 23: 63–72.

Hodgkinson, G.P. and Bown, N.J. (1999) The individual in the strategy process: a cognitive model. Paper presented at the Annual Conference of the British Academy of Management, Manchester, UK, September.

Hodgkinson, G.P. and Herriot, P. (2002) The role of psychologists in enhancing organizational effectiveness, in I. Robertson, M. Callinan and D. Bartram (eds) *Organizational Effectiveness: The Role of Psychology*. Chichester: Wiley.

Hodgkinson, G.P. and Johnson, G. (1994) Exploring the mental models of competitive strategists: the case for a processual approach, *Journal of Management Studies*, 31: 525–51.

Hodgkinson, G.P. and Maule, A.J. (2002) The individual in the strategy process: insights from behavioural decision research and cognitive mapping, in A.S. Huff and M. Jenkins (eds) *Mapping Strategic Knowledge*. London: Sage.

Hodgkinson, G.P. and Sadler-Smith, E. (in press) Complex or unitary? A critique and empirical re-assessment of the Allinson-Hayes Cognitive Style Index, *Journal of Occupational and Organizational Psychology*.

Hodgkinson. G.P. and Thomas, A.B. (eds) (1997) Thinking in organizations, *Journal of Management Studies*, 34 (special issue): 845–952.

Hodgkinson, G.P. and Wright, G. (in press) Confronting strategic inertia in a top management team: learning from failure, *Organization Studies*.

Hodgkinson, G.P., Padmore, J. and Tomes, A.E. (1991) Mapping consumers' cognitive structures: a comparison of similarity trees with multidimensional scaling and cluster analysis, *European Journal of Marketing*, 25(7): 41–60.

Hodgkinson, G.P., Tomes, A.E. and Padmore, J. (1996) Using consumers' perceptions for the cognitive analysis of corporate-level competitive structures, *Journal of Strategic Marketing*, 4: 1–22.

Hodgkinson, G.P., Bown, N.J., Maule, A.J., Glaister, K.W. and Pearman, A.D. (1998) Dual information processing in strategic decision making? A theoretical framework and some empirical data. Paper presented at the 18th International Conference of the Strategic Management Society, Orlando, Florida, 4 November.

Hodgkinson, G.P., Bown, N.J., Maule, A.J., Glaister, K.W. and Pearman, A.D. (1999) Breaking the frame: an analysis of strategic cognition and decision making under uncertainty, *Strategic Management Journal*, 20: 977–85.

Hodgkinson, G.P., Maule, A.J. and Bown, N.J. (2000) Charting the mind of the strategic decision maker: a comparative analysis of two methodological alternatives involving causal mapping. Paper presented at the Annual Meeting of the Academy of Management, Toronto, 4–9 August.

Hofer, C.W. and Schendel, D. (1978) *Strategy Formulation: Analytical Concepts*. St Paul, MN: West.

Hofstede, G. (1980) *Culture's Consequences*. London: Sage.

Hogan, E.A. and Overmyer-Day, L. (1994) The psychology of mergers and acquisitions, in C.L. Cooper and I.T. Robertson (eds) *International Review of Industrial and Organizational Psychology*, vol. 9. Chichester: Wiley.

Hollingshead, A.B. (1998) Retrieval processes in transactive memory systems, *Journal of Personality and Social Psychology*, 74: 659–71.

Honey, P. and Mumford, A. (1982) *The Manual of Learning Styles*. Maidenhead: Honey.

Huber, G.P. (1991) Organizational learning: the contributing process and the literatures, *Organization Science*, 2(1): 88–115.

Huber, G.P. and Daft, R.L. (1987) The information environments of organizations, in F.M. Javlin, L.L. Putnam, K.H. Roberts and L.W. Porter (eds) *Handbook of Organizational Communication*. Newbury Park, CA: Sage.

Huff, A.S. (1982) Industry influences on strategy reformulation, *Strategic Management Journal*, 3: 119–30.

Huff, A.S. (ed.) (1990) *Mapping Strategic Thought*. Chichester: Wiley.

Huff, A.S. (1997) A current and future agenda for cognitive research in organizations, *Journal of Management Studies*, 34(6): 947–52.

Huff, A.S. (2000) Changes in organizational knowledge production, *Academy of Management Review*, 25: 288–93.

References

Huff, A.S. and Jenkins, M. (eds) (2002) *Mapping Strategic Knowledge.* London: Sage.

Huff, A.S. and Schwenk, C. (1990) Bias and sensemaking in good times and bad, in A.S. Huff (ed.) *Mapping Strategic Thought.* Chichester: Wiley.

Huff, A.S., Narapareddy, V. and Fletcher, K.E. (1990) Coding the causal association of concepts, in A.S. Huff (ed.) *Mapping Strategic Thought.* Chichester: Wiley.

Hunt, M.S. (1972) Competition in the major home appliance industry. Unpublished doctoral dissertation, University of Harvard.

Hunt, R.G., Krzystofiak, F.J., Meindl, J.R. and Yousry, A.M. (1989) Cognitive style and decision-making, *Organizational Behavior and Human Decision Processes,* 44: 436–53.

Hurst, D.K., Rush, J.C. and White, R.E. (1989) Top management teams and organizational renewal, *Strategic Management Journal,* 10: 87–105.

Huselid, M.A. (1995) The impact of human resource management practices on turnover, productivity and corporate financial performance, *Academy of Management Journal,* 38(3): 635–72.

Hutchins, E. (1995) *Cognition in The Wild.* Cambridge, MA: MIT Press.

Huysman, M. (1996) *Dynamics of Organizational Learning.* Amsterdam: Thesis Publishers.

Huysman, M. (1999) Balancing biases: a critical review of the literature on organizational learning, in M. Easterby-Smith, J. Burgoyne and L. Araujo (eds) *Organizational Learning and the Learning Organization: Developments in Theory and Practice.* London: Sage.

Ilinitch, A.Y., Lewin, A.Y. and D'Aveni, R.D. (1998) Introduction, in A.Y. Ilinitch, A.Y. Lewin and R.D. D'Aveni (eds) *Managing in Times of Disorder: Hypercompetitive Organizational Responses.* London: Sage.

Inglis, B. (1987) *The Unknown Guest: The Mystery of Intuition.* London: Chatto & Windus.

Ingram, P. and Baum, J.A.C. (1997) Opportunity and constraint: organizations learning from the operating and competitive experience of industries, *Strategic Management Journal,* 18: 75–98.

Inkpen, A. (1996) Creating knowledge through collaboration, *California Management Review,* 39: 123–40.

Inkpen, A. and Crossan, M. (1995) Believing is seeing: organizational learning in joint ventures, *Journal of Management Studies,* 32: 595–618.

Isaacs, W.N. (1993) Taking flight: dialogue, collective thinking and organizational learning, *Organizational Dynamics,* 22(2): 24–39.

Isen, A.M. (1984) Toward understanding the role of affect in cognition, in R.S. Wyer and T.K. Srull (eds) *Handbook of Social Cognition,* vol. 3. Hillsdale, NJ: Lawrence Erlbaum Associates.

Isen, A.M., Daubman, K.A. and Nowicki, G.P. (1987) Positive affect facilitates creative problem solving, *Journal of Personality and Social Psychology*, 52: 1122–31.

Jablin, F.M. (1997) Organizational entry, assimilation and exit, in F. Jablin and L. Putnam (eds) *The New Handbook of Organizational Communication*. Thousand Oaks, CA: Sage.

Jackson, S.E. (1992) Consequences of group composition for the interpersonal dynamics of strategic issue processing, *Advances in Strategic Management*, 8: 345–82.

Jackson, S.E. and Dutton, J.E. (1988) Discerning threats and opportunities, *Administrative Science Quarterly*, 33: 370–87.

James, L.R. and James, L.A. (1989) Causal modelling in organizational research, in C.L. Cooper and I.T. Robertson (eds) *International Review of Industrial and Organizational Psychology*, vol. 4. Chichester: Wiley.

Janis, I. (1982) *Groupthink*, 2nd edn. Boston: Houghton-Mifflin.

Janis, I. and Mann, L. (1977) *Decision Making: A Psychological Analysis of Conflict, Choice and Commitment*. New York: Free Press.

Jenkins, M. and Johnson, G. (1997a) Entrepreneurial intentions and outcomes: a comparative causal mapping study, *Journal of Management Studies*, 34 (special issue): 895–920.

Jenkins, M. and Johnson, G. (1997b) Linking managerial cognition and organizational performance: a preliminary investigation using causal maps, *British Journal of Management*, 8: (special issue) S77–90.

Joe, V.C. (1971) Review of the internal-external control construct as a personality variable, *Psychological Reports*, 28: 619–40.

Johnson, G. (1987) *Strategic Change and the Management Process*. Oxford: Basil Blackwell.

Johnson, G. (1988) Re-thinking incrementalism, *Strategic Management Journal*, 9: 75–91.

Johnson, G. and Scholes, K. (1999) *Exploring Corporate Strategy: Text and Cases*, 5th edn. London: Prentice-Hall.

Johnson, P., Daniels, K. and Asch, R. (1998) Mental models of competition, in C. Eden and J-C. Spender (eds) *Managerial and Organizational Cognition: Theory, Methods and Research*. London: Sage.

Johnson-Laird, P.N. (1983) *Mental Models*. Cambridge: Cambridge University Press.

Johnson-Laird, P.N. (1993) *The Computer and the Mind*, 2nd edn. London: Fontana.

Johnson-Laird, P.N. and Bara, B.G. (1984) Syllogistic inference, *Cognition*, 16(1): 1–61.

Joreskog, K.G. and Sorbom, D. (1993) *LISREL 8: Structural Equation Modelling with the SIMPLIS Command Language*. Hillsdale, NJ: Lawrence Erlbaum Associates.

References

Jung, C.G. (1923) *Psychological Types*. London: Routledge.

Kagan, J. (1965) Individual differences in the resolution of response uncertainty, *Journal of Personality and Social Psychology*, 2: 154–60.

Kagono, T., Nonaka, I. Sakakibara, K. and Okumura, A. (1985) *Strategic vs Evolutionary Management: A US-Japan Comparison of Strategy and Organization*. Amsterdam, North Holland: Elsevier Science Publishers.

Kahneman D. and Tversky A. (1984) Choices, values and frames, *American Psychologist*, 39: 341–50.

Kahneman, D., Slovic, P. and Tversky, A. (eds) (1982) *Judgment Under Uncertainty: Heuristics and Biases*. Cambridge: Cambridge University Press.

Kantrow, A.M. (1987) *The Constraints of Corporate Tradition*. New York: Harper & Row.

Karmiloff-Smith, A. (1992) *Beyond Modularity: A Developmental Perspective on Cognitive Science*. Cambridge, MA: MIT Press.

Keck, S.L. (1997) Top management team structure: differential effects by environmental context, *Organization Science*, 8: 143–56.

Keck, S.L. and Tushman, M.L. (1993) Environmental and organizational context and executive team structure, *Academy of Management Journal*, 36: 314–44.

Keegan, W.J. (1982) *Keegan Type Indicator Form B*. New York: Warren Keegan Associates Press.

Kelloway, E.K. (1996) Common practices in structural equation modeling, in C.L. Cooper and I.T. Robertson (eds) *International Review of Industrial and Organizational Psychology*, vol. 11. Chichester: Wiley.

Kelly, G.A. (1955) *The Psychology of Personal Constructs*. (2 vols) New York: Norton.

Kelly, G.A. (1969) The role of classification in personality theory, in E. Maher (ed.) *Clinical Psychology and Personality: The Selected Papers of George Kelly*. New York: Wiley.

Kempton, W. (1978) Category grading and taxonomic relations: a mug is a sort of cup, *American Ethnologist*, 5: 44–65.

Kets de Vries, M.F.R. (1980) *Organizational Paradoxes: Clinical Approaches to Management*. London: Tavistock.

Kets de Vries, M.F.R. and Miller, D. (1984) *The Neurotic Organization: Diagnosing and Changing Counterproductive Styles of Management*. San Francisco: Jossey-Bass.

Kilduff, M., Angelmar, R. and Mehra, A. (2000) Top management-team diversity and firm performance: examining the role of cognitions, *Organization Science*, 11: 21–34.

Kim, D.H. (1993) *Systems Archetypes: Diagnosing Systemic Issues and Designing High Leverage Interventions*. Cambridge, MA: Pegasus Communications.

Kim, W. and Mauborgne, R. (1991) Implementing global strategies: the role of procedural justice, *Strategic Management Journal*, 12: 125–43.

Kinicki, A.J. and Vecchio, R.P. (1994) Influences on the quality of supervisor-subordinate relations: the role of time-pressure, organizational commitment, and locus of control, *Journal of Organizational Behavior*, 15: 75–82.

Kirton, M.J. (1976) Adaptors and Innovators: a description and measure, *Journal of Applied Psychology*, 61: 622–9.

Kirton, M.J. (ed.) (1989) *Adaptors and Innovators: Styles of Creativity and Problem Solving*. London: Routledge.

Kirton, M.J. (1994) A theory of cognitive style, in M.J. Kirton (ed.) *Adaptors and Innovators: Styles of Creativity and Problem Solving*, revised edn. London: Routledge.

Kleinmuntz, B. (1990) Why we still use our heads instead of formulas: towards an integrative approach, *Psychological Bulletin*: 107(3): 296–310.

Klimoski, R. and Mohammed, S. (1994) Team mental model: construct or metaphor? *Journal of Management*, 20: 403–37.

Knight, D., Pearce, C.L., Smith, K.G. *et al.* (1999) Top management team diversity, group process, and strategic consensus, *Strategic Management Journal*, 20: 445–65.

Kocharekar, R. (2001) K-commerce: knowledge-based commerce architecture with convergence of e-commerce and knowledge management, *Information Systems Management*, 18(2): 30–5.

Kogut, B. and Zander, U. (1992) Knowledge of the firm, combinative capabilities, and the replication of technology, *Organization Science*, 3: 388–97.

Kogut, B. and Zander, U. (1993) Knowledge of the firm and the evolutionary theory of the multinational corporation, *Journal of International Business Studies*, 24: 625–45.

Kolb, D.A. (1976) *The Learning Styles Inventory: Technical Manual*. Englewood Cliffs, NJ: Prentice Hall.

Kolb, D.A. (1984) *Experiential Learning*. Englewood Cliffs, NJ: Prentice Hall.

Krackhardt, D. (1987) Cognitive social structures, *Social Networks*, 9: 109–34.

Krackhardt, D. (1990) Assessing the political landscape: structure, cognition, and power in organizations, *Administrative Science Quarterly*, 35: 342–69.

Kramer, R.M. and Tyler, T.R. (eds) (1996) *Trust In Organizations: Frontiers of Theory and Research*. London: Sage.

Kreft, I. and de Leeuw, J. (1998) *Introducing Multilevel Modelling*. London: Sage.

References

Kris, E. (1952) *Psychoanalytical Explorations in Art*. New York: International Universities Press.

Krishnan, H.A., Miller, A. and Judge, W.Q. (1997) Diversification and top management team complementarity: is performance improved by merging similar or dissimilar teams? *Strategic Management Journal*, 18: 361–74.

Kruskal, J.B. and Wish, M. (1978) *Multidimensional Scaling*. Sage University Paper Series on Quantitative Applications in the Social Sciences, 07–011. Beverley Hills, CA: Sage.

Kuhberger (1998) The influence of framing on risky decisions: a meta analysis, *Organizational Behavior and Human Decision Processes*, 75: 23–55.

Kulik, C.T. and Ambrose, M.C. (1992) Personal and situational determinants of referent choice, *Academy of Management Review*, 17: 212–38.

Lakeoff, G. (1987) *Women, Fire and Dangerous Things: What Categories Reveal About the Mind*. Chicago: University of Chicago Press.

Lakeoff, G. and Johnson, M. (1980) *Metaphors We Live By*. Chicago: University of Chicago Press.

Langer, E.J. (1975) The illusion of control, *Journal of Personality and Social Psychology*, 32(2): 311–38.

Langer, E.J. (1989) Minding matters: the consequences of mindlessness-mindfulness, in L. Berkowitz (ed.) *Advances in Experimental Social Psychology*, vol. 22. New York: Academic Press.

Langfield-Smith, K.M. and Wirth, A. (1992) Measuring differences between cognitive maps, *Journal of the Operational Research Society*, 43: 1135–50.

Langley, A., Mintzberg, H., Pitcher, P., Posada, E. and St. Macary, J. (1995) Opening up decision making: the view from the black stool, *Organization Science*, 6: 260–79.

Lank, A. and Lank, E.A. (1995) Legitimising the gut feeling: the role of intuition in business, *Journal of Managerial Psychology*, 10(5): 18–23.

Lant, T.K. (1999) A situated learning perspective on the emergence of knowledge and identity in cognitive communities, *Advances in Management Cognition and Organizational Information Processing*, 6: 171–94.

Lant, T.K. and Baum, J.C. (1995) Cognitive sources of socially constructed competitive groups: examples from the Manhattan hotel industry, in W.R. Scott and S. Christensen (eds) *The Institutional Construction of Organizations: International and Longitudinal Studies*. Thousand Oaks, CA: Sage.

Lant, T.K. and Phelps, C. (1999) Strategic groups: a situated learning perspective, *Advances in Strategic Management*, 16: 221–47.

Lant, T.K. and Shapira, Z. (eds) (2001a) *Organizational Cognition: Computation and Interpretation*. Mahwah, NJ: Lawrence Erlbaum Associates.

Lant, T.K. and Shapira, Z. (2001b) Introduction: foundations of research on cognition in organizations, in T.K. Lant and Z. Shapira (eds) *Organizational Cognition: Computation and Interpretation*. Mahwah, NJ: Lawrence Erlbaum Associates.

Lant, T.K. and Shapira, Z. (2001c) New research directions on organizational cognition, in T.K. Lant and Z. Shapira (eds) *Organizational Cognition: Computation and Interpretation*. Mahwah, NJ: Lawrence Erlbaum Associates.

Lant, T.K., Milliken, F.J. and Batra, B. (1992) The role of managerial learning and interpretation in strategic persistence and reorientation: an empirical exploration, *Strategic Management Journal*, 13: 585–608.

Larreche, J-C. and Gatignon, H. (1990) *MARKSTRAT2: Instructor's Manual*. Redwood City, CA: The Scientific Press.

Larson, J. and Christensen, C. (1993) Groups as problem-solving units: toward a new meaning of social cognition, *British Journal of Social Psychology*, 32: 5–30.

Larson Jr., J.R., Foster-Fishman, P.G. and Keys, C.B. (1994) Discussion of shared and unshared information in medical decision-making teams, *Journal of Personality and Social Psychology*, 71: 315–30.

Larson Jr., J.R., Christensen, C., Abbott, A.S. and Franz, T.M. (1996) Diagnosing groups: charting the flow of information in medical decision-making teams, *Journal of Personality and Social Psychology*, 71: 315–30.

Lau, J. and Murnighan, J.K. (1998) Demographic diversity and faultlines: the compositional dynamics of organizational groups, *Academy of Management Review*, 23: 325–40.

Lau, R. and Ware, J. (1981) Refinements in the measurement of health-specific locus of control beliefs, *Medical Care*, 19: 1147–58.

Laughlin, R.C. (1991) Environmental disturbances and organizational transitions and transformations: some alternative models, *Organization Studies*, 12: 209–32.

Laukkanen, M. (1994) Comparative cause mapping of organizational cognitions, *Organization Science*, 5: 322–43.

Lave, J. and Wenger, E. (1991) *Situated Learning: Legitimate Peripheral Participation*. New York: Cambridge University Press.

Lawrence, B.S. (1997) The black box of organizational demography, *Organization Science*, 8: 1–22.

Lawrence, P.R. and Lorsch, J.W. (1967) *Organization and Environment: Managing Differentiation and Integration*. Boston, MA: Harvard University Press.

References

Leonard, N.H., Scholl, R.W. and Kowalski, B. (1999) Information processing style and decision making, *Journal of Organizational Behavior*, 20: 407–20.

Leroy, F. and Ramanantsoa, B. (1997) The cognitive and behavioural dimensions of organizational learning in a merger: an empirical study, *Journal of Management Studies*, 34: 871–94.

Lessard, D.R. and Zaheer, S. (1996) Breaking the silos: distributed knowledge and strategic responsiveness to volatile exchange rates, *Strategic Management Journal*, 17(7): 513–34.

Levenhagen, M., Porac, J.F. and Thomas, H. (1993) Emergent industry leadership and the selling of technological visions: a social constructionist view, in J. Hendry and G. Johnson with J. Newton (eds) *Strategic Thinking: Leadership and the Management of Change*. Chichester: Wiley.

Levenson, H. (1981) Differentiating among internality, powerful others and chance, in H.M. Lefcourt (ed.) *Research with the Locus of Control Construct: Volume 1, Assessment Methods*. New York: Academic Press.

Levinthal, D.A. and March, J.G. (1993) Exploration and exploitation in organizational learning, *Strategic Management Journal*, 14(winter): 95–112.

Levitt, B. and March, J.G. (1988) Organizational learning, *Annual Review of Sociology*, 14: 319–40.

Lewicki, P. (1986) *Nonconscious Social Information Processing*. New York: Academic Press.

Lewicki, P., Czyzewska, M. and Hoffman, H. (1987) Unconscious acquisition of complex procedural knowledge, *Journal of Experimental Psychology: Learning, Memory and Cognition*, 13: 523–30.

Lewicki, P., Hill, T. and Bizot, E. (1988) Acquisition of procedural knowledge about a pattern of stimuli that cannot be articulated, *Cognitive Psychology*, 20: 24–37.

Lewicki, P., Hill T. and Czyzewska, M. (1992) Non-conscious acquisition of information, *American Psychologist*, 47: 796–801.

Lewis, D. (1999) *Information Overload: Practical Strategies for Surviving in Today's Workplace*. London: Penguin Books.

Liang, D.W., Moreland, R. and Argote, L. (1995) Group versus individual training and group performance: the mediating role of transactive memory, *Personality and Social Psychology Bulletin*, 21(4): 384–93.

Liebeskind, J.P. (1996) Knowledge, strategy, and the theory of the firm, *Strategic Management Journal*, 17: 93–107.

Lindell, P., Melin, L., Gahmberg, H.J., Hellqvist, A. and Melander, A. (1998) Stability and change in a strategist's thinking, in C. Eden and J-C. Spender (eds) *Managerial and Organizational Cognition: Theory, Methods and Research*. London: Sage.

Littunen, H. and Storhammar, E. (2000) The indicators of locus of control in the small business context, *Journal of Enterprising Culture*, 8: 343–60.

Locke, E. and Latham, G. (1990) *A Theory of Goal Setting and Task Performance*. Englewood Cliffs, NJ: Prentice Hall.

Lohrke, F. and Bruton, G. (1997) Contributions and gaps in international strategic management, *Journal of International Management*, 3: 25–57.

Lord, R. and Foti, R. (1986) Schema theories, information processing and organizational behavior, in H.P. Sims and D.A. Gioia (eds) *The Thinking Organization: Dynamics of Organizational Social Cognition*. San Francisco: Jossey-Bass.

Louis, M.R. and Sutton, R.I. (1991) Switching cognitive gears: from habits of mind to active thinking, *Human Relations*, 44: 55–76.

Löwstedt, J. (1985) Contingencies or cognitions? Two paths for research on organization and technology, *Scandinavian Journal of Management*, 1: 207–25.

Lubit, R. (2001) Tacit knowledge and knowledge management: the keys to sustainable competitive advantage, *Organization Dynamics*, 29(4): 164–78.

Luthans, F., Baack, D. and Taylor, L. (1987) Organizational commitment: analysis of antecedents, *Human Relations*, 40: 219–36.

Lyles, M.A. and Schwenk, C.R. (1992) Top management, strategy and organizational knowledge structures, *Journal of Management Studies*, 29(2): 155–74.

McClelland, D.C. (1961) *The Achieving Society*. Princeton, NJ: Van Nostrand.

MacCleod, C. (1991) Clinical anxiety and the selective coding of threatening information, *International Review of Psychology*, 3: 279–92.

McCrae, R.R. and Costa, P.T. (1987) Validation of the five factor model of personality across instruments and observers, *Journal of Personality and Social Psychology*, 52: 81–90.

McEvily, S.K., Das, S. and McCabe, K. (2000) Avoiding competence substitution through knowledge sharing, *Academy of Management Review*, 25(2): 294–311.

McGee, J. and Segal-Horn, S. (1990) Strategic space and industry dynamics, *Journal of Marketing Management*, 6: 175–93.

McGee, J. and Thomas, H. (1986) Strategic groups: theory, research and taxonomy, *Strategic Management Journal*, 7: 141–60.

McKeen, J.D. (2001) Editorial for the special issue on 'The study of knowledge-based enterprises', *International Journal of Management Reviews*, 3(1): iii–iv.

March, J.G. (1991) Exploration and exploitation in organizational learning, *Organization Science*, 2: 71–87.

References

March, J.G. (1999) *The Pursuit of Organizational Intelligence*. Oxford: Blackwell.

March, J.G. and Simon, H.A. (1958) *Organizations*. New York: Wiley.

Markman, A., Yamauchi, T. and Makin, V. (1997) The creation of new concepts: a multi-faceted approach to category learning, in T. Ward, S. Smith and J. Vaid (eds) *Creative Thought: An Investigation of Conceptual Structures and Processes*. Washington: American Psychological Association.

Markoczy, L. (1995) States and belief states, *International Journal of Human Resource Management*, 6: 249–70.

Markoczy, L. (1997) Measuring beliefs: accept no substitutes, *Academy of Management Journal*, 40: 1228–42.

Markoczy, L. and Goldberg, J. (1995) A method for eliciting and comparing causal maps, *Journal of Management*, 21: 305–33.

Markus, H. (1977) Self-schemata and processing information about the self, *Journal of Personality and Social Psychology*, 35: 63–78.

Markus, H. and Nurius, P. (1986) Possible selves, *American Psychologist*, 41: 954–69.

Markus, H. and Wurf, E. (1987) The dynamic self-concept: a social psychological perspective, *Annual Review of Psychology*, 38: 299–337.

Martindale, C. (1999) Biological bases of creativity, in R.J. Sternberg (ed.) *Handbook of Creativity*. Cambridge: Cambridge University Press.

Martindale, C., Anderson, K., Moore, K. and West, A.N. (1996) Creativity, oversensitivity and rate of habituation, *Personality and Individual Differences*, 20: 423–7.

Mason, E. (1957) *Economic Concentration and the Monopoly Problem*. Cambridge, MA: Harvard University Press.

Matlin, M.W. (1994) *Cognition*, 3rd edn. Orlando, FL: Harcourt Brace Jovanovich.

Matt, G.E., Vazquaz, C. and Campbell, W.K. (1992) Mood congruent recall of affectively toned stimuli: a meta-analytic review, *Clinical Psychology Review*, 12: 227–55.

Maule, A.J. and Hodgkinson, G.P. (2002) Heuristics, biases and strategic decision making, *The Psychologist*, 15: 68–71.

Maule, A.J., Hodgkinson, G.P. and Bown, N.J. (in press) Causal mental models in strategic decision making, in D. Hardman and V. Macchi (eds) *The Psychology of Reasoning and Decision Making: A Handbook*. Chichester: Wiley.

Mayer, R. (1995) The search for insight: grappling with Gestalt psychology's unanswered questions, in R. Sternberg and J. Davidson (eds) *The Nature of Insight*. Cambridge, MA: MIT Press.

367

The competent organization

Meindl, J.R., Stubbart, C. and Porac, J.F. (eds) (1994) Cognition, *Organization Science*, 5 (special issue): 288–477.

Meindl, J.R., Stubbart, C. and Porac, J.F. (eds) (1996) *Cognition Within and Between Organisations*. London: Sage.

Messick, S. (1984) The nature of cognitive styles: problems and promise in educational practice, *Educational Psychologist*, 19(2), 59–74.

Metcalfe, J. and Weibe, D. (1987) Intuition in insight and non-insight problem solving, *Memory and Cognition*, 15: 238–46.

Meyer, J.W. and Rowan, B. (1977) Institutionalized organizations: formal structure as myth and ceremony, *American Journal of Sociology*, 83: 340–63.

Miller, A. (1987) Cognitive styles: an integrated model, *Educational Psychology*, 7: 251–68.

Miller, A. (1991) Personality types, learning styles and educational goals, *Educational Psychology*, 11: 217–38.

Miller, C.C. and Cardinal, L.B. (1994) Understanding the linkage between strategic planning and firm performance: a synthesis of more than two decades of research, *Academy of Management Journal*, 37: 1649–65.

Miller, C.C., Burke, L.M. and Glick, W.H. (1998) Cognitive diversity among upper-echelon executives: implications for strategic decision processes, *Strategic Management Journal*, 19: 39–58.

Miller, D. (1983) The correlates of entrepreneurship in three types of firms, *Management Science*, 29: 770–91.

Miller, D. (1993) The architecture of simplicity, *Academy of Management Review*, 18: 116–38.

Miller, D. (1994) What happens after success: the perils of excellence, *Journal of Management Studies*, 31; 325–58.

Miller, D. and Toulouse, J.M. (1986) Chief executive personality and corporate strategy and structure in small firms, *Management Science*, 32: 1389–409.

Miller, D. and Chen, M-J. (1996) The simplicity of competitive repertoires: an empirical analysis, *Strategic Management Journal*, 17: 419–39.

Miller, D., Kets de Vries, M.F.R. and Toulouse, J.M. (1982) Top executive locus of control and its relationship to strategy-making, structure, and environment, *Academy of Management Journal*, 25: 237–53.

Miller, D., Lant, T.K., Milliken, F.J. and Korn, H.J. (1996) The evolution of strategic simplicity: exploring two models of organizational adaptation, *Journal of Management*, 22: 863–87.

Miller, D., Droge, C. and Vickery, S. (1997) Celebrating the 'essential': the impact of performance on the functional favoritism of CEOs in two contexts, *Journal of Management*, 23: 147–68.

Milliken, F.J. and Lant, T.K. (1991) The effect of an organization's recent performance history on strategic persistence and change: the role of managerial interpretations, in J. Dutton, A.S. Huff and P. Shrivastava (eds) *Advances in Strategic Management*, vol. 7. Greenwich, CT: JAI Press.

Milliken, F.J. and Martins, L.I. (1996) Searching for common threads: understanding the multiple effects of diversity in organizational groups, *Academy of Management Review*, 21: 402–33.

Mintzberg, H. (1973) *The Nature of Managerial Work*. New York: Harper & Row.

Mintzberg, H. (1983) *Power in and Around Organizations*. Englewood Cliffs, NJ: Prentice Hall.

Mintzberg, H. (1990) The design school: reconsidering the basic premises of strategic management, *Strategic Management Journal*, 11: 171–95.

Mintzberg, H. (1994) *The Rise and Fall of Strategic Planning*. London: Prentice Hall.

Mintzberg, H. and Waters, J.A. (1985) Of strategies deliberate and emergent, *Strategic Management Journal*, 6: 257–72.

Mintzberg, H., Ahlstrand, B. and Lampel, J. (1998) *Strategy Safari: A Guided Tour Through the Wilds of Strategic Management*. London: Prentice Hall Europe.

Mitroff, I.I. and Kilmann, R. (1975) Stories managers tell: a new tool for organizational problem solving, *Management Review*, July: 18–28.

Mohammed, S. and Dumville, B.C. (2001) Team mental models in a team knowledge framework: expanding theory and measurement across disciplinary boundaries, *Journal of Organizational Behavior*, 22: 89–106.

Mohammed, S., Klimoski, R. and Rentsch, J. (2000) The measurement of team mental models: we have no shared schema, *Organizational Research Methods*, 3: 123–65.

Moll, L.C. (ed.) (1990) *Vygotsky and Education: Instructional Implications and Applications of Sociohistorical Psychology*. New York: Cambridge University Press.

Molloy, S. and Schwenk, C.R. (1995) The effects of information technology on strategic decision making, *Journal of Management Studies*, 32(3): 283–311.

Morck, R., Shleifer, A. and Vishny, R.W. (1990) Do managerial objectives drive bad acquisitions? *Journal of Finance*, 45: 31–48.

Morecroft, J.D.W (1994) Executive knowledge, models and learning, in J.D.W. Morecroft and J.D. Sterman (eds) *Modelling for Learning Organizations*. Portland, OR: Productivity Press.

Moreland, R.L. (2000) Transactive memory: learning who knows what in work groups and organizations, in L. Thompson, D. Messick and J. Levine (eds) *Shared Cognition In Organizations: The Management of Knowledge*. Hillsdale, NJ: Lawrence Erlbaum Associates.

Morrison, E.W. and Robinson, S.L. (1997) When employees feel betrayed: a model of how psychological contract violation develops, *Academy of Management Review*, 22(1): 226–56.

Mowrer, O.H. (1947) On the dual nature of learning: A reinterpretation of 'conditioning' and 'problem solving', *Harvard Educational Review*, 17: 102–48.

Murray, A. (1989) Top management group heterogeneity and firm performance, *Strategic Management Journal*, 10: 125–41.

Myers, I.B. (1962) *The Myers Briggs Type Indicator*. Palo Alto, CA: Consulting Psychologists Press.

Nahapiet, J. and Ghoshal, S. (1998) Social capital, intellectual capital and the creation of value in firms, *Academy of Management Best Paper Proceedings*, 35–9.

Narayanan, V.K. and Fahey, L. (1990) Evolution of revealed causal maps during decline: a case study of Admiral, in A.S. Huff (ed.) *Mapping Strategic Thought*. Chichester: Wiley.

Nardi, B.A. (ed.) (1996) *Context and Consciousness: Activity Theory and Human-Computer Interaction*. Cambridge, MA: MIT Press.

Neisser, U., Boodoo, G., Bourchard, T.J. *et al.* (1996) Intelligence: knowns and unknowns, *American Psychologist*, 51: 77–101.

Nelson, R.R. and Winter, S.G. (1982) *An Evolutionary Theory of Economic Change*. Cambridge, MA: Harvard University Press.

Neustadt, R.E. and May, E.R. (1986) *Thinking in Time: The Uses of History for Decision Makers*. New York: Free Press.

Nevis, E.C., DiBella, A.J. and Gould, J.M. (1997) Understanding organizations as learning systems, *Sloan Management Review*, 36(2): 73–85.

Newell, S., Scarbrough, H. and Swan, J. (2001) From global knowledge management to internal electronic fences: contradictory outcomes of intranet development, *British Journal of Management*, 12: 97–111.

Nickerson, R., Perkins, D. and Smith, E. (1985) *The Teaching of Thinking*. Hillsdale, NJ: Lawrence Earlbaum Associates.

Nonaka, I. (1991) The knowledge-creating company, *Harvard Business Review*, November–December: 96–104.

Nonaka, I. (1994) A dynamic theory of organizational knowledge-creation, *Organization Science*, 5(1): 14–37.

Nonaka, I. and Takeuchi, H. (1995) *The Knowledge-Creating Company: How Japanese Companies Create the Dynamics of Innovation*. Oxford: Oxford University Press.

Nonaka, I., Takeuchi, H. and Umemoto, K. (1996) A theory of organizational knowledge creation, *International Journal of Technology Management*, 11(7/8): 833–45.

References

Norburn, D. and Birley, S. (1988) The top management team and corporate performance, *Strategic Management Journal*, 9: 225–37.

Norman, D. (1985) Twelve issues for cognitive science, in A.M. Aitkenhead and J.M. Slack (eds) *Issues in Cognitive Modelling*. London: Lawrence Erlbaum Associates.

Norman, D.A. (1988) *The Psychology of Everyday Things*. New York: Basic Books.

Nunnally, J.C. (1978) *Psychometric Theory*. New York: McGraw Hill.

O'Reilly, C.A., Chatman, J. and Caldwell, D.F. (1991) People and organizational culture: a profile comparison approach to assessing person-organization fit, *Academy of Management Journal*, 34: 487–516.

Ocasio, W. (1997) Towards an attention-based view of the firm, *Strategic Management Journal*, 18: 187–206.

Odorici, V. and Lomi, A. (2001) Classifying competition: an empirical study of the cognitive social structure of strategic groups, in T.K. Lant and Z. Shapira (eds) (2001) *Organizational Cognition: Computation and Interpretation*. Mahwah, NJ: Lawrence Erlbaum Associates.

Offsey, S. (1997) Knowledge management: linking people to knowledge for bottom line results, *Journal of Knowledge Management*, 1(2): 113–22.

Orr, J.E. (1990) Sharing knowledge, celebrating identity: community memory in a service culture, in D. Middleton and D. Edwards (eds) *Collective Remembering*. London: Sage.

Osborne, J.D., Stubbart, C.I. and Ramaprasad, A. (2001) Strategic groups and competitive enactment: a study of dynamic relationships between mental models and performance, *Strategic Management Journal*, 22: 435–54.

Oster, S.M. (1990) *Modern Competitive Analysis*. Oxford: Oxford University Press.

Palinscar, A.S. (1998) Social constructivist perspectives on teaching and learning, *Annual Review of Psychology*, 49: 345–75.

Papadakis, V. and Barwise, P. (1998) Research on strategic decisions: where do we go from here? in V. Papadakis and P. Barwise (eds) *Strategic Decisions*. Hingham, MA: Kluwer Academic.

Papadakis, V.M., Lioukas, S. and Chambers, D. (1998) Strategic decision-making processes: the role of management and context, *Strategic Management Journal*, 19: 115–47.

Pask, G. and Scott, B.C.E. (1972) Learning strategies and individual competence, *International Journal of Man-Machine Studies*, 4: 217–53.

Paté-Cornell, M.E. (1993) Learning from the Piper Alpha accident: a post-mortem analysis of technical and organizational factors, *Risk Analysis*, 13(2): 215–32.

Payne, J.W., Bettman, J.R. and Johnson, E.J. (1988) Adaptive strategy selection in decision-making, *Journal of Experimental Psychology: Learning, Memory and Cognition*, 3: 534–52.

Payne, J.W., Bettman, J.R. and Johnson, E.J. (1993) *The Adaptive Decision Maker*. Cambridge: Cambridge University Press.

Pedler, M., Boydell, T. and Burgoyne, J. (1989) Towards the learning company, *Management Education and Development*, 20(1): 1–8.

Pelled, L.H. (1996) Demographic diversity, conflict, and work group outcomes: an intervening process theory, *Organization Science*, 7: 615–31.

Perkins, D. (1997) Creativity's camel: the role of analogy in invention, in T. Ward, S. Smith and J. Vaid (eds) *Creative Thought: An Investigation of Conceptual Structures and Processes*. Washington: American Psychological Association.

Perrow, C. (1984) *Normal Accidents: Living with High-risk Technologies*. New York: Basic Books.

Pesut, D.J. (1990) Creative thinking as a self-regulatory meta-cognitive process: a model for education, training and further research, *Journal of Creative Behavior*, 24: 105–10.

Peteraf, M. and Shanley, M. (1997) Getting to know you: a theory of strategic group identity, *Strategic Management Journal*, 18 (summer special issue): 165–86.

Peters, T.J. and Waterman, R.H. Jr. (1982) *In Search Of Excellence*. New York: Harper & Row.

Pettigrew, A.M. (1973) *The Politics of Organizational Decision Making*. London: Tavistock.

Pettigrew, A.M. (1985) *The Awakening Giant: Continuity and Change in ICI*. Oxford: Blackwell.

Pettigrew, A.M. (1992) On studying managerial élites, *Strategic Management Journal*, 13 (special issue): 163–82.

Pettigrew, A.M. and Fenton, E.M. (2000) Complexities and dualities in innovative forms of organizing, in A.M. Pettigrew and E.M. Fenton (eds) *The Innovating Organization*. London: Sage.

Pettigrew, A.M. and Whipp, R. (1991) *Managing Change for Competitive Success*. Oxford: Blackwell.

Petty, R.E. (1995) Attitude change, in A. Tesser (ed.) *Advanced Social Psychology*. Boston, MA: McGraw-Hill.

Petty, R.E. and Cacioppo, J.T. (1986) The elaboration likelihood model of persuasion, in L. Berkowitz (ed.) *Advances in Experimental Social Psychology*, vol. 19. New York: Academic Press.

Pfeffer, J. (1981a) Management as symbolic action: the creation and maintenance of organizational paradigms, in L.L. Cummings and B.M. Staw

References

(eds) *Research in Organizational Behavior*, vol. 3. Greenwich, CT: JAI Press.

Pfeffer, J. (1981b) *Power in Organizations*. Cambridge, MA: Ballinger.

Pfeffer, J. (1983) Organizational demography, in B.M. Staw and L.L. Cummings (eds) *Research in Organizational Behavior*, vol. 5. Greenwich, CT: JAI Press.

Pfeffer, J. and Salancik, G.R. (1974) Organizational decision making as a political process: the case of a university budget, *Administrative Science Quarterly*, 19: 135–51.

Phares, E.J. (1976) *Locus of Control in Personality*. Morristown, NJ: General Learning Press.

Piaget, J. (1951) *Play, Dreams and Imitation in Childhood*. New York: W.W. Norton.

Pilkington, A. (1996) Learning from joint ventures: the Rover-Honda relationship, *Business History*, 38: 90–116.

Polanyi, M. (1958) *Personal Knowledge: Towards a Post Critical Philosophy*. London: Routledge & Kegan Paul.

Polanyi, M. (1967) *The Tacit Dimension*. Garden City, NY: Anchor Books.

Porac, J.F. and Rosa, A. (1996) Rivalry, industry models, and the cognitive embeddedness of the comparable firm, *Advances in Strategic Management*, 13: 363–88.

Porac, J.F. and Thomas, H. (1987) Cognitive taxonomies and cognitive systematics. Paper presented at the Annual Meeting of the Academy of Management, New Orleans, August.

Porac, J.F. and Thomas, H. (eds) (1989) Managerial thinking in business environments, *Journal of Management Studies*, 26 (special issue): 323–438.

Porac, J.F. and Thomas, H. (1990) Taxonomic mental models in competitor definition, *Academy of Management Review*, 15: 224–40.

Porac, J.F. and Thomas, H. (1994) Cognitive categorization and subjective rivalry among retailers in a small city, *Journal of Applied Psychology*, 79: 54–66.

Porac, J.F., Thomas H. and Emme, B. (1987) Knowing the competition: the mental models of retailing strategists, in G. Johnson (ed.) *Business Strategy and Retailing*. Chichester: Wiley.

Porac, J.F., Thomas, H. and Baden-Fuller, C. (1989) Competitive groups as cognitive communities: the case of Scottish knitwear manufacturers, *Journal of Management Studies*, 26: 397–416.

Porac, J.F., Thomas, H., Wilson, F., Paton, D. and Kanfer, A. (1995) Rivalry and the industry model of Scottish knitwear producers, *Administrative Science Quarterly*, 40: 203–27.

Porter, M.E. (1980) *Competitive Strategy: Techniques for Analyzing Industries and Competitors*. New York: Free Press.

Porter, M.E. (1981) The contributions of industrial organization to strategic management, *Academy of Management Review*, 6: 609–20.

Porter, M.E. (1985) *Competitive Advantage: Creating and Sustaining Superior Performance*. New York: Free Press.

Porter, M.E. (1996) What is strategy? *Harvard Business Review*, 74(6): 61–78.

Powell, W.W. and DiMaggio, P.J. (eds) (1991) *The New Institutionalism in Organizational Analysis*. Chicago, IL: University of Chicago Press.

Prahalad, C.K. and Bettis, R.A. (1986) The dominant logic: a new linkage between diversity and performance, *Strategic Management Journal*, 7: 485–501.

Prange, C. (1999) Organizational learning – desperately seeking theory? in M. Easterby-Smith, J. Burgoyne and L. Araujo (eds) *Organizational Learning and the Learning Organization: Developments in Theory and Practice*. London: Sage.

Preskill, H. and Torres, R. (1999) The role of evaluative enquiry in creating learning organizations, in M. Easterby-Smith, J. Burgoyne and L. Araujo (eds) *Organizational Learning and the Learning Organization: Developments in Theory and Practice*. London: Sage.

Quinn, J.B. (1992) *Intelligent Enterprise: A Knowledge and Service Based Paradigm for Industry*. New York: Free Press.

Ramakrishna, H.V. and Schilhavy, R.A. (1986) Psychological types as a factor in organizational design: some empirical evidence, *Proceedings of the Annual Meeting of the Decision Sciences Institute*, 40–2.

Ramaprasad, A. and Mitroff, I.I. (1984) On formulating strategic problems, *Academy of Management Review*, 9: 597–605.

Rauch, A. and Frese, M. (2000) Psychological approaches to entrepreneurial success: a general model and an overview of findings, in C.L. Cooper and I.T. Robertson (eds) *International Review of Industrial and Organizational Psychology*, vol. 15. Chichester: Wiley.

Reason, P. and Rowan, J. (1981) On making sense, in P. Reason and J. Rowan (eds) *Human Inquiry: A Sourcebook of New Paradigm Research*. Chichester: Wiley.

Reber, A.S. (1993) *Implicit Learning and Tacit Knowledge: An Essay on the Cognitive Unconscious*. New York: Oxford University Press.

Reed, R. and DeFillippi, R.J. (1990) Causal ambiguity, barriers to imitation, and sustainable competitive advantage, *Academy of Management Review*, 15: 88–102.

Reger, R.K. (1990a) Managerial thought structures and competitive positioning, in A.S. Huff (ed.) *Mapping Strategic Thought*. Chichester: Wiley.

References

Reger, R.K. (1990b) The repertory grid for eliciting the content and structure of cognitive constructive systems, in A.S. Huff (ed.) *Mapping Strategic Thought*. Chichester: Wiley.

Reger, R.K. and Huff, A.S. (1993) Strategic groups: a cognitive perspective, *Strategic Management Journal*, 14: 103–24.

Reger, R.K. and Palmer, T.B. (1996) Managerial categorization of competitors: using old maps to navigate new environments, *Organization Science*, 7: 22–39.

Rentsch, J.R. and Hall, R.J. (1994) Members of great teams think alike: a model of team effectiveness and schema similarity among team members, *Advances in Interdisciplinary Studies of Work Teams*, 1: 223–61.

Reuber, A. and Fischer, E. (1997) The influence of top management team's international experience on international behaviors of SMEs, *Journal of International Business Studies*, 28: 807–25.

Reuters (1998) *Out of the Abyss: Surviving the Information Age*. London: Reuters Limited.

Revans, R. (1982) *The Origins and Growth Of Action Learning*. Bromley: Chartwell-Bratt Ltd.

Richmond, B. (1993) Systems thinking: critical thinking skills for the 1990s and beyond, *Systems Dynamics Review*, 9(2): 113–33.

Rickards, T. and Moger, S. (1999) *Handbook of Creative Team Leaders*. Aldershot: Gower.

Riding, R.J. (1991a) *Cognitive Styles Analysis*. Birmingham: Learning and Training Technology.

Riding, R.J. (1991b) *Cognitive Styles Analysis User Manual*. Birmingham: Learning and Training Technology.

Riding, R.J. and Rayner, S.G. (1998) *Cognitive Styles and Learning Strategies*. London: Fulton.

Roberts, F.S. (1976) Strategy for the energy crisis: the case of commuter transport policy, in R. Axelrod (ed.) *The Structure of Decision: Cognitive Maps of Political Elites*. Princeton, NJ: Princeton University Press.

Roberts, K.H. (1989) New challenges in organizational research: high reliability organizations, *Industrial Crisis Quarterly*, 3: 111–25.

Roberts, K.H. (1990) Managing high reliability systems, *California Management Review*, 32(4): 101–13.

Roberts, K.H. and Bea, R.G. (2001) When systems fail, *Organizational Dynamics*, 29(3): 179–91.

Robertson, I.T. (1985) Human information processing strategies and styles, *Behaviour and Information Technology*, 4: 19–29.

Robey, D. and Taggart, W. (1981) Measuring managers' minds: the assessment of style in human information processing, *Academy of Management Review*, 6: 375–83.

Rochlin, G.I., LaPorte, T.R. and Roberts, K.H. (1987) The self-designing high reliability organization: aircraft carrier flight operations at sea, *Naval War College Review*, 40(4): 76–90.

Rogers, Y. and Ellis, J. (1994) Distributed cognition: an alternative framework for analysing and explaining collaborative working, *Journal of Information Technology*, 9: 119–28.

Roos, L.L. and Hall, R.I. (1980) Influence diagrams and organizational power, *Administrative Science Quarterly*, 25: 57–71.

Rosch, E. (1975) Cognitive reference points, *Cognitive Psychology*, 7: 532–47.

Rosch, E. (1978) Principles of categorization, in E. Rosch and B.B. Lloyd (eds) *Cognition and Categorization*. Hillsdale, NJ: Lawrence Erlbaum Associates.

Rosch, E., Mervis, C.B., Gray, W.D., Johnson, D. and Boyes-Braem, P. (1976) Basic objects in natural categories, *Cognitive Psychology*, 8: 382–439.

Rothenberg, A. (1991) Creativity, health and alcoholism, *Creativity Research Journal*, 3: 179–202.

Rothenberg, A. and Hausman, C. (2000) Metaphor and creativity, in M.A. Runco (ed.) *Creativity Research Handbook*, vol. 2. Cresskill, NJ: Hampton.

Rotter, J.B. (1954) *Social Learning Theory in Clinical Psychology*. Englewood Cliffs, NJ: Prentice Hall.

Rotter, J.B. (1966) Generalized expectancies for internal versus external control of reinforcement, *Psychological Monographs: General and Applied*, 80: Whole no. 609.

Rotter, J.B. (1975) Some problems and misconceptions related to the construct of internal versus external control of reinforcement, *Journal of Consulting and Clinical Psychology*, 43: 56–67.

Roure, J.B. and Keeley, R.H. (1990) Predictors of success in new technology-based ventures, *Journal of Business Venturing*, 5: 201–20.

Rousseau, D.M. (1995) *Psychological Contracts in Organizations: Understanding Written and Unwritten Agreements*. Thousand Oaks, CA: Sage.

Ruble, T.L. and Cosier, R.A. (1990) Effects of cognitive styles and decision setting on performance, *Organizational Behavior and Human Decision Processes*, 46: 283–95.

Ruggles, R. (1998) The state of the notion: knowledge management in practice, *California Management Review*, 40(3): 80–9.

Rulke, D. and Zaheer, S. (2001) Shared and unshared transactive knowledge in complex organizations: an exploratory study, in T.K. Lant and Z. Shapira (eds) *Organizational Cognition: Computation and Interpretation*. London: Lawrence Erlbaum Associates.

References

Runco, M.A. and Chand, I. (1995) Cognition and creativity, *Educational Psychology Review*, 7: 243–67.

Ryback, D. (1998) *Putting Emotional Intelligence to Work: Successful Leadership is More Than IQ*. Oxford: Butterworth-Heinemann.

Ryle, G. (1949) *The Concept of Mind*. Chicago: University of Chicago Press.

Sackmann, S.A. (1991) *Cultural Knowledge in Organizations: Exploring the Collective Mind*. Newbury Park, CA: Sage.

Sackmann, S.A. (1992) Culture and sub-cultures: an analysis of organizational knowledge, *Administrative Science Quarterly*, 37, 140–61.

Sadler-Smith, E. (1998) Cognitive style: some human resource implications for managers, *International Journal of Human Resource Management*, 19(1): 185–202.

Sadler-Smith, E. (1999a) Intuition-analysis: cognitive style and learning preferences of business and management students, *Journal of Managerial Psychology*, 14(1): 26–38.

Sadler-Smith, E. (1999b) Intuition-analysis: style and approaches to studying, *Educational Studies*, 25(2): 159–74.

Sadler-Smith, E., Allinson, C.W. and Hayes, J. (2000) Learning preferences and cognitive style: some implications for continuing professional development, *Management Learning*, 31: 239–56.

Sadler-Smith, E., Spicer, D.P. and Tsang, F. (2000) Validity of the cognitive style index: replication and extension, *British Journal of Management*, 11: 175–81.

Salaman, G. (2001) A response to Snell: the learning organization: fact or fiction? *Human Relations*, 54(3): 343–59.

Salancik, G.R. and Pfeffer, J. (1978) A social information processing approach to job attitudes and task design, *Administrative Science Quarterly*, 23: 224–52.

Salancik, G.R. and Porac, J.F. (1986) Distilled ideologies: values derived from causal reasoning in complex environments, in H.P. Sims, Jr. and D.A. Gioia (eds) *The Thinking Organization: Dynamics of Organizational Social Cognition*. San Francisco: Jossey-Bass.

Salomon, G. (1993) *Distributed Cognitions: Psychological and Educational Considerations*. Cambridge: Cambridge University Press.

Salovey, P. and Mayer, J.D. (1990) Emotional intelligence, *Imagination, Cognition and Personality*, 9: 185–211.

Sambharya, R.B. (1996) Foreign experience of top management teams and international diversification strategies of US multinational corporations, *Strategic Management Journal*, 17: 739–46.

Sanchez, R. and Mahoney, I.T. (1996) Modularity, flexibility and knowledge management in product and organization design, *Strategic Management Journal*, 17: 63–76.

Sandelands, L.E. and Larsen, J.R. (1985) When measurement causes task attitudes: a note from the laboratory, *Journal of Applied Psychology*, 70: 116–21.

Sandelands, L.E. and Stablein, R.E. (1987) The concept of organizational mind, in S. Bachrach and N.D. Tomaso (eds) *Research in the Sociology of Organizations*, vol. 5. Greenwich, CT: JAI Press.

Sanders, W. and Carpenter, M. (1998) Internationalization and firm governance: the roles of CEO compensation, top team composition, and board structure, *Academy of Management Journal*, 41: 158–78.

Sattath, S. and Tversky, A. (1977) Additive similarity trees, *Psychometrika*, 42: 319–45.

Savvas, M., El-Kot, G. and Sadler-Smith, E. (2001) Comparative study of cognitive styles in Egypt, Greece, Hong Kong and the UK, *International Journal of Training and Development*, 5: 64–73.

Scaife, M. and Rogers, Y. (1996) External cognition: how do graphical representations work? *International Journal of Human-Computer Studies*, 45: 185–23.

Scarbrough, H. and Swan, J. (2001) Explaining the diffusion of knowledge management: the role of fashion, *British Journal of Management*, 12(1): 3–12.

Scarbrough, H., Swan, J. and Preston, J. (1999) *Knowledge Management: A Literature Review*. London: Chartered Institute of Personnel and Development.

Schank, R.C. (1982) *Dynamic Memory: A Theory of Learning in People and Computers*. Cambridge: Cambridge University Press.

Schein, E.H. (1993) On dialogue, culture, and organizational learning, *Organizational Dynamics*, winter: 40–51.

Schiffman, S.S., Reynolds, M.L. and Young, F.W. (1981) *Introduction to Multidimensional Scaling*. New York: Academic Press.

Schneider, S.C. and De Meyer, A. (1991) Interpreting and responding to strategic issues: the impact of national culture, *Strategic Management Journal*, 12: 307–20.

Schneider, W. and Shiffrin, R.M. (1977) Controlled and automatic human information processing: 1, detection, search and attention, *Psychological Review*, 84: 1–66.

Schoemaker, P.J.H. (1993) Multiple scenario development: its conceptual and behavioral foundation, *Strategic Management Journal*, 14: 193–213.

Schoemaker, P.J.H. (1995) Scenario planning: a tool for strategic thinking, *Sloan Management Review*, winter: 25–40.

Schoemaker, P.J.H. and Mavaddat, V.M. (2000) Scenario planning for disruptive technologies, in G.S. Day and P.J.H. Schoemaker with R.E. Gunther (eds) *Wharton on Managing Emerging Technologies*. New York: Wiley.

References

Schön, D.A (1983) Organizational learning, in G. Morgan (ed.) *Beyond Method: Strategies for Social Research*. Beverly Hills, CA: Sage.

Schuler, R.S. (2001) Human resource issues and activities in international joint ventures, *International Journal of Human Resource Management*, 12(1): 1–52.

Schuler, R.S. and Jackson, S.E. (2001) HR issues and activities in mergers and acquisitions, *European Management Journal*, 19(3): 239–53.

Schultz, A. (1953) Common-sense and scientific interpretation of human action, *Philosophical and Phenomenological Research*, 14: 1–38.

Schultz, A. (1972) *The Phenomenology of the Social World*. London: Heinemann.

Schuman, H. and Scott, J. (1989) Generations and collective memories, *American Sociological Review*, 54, 359–81.

Schwartz, D.G. (1999) When e-mail meets organizational memories: addressing threats to communication in a learning organization, *International Journal of Human-Computer Studies*, 51: 599–614.

Schwenk, C.R. (1982) Why sacrifice rigor for relevance? A proposal for combining laboratory and field research in strategic management, *Strategic Management Journal*, 3: 213–25.

Schwenk, C.R. (1984) Cognitive simplification processes in strategic decision making, *Strategic Management Journal*, 5: 111–28.

Schwenk, C.R. (1985) Management illusions and biases: their impact on strategic decisions, *Long Range Planning*, 18(5): 74–80.

Schwenk, C.R. (1986) Information, cognitive biases and commitment to a course of action, *Academy of Management Review*, 11: 298–310.

Schwenk, C.R. (1988) The cognitive perspective on strategic decision making, *Journal of Management Studies*, 25: 41–55.

Schwenk, C.R. (1995) Strategic decision making, *Journal of Management*, 21: 471–93.

Scott, S.G. and Bruce, R.A. (1995) Decision making style: the development and assessment of a new measure, *Educational and Psychological Measurement*, 55: 818–31.

Scribner, S. (1985) Knowledge at work, *Anthropology and Education Quarterly*, 16: 1999–206.

Scribner, S. (1986) Thinking in action: some characteristics of practical thought, in R. Sternberg and R.K. Wagner (eds) *Practical Intelligence: Nature and Origin of Competence in the Everyday World*. Cambridge: Cambridge University Press.

Senge, P.M. (1990a) *The Fifth Discipline: The Art and Practice of the Learning Organization*. London: Doubleday.

Senge, P.M. (1990b) D.E. Meen and M. Keough: creating the learning organization – an interview with Peter Senge, *McKinsey Quarterly*, 1: 58–78.

Senge, P.M. (1992) The leader's new work: building learning organizations, *Sloan Management Review*, fall: 7–23.

Senge, P.M., Roberts, C., Ross, R.B., Smith, B.J. and Kleiner, A. (1994) *The Fifth Discipline Fieldbook*. New York: Doubleday.

Shadbolt, N. and Milton, N. (1999) From knowledge engineering to knowledge management, *British Journal of Management*, 10: 309–22.

Shannon, C.E. and Weaver, W. (1948) *The Mathematical Theory of Communication*. Urbana, IL: University of Illinois Press.

Sheldon, A. (1980) Organizational paradigms: a theory of organizational change, *Organizational Dynamics*, 8: 61–80.

Shiffrin, R.M. and Schneider, W. (1977) Controlled and automatic information processing, II: perceptual learning, automatic attending, and a general theory, *Psychological Review*, 84: 127–90.

Showers, J.L. and Chakrin, L. (1981) Reducing uncollectable revenue from residential telephone customers, *Interfaces*, 11: 21–31.

Shrivastava, P. and Schneider, S. (1984) Organizational frames of reference, *Human Relations*, 37(10): 795–809.

Simon, H.A. (1947) *Administrative Behavior*. New York: Macmillan.

Simon, H.A. (1957) *Administrative Behavior*, 2nd edn. New York: Macmillan.

Simon, H.A. (1987) Making management decision: the role of intuition and emotion, *Academy of Management Executive*, 1: 57–64.

Simon, H.A. (1997) Designing organizations for an information-rich world, in D.M. Lamberton (ed.) *The Economics of Communication and Information*. Cheltenham: Edward Elgar.

Simons, T., Pelled, L.H. and Smith, K.A. (1999) Making use of difference: diversity, debate and decision comprehensiveness in top management teams, *Academy of Management Journal*, 42: 662–73.

Simontin, D.K. (1994) *Greatness: Who Makes History and Why*. New York: Guilford Press.

Simontin, D.K. (1997) Creativity in personality, developmental, and social psychology: any links with cognitive psychology? in T.B. Ward, S.M. Smith and J. Vaid (eds) *Creative Thought: An Investigation of Conceptual Structures and Processes*. Washington, DC: APA.

Sims, H.P. and Lorenzi, P. (1992) *The New Leadership Paradigm: Social Learning and Cognition in Organizations*. Newbury Park, CA: Sage.

Skinner, B.F. (1938) *The Behavior of Organisms*. New York: Appleton-Century-Crofts.

Slater, P. (ed.) (1976) *The Measurement of Intrapersonal Space by Grid Technique: Vol. I – Explorations of Intrapersonal Space*. Chichester: Wiley.

Slater, P. (ed.) (1977) *The Measurement of Intrapersonal Space by Grid Technique: Vol. II – Dimensions of Intrapersonal Space*. Chichester: Wiley.

References

Slocum, J.W. (1978) Does cognitive style affect diagnosis and intervention strategies of change agents? *Group and Organization Studies*, 3: 199–210.

Slovic, P. and Liechtenstein, S. (1971) Comparison of Bayesian and regression approaches to the study of information processing in judgment, *Organizational Behavior and Human Performance*, 6: 649–744.

Smircich, L. and Stubbart, C. (1985) Strategic management in an enacted world, *Academy of Management Review*, 10: 724–36.

Smith, G.J.W. (1990) Creativity in old age, *Creativity Research Journal*, 3: 249–64.

Smith, G.J.W. and Van der Meer, G. (1997) Perception and creativity, in M.A. Runco (ed.) *Creativity Research Handbook*, vol. 1. Cresskill, NJ: Hampton.

Smith, K.G., Smith, K.A., Olian, J.D. *et al.* (1994) Top management team demography and process: the role of social integration and communication, *Administrative Science Quarterly*, 39: 412–38.

Smith, M. and Gibson, J. (1988) Using repertory grids to investigate racial prejudice, *Applied Psychology: An International Review*, 37: 311–26.

Smith, M. and Stewart, B.J.M. (1977) Repertory grids: a flexible tool for establishing the contents and structure of a manager's thoughts, in D. Ashton (ed.) *Management Bibliographies and Reviews*, 3: 209–29.

Smith, S., Duke, D. and Wright, P.C. (1999) Using the resources model in virtual environment design, in M.D. Harrison and S. Smith (eds) *King's Manor Workshop on User-centred Design and Implementation of Virtual Environments*. York: University of York.

Snell, R.S. (2001) Moral foundations of the learning organization, *Human Relations*, 54(3): 321–44.

Spangler, W.E. (1991) The role of artificial intelligence in understanding the strategic decision-making process, *IEEE Transactions on Knowledge and Data Engineering*, 3(2): 149–59.

Sparrow, J.A. (1989) Graphical displays in information systems: some data properties influencing the effectiveness of alternative forms, *Behaviour and Information Technology*, 8(1): 43–56.

Sparrow, J.A. (1998) *Knowledge in Organizations: Access to Thinking at Work*. London: Sage.

Sparrow, P.R. (1994) The psychology of strategic management: emerging themes of diversity and cognition, in C.L. Cooper and I.T. Robertson (eds) *International Review of Industrial and Organizational Psychology*, vol. 9. Chichester: Wiley.

Sparrow, P.R. (1998a) Information overload, in K. Legge, C. Clegg, and S. Walsh (eds) *The Experience of Managing: A Skills Workbook*. London: Macmillan.

Sparrow, P.R. (1998b) The pursuit of multiple and parallel organizational flexibilities: reconstituting jobs, *European Journal of Work and Organizational Psychology*, 7(1): 79–95.

Sparrow, P.R. (1999a) Strategy and cognition: understanding the role of management knowledge structures, organizational memory and information overload, *Creativity and Innovation Management*, 8(2): 140–8.

Sparrow, P.R. (1999b) Is HRM in crisis? Re-engaging, deterring and regulating the modern organization, in R. Schuler and S. Jackson (eds) *Strategic Human Resource Management: Linking People to the Firm*. New York: Blackwell.

Sparrow, P.R. (2000) Strategic management in a world turned upside down: the role of cognition, intuition and emotional intelligence, in P.C. Flood, T. Dromgoole, S.J. Carroll and L. Gorman (eds) *Managing Strategy Implementation*. Oxford: Blackwell.

Sparrow, P.R. and Cooper, C.L. (1998) New organizational forms: the strategic relevance of future psychological contract scenarios, *Canadian Journal of Administrative Sciences*, 15(4): 1–16.

Sparrow, P.R. and Daniels, K. (1999) Human resource management and the virtual organization: mapping the future research issues, in C.L. Cooper and D. Rousseau (eds) *Trends in Organizational Behaviour*, vol. 6. Chichester: Wiley.

Sparrow, P.R. and Marchington, M. (eds) (1998) *Human Resource Management: The New Agenda*. London: *Financial Times* Pitman Publications.

Sparrow, P.R. and Pettigrew, A. (1988) Strategic HRM in the computer supplier industry, *Journal of Occupational Psychology*, 51: 25–42.

Sparrow, P.R. and West, M. (2002) Psychology and organizational effectiveness, in I. Robertson, M. Callinan and D. Bartram (eds) *Organizational Effectiveness: The Role of Psychology*. Chichester: Wiley.

Spector, P.E. (1982) Behavior in organisations as a function of employees' locus of control, *Psychological Bulletin*, 91: 482–97.

Spector, P.E. (1988) Development of the work locus of control scale, *Journal of Occupational Psychology*, 61: 335–40.

Spector, P.E. and O'Connell, B.J. (1994) The contribution of personality traits, negative affectivity, locus of control and type A to subsequent reports of job stressors and job strains, *Journal of Occupational and Organizational Psychology*, 67: 1–12.

Spender, J-C. (1989) *Industry Recipes: An Enquiry into the Nature and Sources of Managerial Judgement*. Oxford: Blackwell.

Spender, J-C. (1996) Making knowledge the basis for a dynamic view of the firm, *Strategic Management Journal*, 17: 45–62.

Spender, J-C. (1998) The dynamics of individual and organizational knowledge, in C. Eden and J-C. Spender (eds) *Managerial and Organizational Cognition: Theory, Methods and Research*. London: Sage.

Spender, J-C. (2000) Book review of 'Tacit knowledge in organizations' by Philippe Baumard, *Academy of Management Review*, 25(2): 443–6.

Spender, J-C. and Eden, C. (1998) Introduction, in C. Eden and J-C. Spender (eds) *Managerial and Organizational Cognition: Theory, Methods and Research*. London: Sage.

Staples, D.S., Greenaway, K. and McKeen, J.D. (2001) Opportunities for research about managing the knowledge-based enterprise, *International Journal of Management Reviews*, 3(1): 1–20.

Starbuck, W.H. and Hedberg, B. (1977) Saving an organization from a stagnating environment, in H.B. Thorelli (ed.) *Strategy + Structure = Performance*. Bloomington, IN: Indiana University.

Starbuck, W.H. and Hedberg, B. (2001) How organizations learn from success and failure, in M. Dierkes, A.B. Antal, J. Child and I. Nonaka (eds) *Handbook of Organizational Learning and Knowledge*. Oxford: Oxford University Press.

Starbuck, W.H. and Milliken, F.J. (1988) Executives' perceptual filters: what they notice and how they make sense, in D.C. Hambrick (ed.) *The Executive Effect: Concepts and Methods for Studying Top Managers*. Greenwich, CT: JAI Press.

Stasser, G. and Titus, W. (1985) Pooling of unshared information in group decision-making: biased information sampling during discussion, *Journal of Personality and Social Psychology*, 48: 1467–78.

Stasser, G. and Titus, W. (1987) Effects of information load and percentage of shared information on the dissemination of unshared information during group discussion, *Journal of Personality and Social Psychology*, 53: 81–93.

Stasser, G., Stewart, D.D. and Wittenbaum, G.M. (1995) Expert roles and information exchange during discussion: the importance of knowing who knows what, *Journal of Experimental and Social Psychology*, 31: 1–22.

Staw, B.M. (1981) The escalation of commitment to a course of action, *Academy of Management Review*, 6: 577–87.

Staw, B.M. (1997) The escalation of commitment: an update and appraisal, in Z. Shapira (ed.) *Organizational Decision Making*. Cambridge: Cambridge University Press.

Staw, B.M., Sandelands, L.E. and Dutton, J.E (1981) Threat-rigidity effects in organizational behavior: a multilevel analysis, *Administrative Science Quarterly*, 26: 501–24.

Staw, B.M., McKechnie, P.I. and Puffer, S.M. (1983) The justification of organizational performance, *Administrative Science Quarterly*, 28: 582–600.

Steiner, G.A. (1969) *Top Management Planning*. New York: Macmillan.

Sternberg, R.J. (1985) Implicit theories of intelligence, creativity and wisdom, *Journal of Personality and Social Psychology*, 49: 607–27.

Sternberg, R.J. (ed.) (1988) *The Nature of Creativity*. Cambridge: Cambridge University Press.

Sternberg, R .J. (1997) *Thinking Styles*. Cambridge: Cambridge University Press.

Sternberg, R.J. and Davidson, J. (eds) (1985) *The Nature of Insight*. Cambridge, MA: MIT Press.

Sternberg, R.J. and Grigorenko, E.L. (1997) Are cognitive styles still in style? *American Psychologist*, 52(7): 700–12.

Sternberg, R.J. and Lubart, T.I. (1996) Investing in creativity, *American Psychologist*, 51: 677–88.

Sternberg, R.J. and O'Hara, L.A. (1999) Creativity and Intelligence, in R.J. Sternberg (ed.) *Handbook of Creativity*. Cambridge: Cambridge University Press.

Sternberg, R.J. and Wagner, R.K. (1991) MSG thinking styles. Unpublished manual.

Sternberg, R.J. and Wagner, R.K. (1993) The geocentric view of intelligence and job performance is wrong, *Current Directions in Psychological Science*, 2: 1–5.

Sternberg, R.J. and Wagner, R.K. (1994) *Mind in Context: Interactionist Perspectives on Human Intelligence*. Cambridge: Cambridge University Press.

Sternberg, R.J., Wagner, R.K., Williams, W.M. and Horvath, J.A. (1995) Testing common sense, *American Psychologist*, 50: 912–27.

Stewart, D.D. and Stasser, G. (1998) The sampling of critical, unshared information in decision-making groups: the role of an informed minority, *European Journal of Social Psychology*, 28: 95–113.

Stewart, T.A. (1994) Managing in a wired company, *Fortune*, 11 July: 44–56.

Stewart, T.A. (2000) Knowledge worth $1.25 billion, *Fortune*, 302, 27 Nov.

Stewart, V., Stewart, A. and Fonda, N. (1981) *The Business Application of Repertory Grids*. London: McGraw-Hill.

Stohl, C. and Redding, W. (1987) Messages and message exchange processes, in F.M. Jablin, L.L. Putnam, K.H. Roberts and L.W. Porter (eds) *Handbook of Organizational Communication*. London: Sage.

Strata, R. (1989) Organizational learning – the key to management innovation, *Sloan Management Review*, spring: 63–74.

Streufert, S. and Nogami, G.Y. (1989) Cognitive style and complexity: implications for I/O psychology, in C.L. Cooper and I.T. Robertson (eds) *International Review of Industrial and Organizational Psychology*. Chichester: Wiley.

References

Stubbart, C.I. (1989) Managerial cognition: a missing link in strategic management research, *Journal of Management Studies*, 26: 325–47.

Stubbart, C.I. and Ramaprasad, A. (1988) Probing two chief executives' schematic knowledge of the US steel industry using cognitive maps, *Advances in Strategic Management*, 5: 139–64.

Stubbart, C.I. and Ramaprasad, A. (1990) Comments on the empirical articles and recommendations for future research, in A.S. Huff (ed.) *Mapping Strategic Thought*. Chichester: Wiley.

Sutcliffe, K.M. (2001) Commentary: motivational preconditions and intra-organizational barriers to learning in organizational settings, in T.K. Lant and Z. Shapira (eds) *Organizational Cognition: Computation and Interpretation*. Mahwah, NJ: Lawrence Erlbaum Associates.

Sutcliffe, K.M. and Huber, G.P. (1998) Firm and industry as determinants of executive perceptions of the environment, *Strategic Management Journal*, 19: 793–807.

Svenson, O. (1979) Process description of decision making, *Organizational Behavior and Human Performance*, 23: 86 –122.

Swan, J. (1997) Using cognitive mapping in management research: decisions about technical innovation, *British Journal of Management*, 8: 183–98.

Swan, J. and Newell, S. (1998) Making sense of technological innovation: the political and social dynamics of cognition, in C. Eden and J-C. Spender (eds) *Managerial and Organizational Cognition: Theory, Methods and Research*. London: Sage.

Swieringa, J. and Wierdsma, A. (1992) *Becoming a Learning Organization: Beyond the Learning Curve*. Wokingham: Addison-Wesley.

Swink, M. (1995) The influences of user characteristics on performance in a logistics DSS application, *Decision Sciences*, 26(4): 503–29.

Tabachnik, B.G. and Fidell, L.S. (1996) *Using Multivariate Statistics*. New York: HarperCollins.

Tajfel, H. and Turner, J.C. (1985) The social identity theory of intergroup behavior, in S. Worchel and W.G. Austin (eds) *Psychology of Intergroup Relations*, 2nd edn. Chicago: Nelson-Hall.

Tang, M. and Thomas, H. (1992) The concept of strategic groups: theoretical construct or analytical convenience? *Managerial and Decision Economics*, 13: 323–9.

Teece, D.J. (1998) Capturing value from knowledge assets, *California Management Review*, 40(3): 55–79.

Thomas, H. and Venkatraman, N. (1988) Research on strategic groups: progress and prognosis, *Journal of Management Studies*, 25: 537–55.

Tolman, E.C. (1932) *Purposive Behaviour in Animals and Men*. New York: Century.

Tranfield, D. and Starkey, K. (1998) The nature, social organization and promotion of management research: towards policy, *British Journal of Management*, 9: 341–53.

Trice, A.D., Hare, J.R. and Elliott, K.A. (1989) A career locus of control scale for undergraduate students, *Perceptual and Motor Skills*, 69: 555–61.

Tsang, E. (1997) Organizational learning and the learning organization: a dichotomy between descriptive and prescriptive research, *Human Relations*, 50(1): 89.

Tsoukas, H. (1992) Ways of seeing: topographic and network representations in organization theory, *Systems Practice*, 5: 441–56.

Tsoukas, H. (1996) The firm as a distributed knowledge system: a constructionist approach, *Strategic Management Journal*, 17: 11–25.

Tsui, A.S. and Gutek, B.A. (1999) *Demographic Differences in Organizations: Current Research and Future Directions*. Lanham, MD: Lexington Books.

Tulving, E. (1972) Episodic and semantic memory, in E. Tulving and W. Donaldson (eds) *Organization of Memory*. New York: Academic Press.

Turuch, E. (2001) Knowledge management: auditing and reporting intellectual capital, *Journal of General Management*, 26(3): 26–40.

Tushman, M.L. (1977) Special boundary roles in the innovation process, *Administrative Science Quarterly*, 22: 587–605.

Tushman, M.L. and Anderson, P. (1990) Technological discontinuities and dominant designs: a cyclical model of technological change, *Administrative Science Quarterly*, 35: 604–33.

Tushman, M.L. and Romanelli, E. (1985) Organizational evolution: a metamorphosis model of convergence and reorientation, in L.L. Cummings and B.M. Staw (eds) *Research in Organizational Behaviour*, vol. 7. Greenwich, CT: JAI Press.

Tushman, M.L., Virany, B. and Romanelli, E. (1985) Executive succession, strategic reorientation and organizational evolution, *Technology in Society*, 7: 297–314.

Tversky, A. (1977) Features of similarity, *Psychological Review*, 84: 327–52.

Tversky, A. and Gati, I. (1978) Studies of similarity, in E. Rosch and B.B. Lloyd (eds) *Cognition and Categorization*. London: Lawrence Erlbaum Associates.

Tversky, A. and Kahneman, D. (1974) Judgment under uncertainty: heuristics and biases, *Science*, 198: 1124–31.

Tversky, A. and Kahneman, D. (1981) The framing of decisions and the psychology of choice, *Science*, 211: 453–8.

Tyler, B.B. and Steensma, H.K. (1995) Evaluating technological collaborative opportunities: a cognitive modelling perspective, *Strategic Management Journal*, summer special issue, 16: 43–70.

Tyler, B.B. and Steensma, H.K. (1998) The effects of executives' experiences and perceptions on their assessment of potential technological alliances, *Strategic Management Journal*, 19: 939–65.

Unsworth, K. (2001) Unpacking creativity, *Academy of Management Review*, 26(2): 289–97.

Usdiken, B. (1992) The impact of environmental change on the environmental characteristics of top management teams, *British Journal of Management*, 3: 207–20.

Valkenburg, P.M. and Vandervoort, T.H.A. (1995) The influence of television on children's daydreaming styles, *Communication Research*, 22(3): 267–87.

Van de Vliert, A. (1997) Lest we forget, *Management Today*, January: 62–3.

Van der Heijden, K. (1994) Probabilistic planning and scenario planning, in G. Wright and P. Ayton (eds) *Subjective Probability*. Chichester: Wiley.

Van der Heijden, K. (1996) *Scenarios: The Art of Strategic Conversation*. Chichester: Wiley.

Van der Heijden, K. and Eden, C. (1998) The theory and praxis of reflective learning in strategy making, in C. Eden and J-C. Spender (eds) *Managerial and Organizational Cognition: Theory, Methods and Research*. London: Sage.

Van Wijk, R.A. and van den Bosch, F.A.J. (2000) The emergence and development of internal networks and their impact on knowledge flows: the case of Rabobank Group, in A.M. Pettigrew and E.M. Fenton (eds) *The Innovating Organization*. London: Sage.

Vaughan, D. (1996) *The Challenger Launch Decision: Risky Technology, Culture and Deviance at NASA*. Chicago: Chicago University Press.

Vaughan, F.E. (1979) *Awakening Intuition*. New York: Doubleday.

Vermeulen, F. and Barkema, H. (2001) Learning through acquisitions, *Academy of Management Journal*, 44(3): 457–76.

Virany, B. and Tushman, M.L. (1986) Top management teams and corporate success in an emerging industry. *Journal of Business Venturing*, 1: 261–74.

Virany, B., Tushman, M.L. and Romanelli, E. (1992) Executive succession and organization outcomes in turbulent environments: an organizational learning approach, *Organization Science*, 3: 72–91.

Vygotsky, L.S. (1962) *Thought and Language*. Cambridge, MA: MIT Press.

Wack, P. (1985a) Scenarios: uncharted waters ahead, *Harvard Business Review*, Sept.–Oct.: 73–90.

Wack, P. (1985b) Scenarios: shooting the rapids, *Harvard Business Review*, Nov.–Dec.: 131–42.

Wagner, R.K. and Sternberg, R.J. (1985) Practical intelligence in real world pursuits: the role of tacit knowledge, *Journal of Personality and Social Psychology*, 49: 436–58.

Wallach, M. and Kogan, N. (1965) *Modes of Thinking in Young Children*. New York: Holt, Rinehart & Winston.

Waller, M.J., Huber, G.P. and Glick, W.H. (1995) Functional background as a determinant of executives' selective perception, *Academy of Management Journal*, 38: 943–74.

Wallston, B., Wallston, K., Kaplan, G. and Maldes, S. (1976) Development and validation of the health locus of control (HLC) scale, *Journal of Consulting and Clinical Psychology*, 44: 580–9.

Wallston, K.A. and Wallston, B.S. (1982) Who is responsible for your health? The construct of health locus of control, in G.S. Sanders and J. Suils (eds) *Social Psychology of Health and Illness*. Hillsdale, NJ: Earlbaum.

Walsh, J.P. (1988) Selectivity and selective perception: an investigation of managers' belief structures and information processing, *Academy of Management Journal*, 31: 873–96.

Walsh, J.P. (1995) Managerial and organizational cognition: notes from a trip down memory lane, *Organization Science*, 6(3): 280–321.

Walsh, J.P. and Dewar, R.D. (1987) Formalization and the organization life cycle, *Journal of Management Studies*, 24, 216–31.

Walsh, J.P. and Fahay, L. (1986) The role of negotiated belief structures in strategy making, *Journal of Management*, 12: 325–38.

Walsh, J.P. and Ungson, G. (1991) Organizational memory, *Academy of Management Review*, 16(1): 57–91.

Walsh, J.P., Henderson, C.M. and Deighton, J. (1988) Negotiated belief structures and decision performance: an empirical investigation, *Organizational Behavior and Human Decision Processes*, 42: 194–216.

Walton, E.J. (1986) Managers' prototypes of financial firms, *Journal of Management Studies*, 23: 679–98.

Wang, S. (1996) A dynamic perspective of differences between cognitive maps, *Journal of the Operational Research Society*, 47: 538–49.

Ward, T.B., Smith, S.M. and Vaid, J. (eds) (1997) *Creative Thought: An Investigation of Conceptual Structures and Processes*. Washington: American Psychological Association.

Ward, T.B., Smith, S.M. and Finke, R.A. (1999) Creative cognition, in R.J. Sternberg (ed.) *Handbook of Creativity*. Cambridge: Cambridge University Press.

Warr, P. and Allan, C. (1998) Learning strategies and occupational training, in C.L. Cooper and I.T. Robertson (eds) *International Review of Industrial and Organizational Psychology*, vol. 13. Chichester: Wiley.

References

Wasserman, S. and Faust, K. (1994) *Social Network Analysis*. Cambridge: Cambridge University Press.

Wegner, D.M. (1987) Transactive memory: a contemporary analysis of the group mind, in G. Mullen and G. Geothals (eds) *Theories of Group Behavior*. New York: Springer-Verlag.

Weick K.E. (1969) *The Social Psychology of Organizing*. Reading, MA: Addison-Wesley.

Weick K.E. (1979a) *The Social Psychology of Organizing*, 2nd edn. Reading, MA: Addison-Wesley.

Weick, K.E. (1979b) Cognitive processes in organizations, in B.M. Staw (ed.) *Research in Organizational Behavior*, vol. 1. Greenwich, CT: JAI Press.

Weick, K.E. (1987) Organizational culture as a source of high reliability, *California Management Review*, 29: 112–27.

Weick, K.E. (1990) Technology as an equivoque: sensemaking in new technologies, in P. Goodman and L. Sproull (eds) *Technology and Organization*, San Francisco: Jossey-Bass.

Weick, K.E. (1991) The non-traditional quality of organizational learning, *Organization Science*, 2(1): 116–24.

Weick, K.E. (1995) *Sensemaking in Organizations*. Thousand Oaks, CA: Sage.

Weick, K.E. (2001) *Making Sense of the Organization*. Oxford: Blackwell.

Weick, K.E. and Bougon, M.G. (1986) Organizations as cognitive maps, in H.P. Sims, Jr. and D.A. Gioia (eds) *The Thinking Organization: Dynamics of Organizational Social Cognition*. San Francisco: Jossey-Bass.

Weick, K.E. and Roberts, K.H. (1993) Collective mind in organization: heedful interrelating on flight decks, *Administrative Science Quarterly*, 38: 357–81.

Weick, K.E. and Van Orden, P. (1990) Organizing on a global scale, *Human Resource Management*, 29: 49–62.

Weick, K.E. and Westley, F. (1996) Organizational learning: affirming an oxymoron, in S.R. Clegg, C. Hardy and W.R. Nord (eds) *Handbook of Organization Studies*. London: Sage.

Weisberg, R.W. (1995) Case studies of creative thinking: reproduction versus restructuring in the real world, in S.M. Smith, T.B.Ward and R.A. Finke (eds) *The Creative Cognition Approach*. Cambridge, MA: MIT Press.

Weisbord, M. (1992) *Discovering Common Ground*. San Francisco: Berrett-Koehler.

Welford, A.T. (1976) *Skilled Performance*. Glenview, IL: Scott Foresman.

Wells, R.S. and Bantel, K.A. (2000) Competitive external pressures: building top management teams to sustain competitive advantage in a changing world, in R.E. Quinn, R.M. O'Neill and L. St Clair (eds) *Pressing Problems in Modern Organizations (That Keep us up at Night): Transforming Agendas for Research and Practice*. New York: AMACOM.

West, C. and Schwenk, C. (1996) Top management team strategic consensus, demographic homogeneity and firm performance: a report of resounding non-findings, *Strategic Management Journal*, 17: 571–6.

West, M.A. and Farr, J.L. (eds) (1990) *Innovation and Creativity at Work: Psychological and Organizational Strategies*. Chichester: Wiley.

Whetten, D.A., Cameron, K.S. and Woods, M. (1994) *Developing Management Skills for Europe*. London: HarperCollins.

Whitley, R.D. (1987) Taking firms seriously as economic actors: towards a sociology of firm behaviour, *Organization Studies*, 8: 125–47.

Whitley, R.D. (2000) *The Intellectual and Social Organization of the Sciences*, 2nd edn. Oxford: Oxford University Press.

Whittington, R. (1993) *What is Strategy and Does it Matter?* London: Routledge.

Wickens, C.D. (1984) *Engineering Psychology and Human Performance*. Columbus, OH: Merrill.

Wiersema, M.F. and Bantel, K.A. (1992) Top team demography and corporate strategic change, *Academy of Management Journal*, 35: 91–121.

Williams, K.Y. and O'Reilly, C.A. (1998) Demography and diversity in organizations: a review of 40 years of research, in L.L. Cummings and B.M. Staw (eds) *Research in Organizational Behavior – Vol. 20*. Greenwich, CT: JAI Press.

Williams, L.J., Gavin, M.B. and Williams, M.L. (1996) Measurement and non-measurement processes with negative affectivity and employee attitudes, *Journal of Applied Psychology*, 81: 88–101.

Williams, R.J., Barrett, J.D. and Brabston, M. (2000) Managers' business school education and military service: possible links to corporate criminal activity, *Human Relations*, 53: 691–712.

Willman, P., O'Creevy, M.P., Nicholson, N. and Soane, E. (2001) Knowing the risks, theory and practice in financial market trading, *Human Relations*, 54: 887–910.

Witkin, H.A. (1962) *Psychological Differentiation: Studies of Development*. New York: Wiley.

Wood, D. and Latak, J. (1982) A mental health locus of control scale, *Personality and Individual Differences*, 3: 84–7.

Wood, R. and Bandura, A. (1989) Social cognitive theory of organizational management, *Academy of Management Review*, 14: 361–84.

Woolridge, B. and Floyd, S. (1989) Strategic process effects on consensus, *Strategic Management Journal*, 10: 295–302.

References

Woolridge, B. and Floyd, S.W. (1990) The strategy process, middle management involvement, and organizational performance, *Strategic Management Journal*, 11: 231–41.

Wright, G. and Goodwin, P. (1999) Future-focused thinking: combining scenario planning with decision analysis, *Journal of Multi-Criteria Decision Analysis*, 8: 311–21.

Wright, P.C., Fields, R.E. and Harrison, M.D. (2000) Analysing human-computer interaction as distributed cognition: the resource model, *Human Computer Interaction*, 15(1): 1–41.

Wright, P.M. and Snell, S.A. (1998) Toward a unifying framework for exploring fit and flexibility in strategic human resource management, *Academy of Management Review*, 23(4), 756–72.

Wrightson, M.T. (1976) The documentary coding method, in R. Axelrod (ed.) *Structure of Decision: The Cognitive Maps of Political Elites*. Princeton, NJ: Princeton University Press.

Wurman, R.S. (1989) *Information Anxiety*. New York: Doubleday.

Zack, M. (1999) Managing codified knowledge, *Sloan Management Review*, summer: 45–58.

Zajac, E.J. and Bazerman, M.H. (1991) Blindspots in industry and competitor analysis: implications of interfirm (mis)perceptions for strategic decisions, *Academy of Management Review*, 16: 37–56.

Zander, U. and Kogut, B. (1995) Knowledge and the speed of the transfer and imitation of organizational capabilities: an empirical test, *Organization Science*, 6: 76–92.

Zhang, J. (1996) A representational analysis of relational information displays, *International Journal of Human-Computer Studies*, 45: 59–74.

Zhang, J. (1997) The nature of external representations in problem solving, *Cognitive Science*, 21: 179–217.

Zhang, J. and Norman, D.A. (1994) Representations in distributed cognitive tasks, *Cognitive Science*, 18: 87–122.

Zohar, A. and Morgan, G. (1998) Refining our understanding of hyper-competition and hyperturbulence, in A.Y. Ilinitch, A.Y. Lewin and R. D'Aveni (eds) *Managing in Times of Disorder: Hypercompetitive Organizational Responses*. London: Sage.

Zuboff, S. (1988) *In the Age of the Smart Machine: The Future of Work and Power*. Oxford: Heinemann.

AUTHOR INDEX

Author index

393

Author index

Author index

SUBJECT INDEX